ANALECTA BIBLICA
INVESTIGATIONES SCIENTIFICAE IN RES BIBLICAS

144

D0207424

JOHN PAUL HEIL

THE TRANSFIGURATION OF JESUS:
Narrative Meaning and Function of
Mark 9:2-8, Matt 17:1-8 and Luke 9:28-36

EDITRICE PONTIFICIO ISTITUTO BIBLICO - ROMA 2000

IMPRIMI POTEST

Romae, die 12 octobris 2000

R.P. ROBERT F. O'TOOLE, S.J.

Rector Pontificii Instituti Biblici

ISBN 88-7653-144-0

© E.P.I.B. – Roma – 2000

EDITRICE PONTIFICIO ISTITUTO BIBLICO

Piazza della Pilotta, 35 - 00187 Roma, Italia

PREFACE

The following investigation of the stories of the transfiguration of Jesus in the Gospels of Mark, Matthew, and Luke assumes no particular theory of literary dependency among the Synoptic Gospels. It is primarily a narrative-critical study that concentrates on the meaning and function of each account within its respective Gospel. Because of the similarities of the three accounts, a certain amount of repetition in the presentation is to be expected. On the other hand, what often appears on the surface as mere repetition from one account to the other sometimes involves subtle differences and nuances. One of the advantages of retaining the repetition is that the chapters on the individual accounts can be read as continuous and autonomous wholes, without the annoyance of numerous cross references.

The abbreviations, footnotes, and bibliographical entries are given according to the conventions adopted by the *Catholic Biblical Quarterly* 60 (1998) 829-56.

The stories of the transfiguration of Jesus were of special interest to the late Fritzleo Lentzen-Deis, S.J. This investigation is dedicated to his memory.

John Paul Heil

TABLE OF CONTENTS

ABBREVIATIONS

AB	Anchor Bible
ABD	*Anchor Bible Dictionary*
ABRL	Anchor Bible Reference Library
AGAJU	Arbeiten zur Geschichte des antiken Judentums und des Urchristentums
A.J.	*Antiquitates judaicae* by Josephus
AnBib	Analecta biblica
ANTC	Abingdon New Testament Commentaries
ASNU	Acta Seminarii neotestamentici Upsaliensis
ATANT	Abhandlungen zur Theologie des Alten und Neuen Testaments
BAGD	Bauer, Arndt, Gingrich, and Danker, *Greek-English Lexicon of the NT*
BBB	Bonner biblische Beiträge
B.C.	Before Christ
BDB	Brown, Driver, and Briggs, *Hebrew and English Lexicon of the Old Testament*
BDF	Blass, Debrunner, and Funk, *A Greek Grammar of the NT*
BECNT	Baker Exegetical Commentary on the New Testament
BETL	Bibliotheca Ephemeridum theologicarum Lovaniensium
BGBE	Beiträge zur Geschichte der biblischen Exegese
Bib	*Biblica*
BIS	Biblical Interpretation Series
BJS	Brown Judaic Studies
BK	*Bibel und Kirche*

BR	*Biblical Research*
BSac	*Bibliotheca Sacra*
BTB	*Biblical Theology Bulletin*
BTN	Bibliotecta Teologica Napoletana
BZ	*Biblische Zeitschrift*
BZAW	Beihefte zur ZAW
BZNW	Beihefte zur ZNW
CahRB	Cahiers de la Revue biblique
CBQ	*Catholic Biblical Quarterly*
CBQMS	CBQ, Monograph Series
C.E.	Common Era
ConBNT	Coniectanea biblica, New Testament
ConBOT	Coniectanea biblica, Old Testament
DRev	*Downside Review*
EBib	*Études bibliques*
EDNT	*Exegetical Dictionary of the New Testament*
EKKNT	Evangelisch-katholischer Kommentar zum Neuen Testament
ETL	*Ephemerides theologicae Lovanienses*
ETR	*Études théologiques et religieuses*
EvT	*Evangelische Theologie*
ExpTim	*Expository Times*
FB	Forschung zur Bibel
FFNT	Foundations and Facets, New Testament
FTS	Frankfurter Theologische Studien
HAT	Handbuch zum Alten Testament
HeyJ	*Heythrop Journal*
HTKNT	Herders theologischer Kommentar zum Neuen Testament
HTR	*Harvard Theological Review*
ICC	International Critical Commentary

IDBSup	Supplementary volume to *Interpreter's Dictionary of the Bible*
Int	*Interpretation*
JBL	*Journal of Biblical Literature*
JETS	*Journal of the Evangelical Theological Society*
JJS	*Journal of Jewish Studies*
JQR	*Jewish Quarterly Review*
JSJ	*Journal for the Study of Judaism in the Persian, Hellenistic, and Roman Periods*
JSJSup	JSJ, Supplement Series
JSNT	*Journal for the Study of the New Testament*
JSNTSup	JSNT, Supplement Series
JSOT	*Journal for the Study of the Old Testament*
JSOTSup	JSOT, Supplement Series
JSP	*Journal for the Study of the Pseudepigrapha*
JSPSup	JSP, Supplement Series
JTS	*Journal of Theological Studies*
L.A.B.	*Liber antiquitatum biblicarum* by Pseudo-Philo
LCL	Loeb Classical Library
LD	Lectio divina
LXX	Septuagint
Mos.	*De vita Moysis* by Philo
MT	masoretic text
Neot	*Neotestamentica*
NICNT	New International Commentary on the New Testament
NICOT	New International Commentary on the Old Testament
NIGTC	New International Greek Testament Commentary
NJBC	*New Jerome Biblical Commentary*
NovT	*Novum Testamentum*
NovTSup	NovT, Supplement Series

NRSV	*New Revised Standard Version*
NTL	New Testament Library
NTOA	Novum Testamentum et orbis antiquus
NTS	*New Testament Studies*
NTTS	New Testament Tools and Studies
OBO	Orbis biblicus et orientalis
OBT	Overtures to Biblical Theology
OTL	Old Testament Library
OTP	*The Old Testament Pseudepigrapha*
OTS	Oudtestamentische studiën
PVTG	Pseudepigrapha Veteris Testamenti Graece
Q.G.	*Questiones et solutiones in Genesin* by Philo
RAC	*Reallexikon für Antike und Christentum*
RB	*Revue biblique*
RivB	*Rivista biblica*
RTL	*Revue théologique de Louvain*
SA	Studia Anselmiana
SacPag	Sacra Pagina
SANT	Studien zum Alten und Neuen Testament
SB	Sources bibliques
SBEC	Studies in the Bible and Early Christianity
SBLDS	Society of Biblical Literature Dissertation Series
SBLMS	Society of Biblical Literature Monograph Series
SBLSCS	Society of Biblical Literature Septuagint and Cognate Studies
SBLSP	*Society of Biblical Literatrue Seminar Papers*
SBLTT	Society of Biblical Literature Texts and Translations
ScEs	*Science et esprit*
SJLA	Studies in Judaism in Late Antiquity
SJOT	*Scandinavian Journal of the Old Testament*

SJT	*Scottish Journal of Theology*
SNT	Studien zum Neuen Testament
SNTSMS	Society for New Testament Studies Monograph Series
SVTP	Studia in Veteris Testamenti pseudepigrapha
T. Abr.	*Testament of Abraham*
TDNT	*Theological Dictionary of the New Testament*
TDOT	*Theological Dictionary of the Old Testament*
Tg. Neof.	*Targum Neofiti 1*
Tg. Onq.	*Targum Onqelos*
Tg. Ps.-J.	*Targum Pseudo-Jonathan*
THKNT	Theologischer Handkommentar zum Neuen Testament
TSAJ	Texte und Studien zum antiken Judentum
TWAT	*Theologisches Wörterbuch zum Alten Testament*
TynBul	*Tyndale Bulletin*
USQR	*Union Seminary Quarterly Review*
Vg	Vulgate
VMSAB	Veröffentlichungen Des Missionspriesterseminars St. Augustin bei Bonn
VT	*Vetus Testamentum*
VTSup	VT, Supplements
WBC	Word Biblical Commentary
WMANT	Wissenschaftliche Monographien zum Alten und Neuen Testament
WTJ	*Westminster Theological Journal*
WUNT	Wissenschaftliche Untersuchungen zum Neuen Testament
ZAW	*Zeitschrift für die alttestamentliche Wissenschaft*
ZKT	*Zeitschrift für katholische Theologie*
ZNW	*Zeitschrift für die neutestamentliche Wissenschaft*
ZTK	*Zeitschcrift für Theologie und Kirche*

CHAPTER ONE

INTRODUCTION

A. STATE OF THE RESEARCH

Source- and redaction-critical issues have dominated modern research on the three synoptic accounts of the transfiguration of Jesus. Recent studies of the transfiguration narrative recount the past research and usually offer their own new source and redaction-critical theories along with other contributions. Studies of the transfiguration narrative normally focus mainly on one of the three versions – Mark,[1] Matthew,[2] or Luke.[3] There has also been recent study of the relationship between

---

[1] C. CLIVAZ, "La Transfiguration au risque de la compréhension du disciple: Mc 9/2-10," *ETR* 70 (1995) 493-508; M. ÖHLER, "Die Verklärung (Mk 9:1-8): Die Ankunft der Herrschaft Gottes auf der Erde," *NovT* 38 (1996) 197-217; IDEM, *Elia im Neuen Testament: Untersuchungen zur Bedeutung des alttestamentlichen Propheten im frühen Christentum* (BZNW 88; Berlin: De Gruyter, 1997) 118-35; D. ZELLER, "La métamorphose de Jésus comme épiphanie (Mc 9,2-8)," *L'évangile exploré: Mélanges offerts à Simon Légasse à l'occasion de ses soixante-dix ans* (LD 166; ed. A. Marchadour; Paris: Cerf, 1996) 167-86; IDEM, "Bedeutung und religionsgeschichtlicher Hintergrund der Verwandlung Jesu (Markus 9:2-8)," *Authenticating the Activities of Jesus* (NTTS 28; eds. B. Chilton and C. A. Evans; Leiden: Brill, 1999) 303-21.

[2] J.A. PENNER, "Revelation and Discipleship in Matthew's Transfiguration Account," *BSac* 152 (1995) 201-10; A.D.A. MOSES, *Matthew's Transfiguration Story and Jewish-Christian Controversy* (JSNTSup 122; Sheffield: Sheffield Academic Press, 1996).

[3] S.H. RINGE, "Luke 9:28-36: The Beginning of an Exodus," *The Bible and Feminist Hermeneutics* (Semeia 28; ed. M.A. Tolbert; Chico: Scholars Press, 1983) 83-99; A.A. TRITES, "The Transfiguration in the Theology of Luke: Some Redactional Links," *The Glory of Christ in the New Testament* (eds. L.D. Hurst and N.T. Wright; Oxford: Claredon, 1987) 71-81; B.E. REID, "Voices and Angels: What Were They Talking About at the Transfiguration?: A Redaction-Critical Study of Luke 9:28-36," *BR* 34 (1989) 19-31; IDEM, *The Transfiguration: A Source- and Redaction-Critical Study of Luke 9:28-36* (CahRB 32; Paris: Gabalda, 1993). For a critique of Reid, see R.J. MILLER, "Historicizing the Trans-Historical: The Transfiguration

the synoptic accounts and the apparent reference to the transfiguration in 2 Pet 1:16-17.[4]

B. New Methodological Approach

The present study offers a comprehensive treatment of each of the three versions of the transfiguration of Jesus from a narrative-critical perspective with focus on the response of the implied audience.[5] Our goal is to determine the narrative meaning and function of each version of the transfiguration story by considering its impact upon its respective implied audience, after determining its more precise literary genre and the intertextual background of its main literary motifs. The investigation begins with a preliminary analysis and comparison of the three versions to demonstrate that they all are basically of the same literary genre and to determine the distinctive features of each (chap. 1).

There is no consensus on the literary genre of the transfiguration narratives. Are they misplaced resurrection accounts[6], misplaced ascension stories,[7] pronouncement stories,[8] "magical stories,"[9] "derashic sce-

---

Narrative (Mark 9:2-8, Matt 17:1-8, Luke 9:28-36)," *Forum* 10 (1994) 219-48; IDEM, "Source Criticism and the Limits of Certainty: The Lukan Transfiguration Story as a Test Case," *ETL* 74 (1998) 127-44. See also J.A. McGUCKIN, *The Transfiguration of Christ in Scripture and Tradition* (SBEC 9; Lewiston: Mellen, 1986); H.W. BASSER, "The Jewish Roots of the Transfiguration," *Bible Review* 14 (1998) 30-35; G. BRAY, "La transfiguration," *Revue Réformée* 50 (1999) 85-91.

[4] R.J. MILLER, "Is There Independent Attestation for the Transfiguration in 2 Peter?" *NTS* 42 (1996) 620-25. See also J.H. NEYREY, "The Apologetic Use of the Transfiguration in 2 Peter 1:16-21," *CBQ* 42 (1980) 504-19.

[5] For the narrative-critical, audience-oriented approach we are employing, see W. CARTER and J.P. HEIL, *Matthew's Parables: Audience-Oriented Perspectives* (CBQMS 30; Washington: Catholic Biblical Association, 1998) 8-17. For a new and provocative thesis that the Gospels were written for a much wider audience than the narrowly defined "communities" of each evangelist, see R. BAUCKHAM, ed., *The Gospels for All Christians: Rethinking the Gospel Audiences* (Grand Rapids: Eerdmans, 1998).

[6] R.H. STEIN, "Is the Transfiguration (Mark 9:2-8) a Misplaced Resurrection Account?" *JBL* 95 (1976) 79-96.

[7] F.R. McCURLEY, "'And After Six Days' (Mark 9:2): A Semitic Literary Device," *JBL* 93 (1974) 67-81.

[8] For a proposal that the final redaction of Luke's transfiguration narrative is a pronouncement story, see REID, *Transfiguration*, 97-98.

[9] M. SMITH, "The Origin and History of the Transfiguration Story," *USQR* 36 (1980) 39-44.

nifications,"[10] theophanies, apocalyptic visions,[11] epiphanies, or something else? Chapter 2 demonstrates that the transfiguration narratives can be categorized under the general "epiphany" genre in distinction to a "vision" or "theophany" understood as modern, technical designations for very specific, ancient literary genres. Through analysis and comparison with Num 22:31-35, Josh 5:13-15, and 2 Macc 3:22-34 chapter 3 narrows the definition of the literary genre to a special type of "mandatory epiphany." Chapter 4 analyzes the mysterious and enigmatic "transfiguration" of Jesus as a literary motif within the epiphany genre.

Key to the meaning of the transfiguration narratives is the significance of the appearance of Moses and Elijah in conversation with the transfigured Jesus. Do they simply represent the Law and the Prophets? Are they merely examples of the glorified righteous? Chapter 5 explains the appearance of Moses and Elijah as prophetic figures who attained heavenly glory without being put to death in the manner that Jesus will be. The exposition centers upon a detailed investigation of the various biblical traditions surrounding the mysterious death of Moses.

Each version of the transfiguration narrative includes Peter's puzzling offer to build a tent each for Jesus, Moses, and Elijah, interrupted by an additional epiphanic action – the sudden and unexpected appearance of an overshadowing cloud out of which the voice of God utters a climactic command. Chapters 6 and 7 investigate the biblical background of the "tents" and the "cloud" respectively to help determine their significance and function in the transfiguration epiphany.

With the precise determination of the literary genre, the explanation of the key role of the appearance of Moses and Elijah, and the background of the tents and the overshadowing cloud, the remaining chapters (8-13) demonstrate the narrative meaning and function of each version of the transfiguration story. This includes a detailed exegesis

---

[10] A. DEL AGUA, "The Narrative of the Transfiguration as a Derashic Scenification of a Faith Confession (Mark 9.2-8 Par.)," *NTS* 39 (1993) 340-54.

[11] MOSES, *Matthew's Transfiguration Story*, 89-91; W.R. STEGNER, "The Use of Scripture in Two Narratives of Early Jewish Christianity (Matthew 4.1-11; Mark 9.2-8)," *Early Christian Interpretation of the Scriptures of Israel: Investigations and Proposals* (JSNTSup 148; eds. C.A. Evans and J.A. Sanders; Sheffield: Sheffield Academic Press, 1997) 111-12.

of each version in itself as well as a demonstration of the role each version plays in the broader narrative context of its respective Gospel. Chapter 14 summarizes and concludes the investigation with a discussion of the pragmatic effects and profound theological significance the transfiguration narrative has for its implied audiences.

C. PRELIMINARY ANALYSIS AND COMPARISON

Each version of the transfiguration follows closely upon Jesus' first prediction of his passion, death, and resurrection (Mark 8:27-33; Matt 16:13-23; Luke 9:18-22) with its challenging call for anyone who would come after Jesus to deny himself, take up his cross, and follow Jesus in order to gain eschatological salvation and life in God's kingdom (Mark 8:34-9:1; Matt 16:24-28; Luke 9:23-27). In each case the transfiguration narrative immediately follows Jesus' promise that "there are some standing here who will not taste death until they see the kingdom of God" (Luke 9:27) or "until they see that the kingdom of God has come in power" (Mark 9:1) or "until they see the Son of Man coming in his kingdom" (Matt 16:28).[12]

In Mark and Matthew the transfiguration narrative proper is followed by the report of the descent of Jesus with his three disciples from the mountain, during which they discuss the coming of Elijah (Mark 9:9-13; Matt 17:9-13).[13] This is followed by Jesus' exorcism of a boy his disciples could not heal (Mark 9:14-29; Matt 17:14-21). Luke lacks the discussion about the coming of Elijah, so that his transfiguration

---

[12] Some treat this promise as already part of the transfiguration narrative or as a very closely connected transition to it. See, for example, ÖHLER, "Verklärung," 197-98; D. WENHAM and A.D.A. MOSES, "'There Are Some Standing Here..': Did They Become the 'Reputed Pillars' of the Jerusalem Church? Some Reflections on Mark 9:1, Galatians 2:9 and the Transfiguration," *NovT* 36 (1994) 146-63; E. NARDONI, "A Redactional Interpretation of Mark 9:1," *CBQ* 43 (1981) 365-84.

[13] Some treat this discussion as part of the transfiguration scene. See, for example, U. LUZ, *Das Evangelium nach Matthäus* (EKKNT 1/2; Zürich: Benziger, 1990) 503-18. The original place of the discussion about the coming of Elijah is immediately following Matt 16:28 and Mark 9:1, so that the transfiguration narrative is a later insert, according to J. TAYLOR, "The Coming of Elijah, Mt 17,10-13 and Mk 9,11-13: The Development of the Texts," *RB* 98 (1991) 107-19.

narrative is followed immediately by this especially difficult exorcism (Luke 9:37-43a). Thus, the transfiguration narrative occurs in basically the same place in each version – after the first prediction of the passion and before Jesus' exorcism of a boy severely possessed by a demon.

Each version of the transfiguration narrative exhibits essentially the same sequence of literary motifs, but with notable variations. We will now closely compare the three versions, observing their similarities and differences.[14]

1. *Introduction: Jesus takes Peter, James and John up a mountain*

Mark 9:2a: And after six days Jesus took along Peter and James and John, and led them up to a high mountain privately, alone.

Matt 17:1: And after six days Jesus took along Peter and James and John his brother, and led them up to a high mountain privately.

Luke 9:28: About eight days after these words, taking along Peter and John and James, he went up to the mountain to pray.

Each version begins with a temporal notice that links the event of the transfiguration to the previous scene. In Mark and Matthew it occurs "after six days," whereas in Luke it occurs after "about eight days." Luke makes explicit what Mark and Matthew imply, that the transfiguration takes place "after these words," that is, the words of Jesus predicting his suffering, death and resurrection as well as calling for others to follow him (Mark 8:27-9:1; Matt 16:13-28; Luke 9:18-27).

In each version Jesus takes along the same three disciples – Peter, James and John. Matthew adds the note that John is the brother of James ("his brother"). Luke has a different order – Peter, John and James – and does not explicitly name Jesus.

A mountain is the location for the transfiguration in each version. In Mark and Matthew it is a "high" mountain, in Luke simply "the mountain."[15] Whereas in Mark Jesus led them up a high mountain

---

[14] Unless otherwise noted, all translations of biblical texts used in this study are my own.

[15] Some translate τὸ ὄρος in Luke 9:28 as "the hill country," "the hills," or "the mountains;" see M. ZERWICK and M. GROSVENOR, *A Grammatical Analysis of the Greek New Testament* (Rome: Biblical Institute, 1974) 1.214. REID, *Transfiguration*, 102-3: "In the Galilean setting of the transfiguration story, τὸ ὄρος designates the hilly ring surrounding Lake Gennesaret."

"privately, alone," in Matthew it is simply "privately."[16] Instead of noting the privacy of the event, Luke states that the purpose of Jesus' ascent to the mountain with the three disciples was "to pray."

2. *Jesus is transfigured before Peter, James and John*

Mark 9:2b-3: And he was transfigured before them, that is, his clothes became very radiantly white, such as no bleacher on the earth could thus whiten.

Matt 17:2: And he was transfigured before them, that is, his face shone as the sun, while his clothes became white as the light.[17]

Luke 9:29: And while he was praying the appearance of his face became different and his clothing dazzling white.

In each version the external appearance of Jesus is dramatically changed. In Mark and Matthew he was "transfigured" or "transformed" (μετεμορφώθη) "before them," that is, before Peter, James and John. In Luke it was while Jesus was praying, the stated purpose of his ascent to the mountain (9:28), that the appearance of his face became "different" or "other" (ἕτερον). In Luke it is not explicitly stated but implied that this happened before the three disciples.

Only in Matthew and Luke does the description of Jesus' transfiguration explicitly include his face. In Matthew "his face (πρόσωπον) shone like the sun," while in Luke "the appearance of his face (προσώπου) became different." That Mark lacks an explicit notice that the "face" of Jesus was involved in his transfiguration suggests that this element may be of lesser importance in the determination of the literary genre.

In each version Jesus' transfiguration is further described in terms of his clothing becoming extremely white. Mark's statement that his

---

[16] Such dual expressions are typical of Mark; see R.H. GUNDRY, *Mark: A Commentary on His Apology for the Cross* (Grand Rapids: Eerdmans, 1993) 457-58.

[17] We translate the καὶ that follows the statement of Jesus' transfiguration in Mark 9:3 and Matt 17:2 as "that is," understanding it in an epexegetical sense as a definition and further description of the transfiguration; see BDF, 228-29; M. ZERWICK, *Biblical Greek* (Rome: Biblical Institute, 1963) 154; C. NIEMAND, *Studien zu den Minor Agreements der synoptischen Verklärungsperikopen: Eine Untersuchung der literarkritischen Relevanz der gemeinsamen Abweichungen des Matthäus und Lukas von Markus 9,2-10 für die synoptische Frage* (Frankfurt: Lang, 1989) 82.

clothes became more radiantly white than any bleacher "on the earth" could whiten them suggests a heavenly apparel for Jesus while still on earth. Matthew's comparison that his clothes became white "as the light" parallels his comparison that his face shone "as the sun." Luke likewise closely coordinates the clothing that became dazzling white with the face that became different.

3. *Moses and Elijah appear and speak with the transfigured Jesus*

Mark 9:4: Then there appeared to them Elijah with Moses, and they were talking with Jesus.
Matt 17:3: Then behold there appeared to them Moses and Elijah talking with him.
Luke 9:30-32: Then behold two men were talking with him, who were Moses and Elijah, who, appearing in glory, were speaking about his exodus, which he was about to accomplish in Jerusalem. Now Peter and those with him had been overcome with sleep, but when they became wide awake,[18] they saw his glory and the two men standing with him.

In each version Moses and Elijah appear and talk with the transfigured Jesus. Whereas Matthew and Luke have as the order of appearance, "Moses and Elijah," Mark has "Elijah with Moses" and explicitly mentions Jesus by name. Matthew and Luke introduce the sudden appearance with the word "behold" (ἰδού), which Mark lacks. Moses and Elijah appeared explicitly to "them" (αὐτοῖς), the three disciples, in Mark and Matthew. That their appearance was to the three disciples also in Luke becomes evident after the three awoke and saw the two men (Moses and Elijah), who were appearing in glory (9:31), standing with Jesus.

Luke elaborates upon the motif of the appearance and conversation of Moses and Elijah in a manner that goes well beyond Mark and Matthew. Before Moses and Elijah are named, they are introduced as "two men" talking with Jesus. In Luke Moses and Elijah appear explicitly "in glory" (ἐν δόξῃ). Only Luke reports the content of their conversa-

---

[18] At this point the NRSV translates, "but since they had stayed awake," offering as an alternative, "but when they were fully awake."

tion with Jesus, "his exodus (ἔξοδον), which he was about to accomplish in Jerusalem." But Peter and his companions had been asleep, so that they did not hear the conversation. Upon awakening, they saw Jesus' "glory" (δόξαν) and the "two men" (Moses and Elijah) standing with him, who were also appearing in glory.

4. *Peter offers to build a tent each for Jesus, Moses, and Elijah*

Mark 9:5-6: Then replying, Peter said to Jesus, "Rabbi, it is good that we are here, so let us make three tents, for you one and for Moses one and for Elijah one." He did not know what to reply, for they had become terrified.

Matt 17:4: Replying, Peter spoke to Jesus, "Lord, it is good that we are here. If you wish, I will make here three tents, for you one and for Moses one and for Elijah one."

Luke 9:33: As they were separating from him, Peter spoke to Jesus, "Master, it is good that we are here, so let us make three tents, one for you and one for Moses and one for Elijah," not knowing what he was saying.

Although Peter tells Jesus in each version that "it is good that we are here," he addresses Jesus differently – in Mark as "Rabbi" (ῥαββί), in Matthew as "Lord" (κύριε), and in Luke as "Master" (ἐπιστάτα). In Luke Peter's statement occurs after the notice that Moses and Elijah were separating from Jesus.

In each version Peter offers to make three tents, one each for Jesus, Moses, and Elijah. In Mark and Luke Peter speaks in the first person plural, "let us make three tents." But in Matthew, after a deferential, "If you wish," Peter addresses Jesus in the first person singular, "I will make here three tents." Peter's repetition of "here" (ὧδε) in his statement that "I will make *here* three tents," after stating that "it is good that we are here (ὧδε)," places a certain emphasis upon the location in Matthew. Luke has a subtle stylistic variation in the enumeration of the tents, placing the number "one" (μίαν) before rather than after each person.

In Mark and Luke a parenthetical remark by the narrator indicates to the audience Peter's lack of knowledge about how to respond to the event. In Mark he did not know "what to reply," while in Luke he did not know "what he was saying." Only Mark includes a fear motif as the reason for Peter's unknowing response: "For they (Peter, James and John) had become terrified."

5. *A cloud overshadows them*

> Mark 9:7a: Then there came a cloud overshadowing them,
> Matt 17:5a: While he was still speaking, behold a bright cloud overshadowed them,
> Luke 9:34: While he was saying these things, a cloud came and was overshadowing them. They were frightened as they entered into the cloud.

All three versions contain the motif of an overshadowing cloud at this point, but the "overshadowing" is expressed with a different tense of the same verb – in Mark the present participle, "overshadowing" (ἐπισκιάζουσα), in Matthew the aorist, "overshadowed" (ἐπεσκίασεν), and in Luke the imperfect, "was overshadowing" (ἐπεσκίαζεν). Whom the cloud overshadows is somewhat nebulous grammatically at this point in Mark and Matthew, in each case expressed by a vague "them." Luke, however, has already stated that "they" (αὐτούς), referring to Moses and Elijah, were separating from him" (ἀπ᾽ αὐτοῦ), referring to Jesus (9:33). When Luke then states that the cloud was overshadowing "them" (αὐτούς), it is logical grammatically for "them" to refer again to Moses and Elijah. "They" (the disciples) then became afraid when "they" (αὐτούς), again referring to Moses and Elijah, entered into the cloud to complete the process of their separation from Jesus.[19]

In Matthew and Luke the cloud appears explicitly while Peter is still speaking about building three tents. For Matthew it is a "bright" cloud introduced by his characteristic "behold" (ἰδού), paralleling the "behold" (ἰδού) that introduced the appearance of Moses and Elijah (17:3).[20] Whereas in Mark the three disciples "had become terrified (ἔκφοβοι)" (9:6) at the appearance of Moses and Elijah in conversation with the transfigured Jesus, in Luke "they were frightened (ἐφοβήθησαν) as they (Moses and Elijah) entered into the cloud."

---

[19] Each occurrence of αὐτούς in Luke 9:33-34, then, refers to Moses and Elijah. For different interpretations, see REID, *Transfiguration*, 137; I.H. MARSHALL, *The Gospel of Luke* (Grand Rapids: Eerdmans, 1978) 387; J.A. FITZMYER, *The Gospel According to Luke I-IX* (AB 28; Garden City: Doubleday, 1981) 802; J.B. GREEN, *The Gospel of Luke* (NICNT; Grand Rapids: Eerdmans, 1997) 383-84.

[20] R.H. GUNDRY, *Matthew: A Commentary on His Literary and Theological Art* (Grand Rapids: Eerdmans, 1982) 343-44.

6. *A voice from the cloud commands them to listen to God's Son*

Mark 9:7b: then there came a voice from the cloud, "This is my beloved Son; listen to him!"
Matt 17:5b-7: and behold a voice from the cloud saying, "This is my beloved Son, with whom I am well pleased; listen to him!" Hearing this the disciples fell upon their face and were greatly frightened. But Jesus approached, and touching them, said, "Arise and do not be afraid."
Luke 9:35: Then a voice came from the cloud saying, "This is my chosen Son; to him listen!"

In each version God's voice comes from the cloud commanding the three disciples to listen to Jesus as God's Son. Luke differs from Mark and Matthew in having the voice refer to "my chosen Son" rather than "my beloved Son." God's command in Luke, "to him listen!," exhibits a reversal of the word order in the Matthean and Markan versions, "listen to him!" Matthew introduces the voice with his characteristic "behold" (ἰδού), paralleling its use for the appearance of Moses and Elijah (17:3) as well as for the appearance of the cloud (17:5).

Only Matthew reports that when the disciples heard the voice "they fell upon their face and were greatly frightened." Thus, the fear motif occurs at a different place in each version. For Mark the three disciples "had become terrified (ἔκφοβοι)" (9:6) at the appearance of Moses and Elijah in conversation with the transfigured Jesus. For Luke "they were frightened (ἐφοβήθησαν) as they entered into the cloud" (9:34). And for Matthew "they were greatly frightened (ἐφοβήθησαν)" (17:6) upon hearing the voice from the cloud. But only in Matthew does Jesus approach, touch the three prostrate disciples, and utter the comforting motif, "Arise and do not be afraid."

7. *Jesus alone is with them*

Mark 9:8: Then suddenly, looking around, they no longer saw anyone but Jesus alone with them.
Matt 17:8: Raising their eyes they saw no one but him, Jesus alone.
Luke 9:36: When the voice came there was found Jesus alone. And they kept silent and reported to no one in those days any of the things they had seen.

Each version concludes with the notice that after the voice from the cloud "Jesus alone" was there before the three disciples, so that the command to listen refers to him in distinction to Moses and Elijah, who have now disappeared. In Mark after the dramatic voice from the cloud the three disciples look around and suddenly no longer see Moses and Elijah. To the notice that they saw "Jesus alone" only Mark adds the words "with them." In Matthew the prostrate disciples raise their eyes and see no one but "him," the one who came forward, touched them, and urged them to rise and not be afraid (17:7), that is, "Jesus alone" without Moses and Elijah. In Luke "Jesus alone" was found after the voice came, so that the command to listen can only refer to Jesus. Luke's conclusion underlines the secrecy of the event, at least during "those days," as the disciples tell no one at that time what they had witnessed. The implication is that they reported it at a later time. The conclusion of each version leaves the audience in suspense as to whether or not the disciples will obey the command to listen to Jesus.

D. CONCLUSION

Each version of the transfiguration narrative exhibits its own note-worthy characteristics. Of all three versions Mark is the most concise. In Mark the motif of Jesus' transfiguration does not involve any explicit change in Jesus' face, but his clothes became very radiantly white. Only Mark notes that this "whiteness" was unlike anything on earth, thus implying a heavenly apparel for Jesus (9:3). Only Mark has the appearance of "Elijah with Moses" (9:4) rather than "Moses and Elijah." Only in Mark does Peter address the transfigured Jesus as "Rabbi" (9:5). Only in Mark do the three disciples become terrified at the point where Elijah appears with Moses in conversation with the transfigured Jesus, so that Peter did not really know what to say when he suggested that they build a tent for each (9:4-6).

Matthew and Mark's versions are closer to one another than either is to Luke's version. Only Matthew mentions that John is the brother of James (17:1). Matthew's description of Jesus' transfiguration is characterized by a double comparison: his face shone "as the sun" and his clothes became white "as the light" (17:2). Only Matthew employs the word "behold" three times to introduce the appearances of Moses and Elijah (17:3), of the bright cloud (17:5), and of the voice from the cloud (17:5). Only in Matthew does Peter address the transfigured Jesus as "Lord" (17:4). Only in Matthew does Peter offer to build the three tents by himself "here," in correspondence to his statement that it is good that we are "here" (17:4). Only Matthew refers to the overshadowing cloud as "bright" (17:5). Only in Matthew does the voice from the cloud refer to "my beloved Son" as the one "with whom I am well pleased" (17:5).

But the main characteristic of Matthew's version is his unique elaboration upon the disciples' response to the voice from the cloud. This is the point where Matthew places the motif of the fear of the disciples. Upon hearing the voice, the disciples fall upon their face and become greatly frightened (17:6). Then, only in Matthew does Jesus come forward, touch the disciples, and speak to them the comforting motif, "Arise and do not be afraid" (17:7). Only in Matthew's version, then, does Jesus actually speak.

In contrast to Mark and Matthew, Luke's version takes place "about eight days after these words" (9:28) rather than "after six days" (Mark 9:2; Matt 17:1). Only Luke mentions that Jesus ascended the mountain with the three disciples explicitly "to pray" (9:28), so that Jesus' transfiguration occurs while he is praying (9:29). In contrast to Mark and Matthew, where Jesus "was transfigured before them" (Mark 9:2; Matt 17:2), in Luke "the appearance of his face became different" (9:29).

But the main characteristic of Luke's version is his unique elaboration upon the transfigured Jesus' conversation with Moses and Elijah. Only in Luke do Moses and Elijah appear explicitly "in glory" and speak with Jesus about his "exodus" that he is about to accomplish in Jerusalem (9:31). Only in Luke are Peter and his companions overcome by sleep, with the implication that they thus do not hear the conversation. When they awaken, they see Jesus' glory and the two men (Moses and Elijah), who also appeared in glory (9:31), standing with him (9:32). Only in Luke does Peter's suggestion that we build three tents come in response to the separation of Moses and Elijah from Jesus (9:33). Only in Luke does Peter address the transfigured Jesus as "Master" (9:33).

Luke places the motif of the fear of the disciples at the point where "they" (Moses and Elijah) entered the overshadowing cloud (9:34). Only in Luke does the voice from the cloud command the disciples, "To him listen!" (9:35), rather than, "Listen to him!" (Mark 9:7; Matt

17:5). Only Luke links the mention that Jesus alone was found there explicitly with the coming of the voice (9:36). And only Luke concludes with the notice that the disciples kept silent and told no one at that time what they had seen (9:36).[21]

Although all three versions of the transfiguration narrative exhibit their own unique characteristics, each narrates essentially the same sequence of literary motifs for its respective Gospel audience. After an introduction that locates the event temporally and spatially, each version begins with a stunning transfiguration of Jesus' external appearance before three of his disciples followed by a dramatic appearance of Moses and Elijah in conversation with Jesus. In response Peter suggests the building of three tents, one for Jesus, one for Moses, and one for Elijah. Then in each version a cloud overshadows "them." A voice from the cloud announces that this is my beloved or chosen Son and commands the disciples to listen to him. Each version concludes with a notice that Jesus alone was left there. Each version, then, presents a unified, consistent narrative that is of the same basic literary genre, evoking in general the same basic responses from their respective implied Gospel audiences familiar with the genre. The determination and description of that basic genre is the focus of the next chapter.

---

[21] REID (*Transfiguration*, 34-36) sees "several inconsistencies and tensions" in Luke's version, which leads her to posit the combination of "two separate pieces of tradition." According to Reid the focus shifts from Jesus to the disciples, so that "the disciples move to center stage in vv 33b-35." But in Peter's statement that "it is good that we are here" and his offer to build three tents (Luke 9:33), the focus and center of the stage, as in Mark and Matthew, remain Jesus, Moses, and Elijah, the ones for whom the tents are to be built! In Luke 9:34-35, as in the parallels in Mark and Matthew, the overshadowing cloud and commanding voice from the cloud that dramatically points to Jesus are the focus and center of the stage, not the disciples. In each version the disciples consistently remain throughout the entire narrative the recipients who witness the events that are the main focus and center of the stage — the transfiguration of Jesus, the appearance of Moses and Elijah, the appearance of the overshadowing cloud, and the dramatic voice from the cloud that directs them to Jesus. Luke's manner of narration and stylistic variations from Mark and Matthew do not destroy the fundamental unity and consistency of his transfiguration story.

CHAPTER 2

THE EPIPHANY GENRE OF THE TRANSFIGURATION NARRATIVE

A. LITERARY GENRES

One of the main goals of this investigation is a more precise determination of the literary genre of each version of the story of Jesus' transfiguration. We must first determine the literary genre if we are to understand what the story is communicating to its implied audience.[1] We propose that each version of the transfiguration narrative can be best interpreted as a form of the general category of "epiphany," understood as a modern, technical designation for a precise, ancient literary genre within the biblical tradition.[2]

There is much confusion both among scholars and in common parlance in the use of the terms "epiphany," "theophany," and "vision" in reference to narratives involving the appearances of divine or heavenly beings. The literary units that some call theophanies may be referred to by others as epiphanies or visions. The three terms are often employed

---

[1] R.A. BURRIDGE, "About People, by People, for People: Gospel Genre and Audiences," *The Gospels for All Christians: Rethinking the Gospel Audiences* (ed. R. Bauckham; Grand Rapids: Eerdmans, 1998) 114: "Genre forms a kind of 'contract' or agreement, often unspoken or unwritten, or even unconscious, between an author and a reader, by which the author sets out to write according to a whole set of expectations and conventions, giving us an initial idea of what we might expect to find."

[2] Thus we are not using the word "epiphany" as a term connoting the hellenistic concept of divinization in antiquity; see H.C. KEE, "The Transfiguration in Mark: Epiphany or Apocalyptic Vision?" *Understanding the Sacred Text: Essays in Honor of Morton S. Enslin on the Hebrew Bible and Christian Beginnings* (ed. J. Reumann; Valley Forge: Judson, 1972) 137-38.

without precision, in somewhat synonymous and overlapping ways. Before illustrating how each version of the transfiguration story exhibits the essential characteristics of the epiphany genre, we need to define, describe, and distinguish the terms "theophany," "vision," and "epiphany" as modern, technical designations for very specific and different literary genres in the biblical tradition.

1. *Theophany*

Understood as a technical designation for a biblical literary genre, "theophany" refers to a disposition of literary motifs which describes a coming of God recognized by the terrifying circumstances that accompany it rather than by seeing the actual figure of God. In its oldest and most concise form the theophany genre follows a twofold pattern: 1) a going forth or descent of Yahweh from various places, e.g., heaven, Sinai, Zion, Seir, Edom; 2) the dramatic and terrifying effects that this coming has on nature, e.g., earthquakes, volcanic phenomena, storms, thunder, lightning, fire, etc.[3] From the Song of Deborah in Judges comes an excellent example of a theophany:[4]

Judges 5:4-5

4 Lord, when you went out from Seir, when you marched from the region of Edom, the earth trembled, and the heavens poured, the clouds indeed poured water.

5 The mountains quaked before the Lord, the One of Sinai, before the Lord, the God of Israel (*NRSV*).

Here we have a twofold expression of the coming of Yahweh ("went out" and "marched"), illustrating the first part of a theophany. Although Yahweh comes, he is not directly seen. Rather, his coming is

---

[3] J. JEREMIAS, "Theophany in the OT," *IDBSup*, 897-98; T. HIEBERT, "Theophany in the OT," *ABD* 6.505-11; F. LENTZEN-DEIS, *Die Taufe Jesu nach den Synoptikern: Literarkritische und gattungsgeschichtliche Untersuchungen* (FTS 4; Frankfurt: Knecht, 1970) 100-101.

[4] Judges 5:4-5 represents the most original form of a theophany from which all others developed, according to J. JEREMIAS, *Theophanie: Die Geschichte einer alttestamentlichen Gattung* (WMANT 10; Neukirchen: Neukirchener Verlag, 1977) 7. See also A. GLOBE, "The Text and Literary Structure of Judges 5,4-5," *Bib* 55 (1974) 168-78; C. HOUTMAN, *Der Himmel im Alten Testament: Israels Weltbild und Weltanschauung* (OTS 30; Leiden: Brill, 1993) 140-42. Exemplifying the terminological confusion, Judg 5:4-5 is referred to as an "epiphany" by R.H. O'CONNELL, *The Rhetoric of the Book of Judges* (VTSup 63; Leiden: Brill, 1996) 115.

registered by the effect it has on nature. In this case, the trembling of the earth, the pouring forth of rain from the clouds in the heavens, and the quaking of the mountains demonstrate the second part of a theophany, the response of nature to the powerful coming of God.[5]

2. *Vision*

We define "vision" as a disposition of literary motifs which narrates the seeing by a privileged individual or group of supernatural phenomena located mainly in the heavenly realm. Whereas a theophany involves a coming of God to earth independent of whether or not the event is seen, a vision employs a verb of seeing or its equivalent and centers upon a seeing of heavenly realities reserved to the viewer. Although the heavenly phenomena seen in a vision may descend or touch upon the earth, e.g., Isa 6:1; Acts 10:11, they are mainly witnessed as heavenly phenomena. A vision is thus an experience of heavenly realities, which, even if reaching to and involving the earth, are viewed mainly within a supernatural, transcendent, or heavenly context.

In some cases the viewer remains on earth and has the vision into heaven as the "heavens are opened" (Ezek 1:1; Matt 3:16; Mark 1:10; Acts 7:55-56; 10:11).[6] In other cases the viewer is transported to heaven for the vision. For example, after John had a vision of an open door to heaven, he was invited to "come up here" (Rev 4:1) for a vision of heavenly things. Visions give their viewers a role to play in God's plan of salvation. The literary genre of "vision" can be subdivided into a number of varieties, e.g., dream vision, call vision, apocalyptic vision, interpretive vision, heavenly journey, etc.[7]

The literary genre of the transfiguration narrative is not that of a "vision," since it does not narrate a seeing of heavenly realities or phe-

---

[5] For other examples of theophanies, see Exod 19:16-19; Deut 33:2; Isa 30:27-28; Jer 25:30-31; Amos 1:2; Mic 1:3-4; Hab 3:3-15; Pss 18:8-20; 50:2-3; 68:8-9. There is no example of a complete theophany in accord with this precise definition in the New Testament, although there are what may be termed theophanic elements or perhaps partial theophanies (e.g. Matt 8:24; 27:51; 28:2).

[6] For the definition of "vision" and a discussion of the motif of "opened heavens" in visions, see LENTZEN-DEIS, *Taufe*, 105-6.

[7] On different types of apocalyptic visions, see C. ROWLAND, *The Open Heaven: A Study of Apocalyptic in Judaism and Early Christianity* (New York: Crossroad, 1982) 52-58.

nomena taking place in heaven. The transfiguration of Jesus into a heavenly being, the appearance of the heavenly figures of Moses and Elijah, and the appearance of the divine overshadowing cloud out of which comes the voice of God are all narrated as events that take place in the earthly (on a mountain) rather than heavenly realm. Although the heavenly figures of Moses and Elijah "appear" (ὤφθη in Matt 17:3; Mark 9:4; ὀφθέντες in Luke 9:31) before the three disciples, their appearance is narrated as an epiphanic rather than visionary event. The three disciples do not "see" these heavenly events through the opened heavens. Rather, these heavenly events take place on the mountain, independent of their being seen by the disciples. They take place there for anyone to see, but only the disciples are there to witness them. In Luke Jesus has already been transfigured while praying (9:29), and Moses and Elijah have already appeared in glory (9:31), before the disciples awaken from their sleep and "see" (εἶδον) Jesus' glory and the two men standing with him (9:32) as epiphanic events.[8]

3. *Epiphany*

By "epiphany" as a modern, technical designation for an ancient literary genre we mean a disposition of literary motifs which narrates a sudden and unexpected manifestation of a divine or heavenly being experienced by certain selected persons as an event independent of their seeing, in which the divine being reveals a divine attribute, action, or message. Similar to a vision, an epiphany presents a particular revelation or message to certain people, offering them an opportu-

---

[8] MOSES (*Matthew's Transfiguration Story*, 89-91) draws an analogy between the transfiguration narrative in Matthew and the "vision-form" in Daniel 7. But Daniel has a "vision" (he "was terrified by the visions of his mind," 7:1) of heavenly, intangible realities, while in the transfiguration the disciples see heavenly, tangible figures. Although Matt 17:9 refers to what the disciples have seen within the transfiguration narrative as a "vision" (ὅραμα), this is parallel to Mark 9:9, "what they have seen" (ἃ εἶδον), and should not be understood as a technical designation for the literary genre of the entire transfiguration narrative. On ὅραμα, W.D. DAVIES and D.C. ALLISON, *The Gospel According to Saint Matthew: Volume II: Commentary on Matthew VIII-XVIII* (ICC; Edinburgh: Clark, 1991) 713: "The word itself may indicate either a vision or a solid manifestation or sight [i.e., what we would call an epiphany]. That the latter may be intended here is perhaps indicated by Peter's request to build tents or booths. One does not make dwellings for intangible beings."

nity to play a role in God's salvific dealings with his people.[9] There are various types of the literary genre of "epiphany," e.g., "angelophanies," in which the divine being is an angel or angels who deliver a message about God's plan of salvation to selected persons (Gen 18:1-15; Num 22:22-35; Josh 5:13-15; Judg 6:11-24; 13:1-24; Matt 1:20-25; 2:12, 13-15, 19-23; Luke 1:8-20, 26-38; 2:8-15; 24:1-11; Matt 28:1-8; Mark 16:1-8; Acts 1:10-11), "sea-rescue epiphanies," in which Jesus functions as the epiphanic being who rescues his disciples by the revelation of a divine action (Matt 8:23-27; 14:22-33; Mark 4:35-41; 6:45-52; Luke 8:22-25; John 6:15b-21),[10] resurrectional "christophanies," in which the risen Jesus appears as the divine being from the heavenly realm (Matt 28:9-10; Luke 24:36-43; John 20:11-18, 19-23, 24-29; 21:1-14); etc.

Like the literary genre of theophany, an epiphany narrates a coming of a divine being. In a theophany the divine being remains invisible and his coming is recognized only by its effects on nature. But in an epiphany the divine being assumes visible form and appears before the eyes of human beings.[11] Like the literary genre of vision, an epiphany narrates the viewing of heavenly realities. In

---

[9] E. PAX, *Epiphaneia: Ein religionsgeschichtlicher Beitrag zur Biblischen Theologie* (Munich: Zink, 1955) 20; IDEM, "Epiphanie," *RAC* 5 (1962) 832-909; LENTZEN-DEIS, *Taufe*, 103-5; D. LÜHRMANN, "Epiphaneia: Zur Bedeutungsgeschichte eines griechischen Wortes," *Tradition und Glaube: Das frühe Christentum in seiner Umwelt: Festgabe für Karl Georg Kuhn zum 65. Geburtstag* (G. Jeremias, et al.; Göttingen: Vandenhoeck & Ruprecht, 1971) 185-99; G. THEISSEN, *Urchristliche Wundergeschichten: Ein Beitrag zur formgeschichtlichen Erforschung der synoptischen Evangelien* (SNT 8; Gütersloh: Mohn, 1974) 102-7; J. P. HEIL, *Jesus Walking on the Sea: Meaning and Gospel Functions of Matt 14:22-33, Mark 6:45-52 and John 6:15b-21* (AnBib 87; Rome: Biblical Institute, 1981) 8; IDEM, *The Gospel of Mark as a Model for Action: A Reader-Response Commentary* (New York: Paulist, 1992) 115. For a discussion of the recurring literary motifs in epiphanies, see M. FRENSCHKOWSKI, *Offenbarung und Epiphanie: Band 2: Die verborgene Epiphanie in Spätantike und frühen Christentum* (WUNT 80; Tübingen: Mohr Siebeck, 1997) 52-111.

[10] For an extensive discussion of these "sea-rescue epiphanies," see HEIL, *Jesus Walking on the Sea.*

[11] What we are referring to as an "epiphany" some scholars refer to as a type of theophany, see HIEBERT, "Theophany," 510-11; J.E. ALSUP, "Theophany in the NT," *IDBSup*, 898-900; H.M. OHMANN, "Some Remarks on the Use of the Term 'Theophany' in the Study of the Old Testament," *Unity in Diversity: Studies Presented to Dr. Jelle Faber on the Occasion of His Retirement* (ed. R. Faber; Hamilton, Ont.: Senate of the Theological College of the Canadian Reformed Churches, 1989) 2-12.

a vision the viewing is of heavenly realities or phenomena seen only through the eyes of a selected viewer mainly within a heavenly location or context. But in an epiphany the heavenly phenomena take place on earth as an event visible to anyone privileged to witness it.[12]

We may illustrate the difference between the closely related literary genres of vision and epiphany by a couple of examples. In Matthew and Mark the descent from heaven of the holy Spirit like a dove upon Jesus after his baptism by John is narrated as an "interpretive vision." In each case there is the use of an explicit verb for the "seeing" by Jesus. In Matt 3:16 "the heavens were opened" and Jesus "saw" (εἶδεν) "the Spirit of God descending like a dove, coming upon him." In Mark 1:10 Jesus "saw" (εἶδεν) "the heavens being torn open and the Spirit, like a dove, descending upon him." Matthew and Mark narrate a visionary experience of Jesus; only Jesus and no one else who may be present sees the Spirit descending upon him. But Luke at this point employs the literary genre of an epiphany rather than a vision. In Luke 3:21-22 the baptized Jesus is praying while "the heaven is opened and the holy Spirit descends in bodily form like a dove upon him".[13] Luke lacks a verb for the "seeing" by Jesus, so that the descent of the Spirit is narrated as an event visible to anyone present. By describing the descent of the Spirit "in bodily form" (σωματικῷ εἴδει, 3:22), Luke underlines the earthly reality of the event characteristic of the epiphany genre.[14]

Acts 10 provides another excellent example of the difference between the literary genres of "epiphany" and "vision." First the devout gentile centurion, Cornelius, experiences an angelophany:

---

[12] Although in Matt 1:20-25; 2:13-15, 19-23 the angel of the Lord appears to Joseph repeatedly "in a dream" (κατ' ὄναρ), which may seem to be "visions," they are actually angelophanies, since the angel leaves the heavenly realm and enters into the earthly domain, rather than giving Joseph a view of events originating and/or taking place in heaven. Furthermore, these Matthean angelophanies lack an explicit verb for "seeing," which is characteristic of visions. See R. GNUSE, "Dream Genre in the Matthean Infancy Narratives," *NovT* 32 (1990) 97-120.

[13] Note that Jesus was also praying while being transformed in the transfiguration epiphany in Luke 9:29.

[14] On Luke's use of the literary genre of epiphany rather than vision here, see LENTZEN-DEIS, *Taufe*, 286.

Acts 10:3-8

3 He saw in a vision clearly about the ninth hour of the day an angel of God coming in toward him and saying to him, "Cornelius." 4 Looking intently at him and becoming fearful, he said, "What is it, sir?" He said to him, "Your prayers and alms-giving have ascended as a memorial before God. 5 Now send men to Joppa and summon a certain Simon who is called Peter. 6 He is lodging with another Simon, a tanner, who has a house by the sea." 7 When the angel who spoke to him departed, he called two of his servants and a devout soldier from his staff. 8 And explaining everything to them, he sent them to Joppa.

At first sight we might think that this narrative surely has the literary genre of a "vision." After all it begins with an explicit notice of what Cornelius "saw" (εἶδεν) in a "vision" (ὁράματι) (10:3).[15] But a closer consideration reveals that it is actually an "epiphany," or more precisely, an "angelophany." Rather than a seeing by Cornelius into the heavenly realm through opened heavens, it narrates his seeing of the earthly event of a heavenly being, an angel, not remaining in heaven but "coming in toward him" and speaking to him (10:3). Indeed, the use of the epiphany genre here, in which the angel actually came in and, as later reported, "was standing in his house" (11:13), better serves the purpose of demonstrating the acceptability for Jews to enter into the homes of Gentiles than the primarily heavenly event of a vision.[16] In accord with the epiphany genre, the angel offers Cornelius an opportunity to play a role in God's salvific plan by summoning Simon Peter to his house from Joppa (10:5-6). After the angel returns to heaven, Cornelius, who, in accord with the epiphany genre is free to accept or reject the heavenly message, accepts his role and obeys the angel's instructions (10:7-8).

In the very next scene Peter's very private experience of heavenly realities exemplifies the literary genre of a vision:

---

[15] The modern terminology that we are employing to designate the ancient literary genres of "theophany," "epiphany," and "vision" does not necessarily correspond to the ancient vocabulary. The Greek word for "vision" (ὅραμα), for example, can refer to either an "epiphany" (Matt 17:9; Acts 7:31; 10:3) or a "vision" (Acts 9:10, 12; 10:17, 19; 11:5; 12:9; 16:9-10; 18:9).

[16] On the detail of God's angel as the first to cross the line into the house of the Gentile, thus providing an example for Peter and his Jewish companions to follow, see E.M. HUMPHREY, "Collision of Modes? — Vision and Determining Argument in Acts 10:1-11:18," *Textual Determinacy Volume II* (*Semeia* 71; eds. R.B. Robinson and R.C. Culley; Atlanta: Scholars Press, 1995) 77.

Acts 10:9-16

9 The next day, while they were making their way and nearing the city, Peter went up to the house top to pray about the sixth hour. 10 He became hungry and wanted to eat. While they were making preparations, a trance came upon him. 11 He saw heaven opened and an object like a great sheet with four corners being lowered to the earth. 12 In it were all the four-legged animals and reptiles on the earth and birds of the sky. 13 A voice said to him, "Rise, Peter, slaughter and eat!" 14 But Peter said, "Certainly not, sir, for I have never eaten anything profane and unclean." 15 The voice again, a second time, spoke to him, "What God has made clean, you are not to make profane!" 16 This happened three times, then immediately the object was taken up to heaven.

In contrast to the previous epiphany, in which an angel actually enters into earthly reality by coming and standing in the house of Cornelius, Peter has a purely visionary experience.[17] The hunger-induced trance that came upon Peter (10:10) places the event squarely within a visionary framework. Peter "saw" (θεωρεῖ) through the opened heaven an object like a great sheet (10:11) within the heavenly realm. Although the object was "being lowered to the earth" (10:11), it never actually enters into earthly reality but remains within the heavenly framework of the vision. No one else on earth but Peter would be able to see it. That the great sheet contained an exaggerated "all" (πάντα) of the animals of the earth adds to the surrealistic nature of this vision. Whereas the message and instructions of the epiphany were clear to Cornelius, who promptly obeyed them, Peter's vision, as is often the case with visions, still needs to be clarified and interpreted. He was in doubt about its meaning (10:17) and still pondering it when the Spirit gave him further instructions (10:19).

In this case both the epiphany (10:3-8) and the vision (10:9-16) offer selected individuals an opportunity to play their parts in God's plan of salvation. The voice of the angel instructs Cornelius to summon Peter from Joppa, and he obeys (10:5-8). The voice from heaven thrice commands Peter not to make profane what God has made clean (10:15-16). By the end of the vision, however, there still remains the suspense for the audience of whether or how Peter will accept the rather mysterious role the heavenly voice commands for him.

---

[17] The distinction between an epiphany, in which a heavenly being or angel actually enters into the reality of the earthly domain, as opposed to a vision is evident in Acts 12:9, where Peter followed an angel out of prison, not realizing that what was happening through the angel was "real" (ἀληθές); he thought he was seeing a "vision" (ὅραμα).

B. The Transfiguration Narrative as an Epiphany

Each version of the transfiguration narrative exhibits the essential characteristics of the literary genre of an "epiphany." The seven literary motifs common to each version, which we analyzed in chapter 1, play their respective roles within this rather unique epiphany.

The introduction of each account situates the epiphanic action temporally for the audience, either six (Mark 9:2; Matt 17:1) or about eight (Luke 9:28) days after Jesus' previous prediction of his passion, death, and resurrection and his call for disciples to follow him. A nameless and vaguely located mountain, a place isolated from the public domain and close to the heavenly realm, provides the setting appropriate for a private manifestation of heavenly phenomena to specially chosen individuals. In each version Jesus takes along Peter, James and John, three of the specially chosen twelve apostles, who function as the recipients especially privileged to witness the epiphanic activity.

The epiphanic action commences with the sudden and unexpected transfiguration of Jesus' external appearance, so that he resembles a heavenly being but remains on the earth (Mark 9:2-3; Matt 17:2; Luke 9:29). Jesus' transfiguration into a heavenly being is only the beginning of a complex epiphanic action. It facilitates the sudden and unexpected appearance of Moses and Elijah as heavenly figures, who converse with the heavenly transfigured Jesus (Mark 9:4; Matt 17:3; Luke 9:30-32).

This epiphanic appearance privileges the three disciples, the recipients chosen to witness the epiphany, with a special private revelation of heavenly phenomena on the earth. As spokesman for the three, Peter responds to the epiphanic action by offering to build three tents on the mountain, one for each of the heavenly figures (Mark 9:5-6; Matt 17:4; Luke 9:33).

But then suddenly occurs yet another unexpected epiphanic action, as a heavenly cloud overshadows them (Mark 9:7; Matt 17:5; Luke 9:34). This further epiphanic action continues as God's voice comes from the cloud identifying Jesus, in distinction from Moses and Elijah, as "my beloved/chosen Son" and commanding the three disciples to listen to him (Mark 9:7; Matt 17:5-7; Luke 9:35). This commanding voice of God from the cloud brings the entire epiphany to its climactic conclusion. This is confirmed as Jesus alone is left with the three disciples after they hear this dramatic command from the voice of God (Mark 9:8; Matt 17:8; Luke 9:36). That Jesus alone is left there underlines that the command is to listen to him alone as God's Son. The epiphany has ended as the heavenly figures of Moses and Elijah have disappeared with the cloud and Jesus no longer appears to be in a transfigured state.

Reactions of fear on the part of the witnesses to the sudden and awesome appearances of heavenly phenomena in theophanies, visions, and epiphanies are a common occurrence, well known by the Gospel audiences.[18] The transfiguration epiphany exhibits the fear motif, but it occurs in a different place in each version. In Mark 9:6 the three disciples "had become terrified" at the appearance of Moses and Elijah in conversation with the transfigured Jesus. In Luke 9:34 "they were frightened as they entered into the cloud." And in Matt 17:6 "they were greatly frightened" upon hearing the voice from the cloud. Only in Matt 17:7 does Jesus speak the comforting motif, "Arise and do not be afraid," another common occurrence familiar to the audiences of these literary genres.[19]

The transfiguration narrative presents the Gospel audiences with a rather unique type of epiphany. It begins with an initial epiphanic action, the transfiguration of Jesus, closely coordinated with the epiphanic appearance of Moses and Elijah. The transfiguration of Jesus into a heavenly being enables him to converse, while still on earth, with the heavenly figures of Moses and Elijah. But this initial intricate epiphanic appearance of Jesus, Moses, and Elijah is followed by the closely related, further epiphanic action of the divine voice coming out of the sudden appearance of an overshadowing heavenly cloud. The transfiguration narrative, then, is a complex epiphany with more than one epiphanic appearance of heavenly phenomena. Are there any precedents for this type of complex epiphany that would be familiar to the Gospel audiences from their literary traditions?

---

[18] For examples of the fear motif in epiphanies, see Matt 14:26; 28:4; Mark 4:41; 6:50; 16:5; Luke 1:12, 29; 2:9; 8:25; 24:5, 37; Acts 10:4; HEIL, *Jesus Walking on the Sea*, 11.

[19] For examples of the comfort motif in epiphanies, see Matt 14:27; 28:5, 10; Mark 6:50; 16:6; Luke 1:13, 30; 2:10; Heil, *Jesus Walking on the Sea*, 12.

1. *The Angelophany in Judges 6:11-24 and the Transfiguration Epiphany*

As a complex or compounded epiphany the transfiguration narrative follows a general sequence of 1) an initial epiphanic action comprising the appearance of Moses and Elijah as heavenly figures in conversation with Jesus, who has been transfigured into a heavenly figure on earth. 2) In response to this initial epiphanic appearance the recipients offer to build a tent for each heavenly figure, apparently to prolong their appearance on earth and to present them with appropriate homage. 3) Following upon this offer there is a further epiphanic appearance comprising an overshadowing heavenly cloud and God's voice from the cloud. This further epiphanic appearance intends to bring the recipients to a proper recognition of the significance of the initial epiphanic appearance, especially the proper identification of the epiphanic figure of Jesus.

The angelophany in Judg 6:11-24, the call of Gideon, familiar to the Gospel audiences from their scriptural knowledge, demonstrates a comparable general sequence with at least some very rough similarities to the transfiguration epiphany.[20] Its initial epiphanic action consists of the angel or messenger of the Lord appearing to Gideon, much like the initial, but more complex, appearance to the three disciples of Moses and Elijah in conversation with the transfigured Jesus in the transfiguration epiphany:[21]

MT Judg 6:12: וירא אליו מלאן יהוה

LXX Judg 6:12: καὶ ὤφθη αὐτῷ ἄγγελος κυρίου[22]

---

[20] For recent discussions of the Gideon narrative, see P. KÜBEL, "Epiphanie und Altarbau," *ZAW* 83 (1971) 225-31; J.P. TANNER, "The Gideon Narrative as the Focal Point of Judges," *BSac* 149 (1992) 146-61; B. STANDAERT, "Adonai Shalom (Judges 6-9): The Persuasive Means of a Narrative and the Strategies of Inculturation of Yahwism in a New Context," *Rhetoric, Scripture, & Theology: Essays from the 1994 Pretoria Conference* (JSNTSup 133; eds. S.E. Porter and T.H. Olbricht; Sheffield: Sheffield Academic Press, 1996) 195-202; D.I. BLOCK, "Will the Real Gideon Please Stand Up?: Narrative Style and Intention in Judges 6-9," *JETS* 40 (1997) 353-66; J. MARAIS, *Representation in Old Testament Narrative Texts* (BIS 36; Leiden: Brill, 1998) 108-10.

[21] J.A. SOGGIN, *Judges: A Commentary* (OTL; Philadelphia: Westminster, 1981) 114: "...the 'messenger' is a being who is interchangeable with Yahweh, identical to him, and does not exist in a separate form, being his visible manifestation."

[22] According to SOGGIN (*Judges*, 115) the verb "appeared" (וירא; ὤφθη) here "is a technical term for the divine manifestation: it is not enough that the person is present; he needs to reveal himself, to 'appear' to man in the sense of being perceived by him."

Mark 9:4: καὶ ὤφθη αὐτοῖς Ἠλίας σὺν Μωϋσεῖ
Matt 17:3: καὶ ἰδοὺ ὤφθη αὐτοῖς Μωϋσῆς καὶ Ἠλίας
Luke 9:30-31: Μωϋσῆς καὶ Ἠλίας, οἳ ὀφθέντες ἐν δόξῃ[23]

Although Gideon engages in a lively conversation with the angel of the Lord about his calling to play a role in God's salvific plan (6:12-16), he does not seem to be certain of the angel's true identity. Gideon asks for "a sign that it is you who speak with me" (6:17).[24] He goes on to request that the angel "not depart from here" until Gideon returns with an offering of food to set before the angel, who agrees to stay (6:18). Gideon's attempt to detain the angel of the Lord and pay him the homage of a hospitable meal offering in order to see if this is really the angel of the Lord is roughly similar to Peter's attempt to detain the three epiphanic figures — Jesus, Moses, and Elijah — and pay them hospitable homage by building a tent for each of them.[25]

After Gideon returns with the offering of food (6:19-20), there occurs a further epiphanic action. The angel of the Lord reaches out the tip of the staff that was in his hand and touches the food. Immediately fire springs up from the rock and consumes the food, thus transforming it into a sacrificial offering accepted by God. Then the angel of the Lord vanishes from Gideon's eyes (6:21). This further epiphanic action and disappearance of the angel results in Gideon's recognition of the angel's true identity, as he "saw that it was the angel of the Lord" (6:22).[26] Gideon then fearfully cries out for God's help, "for I

---

[23] This contradicts the contention that Moses and Elijah do not "appear" in the Lukan version, as asserted by M. MACH, "Christus Mutans: Zur Bedeutung der 'Verklärung Jesu' im Wechsel von jüdischer Messianität zur neutestamentlichen Christologie," *Messiah and Christos: Studies in the Jewish Origins of Christianity: Festschrift D. Flusser* (TSAJ 32; ed. I. Gruenwald, et al.; Tübingen: Mohr Siebeck, 1992) 182.

[24] SOGGIN, *Judges*, 116: "Gideon's affirmation, 'That it is really you who are talking with me' might seem to be a tautology: who else could be talking with him? It is not. More than once we have accepted that Gideon would already have some suspicions about the true identity of the person talking to him."

[25] The attempt to prevent the epiphanic figures from departing is most explicitly stated in the Lukan version, where Moses and Elijah are separating from Jesus, when Peter suggests the building of the tents (9:33). Although Peter seems to recognize the identities of the three epiphanic figures, he does not seem certain in Mark 9:6 and Luke 9:33 that the offer to build each of them a tent is appropriate.

[26] SOGGIN, *Judges*, 122: "...once the messenger has revealed his true identity, he has to disappear, given that his action now transcends the human form which he has assumed."

have seen the angel of the Lord face to face" (6:22). But God assures him with a comforting formula common to epiphanies, "Peace be to you; do not be afraid, you shall not die" (6:23).

This further epiphanic action in the angelophany to Gideon corresponds to the further epiphanic action of the divine voice from the overshadowing cloud in the transfiguration epiphany, which is similarly oriented to the recognition of the true identity of an epiphanic being, in this case of Jesus as God's beloved/chosen Son (Mark 9:7; Matt 17:5; Luke 9:35). The conclusion of the angelophany to Gideon with the disappearance of the angel of the Lord (Judg 6:21) corresponds to the conclusion of the transfiguration epiphany with the disappearance of Moses and Elijah along with the cloud, as Jesus alone remains before the eyes of the disciples (Mark 9:8; Matt 17:8; Luke 9:36). The comforting formula uttered by God to Gideon after he has seen the angel of the Lord face to face in Judg 6:23, "do not be afraid" (אַל־תִּירָא; μὴ φοβοῦ), corresponds to the comforting formula uttered by Jesus to the three disciples after they have heard the voice of God from the overshadowing cloud in Matt 17:7, "do not be afraid" (μὴ φοβεῖσθε).

2. *The Angelophany in Judges 13:2-24 and the Transfiguration Epiphany*

The angelophany in Judg 13:2-24, the announcement of the birth of Samson to Manoah and his wife, provides the Gospel audiences with another example of epiphanic features comparable to the general sequence of epiphanic activity in the transfiguration narrative.[27] As in the Gideon angelophany, the initial epiphanic action consists of the sudden appearance of the angel of the Lord to the wife of Manoah, similar to the sudden appearance of Moses and Elijah to the three disciples:

MT Judg 13:3: וַיֵּרָא מַלְאַךְ־יְהוָה אֶל־הָאִשָּׁה

LXX Judg 13:3: καὶ ὤφθη ἄγγελος κυρίου πρὸς τὴν γυναῖκα

---

[27] For recent discussions of the Samson narrative, see K.F.D. RÖMHELD, "Von den Quellen der Kraft (Jdc 13)," *ZAW* 104 (1992) 28-52; H.-J. STIPP, "Samson, der Nasiräer," *VT* 45 (1995) 337-69; MARAIS, *Representation*, 122-32; Y. AMIT, *The Book of Judges: The Art of Editing* (BIS 38; Leiden: Brill, 1999) 289-304. On the correspondence between Judg 6:11-24 and 13:2-24, see O'CONNELL, *Judges*, 149 n. 183.

Mark 9:4: καὶ ὤφθη αὐτοῖς ᾽Ηλίας σὺν Μωϋσεῖ
Matt 17:3: καὶ ἰδοὺ ὤφθη αὐτοῖς Μωϋσῆς καὶ ᾽Ηλίας
Luke 9:30-31: Μωϋσῆς καὶ ᾽Ηλίας, οἵ ὀφθέντες ἐν δόξῃ

After the angel informs the wife of Manoah that she will give birth to a son who will be a Nazirite (13:3-5), she reports the angelophany to her husband. But her report discloses her uncertainty about the true identity of the angel: "A man of God came to me, and his appearance was like that of an angel of God, most fearful; I did not ask him where he came from, and he did not tell me his name" (13:6). After Manoah prays, the angel comes again to the woman alone (13:9), who then fetches her husband. Like Gideon, Manoah tries to detain the angel with a hospitable offering of food, "not knowing that it was the angel of the Lord" (13:16). The angel declines to eat the food, but suggests that Manoah offer it as a sacrifice to the Lord (13:15-16). This corresponds more or less to Peter's hospitable offer to Jesus in the transfiguration epiphany to detain the three epiphanic figures by building a tent for each of them, although he does not really know how to respond to the epiphanic appearances (Mark 9:6; Luke 9:33).

After Manoah offers the sacrifice of food to the Lord (13:19), there occurs a further epiphanic action. When the flame consuming the sacrifice of food ascends to heaven, the angel of the Lord ascends in the flame of the altar while Manoah and his wife look on. They respond to this further epiphanic (dis)appearance by falling on their face to the ground (13:20). This further epiphanic action brings the entire angelophany to its conclusion, as the narrator notes that "the angel of the Lord did not appear again to Manoah and his wife" (13:21). The further epiphanic action of the ascension of the angel to heaven results in the recognition of the true identity of the epiphanic being in the initial epiphanic appearance: "Then Manoah knew that it was the angel of the Lord" (13:21).

Like in the angelophany to Gideon, the further epiphanic action of the disappearance of the angel, resulting in the recognition of his true identity, corresponds to the further epiphanic action of the divine voice from the overshadowing cloud in the transfiguration epiphany, which calls for the recognition of the true identity of the transfigured Jesus as God's beloved/chosen Son (Mark 9:7; Matt 17:5; Luke 9:35). Just as Manoah "knew that it was the angel of the Lord" after the angel ascended to heaven and "did not appear again" (13:21), so the three disciples are to know that the transfigured Jesus is God's beloved/chosen Son after Moses and Elijah disappear along with the overshadowing cloud, and Jesus alone is left there (Mark 9:8; Matt 17:8; Luke 9:36). The response to the further epiphanic action of the angel by Manoah and his wife, who "fell on their face (ἔπεσαν ἐπὶ πρόσωπον αὐτῶν) to the ground" in Judg 13:20 corresponds to the response of the disciples, who, when they heard the further epiphanic action of God's voice from the cloud, "fell upon their faces (ἔπεσαν ἐπὶ πρόσωπον αὐτῶν) and were greatly frightened" in Matt 17:6.

C. CONCLUSION

The angelophanies to Gideon (Judg 6:11-24) and to Manoah and his wife (Judg 13:2-24) provide the Gospel audiences with a literary precedent to recognize and understand what is going on in the transfiguration narrative. Both these angelophanies and the transfiguration epiphany begin with an initial epiphanic appearance, and then, after an attempt to detain or prolong the appearance, a further epiphanic action is oriented toward the recognition of the true identity of the initially appearing epiphanic figure. But can we further delineate the specific type of epiphany we have in the transfiguration narrative?

Although the transfiguration epiphany centers upon the recognition of the transfigured Jesus' true identity, the climactic accent of the divine voice from the epiphanic cloud falls on the command: "Listen to him!" (Mark 9:7; Matt 17:5; Luke 9:35). This command creates the final dramatic tension of the epiphany and leaves the Gospel audiences in suspense as to whether the disciples will listen to Jesus as God's beloved/chosen Son. Since the entire transfiguration epiphany is oriented to and issues in this climactic, authoritative command from the epiphanic voice, we may label it as a "mandatory epiphany." We will now demonstrate that the transfiguration narrative is a special type of mandatory epiphany by comparing it with similar mandatory epiphanies well known to the Gospel audiences from Num 22:31-35, Josh 5:13-15, and 2 Macc 3:22-34.

CHAPTER 3

THE TRANSFIGURATION NARRATIVE AS A PIVOTAL MANDATORY EPIPHANY

A. DEFINITION OF A PIVOTAL MANDATORY EPIPHANY

In this chapter we will demonstrate that the literary genre of each version of the transfiguration narrative can be more narrowly classified as a special type of "mandatory epiphany," that is, a "pivotal mandatory epiphany." The Gospel audiences would recognize and understand this literary genre from their thorough familiarity with their scriptural traditions. First, we define "mandatory epiphany" as any epiphany whose whole orientation and final focus centers upon a specific mandate, a *climactic command*, of an epiphanic being or voice to the recipient(s) of the epiphanic activity. The climactic command, emerging from and closely related to the epiphanic appearance, instructs the recipient(s) on how they are to play their role in God's plan of salvation. There may or may not be a final notice of obedience to the command, which indeed is subordinate to the central emphasis upon the command itself.

Secondly, the climactic command of the special type of mandatory epiphany with which we are concerned not only represents the final focus of the epiphany itself, but enunciates and refers the audience to a theme or topic of recurring central importance within the broader narrative context in which the mandatory epiphany is located. Because the command of this type of mandatory epiphany occurs at a pivotal point in the overall narrative, with significant contextual relations both prior and subsequent to the command, we label it as a "pivotal mandatory epiphany." We will now analyze three examples of pivotal mandatory epiphanies found in Num 22:31-35, Josh 5:13-15, and 2 Macc 3:22-34, and compare them to the three versions of the transfiguration narrative to demonstrate how they also exhibit this special type of mandatory epiphany.[1]

1. *The Pivotal Mandatory Epiphany in Numbers 22:31-35 and the Transfiguration Epiphany*

The pivotal mandatory epiphany in Num 22:31-35 occurs within the broader context of the Balaam narrative in Numbers 22-24.[2] Threatened by the great number of the people of Israel camped in the plains of Moab, Balak, the king of Moab, sent messengers to Balaam, the son of Beor at Pethor, which is on the Euphrates, inviting him to come and curse the people of Israel (Num 22:1-6).[3] Prompted by a

---

[1] These are not the only mandatory epiphanies in the biblical literature, but especially appropriate examples of a special type with pivotal narrative functions that are very comparable to the transfiguration narrative. REID (*Transfiguration*, 82-83) classifies Num 22:31-35 and 2 Macc 3:22-34 as "interpretative angelophanies." But the "interpretations" (Num 22:32-33; 2 Macc 3:33-34) are subordinate to the climactic commands (Num 22:35; 2 Macc 3:34) that serve as the final and enduring focus of these epiphanies, so that they are best designated as mandatory epiphanies. For additional examples of mandatory epiphanies, see Gen 19:1-22; 1 Chr 21:15-30; Matt 1:20-25; 2:13-15, 19-21; 28:1-10, 16-20; Mark 16:1-8; John 20:11-18; Acts 10:1-8.

[2] On Numbers 22-24, see W. GROSS, *Bileam: Literar- und formkritische Untersuchung der Prosa in Num 22-24* (SANT 38; Munich: Kösel, 1974); H. ROUILLARD, "L'ânesse de Balaam: Analyse littéraire de Nomb., XXII, 21-35," *RB* 87 (1980) 5-37, 211-41; IDEM, *La péricope de Balaam (Nombres 22-24): La prose et les "oracles"* (EBib 4; Paris: Gabalda, 1985); G. CASTELLO, "Balaam e Balak: Approccio narrativo a Nm 22-24," *Oltre il Racconto: Esegesi ed ermeneutica: alla ricerca del senso* (BTN; Naples: M. D'Auria Editore, 1994) 29-48; H.-C. SCHMITT, "Der heidnische Mantiker als eschatologischer Jahweprophet: Zum Verständnis Bileams in der Endgestalt von Num 22-24," *"Wer ist wie du, HERR, unter den Göttern?": Studien zur Theologie und Religionsgeschichte Israels für Otto Kaiser zum 70. Geburtstag* (ed. I. Kottsieper, et al.; Göttingen: Vandenhoeck & Ruprecht, 1994) 180-98; K.A.D. SMELIK, "Een ezel stoot zich in't gemeen..Een verkenning van Numeri 22-24," *Amsterdamse Cahiers voor Exegese en Bijbelse Theologie* 13 (1994) 14-30; H. SEEBASS, "Zur literarischen Gestalt der Bileam-Perikope," *ZAW* 107 (1995) 409-19; M. BARRÉ, "The Portrait of Balaam in Numbers 22-24," *Int* 51 (1997) 254-66; C. DESPLANQUE, "Mystère divin et ambiguïté humaine dans l'historie de Balaam," *Hokhma* 64 (1997) 1-16; J. VAN SETERS, "From Faithful Prophet to Villain: Observations on the Tradition History of the Balaam Story," *A Biblical Intinerary: In Search of Method, Form and Content: Essays in Honor of George W. Coats* (JSOTSup 240; ed. E.E. Carpenter; Sheffield: Sheffield Academic Press, 1997) 126-32; M. RÖSEL, "Wie einer vom Propheten zum Verführer wurde: Tradition und Rezeption der Bileamgestalt," *Bib* 80 (1999) 506-24.

[3] For the significance and various functions of curses, see J.S. ANDERSON, "The Social Function of Curses in the Hebrew Bible," *ZAW* 110 (1998) 223-37.

message from God, Balaam refused to come and curse the people (22:7-14). A second time Balak sent more messengers to persuade Balaam to come and curse the people (22:15-19). This time, during a nocturnal encounter – "that night," God told Balaam, "If the men have come to summon you, get up and go with them; but only the word that I will speak to you shall you do" (22:20).[4] So Balaam got up in the morning, saddled his donkey, and went with the officials of Moab (22:21).

Although God commanded Balaam to go, God became angry when Balaam actually set out on his journey to Balak. A rather unique angelophany then takes place, in which only Balaam's donkey sees the angel of the Lord standing in the road as an adversary with a drawn sword in his hand. Each of three times that the angel blocked the progress of the donkey, Balaam struck his donkey. Then the Lord opened the mouth of the donkey to ask Balaam why he has struck his donkey these three times. After Balaam vents his desire to kill his donkey, the speaking donkey persuades Balaam to admit that he has never treated Balaam like this in the past (22:22-30). Then occurs our mandatory epiphany:

Numbers 22:31-35

31 Then the Lord unveiled the eyes of Balaam, and he saw the angel of the Lord standing in the road with his drawn sword in his hand, and he bowed down and prostrated himself upon his face.

32 The angel of the Lord said to him, "Why have you struck your donkey these three times? It is I who have come out as an adversary, because your way is evil before me.[5] 33 The donkey saw me and turned away from me these three times. If it had not turned away from me, surely now, you I would have killed but it I would let live."

34 Then Balaam said to the angel of the Lord, "I have sinned, for I did not know that it was you who were standing in the road to oppose me. So now, if it is evil in your eyes, I will return home."

35 The angel of Lord said to Balaam, "*Go with the men, but only the word that I will speak to you shall you speak!*" So Balaam went with the officials of Balak.

Balaam's epiphanic experience began as God unveiled his eyes so that he could now see the angel of the Lord, who had previously

---

[4] On the prophetic character of this nocturnal consultation, see J.-M. HUSSER, *Le songe et la parole: Etude sur le rêve et sa fonction dans l'ancien Israël* (BZAW 210; Berlin: De Gruyter, 1994) 194-95.

[5] For this reading and explanation of the textual evidence, see T.R. ASHLEY, *The Book of Numbers* (NICOT; Grand Rapids: Eerdmans, 1993) 453 n. 9.

appeared as an epiphanic being, but was visible only to Balaam's donkey (22:22-23).[6] When epiphanic beings are made visible, their appearance is often registered in terms of the viewer's response of overwhelming awe and/or humble homage. In this case, when Balaam saw the angel of the Lord standing in the road with his drawn sword in his hand, he responded to this epiphanic appearance with a gesture of humble homage: "he bowed down and prostrated himself upon his face" (22:31).[7]

As a motif common to epiphanies, Balaam's gesture of homage is roughly similar to Peter's offer to build three tents in order to pay homage to the epiphanic figures of Jesus, Moses, and Elijah in the transfiguration narrative (Mark 9:5-6; Matt 17:4; Luke 9:33). But even closer to Balaam's gesture of homage is the disciples' response to the epiphanic voice of God in the Matthean version. Just as Balaam bowed down and "prostrated himself upon his face" (וישתחו לאפיו; προσεκύνησεν τῷ προσώπῳ αὐτοῦ) in response to the epiphanic appearance of the angel (22:31), so the disciples "fell upon their faces" (ἔπεσαν ἐπὶ πρόσωπον αὐτῶν) and were greatly frightened in response to the epiphanic appearance of God's voice from the overshadowing cloud (Matt 17:6).

Very often epiphanies involve some confusion, misunderstanding, or ignorance on the part of the recipient(s) regarding the true identity of the epiphanic being. Balaam is ignorant of the angel's true identity as the one who is ultimately responsible, rather than his donkey, for blocking his progress on the road to Balak. Employing an identification formula common to epiphanies, in which the epiphanic being eliminates the confusion or ignorance regarding his identity, the angel emphatically announces to Balaam that "it is I" (הנה אנכי; ἰδοὺ ἐγώ), not Balaam's donkey whom he struck three times, who has come

---

[6] M. NOTH, *Numbers: A Commentary* (OTL; Philadelphia: Westminster, 1968) 178: "Yahweh's messenger was in himself 'visible' in the usual way, just as elsewhere in the Old Testament the messenger of Yahweh, when he appears, is thought of as visible and in human form and, in the present context, with a drawn sword held threateningly in his hand." Noth expresses well here the earthly reality of the appearance of the angel of the Lord, characteristic of epiphanies, even though the angel was not visible to Balaam until now.

[7] The pair of verbs employed here, "bowed down and prostrated," are used together many times elsewhere in the OT, "always of someone lesser before someone greater, ten times of a person before Yahweh," according to ASHLEY, *Numbers*, 458.

out as the adversary blocking his way (22:32).[8] The angel then explains that the donkey, whom Balaam ironically wanted to kill (22:29), actually saved Balaam's life by turning away from the angel three times (22:33).

Similarly, in the transfiguration epiphany there is some confusion or ignorance on the part of the disciples regarding the true identity of the transfigured Jesus as an epiphanic being in distinction to Moses and Elijah. Consequently, out of the further epiphanic appearance of the overshadowing cloud God's voice emphatically announces that, rather than Moses or Elijah, "*this* is my Son" (οὗτός ἐστιν ὁ υἱός μου; Mark 9:7; Matt 17:5; Luke 9:35).

In response to the angel's identification of himself, Balaam admits that he was ignorant of the angel's true identity as the adversary: "I have sinned, for *I did not know* that it was *you* who were standing in the road to oppose me."[9] Balaam then presumes that his journey to Balak must be displeasing to God, so he offers to return home (22:34).

After Peter offers to build a tent each for Jesus, Moses, and Elijah in the transfiguration epiphany, his ignorance as to whether this is the proper response to the epiphanic appearance, while only implied in Matthew, is explicitly recorded in Mark and Luke: "He did not know what to reply" in Mark 9:6 and "not knowing what he was saying" in Luke 9:33. That Peter's ignorance involves his failure to recognize Jesus' true identity is then confirmed as the epiphanic voice of God announces in each version that "*this one* (not Moses or Elijah) is my Son."

Then occurs the angel's climactic command that defines this angel-ophany as a "mandatory epiphany": "Go with the men, but only the word that I will speak to you shall you speak!" This climactic command represents the whole point and purpose of this extended epiphany, in which the angel is made visible first to the donkey and then to Balaam himself. In this case the mandatory epiphany concludes with a notice of Balaam's partial obedience to the command, as Balaam conti-

---

[8] On the identification formula in epiphanies, see HEIL, *Jesus Walking on the Sea*, 12.

[9] On Balaam's "sin" here ASHLEY (*Numbers*, 459) states that it "does not involve a willful transgression of Yahweh's will and way, but rather a missing of the right way, a mistake....Balaam is simply saying that he made a mistake by not perceiving Yahweh's angel in the road."

nued on his journey to Moab with the officials of Balak (22:35). But still in suspense for the audience is whether or not Balaam will obey the rest of the command by speaking only the word that God/the angel of the Lord speaks to him.[10]

The climactic command of this mandatory epiphany performs a threefold pivotal function for the audience of the Balaam narrative. 1) Within the immediate context of the mandatory epiphany itself the command (22:35) corrects Balaam's false conclusion that he should return home rather than continue his journey to Moab with the men sent by Balak (22:34).

2) In relation to the previous context of the Balaam narrative the command of the angel in 22:35 reinforces and complements the previous command of God himself in 22:20. Note the close verbal relationship between these two commands centered upon "speaking" and "doing" the "word" of God:

> Num 22:20: "but only the word that I will speak to you shall you do!"
>
> MT Num 22:20:   את־הדבר אשר־אדבר אליך אתו תעשה ואך
>
> LXX Num 22:20: ἀλλὰ τὸ ῥῆμα, ὅ ἄν λαλήσω πρὸς σέ, τοῦτο ποιήσεις
>
> Num 22:35: "but only the word that I will speak to you shall you speak!"
>
> MT Num 22:35:   את־הדבר אשר־אדבר אליך אתו תדבר ואפס
>
> LXX Num 22:35: πλὴν τὸ ῥῆμα, ὅ ἐὰν εἴπω πρὸς σέ, τοῦτο φυλάξῃ λαλῆσαι

The mandate of the mandatory epiphany in 22:35 for Balaam "to speak" (תדבר; λαλῆσαι) only the word that the angel of the Lord will speak to him not only reinforces but complements the command in

---

[10] NOTH, *Numbers*, 179: "The messenger of Yahweh ('angel of Yahweh'), here, as elsewhere in the Old Testament, not a particular individual figure but a being of unknown origin sent by Yahweh from time to time, represents Yahweh himself and is introduced particularly at those points where too extended a speech by Yahweh was to be avoided; the messenger of Yahweh, then, acts and speaks in place of Yahweh, but always in such a manner as if it were an action or speech of Yahweh himself."

22:20 for Balaam "to do" (תַּעֲשֶׂה; ποιήσεις) only the word that God will speak to him. It is, therefore, by "speaking" the word of God that Balaam will be "doing" the word/will of God.[11] This complementarity between "doing" and "speaking" the word of God is directed not only to Balaam but to the implied audience.[12]

3) The command of this particular mandatory epiphany provides the audience with a focal point for the remainder of the Balaam narrative. The pivotal importance of the command becomes evident in the repeated statements to Balak by Balaam himself, which dramatically resolve the suspense for the audience as to whether Balaam will obey the command of God to bless rather than curse the people of Israel:

> Num 22:38: "The word God puts in my mouth, that is what I must say."
> Num 23:12: "Must I not take care to say what the Lord puts into my mouth?"
> Num 23:26: "Did I not tell you, 'Whatever the Lord says, that I must do?'"
> Num 24:13: "What the Lord says, that is what I will say."

Like the Balaam angelophany so the transfiguration epiphany exhibits a climactic command that defines it as a "mandatory epiphany": "This is my beloved/chosen Son, with whom I am well pleased; listen to him!" (Matt 17:5; Mark 9:7; Luke 9:35). This climactic command represents the whole point and purpose of this complex epiphany, in which the epiphanic appearances of Jesus, Moses, and Elijah as heavenly figures are followed by the epiphanic appearance of an overshadowing divine cloud from which God's voice issues the command to Peter, James and John, the recipients of the epiphanic activity. At the

---

[11] Note the additional subtle progression in the two commands in the Greek version from "doing" (ποιήσεις) the word in 22:20 to "being careful to speak" (φυλάξῃ λαλῆσαι) the word in 22:35. On the significance of the command of this mandatory epiphany ROUILLARD ("L'ânesse," 230) states: "Tout se passe comme si notre épisode n'était que la démonstration, en actes, le mime, de cet ordre." On 22:35 as the "resumptive repetition" or "reprise" of 22:20-21, see M. ANBAR, "La 'reprise'," VT 38 (1988) 388.

[12] ROUILLARD, "L'ânesse," 231: "Le rédacteur a instauré un suspens narratif, captant l'esprit disponible des auditeurs ou des lecteurs pour transférer dans le domaine du *faire* ce qui relevait de l'ordre du *dire*" (Rouillard's emphasis).

conclusion of the transfiguration epiphany the audience remains in suspense as to whether or how the disciples will obey the command.

The climactic command of the mandatory epiphany that comprises the transfiguration narrative performs for the Gospel audiences a pivotal threefold function analogous to the climactic command in the Balaam mandatory epiphany. 1) Within the immediate context of the transfiguration epiphany itself the command interrupts, overrides, and corrects Peter's offer to build a tent each for Jesus, Moses, and Elijah. Peter's offer makes no distinction between Jesus on the one hand and Moses and Elijah on the other, placing them all on the same level or in the same category as equally worthy of a tent. From the cloud God's voice corrects Peter's ignorance, much like the command of the angel corrected Balaam, by commanding the disciples to listen to Jesus, who is God's own Son in distinction to Moses and Elijah.

2) In the Balaam mandatory epiphany the climactic command of the angel (22:35) very deliberately and emphatically pointed Balaam as well as the audience of the narrative back to God's previous similar command for Balaam to do only what God tells him (22:20). Similarly, in each version of the transfiguration epiphany the climactic command of God's voice from the cloud functions as a pivotal point in the narrative. It very dramatically directs the disciples as well as the Gospel audiences back to listen again to the words Jesus has just spoken before the scene of his transfiguration, the words that predict his passion, death and resurrection, and that call for disciples to follow him (Mark 8:27-9:1; Matt 16:13-28; Luke 9:18-27).[13] The climactic command of the transfiguration mandatory epiphany, then, emphatically underlines the urgent and serious need for the disciples and the audience to carefully heed these words of Jesus.

3) The climactic command in the Balaam mandatory epiphany not only pointed the audience backward to the previous command of God, but also forward by creating suspense for the audience as to whether and how Balaam will obey the angel of the Lord's command. Similarly, the climactic command of God's voice from the cloud plays a pivotal role in the overall Gospel narratives. In each version of the

---

[13] Note again how Luke 9:28 begins the transfiguration epiphany by making explicit what Mark and Matthew imply, that Jesus' transfiguration takes place shortly "after these words" (μετὰ τοὺς λόγους τούτους) that Jesus has just uttered in Luke 9:18-27.

transfiguration mandatory epiphany the command arouses suspense for the audience as to whether or not the disciples will truly heed and understand the subsequent predictions of the passion, death and resurrection of Jesus as God's beloved/chosen Son.

2. *The Pivotal Mandatory Epiphany in Joshua 5:13-15 and the Transfiguration Epiphany*

The pivotal mandatory epiphany in Josh 5:13-15 follows the scene in which the Israelites began to eat from the produce of the promised land of Canaan rather than the manna, the day after they kept the Passover while camped in Gilgal in the plains of Jericho (5:10-12).[14]   It introduces Joshua's conquest of Jericho (6:1-27).

Joshua 5:13-15

13 When Joshua was by Jericho,[15] he raised his eyes and saw – and behold! – a man standing before him with a drawn sword in his hand. Joshua went up to him and said to him, "Are you one of us, or one of our enemies?"

14 He said, "Neither![16] For I am the commander of the army of the Lord. I have now arrived!"

---

[14] On Josh 5:13-15, see F.-M. ABEL, "L'apparition du chef de l'armée de Yahveh à Josué (Jos. V,13-15)," *Miscellanea Biblica et Orientalia: Athanasio Miller Oblata* (SA 27; Rome: Herder, 1951) 109-13; H. JAGERSMA, "Doe je schoen van je voet: Een onderzoek naar de achtergrond en betekenis van Jozua 5:13-15," *Tekst & Interpretatie: Studies over getallen, teksten, verhalen en geschiednis in het Oude Testament* (Nijkerk: Callenbach, 1990) 108-18; L.D. HAWK, *Every Promise Fulfilled: Contesting Plots in Joshua* (Louisville: Westminster John Knox, 1991) 21-24; K. BIEBERSTEIN, Josua-Jordan-Jericho: *Archäologie, Geschichte und Theologie der Landnahmeerzählungen Josua 1-6* (OBO 143; Göttingen: Vandenhoeck & Ruprecht, 1995) 223-29, 413-18; E. JACOB, "Une théopanie mysterieuse: Josué 5,13-15," *Ce Dieu Qui vient: Mélanges offerts à Bernard Renaud* (LD 159; Paris: Cerf, 1995) 130-35; V. FRITZ, *Das Buch Josua* (HAT 7; Tübingen: Mohr Siebeck, 1994) 63-65; C. SCHÄFER-LICHTENBERGER, *Josua und Salomo: Eine Studie zu Autorität und Legitimität des Nachfolgers im Alten Testament* (VTSup 58; Leiden: Brill, 1995) 210-11; N. WINTHER-NIELSEN, *A Functional Discourse Grammar of Joshua: A Computer-Assisted Rhetorical Structure Analysis* (ConBOT 40; Stockholm: Almqvist & Wiksell, 1995) 193-94.

[15] The phrase "by" or "in" Jericho (בִּירִיחוֹ), according to WINTHER-NIELSEN (*Functional Discourse*, 194 n. 70), "probably refers to the city state area, which they had reached on its eastern border at Gilgal by 4:13 and 19."

[16] R.D. NELSON, *Joshua: A Commentary* (OTL; Louisville: Westminster John Knox, 1997) 73-74: "The commander's "no" [לֹא] is best understood as "neither," that is, that he

Then Joshua fell on his face to the earth and worshiped, and said to him, "What has my lord to say to his servant?"

15 The commander of the army of the Lord said to Joshua, *"Remove your sandals from your feet, for the place on which you are standing is holy!"* And Joshua did so.

The epiphany begins as Joshua raised his eyes and suddenly and unexpectedly saw the appearance of an epiphanic being, "a man standing before him with a drawn sword in his hand" (5:13), reminiscent of "the angel of the Lord standing in the road with his drawn sword in his hand" (Num 22:31; cf. 1 Chr 21:16) that Balaam saw in his epiphany.[17] In accord with the epiphany genre there is frequently some confusion on the part of the recipient(s) regarding the true identity of the epiphanic figure. Here Joshua mistakes the epiphanic being for a merely human soldier, as he asked him, "Are you one of us, or one of our enemies?" (5:13). In accord with the identification formula common to epiphanies, the epiphanic being emphatically reveals his true identity: *"I am* the commander of the army of the Lord (יהוה־ אֲנִ֣י שַׂר־צְבָא; Ἐγὼ ἀρχιστράτηγος δυνάμεως κυρίου)" (5:14). After dramatically disclosing his true identity, the commander of God's army solemnly and emphatically announces that "I have *now* arrived" (עַתָּ֥ה בָֽאתִי; νυνὶ παραγέγονα, 5:14).[18] This means that

---

represents a third force in the conflict, the army of Yahweh." See also R.G. BOLING and G.E. WRIGHT, *Joshua: A New Translation with Notes and Commentary* (AB 6; New York: Doubleday, 1982) 197; BIEBERSTEIN, *Josua*, 226.

[17] For a comparison of the epiphany in Josh 5:13-15 with the similar epiphanies to Moses in Exod 3:2-5, to Balaam in Num 22:31-35, and to David in 1 Chr 21:16-17, see BIEBERSTEIN, *Josua*, 414-18.

[18] Many interpreters view the solemn and dramatic announcement of the arrival of the commander of the army of Lord as an abrupt break-off, indicating that an expected further communication has been lost, see NELSON, *Joshua*, 81; J.A. SOGGIN, *Joshua* (OTL; Philadelphia: Westminster, 1972) 78. According to WINTHER-NIELSEN (*Functional Discourse*, 193), "the segment is frequently isolated as an independent and incomplete fragment of unknown Canaanite origin legitimizing a holy place." See, for example, M. NOTH, *Das Buch Josua* (HAT 7; Tübingen: Mohr Siebeck, 1953) 23, 39-40. For a critique of Noth's view, see NELSON, *Joshua*, 82. The abruptness, however, is most appropriate to the emphatic and solemn character of the announcement. Some recent interpreters of Josh 5:13-15, including BIEBERSTEIN (*Josua*, 229), recognize its basic literary unity: "Doch wurden diese Versuche, der als fragmentarisch angesehenen Einheit die erwartete Form zu geben, von jüngeren Kommentatoren zu Recht nicht wiederholt, und die Einheit kann, obgleich möglicherweise fragmentarisch, als literarisch einheitlich gelten."

from now on Joshua will have divine military assistance in his conquest of the promised land.[19]

The transfiguration epiphany exhibits a similar confusion on the part of the disciples regarding the true identity of the transfigured Jesus as an epiphanic being in distinction to Moses and Elijah. Indeed, Peter did not really know how to respond, when he offered to build a tent each for Jesus, Moses, and Elijah (Mark 9:6; Luke 9:33), placing all three in the same category. The identification formula occurs when God's voice out of the further epiphanic appearance of the overshadowing cloud emphatically announces that, "*this one* (οὗτος)" (not Moses or Elijah) is "*my Son*" (Mark 9:7; Matt 17:5; Luke 9:35), in distinction to the prophets Moses and Elijah.

In accord with the homage motif common to epiphanies, Balaam bowed down and "prostrated himself upon his face" (וישתחו לאפיו; προσεκύνησεν τῷ προσώπῳ αὐτοῦ) in response to the epiphanic appearance of the angel of the Lord (Num 22:31). Similarly, after the commander of the army of the Lord identified himself, Joshua "fell on his face to the earth and worshiped" (ויפל אל־פניו ארצה וישתחו; ἔπεσεν ἐπὶ πρόσωπον ἐπὶ τὴν γῆν, 5:14).[20] In the Matthean version of the transfiguration epiphany the disciples "fell upon their faces" (ἔπεσαν ἐπὶ πρόσωπον αὐτῶν) and were greatly frightened in response to the epiphanic appearance of God's voice from the overshadowing cloud (Matt 17:6).

After Joshua in humble homage asks, "What has my lord to say to his servant?" (5:14), there occurs the climactic command that defines this particular epiphany as a "mandatory epiphany": "Remove your sandals from your feet, for the place on which you are standing is holy!" (5:15). This climactic command represents the whole point and purpose of this concise epiphany, in which the commander of the army of the Lord dramatically announces his decisive arrival in the promised, "holy" land. In the Hebrew text Joshua's immediate obedience to the command is explicitly stated: "And Joshua did so" (5:15). But in the Greek text a statement of Joshua's obedience to the command is lacking, thus making this version closer to both the Balaam and the

---

[19] For similar heavenly visitations as signs of divine participation in warfare, see J. VAN SETERS, "Joshua's Campaign of Canaan and Near Eastern Historiography," *SJOT* 4 (1990) 1-12.

[20] That Joshua "worshiped" is lacking in the LXX of Josh 5:14.

transfiguration mandatory epiphanies, which likewise leave their audiences in suspense regarding the obedience to the command.[21]

Like the climactic command of the Balaam mandatory epiphany (Num 22:35) so the climactic command of the Joshua mandatory epiphany (5:15) performs for the audience a pivotal threefold narrative function. 1) Within the immediate context of the mandatory epiphany itself, in answering Joshua's request for what the commander of the army of the Lord has to say to him (5:14), the climactic command further discloses the significance of the epiphanic appearance. Joshua is to remove the sandals from his feet as appropriate recognition that the place on which he is standing is now holy (5:15), because the commander of the army of the Lord has now arrived (5:14) in the land of Canaan with a drawn sword in his hand (5:13), ready to fight with and for Joshua to make this promised land of Canaan the sacred possession of the people of God.

2) With regard to the previous narrative context the command of the commander of the army of the Lord to Joshua reminds the audience of the biblical narrative of the almost identical command that the angel of the Lord issued to Moses from the burning bush:

> Exod 3:5: "Remove your sandals from your feet, for the place on which you are standing is holy ground!"
>
> MT Exod 3:5: אֲשֶׁר אַתָּה עוֹמֵד עָלָיו אַדְמַת־קֹדֶשׁ הוּא שַׁל־נְעָלֶיךָ מֵעַל רַגְלֶיךָ כִּי הַמָּקוֹם
>
> LXX Exod 3:5: λῦσαι τὸ ὑπόδημα ἐκ τῶν ποδῶν σου· ὁ γὰρ τόπος, ἐν ᾧ σὺ ἕστηκας, γῆ ἁγία ἐστίν.
>
> Josh 5:15: "Remove your sandals from your feet, for the place on which you are standing is holy!"
>
> MT Josh 5:15: כִּי הַמָּקוֹם אֲשֶׁר אַתָּה עוֹמֵד עָלָיו קֹדֶשׁ הוּא שַׁל־נַעַלְךָ מֵעַל רַגְלֶךָ
>
> LXX Josh 5:15: λῦσαι τὸ ὑπόδημα ἐκ τῶν ποδῶν σου· ὁ γὰρ τόπος, ἐφ' ᾧ σὺ ἕστηκας, ἅγιός ἐστιν.

That the commander of the army of the Lord issues to Joshua the nearly identical command that the angel of the Lord issued to Moses underlines for the audience that Joshua has become the legitimate suc-

---

[21] Which version of Josh 5:15 is the original is not able to be decided with certainty, according to BIEBERSTEIN, *Josua*, 228.

cessor of Moses.[22] The command to Joshua climactically confirms that the promise that God will be with Joshua like he was with Moses, which has been repeatedly emphasized in the previous context, is being further fulfilled and confirmed with the arrival of the commander of the army of the Lord:

Josh 1:5: "As I was with Moses, so I will be with you."
Josh 1:17: "May the Lord your God be with you, as he was with Moses!"
Josh 3:7: "This day I will begin to exalt you in the sight of all Israel, that they may know that I will be with you as I was with Moses."
Josh 4:14: On that day the Lord exalted Joshua in the sight of all Israel; and all the days of his life they revered him, as they had revered Moses.

The pivotal command of the mandatory epiphany to Joshua also reminds the audience of God's previous promise to Joshua at the beginning of the book:

Josh 1:3: "Every place (מקום; τόπος) that the sole of your foot/feet (רגלכם; τῶν ποδῶν ὑμῶν) will tread upon I have given to you, as I promised to Moses."
Josh 5:15: "Remove your sandals from your feet (רגלך; τῶν ποδῶν σου), for the place (המקום; τόπος) on which you are standing is holy!"

That Joshua is to remove the sandals from his "feet," for "the place" on which he is standing is holy (5:15), signals to the audience that God is fulfilling his previous promise to Joshua that every "place" upon which Joshua's "foot/feet" walks God has given him, as promised

---

[22] The main, hardly significant, difference between the two commands is that Josh 5:15 lacks the word "ground" (אדמה) in Exod 3:5. That Josh 5:15 abruptly ends with the climactic command and does not go on to include the promise of the land as in Exod 3:8 is not an ominous sign, as HAWK (*Every Promise Fulfilled*, 23-24) proposes, but accords with the statement of SCHÄFER-LICHTENBERGER (*Josua und Salomo*, 210): "Die Epiphanie eines ranghohen JHWH-Boten, sein Rang entspricht dem Gebot der Situation, läßt Josua in puncto Gottesbeziehung sichtbar eine Stufe hinter Mose zurücktreten. In dieses Bild fügt sich gut die Abweisung der auf weitere Instruktion harrenden Frage Josuas ein, deren lakonische, allein die Umstände der Erscheinung betreffende Antwort 'Ziehe deine Schuhe von deinen Füßen, denn der Platz auf dem du stehst, heilig ist er' (5,15) eher eine Maßregelung als die erbetene Auskunft darstellt."

to Moses (1:3). The command of the mandatory epiphany indicates further to the audience that the promised land has been set apart to be the "holy" land that God has given to the people of Israel.[23]

3) The pivotal command of the mandatory epiphany to Joshua prepares the audience for Joshua's conquest not only of Jericho but of the rest of the promised land through the divine military assistance now to be provided with the dramatic arrival of the commander of the army of the Lord with his drawn sword. The announcement by the commander of the Lord's army that the place on which Joshua is standing is "holy" (קָדֹשׁ; ἅγιός), which place is in or by Jericho (5:13), prepares for the Lord's instruction to Joshua regarding the metal objects taken from Jericho after its conquest: "But all silver and gold, and vessels of bronze and iron, are holy (קָדֹשׁ; ἅγιον) to the Lord; they shall go into the treasury of the Lord" (6:19).[24]

And that God's army assisted Joshua in his military conquest of the promised land is indicated by the announcements of God himself to Joshua:

> Josh 6:2: "See, I have handed Jericho over to you, along with its king and soldiers."
> Josh 8:1: "See, I have handed over to you the king of Ai with his people, his city, and his land."
> Josh 10:8: "Do not fear them, for I have handed them over to you; not one of them will stand before you."
> Josh 11:6: "Do not be afraid of them, for tomorrow at this time I will hand over all of them, slain, to Israel; you will hamstring their horses, and burn their chariots with fire."

The narrator confirms these promises of God: "Joshua took all these kings and their land at one time, because the Lord God of Israel fought for Israel" (10:42; see also 10:9-14).[25]

---

[23] With reference to the command of Josh 5:15 NELSON (*Joshua*, 82) states: "What was once alien land has now become Yahweh's land, holy land (compare 22:19; 1 Sam 26:19-20; 2 Kings 5:15-19)."

[24] As NELSON (*Joshua*, 83) further remarks: "Jericho as a 'shoes-off place' is off-limits to ordinary human usage, in accord with the curse of 6:26."

[25] SCHÄFER-LICHTENBERGER, *Josua und Salomo*, 211 n. 525: "Die Szene Jos 5,13-15 bietet eine Erklärung an für die stereotypen Zusagen JHWHs an Josua, daß er die Feinde Josua ausliefern werde, sowie für die Aussagen JHWHs aktiven kriegerischen Einsatz für Israel."

The climactic command of the transfiguration mandatory epiphany to the disciples performs for the Gospel audiences a pivotal threefold function comparable to the climactic command in the mandatory epiphany to Joshua. 1) The command for Joshua to honor the land the Israelites are now in as holy clarifies the significance of the epiphanic appearance as the decisive arrival of the commander of the army of the Lord to assist in making the promised land the holy land of the people of Israel. Similarly, the command given to the disciples in the transfiguration epiphany, "this is my beloved/chosen Son; listen to him!" (Mark 9:7; Matt 17:5; Luke 9:35), clarifies for the audience the significance of the initial epiphanic appearance. The disciples are to listen to Jesus as God's Son in order to understand the meaning of the epiphanic appearance in which the earthly Jesus suddenly appears as a heavenly figure in conversation with the heavenly figures of Moses and Elijah.

2) In the Joshua mandatory epiphany the pivotal command to Joshua pointed the audience of the biblical narrative back to the nearly identical command to Moses (Exod 3:5), as well as to the previous promise that God has given the land to Joshua (Josh 1:3). Similarly, in each version of the transfiguration mandatory epiphany the pivotal command directs the disciples as well as the Gospel audiences back to the words Jesus has just spoken before the scene of his transfiguration, the words that predict his passion, death and resurrection, and that call for disciples to follow him (Mark 8:27-9:1; Matt 16:13-28; Luke 9:18-27). The implication is that these words provide the key for understanding the epiphanic appearance of the transfigured Jesus in conversation with Moses and Elijah.

3) The pivotal command of the mandatory epiphany to Joshua that he should recognize the land he is standing on as holy pointed the audience forward to Joshua's conquest not only of Jericho but of the entire "holy" land with the divine military assistance of God. Similarly, the pivotal command of the transfiguration mandatory epiphany for the disciples to listen to Jesus as God's Son points the disciples and the audience forward to the additional predictions of Jesus' passion, as well as to anything else he will say that may reveal the significance of his epiphanic appearance with Moses and Elijah.

3. *The Pivotal Mandatory Epiphany in 2 Maccabees 3:22-34 and the Transfiguration Epiphany*

The pivotal mandatory epiphany in 2 Macc 3:22-34 is located within the account of God's miraculous protection of the Jerusalem temple in 3:1-40.[26] A certain Simon, who had been made captain of the temple, had a disagreement with the current high priest Onias. Simon had King Seleucus informed that he could confiscate from the temple treasury certain funds not belonging to the account of the sacrifices. King Seleucus commissioned Heliodorus to remove the reported wealth (3:1-8). When Heliodorus arrived in Jerusalem, Onias informed him that the funds in question included deposits belonging to widows and orphans, as well as to a man of very prominent position. Onias urged Heliodorus that these people who had trusted in the holiness of the temple that is honored throughout the whole world should not be wronged (3:9-12). Nevertheless, Heliodorus decided that the money must be confiscated for the king. Consequently, the entire populace was distressed and began to pray in supplication (3:13-21). Then occurs our mandatory epiphany:

2 Maccabees 3:22-34

22 While they were calling upon the almighty Lord to keep what had been entrusted safe and secure for those who had entrusted it, 23 Heliodorus went on with what had been decided.

24 But just when he arrived with his bodyguards at the treasury, the sovereign of spirits and of all authority made so great a manifestation that those who had been so bold as to accompany him were astounded at the power of God, becoming faint and fearful. 25 There appeared to them a horse having an awesome rider and adorned with a magnificent harness. Charging furiously, it attacked Heliodorus with its front hoofs. The rider was seen to have golden armor.

---

[26] On 2 Macc 3:22-34, see F.-M. ABEL, *Les Livres des Maccabées* (EBib; Paris: Gabalda, 1949) 322-27; S. ZEITLIN, *The Second Book of Maccabees* (New York: Harper & Brothers, 1954) 125-29; R. DORAN, *Temple Propaganda: The Purpose and Character of 2 Maccabees* (CBQMS 12; Washington: Catholic Biblical Association of America, 1981) 48-51, 98-100; J.A. GOLDSTEIN, *II Maccabees: A New Translation with Introduction and Commentary* (AB 41A; New York: Doubleday, 1983) 210-15; T. FISCHER, "Heliodor im Tempel zu Jerusalem: Ein 'hellenistischer' Aspekt der 'frommen Legende'," *Prophetie und geschichtliche Wirklichkeit im alten Israel: Festschrift für Siegfried Herrmann zum 65. Geburtstag* (eds. R. Liwak and S. Wagner; Stuttgart: Kohlhammer, 1991) 122-33.

26 Then appeared to him two other young men, remarkably strong, gloriously beautiful and splendidly attired, who, standing on each side, flogged him unceasingly, inflicting many blows upon him. 27 When he suddenly fell to the ground, enveloped in deep darkness, they picked him up and placed him on a stretcher. 28 The one who had just entered the aforesaid treasury with a large entourage and a full bodyguard they carried out unable to help himself, having come to experience clearly the sovereign power of God.

29 While he lay speechless because of the divine intervention and deprived of any hope of recovery, 30 they praised the Lord who had acted marvelously for his own place. And the temple, which shortly before had been full of fear and trepidation, was filled with joy and gladness, now that the almighty Lord had appeared.

31 Soon some of the companions of Heliodorus begged Onias to call upon the Most High to grant life to one who was lying at the point of his last breath. 32 So the high priest, suspecting that the king might get the notion that some foul play had been perpetrated by the Jews with regard to Heliodorus, offered sacrifice for the man's recovery.

33 While the high priest was making the atonement, the same young men dressed in the same clothing appeared again to Heliodorus, and they stood and said, "Be very grateful to the high priest Onias, for on his account the Lord has granted you your life. 34 As for you, who have been scourged from heaven, *proclaim to all the majestic power of God.*" Having said these things, they disappeared.[27]

Before narrating the actual epiphanic appearance, the narrator employs the fear motif commonly exhibited by the recipients of epiphanies. Those who had been so bold as to accompany Heliodorus as his bodyguards also became recipients of the epiphany along with Heliodorus. They were so astounded at the great manifestation of the power of God that they "became faint and fearful" (3:24).[28] As we

---

[27] For a discussion of past source-critical theories that view 2 Maccabees 3 as a compilation of at least two sources, see DORAN, *Temple Propaganda*, 20-21. These source theories are not convincing according to FISCHER ("Heliodor," 123), who concludes: "Der ganze Bericht ist in sich schlüssig und nicht ohne einen gewissen Effekt zum Ende hin entwickelt."

[28] Although we are using the word "epiphany" as a modern designation of an ancient literary genre, the use here of the Greek word ἐπιφάνεια for the "manifestation" of God's power (3:24) that will occur in the epiphanic appearance is noteworthy. It indicates how epiphanic appearances take place as earthly realities in contrast to the heavenly appearances that occur in the literary genre of a "vision" (see chap. 2). On the meaning of the word ἐπιφάνεια, BAGD (304) states: "As a religious technical term it means a visible manifestation of a hidden divinity, either in the form of a personal appearance, or by some deed of power by which its presence is made known." On its meaning and use in 2 Maccabees, GOLDSTEIN (*II Maccabees*, 192) notes that ἐπιφάνεια "was a tangible event in which a supernatural being or force was perceived to act...Jason of Cyrene reports such interventions at 3:24-25, 10:29-30, 11:8, 12:22, 15:27; cf. 5:2-4 and 14:15. The word is used of a less tangible apparition at 5:4." See also P.-G. MÜLLER, "ἐπιφάνεια," *EDNT* 2.44-45.

have seen, the fear motif occurs at various places in the three versions of the complex transfiguration epiphany (Mark 9:6; Matt 17:6; Luke 9:34).

The report of the sudden and unexpected appearance to Heliodorus and his companions of a horse and rider resembles the report of the epiphanic appearance to the three disciples of Moses and Elijah in conversation with the transfigured Jesus:

2 Macc 3:25: ὤφθη γάρ τις ἵππος αὐτοῖς
Mark 9:4: καὶ ὤφθη αὐτοῖς ᾽Ηλίας σὺν Μωϋσεῖ
Matt 17:3: καὶ ἰδοὺ ὤφθη αὐτοῖς Μωϋσῆς καὶ ᾽Ηλίας
Luke 9:30-31: Μωϋσῆς καὶ ᾽Ηλίας, οἳ ὀφθέντες ἐν δόξῃ

The epiphany to Heliodorus begins with a double epiphanic appearance. After the appearance of the epiphanic horse with awesome rider (3:25) two other young men appeared (προσεφάνησαν) to Heliodorus, flogging him and inflicting him with many blows (3:26).[29] Similarly, the transfiguration epiphany begins with a double epiphanic appearance. After the appearance of the transfigured Jesus before the three disciples (Mark 9:2; Matt 17:2; Luke 9:29) there appeared to them Moses and Elijah in conversation with the transfigured Jesus (Mark 9:4; Matt 17:3; Luke 9:30-31).

Both of the epiphanic appearances to Heliodorus exhibit a noteworthy focus upon the clothing of the epiphanic figures, which underscores their origin and status as heavenly figures.[30] The epiphanic horse was "adorned with a magnificent harness" and its awesome rider was clothed in "golden armor" (3:25). The two other young men were "gloriously beautiful and splendidly attired" (3:26). Similarly, the focus upon the remarkably white clothing of the transfigured Jesus indicates his transformation into a heavenly figure. In Mark 9:3 "his

---

[29] For the suggestion that the two young men could be identified by an educated Hellenistic audience as the Dioscuri, the twin brothers Castor and Pollux, the sons of Zeus, see FISCHER, "Heliodor," 125.

[30] On the description of the figures as indicative of their heavenly character, see ABEL, *Maccabées*, 324-25. For similarities to epiphanies in Greek literature, see DORAN, *Temple Propaganda*, 99-100. According to GOLDSTEIN (*II Maccabees*, 213): "Interest in the personal appearance and clothing of supernatural beings is common to both pagans and Jews." See also J.W. VAN HENTEN, *The Maccabean Martyrs as Saviours of the Jewish People: A Study of 2 and 4 Maccabees* (JSJSup 57; Leiden: Brill, 1997) 246.

clothes became very radiantly white, such as no bleacher on the earth could thus whiten." In Matt 17:2 "his clothes became white as the light." And in Luke 9:29 "his clothing became dazzling white."

Not only does the epiphany to Heliodorus begin with a double epiphanic appearance, but it concludes with an additional epiphanic appearance, rendering it a complex epiphany similar to the transfiguration epiphany. While the high priest Onias was offering a sacrifice for the recovery of the wounded Heliodorus, "the same young men dressed in the same clothing appeared (ἐφάνησαν) again to Heliodorus" (3:33).[31] Similarly, in the transfiguration epiphany the opening double epiphanic appearance of the transfigured Jesus with Moses and Elijah is followed by the additional epiphanic appearance of the divine overshadowing cloud (Mark 9:7; Matt 17:5; Luke 9:34).

The second epiphanic appearance to Heliodorus of the two young men from heaven issues in the climactic command that defines this epiphany as a "mandatory epiphany." After the two epiphanic young men tell Heliodorus to be grateful to the high priest Onias for the sparing of his life (3:33), they announce to Heliodorus, who "has been scourged from heaven," the climactic command: "Proclaim to all the majestic power of God" (3:34).[32] Once the epiphanic beings have uttered the climactic command, "they disappeared" (3:34), confirming that the *command* is the ultimate point and purpose of this "mandatory" epiphany.[33] Similarly, in the transfiguration epiphany the additional epiphanic appearance of the overshadowing cloud issues in the climactic command that defines it as a "mandatory epiphany." God's voice from the cloud commands the disciples to listen to Jesus as God's beloved/chosen Son (Mark 9:7; Matt 17:5; Luke 9:35). This command represents the ultimate point and purpose of the transfigura-

---

[31] Note again the focus on the glorious clothing of the epiphanic young men indicative of their heavenly character.

[32] That Heliodorus has been scourged *from heaven* further reinforces the heavenly character of the epiphanic beings.

[33] On the overriding significance of the "word" and "proclamation" of the climactic command FISCHER ("Heilodor," 123-24) remarks: "Nicht nur das Heiligtum und Heliodor werden 'errettet' (der sich zudem dem biblischen Glauben zuwendet), sondern auch das 'Wort' wird jetzt über das 'Werk' gestellt! Die aktive, in jeder Hinsicht beredte und persönlich engagierte 'Verkündigung' des noch kurz zuvor 'gelämten' Heliodor ersetzt nämlich die eigentliche 'Tat'."

tion epiphany. Once the command has been uttered, the epiphanic appearances cease, as the disciples no longer see Moses and Elijah or the cloud but Jesus alone (Mark 9:8; Matt 17:8; Luke 9:36).

As in the mandatory epiphanies to Balaam (Num 22:35) and to Joshua (Josh 5:15), so in the mandatory epiphany to Heliodorus the climactic command performs for the audience a pivotal threefold narrative function. 1) Within the immediate context of the mandatory epiphany itself, the command for Heliodorus to proclaim to all the majestic power of God (3:34) indicates to the audience the ultimate significance of the epiphanic appearances of the two young men along with the horse and rider. These epiphanic appearances have not only prevented Heliodorus from plundering the temple treasury, but they have given him a unique experience of the majestic power of God. This experience will ironically transform the pagan enemy Heliodorus into a prime proclaimer to all peoples of the magnificent power of the God of Israel![34]

2) With regard to the previous narrative context the pivotal command to Heliodorus points the audience back to the prayer uttered by the Jewish people that introduced the theme of the Gentiles coming to know the power of the God of Israel:

> 1:27: "May the Gentiles know that you are our God!"
> 3:34: "Proclaim to all the majestic power of God!"

The command answers the prayer in a double way: Heliodorus himself is a Gentile who has come to know the power of God and now he will proclaim that power to all the Gentiles.[35]

3) With regard to the succeeding narrative context the pivotal command for Heliodorus to proclaim to all (πᾶσι) the majestic power of God (3:34) receives a prompt obedience. When Heliodorus returned to King Seleucus (3:35), "he gave witness to all (πᾶσιν) of the deeds of the most high God that he had seen with his own eyes" (3:36). The command for Heliodorus to proclaim (διάγγελλε) to all the majestic

---

[34] FISCHER ("Heliodor," 123) expresses well this significance of the climactic command: "...freilich mit der ernsten 'Abmahnung', ja dem ausdrücklichen 'Befehl', Heliodor solle andauernd dem Hohenpriester Onias dankbar sein und die Herrlichkeit der Macht des Herrn in aller Welt verkünden!"

[35] Note how the prayer's additional request for the punishment of oppressors (1:28) began to be answered in the punishment of Heliodorus by the epiphanic appearances (3:25-28).

power of God (τὸ μεγαλεῖον τοῦ θεοῦ κράτος) also prepares the audience for a recurring theme of other prominent Gentiles attesting to the majestic power of the God of the Jews. After being humiliated by God in his attempt to capture the people of Jerusalem to provide tribute for the Romans, Nicanor proclaimed (κατήγγελλεν) that the Jews had a Defender, and that they were invulnerable, because they followed the laws ordained by him (8:36). The all-seeing Lord, the God of Israel, struck Antiochus, who was intent on making Jerusalem a cemetery of Jews, with an incurable and invisible blow (9:4-5). Consequently, this gentile oppressor vowed that he would become a Jew and visit every inhabited place to proclaim (καταγγέλλοντα) the power of God (τὸ τοῦ θεοῦ κράτος) (9:17).[36]

The climactic command of the transfiguration mandatory epiphany to the disciples performs for the Gospel audiences an analogous pivotal threefold narrative function. 1) The command to Heliodorus (3:34), which emerged as the main reason for the second epiphanic appearance of the two young men, indicated to the audience the ultimate significance of the initial double epiphanic appearances of the horse and rider along with the two young men (3:25-26). Similarly, the command for the three disciples to listen to Jesus as God's beloved/chosen Son, which emerges as the main reason for the additional epiphanic appearance of the overshadowing cloud, indicates to the audience that the key to the ultimate significance of the initial double epiphanic appearance of the transfigured Jesus in conversation with Moses and Elijah lies in listening to the words of Jesus.

2) In the mandatory epiphany to Heliodorus the pivotal command (3:34) pointed the audience back to the prayer (1:27) that introduced the theme of the command, that Gentiles come to know the power of the God of Israel. Similarly, in the transfiguration mandatory epiphany the pivotal command directs the disciples as well as the audience back to the words Jesus has just spoken, which introduce a recurring theme — Jesus' predictions of his passion, death and resurrection, and call for disciples to follow him (Mark 8:27-9:1; Matt 16:13-28; Luke 9:18-27).

---

[36] VAN HENTEN (*Maccabean Martyrs*, 247) alludes to this connection to the command to Heliodorus when he points out "Heliodorus' and Antiochus IV's final recognition that the God of the Jerusalem temple and the Jewish people is the ultimate ruler on earth (3:34-39; 9:12, 17)."

3) The pivotal command of the mandatory epiphany for Heliodorus to proclaim to all the majestic power of God (3:34) prepared and pointed the audience not only to Heliodorus's prompt obedience of the command (3:36) but to further demonstrations of this recurring theme in the similar proclamations by the Gentiles Nicanor (8:36) and Antiochus (9:17). Similarly, the pivotal command of the transfiguration mandatory epiphany for the disciples to listen to Jesus as God's Son prompts the disciples as well as the audience to pay close attention to the additional expressions of the recurring theme of the predictions of Jesus' passion, death and resurrection as the key to understanding the significance of the initial epiphanic appearance of the transfigured Jesus in conversation with the heavenly Moses and Elijah.

B. CONCLUSION

The mandatory epiphanies to Balaam (Num 22:31-35), to Joshua (Josh 5:13-15), and to Heliodorus (2 Macc 3:22-34) provide literary precedents for the Gospel audiences to recognize and understand the literary genre of the transfiguration narrative as that of a similar "pivotal mandatory epiphany," in which the climactic mandate serves as a pivotal focus.[37] But these are all examples of a special kind of manda-

---

[37] REID (*Transfiguration*, 78-86) proposes that the literary genre of Luke's "L source" for the transfiguration narrative, which comprises only the appearance of the "two men" (angels) with Jesus (Luke 9:28-33a, 36b), is that of a "predictive angelophany." But the two men/angels do not announce any predictions to the disciples, the recipients, as do the angels in the examples she offers (Gen 16:1-16; 18:1-16; Judg 13:2-23; *2 Enoch* 1:1-10; Luke 1:5-23, 26-38). Furthermore, although the two men talk to Jesus about his exodus, which he was about to accomplish in Jerusalem (Luke 9:31), they do not *predict* it, either to Jesus or the disciples; indeed, Jesus himself already predicted it in 9:22! Equally unconvincing is Reid's proposal (97-98) that the final form of Luke 9:28-36 is that of a "correction pronouncement story." In pronouncment stories Jesus makes the pronouncement after some objection on the part of opponents to his and/or his disciples' behavior. But the "pronouncement" of the transfiguration story does not follow such an objection and is uttered not by Jesus but by the voice of God from the cloud. Furthermore, the climax of the transfiguration story is not just the pronouncement that Jesus is God's Son but the *command* to listen to him. On pronouncement stories, see R.C. TANNEHILL, "Attitudinal Shift in Synoptic Pronouncement Stories," *Orientation by Disorientation: Studies in Literary Criticism and Biblical Literary Criticism* (ed. R.A. Spencer; Pittsburgh: Pickwick, 1980) 183-97; idem, "Introduction: The Pronouncement Story

tory epiphany. The climactic commands that represent the whole point and purpose of the epiphanies closely relate to and clarify the meaning of the epiphanic appearances. The climactic commands also enunciate and refer the audience to key recurring themes that play pivotal roles in the broader narrative contexts in which these mandatory epiphanies are located.

In the case of the transfiguration mandatory epiphany the pivotal mandate not only points out that Jesus, rather than Moses or Elijah, is God's beloved/chosen Son, but also directs the disciples and the audience to listen to Jesus in order to understand the significance of the epiphanic appearance of the transfigured Jesus in conversation with Moses and Elijah. The words of Jesus that the disciples and the audience are to heed are the words predicting his passion, death and resurrection, a recurring theme of pivotal significance in each of the Gospel narratives in which the transfiguration occurs. Having established the literary genre of each version of the transfiguration narrative as that of a pivotal mandatory epiphany, we now turn our attention to the meaning and significance of the remarkable external change in Jesus' face and clothing, the actual transformation or "transfiguration" of Jesus as an epiphanic motif.

---

and Its Types," *Pronouncement Stories* (*Semeia* 20; ed. R.C. Tannehill; Chico: Scholars Press, 1981) 1-13; IDEM, "Varieties of Synoptic Pronouncement Stories," *Pronouncement Stories* (*Semeia* 20; ed. R.C. Tannehill; Chico: Scholars Press, 1981) 101-19; V.K. ROBBINS, "Pronouncement Stories from a Rhetorical Perspective," *Forum* 4,2 (1988) 3-32.

CHAPTER 4

JESUS' TRANSFIGURATION AS AN EPIPHANIC MOTIF

In this chapter we investigate the literary background that enables the Gospel audiences to understand the significance of the "transformation" or "transfiguration" of Jesus as a rather unique epiphanic motif. After an introductory temporal notice each version of the transfiguration narrative reports that Jesus took along three disciples – Peter, James and John – and led them up a mountain. These three disciples then serve as the specially chosen recipients of this pivotal mandatory epiphany. In each version the sudden and unexpected epiphanic appearances commence immediately with the spectacular "transfiguration" of Jesus:

> Mark 9:2b-3: And he was transfigured before them, that is, his clothes became very radiantly white, such as no bleacher on the earth could thus whiten.
> Matt 17:2: And he was transfigured before them, that is, his face shone as the sun, while his clothes became white as the light.
> Luke 9:29: And while he was praying the appearance of his face became different and his clothing dazzling white.

As noted in the preliminary analysis (chap. 1), Mark and Matthew report that Jesus was "transfigured" or "transformed" (μετεμορφώθη) before the three disciples, whereas Luke reports that while Jesus was praying "the appearance" (τὸ εἶδος) of his "face" (προσώπου) became "different" or "other" (ἕτερον), later referred to as "his glory" (τὴν δόξαν αὐτοῦ) seen by the disciples (Luke 9:32). Only in Matthew and Luke does the description of Jesus' transfiguration explicitly include his face. In each version Jesus' transfiguration is further described in terms of his "clothing" (ἱμάτια in Mark and Matthew; ἱματισμὸς in

Luke) becoming extremely white. Common to all three versions is an aspect of "shining radiance" involving either the face or the clothes. In Matthew Jesus' face "shone" (ἔλαμψεν) as the sun; while in Mark Jesus' clothes became so white that they were "glistening," "gleaming" or "shining" (στίλβοντα); and in Luke his white clothing was "flashing," "gleaming" or "dazzling" like lightning (ἐξαστράπτων).[1]

We propose that the "transfiguration" of Jesus is an epiphanic motif describing his external, proleptic, and temporary transformation by God into a heavenly being while still on earth. This epiphanic "transfiguration" of Jesus performs a twofold narrative function: It enables Jesus, while still on earth, to appear and speak with the heavenly figures of Moses and Elijah before the eyes of the disciples; and it points to Jesus' future and permanent attainment of glory in heaven. To confirm this proposal we will investigate the background and meaning of (1) the statement of Jesus' *transfiguration*, (2) the change in the appearance of his *face*, (3) his extremely *white clothing*, and (4) the *shining radiance* of his face/clothes.

A. TRANSFIGURATION OF JESUS

The verb μεταμορφόω, employed by Mark and Matthew to describe the "transfiguration" of Jesus, refers in a very general sense to a "transformation" or "change in form" of some kind. What it means more specifically must be determined by the context. Thus, Jesus' transfiguration is further defined as his clothing becoming extremely white in Mark 9:3 and as both his face shining and clothes becoming white in Matt 17:2.[2] Since it is seen by the disciples, the transfiguration of Jesus refers to an external transformation outwardly visible

---

[1] According to BAGD, 273, ἐξαστράπτω means "flash or gleam like lightning."

[2] The "and" (καὶ) that follows the statements of the transfiguration in Mark 9:3 and Matt 17:2 should be understood in an epexegetical sense as further defining the transfiguration rather than as a separate addition to it. This is recognized for Mark by GUNDRY, *Mark*, 477: "Thus, the 'and' which introduces a description of Jesus' garments introduces a definition of the Transfiguration." And NIEMAND (*Verklärungsperikopen*, 82) understands Matthew's version to say that Jesus was transfigured, that is ("das heißt"), his face shone and his clothes became white.

rather than an internal transformation invisible to the physical eye, as in 2 Cor 3:18 and Rom 12:2, the only other occurrences of the verb in the NT.[3] The aorist passive form (μετεμορφώθη) indicates that this external transformation of the physical appearance of Jesus was effected objectively, from outside, by God (divine passive) rather than subjectively or interiorly by Jesus himself.[4]

Although it was while Jesus was praying that the appearance of his face became different in Luke 9:29, this transformation should not be understood as a further description of the prayer itself. It is not part of a mystical-like prayer experience, nor is it an answer to an implicitly voiced petition by Jesus. Rather, it is an external transformation effected by God in response to the praying of Jesus. This accords with the Lukan pattern, in which important events occur in the context of and as God's response to the praying of Jesus (Luke 3:21; 5:16; 6:12; 9:18, 28; 11:1; 22:41; 23:46) as an indication of his openness to God's plan.[5] That the change is in "the appearance (τὸ εἶδος) of his face" rather than just in his "face" underscores the external rather than internal nature of the transformation.[6] That Jesus' transfigured state is later

---

[3] W. WIEFEL, *Das Evangelium nach Matthäus* (THKNT 1; Leipzig: Evangelische Verlagsanstalt, 1998) 309: "μετεμορφώθη kennzeichnet eine Verwandlung, also ein objektives Geschehen, das nicht in visionärer Schau aufgeht."

[4] BAGD, 511; J. M. NÜTZEL, "μεταμορφόω" *EDNT* 2.415. According to PHILO (*Mos.* 1.57), while Moses was warning some shepherds who were harassing maidens at a well, he grew inspired and "was transfigured (μεταμορφούμενος) into a prophet." But this "transfiguration" refers to a change in the manner of Moses's speech — he began to speak like a prophet; it is not an epiphanic transfiguration into a heavenly being as we have for Jesus.

[5] LENTZEN-DEIS, *Taufe*, 286; FITZMYER, *Luke I-IX*, 798: "As often elsewhere in this Gospel, the picture of Jesus at prayer precedes an event of importance." The epiphanic transfiguration of Jesus, like the epiphanic descent of the Holy Spirit in bodily form like a dove upon Jesus (Luke 3:21-22), occurs while Jesus is praying. The relation between these epiphanic events and the praying of Jesus is clarified by L. FELDKÄMPER, *Der betende Jesus als Heilsmittler nach Lukas* (VMSAB 29; St. Augustin, West Germany: Steyler, 1978) 50: "Wir dürfen die himmlische Manifestation als Antwort auf Jesu Beten verstehen; allerdings nicht im Sinne der Erfüllung einer Bitte. Von einem Bittgebet ist ja auch gar nicht die Rede. Statt als ausdrückliche oder auch nur implizite Bitte ist Gebet hier wohl nur zu verstehen als grundsätzliche Hinwendung zu und radikale Bereitschaft für Gott, als Hörwilligkeit für sein Wort und Offenheit für seinen Auftrag, als Empfangsbereitschaft."

[6] "Form, outward appearance" is the meaning of εἶδος; see BAGD, 221; G. SCHNEIDER, "εἶδος," *EDNT* 1.385. Just as the descent of the Spirit "in bodily form" (σωματικῷ εἴδει, Luke 3:22) so also "the appearance (εἶδος) of his face" underlines the visible, external reality of these epiphanic events. On the epiphany in Luke 3:21-22, see chap. 2.

referred to as "his glory" (τὴν δόξαν αὐτοῦ, 9:32) indicates how he has been transformed into a heavenly being like Moses and Elijah, who likewise were appearing "in glory" (ἐν δόξῃ, 9:31).[7]

The depiction of Jesus' transfiguration in all three versions as an external change, a transformation from outside of Jesus effected by God, does not support those interpretations that speak in terms of a "revelation," or "disclosure," or "unveiling" of an inner, permanent glory or heavenly status which Jesus already possesses.[8] Although the transfiguration of Jesus takes place on a mountain that he ascends together with three of his disciples, it does not represent an "ascension" into heaven.[9] Rather, he has been temporarily transfigured into a heavenly being while on a mountain still on the earth.

With regard to the background of Jesus being "transfigured" by God many appeal to a Mosaic connection, in which Jesus is seen to be a second or greater Moses.[10] In Exod 34:29 (LXX) when Moses

---

[7] C. SPICQ, *Theological Lexicon of the New Testament* (3 vols.; Peabody: Hendrickson, 1994) 1.367-68: "This glory is luminous, like that of Moses and Elijah at Tabor, signaling a heavenly appearance, a divine manifestation....This is a divine state, a condition of honor, of preeminent dignity, of splendor." See also H. HEGERMANN, "δόξα," *EDNT* 1.346.

[8] GREEN, *Luke*, 380: "...his inner being was made transparent to those who accompanied him. In other words, the change Luke describes is a disclosure of Jesus' status." C.H.T. FLETCHER-LOUIS, *Luke-Acts: Angels, Christology and Soteriology* (WUNT 94; Tübingen: Mohr Siebeck, 1997) 49: "Jesus does not experience transformation into a *new* (or temporary) identity, at the transfiguration. Rather this is the revelation of an identity he already possesses." B. BLACKBURN, *Theios Aner and the Markan Miracle Traditions: A Critique of the Theios Aner Concept as an Interpretative Background of the Miracle Traditions Used by Mark* (WUNT 40; Tübingen: Mohr Siebeck, 1991) 121: "...an indirect reference to the earthly Jesus' hidden dignity, honor, and intimate communion with God." But as GUNDRY (*Mark*, 477) rightly asserts: "Nothing in the text implies that Jesus possesses a glory hidden at other times by his clothes and flesh."

[9] *Contra* J.E. FOSSUM, "Ascensio, Metamorphosis: The 'Transfiguration' of Jesus in the Synoptic Gospels," *The Image of the Invisible God: Essays on the Influence of Jewish Mysticism on Early Christology* (NTOA 30; Göttingen: Vandenhoeck & Ruprecht, 1995) 71-94.

[10] For alleged Mosaic parallels in Matthew see DAVIES and ALLISON, *Matthew*, 2.696; D.A. HAGNER, *Matthew 14-28* (WBC 33B; Dallas: Word Books, 1995) 492-93; F. REFOULÉ, "Jésus, nouveau Moïse, ou Pierre, nouveau Grand Prêtre? (Mt 17,1-9; Mc 9,2-10)," *RTL* 24 (1993) 145-62. The Mosaic connections for Matthew have been greatly exaggerated by MOSES, *Matthew's Transfiguration Story*; for critiques see R.H GUNDRY, *JBL* 116 (1997) 560-62; M.A. POWELL, *CBQ* 59 (1997) 585-87; B.T. VIVIANO, *RB* 105 (1998) 618-20. For alleged Mosaic associations in Mark, see J. MARCUS, T*he Way of the Lord: Christological Exegesis of the Old Testament in the Gospel of Mark* (Louisville: Westminster/Knox, 1992) 80-93. For

descended from Mount Sinai he did not know that "the appearance of the complexion of his face had become glorified" (δεδόξασται ἡ ὄψις τοῦ χρώματος τοῦ προσώπου αὐτοῦ) while he spoke with God. The linguistic associations are inexact. But the fatal flaw of this interpretation is that the transformation involves only the face of Moses and *follows* his speaking with God. Jesus' transfiguration involves not only his face but his clothing and *precedes* his conversation with the heavenly figures of Moses and Elijah. The "glorification" of the face of Moses was a result of his encounter with God on Mount Sinai and not, like for Jesus, an epiphanic appearance that enabled him to have a heavenly encounter on a mountain.[11]

More relevant as background to Jesus' transfiguration is the radical transformation that Moses underwent at his death in order to enter heaven according to Philo. When Moses had to leave this mortal life and enter into heaven (εἰς οὐρανὸν), God summoned him and "resolved his twofold nature of soul and body into a single unity, transforming (μεθαρμοζόμενος) his whole being into mind, pure as sunlight" (*Mos.* 2.288).[12] Although the differences to the transfiguration of Jesus are obvious, the point of comparison is the necessity to be transformed in order to become a heavenly being.

Transformation in order to become a heavenly being is not, however, limited to Moses, but extends to all the righteous:

2 Apocalypse of Baruch 51:3, 10

3 Also, as for the glory of those who proved to be righteous on account of my law, those who possessed intelligence in their life, and those who planted the root of wisdom in their

---

a denial of Mosaic allusions in Mark, see GUNDRY, *Mark*, 475-76. For assertions of a Mosaic background in Luke, see MARSHALL, *Luke*, 383; J. NOLLAND, *Luke 9:21-18:34* (WBC 35B; Dallas: Word Books, 1993) 498; D.L. BOCK, *Luke 1:1-9:50* (BECNT 3A; Grand Rapids: Baker Books, 1994) 867. For a denial of Mosaic associations in Luke, see FITZMYER, *Luke I-IX*, 799; REID, *Transfiguration*, 105.

[11] MACH, "Christus Mutans," 185: "Die Metamorphose des Mose ist also Folge seines Zusammentreffens mit Gott. Dagegen ist die Verwandlung Jesu zunächst unabhängig von der direkten Begegnung." See also W.H. PROPP, "The Skin of Moses' Face — Transfigured or Disfigured?" *CBQ* 49 (1987) 375-86.

[12] Translation from LCL. E.R. GOODENOUGH, *By Light, Light: The Mystic Gospel of Hellenistic Judaism* (Amsterdam: Philo, 1969) 195: "The death of Moses was a 'change.' Moses was...wholly transformed."

heart — their splendor will then be glorified by transformations, and the shape of their face will be changed into the light of their beauty so that they may acquire and receive the undying world which is promised to them....

10 For they will live in the heights of that world and they will be like the angels and be equal to the stars. And they will be changed into any shape which they wished, from beauty to loveliness, and from light to the splendor of glory.[13]

From the same general apocalyptic-eschatological milieu as the New Testament, this text provides more evidence for the necessity to be transfigured by God in order to become a heavenly being. The similarities to the transfiguration of Jesus are evident in the vocabulary: The righteous will be "glorified by transformations" and the "shape of their face will be changed" (v. 3); "they will be changed...to the splendor of glory" (v. 10). Just as for the transfiguration of Jesus these verbs are in the divine passive, indicating that the transformations will be effected by God. But most noteworthy is the reason for these glorious transformations – "*so that* they may acquire and receive the undying world" (v. 3). The motif of Jesus being temporarily transfigured by God in a similar way while still on earth indicates to the audience the anticipation of his future acquisition and reception of the "undying world" of heaven.[14] His transformation into a heavenly figure facilitates his appearance and conversation with Moses and Elijah, who have already become members of the heavenly world.

B. Face of the Transfigured Jesus

The transfiguration of Jesus involves an explicit change in his face in Matthew and Luke but not in Mark. In Matt 17:2 "his face shone as the sun" (cf. 13:43) while in Luke 9:29 "the appearance of his face became different." Luke does not explicitly specify how Jesus' face

---

[13] Translation by A.F.J. KLIJN, "2 (Syriac Apocalypse of) Baruch," *OTP* 1.638. As for dating, Klijn (p. 617) states: "the Apocalypse of Baruch seems to come from the first or second decade of the second century." Although dated slightly later than the Gospels, *2 Apocalypse of Baruch* does not appear to be literarily dependent upon the Gospels, but rather drawing from a common apocalyptic-eschatological tradition and milieu.

[14] On these glorious transformations of the righteous as implying their membership in the heavenly world, see F.J. MURPHY, *The Structure and Meaning of Second Baruch* (SBLDS 78; Atlanta: Scholars Press, 1985) 60-62.

became different, but the context strongly implies that his face, as in Matthew, became gloriously radiant. First, the change in his face is paralleled by "his clothing became dazzling white" (9:29) and later his transfigured state is referred to as "his glory" (9:32).[15]

We have already seen background above for the general facial change in the Lukan transfiguration of Jesus as indicative of his heavenly status:

2 Apoc. Bar. 51:3: ...the shape of their face will be changed...

Luke 9:29: ...the appearance of his face became different...

Now we look at several other texts that provide background that the "shining face" of Jesus, explicit in Matthew and implicit in Luke, indicates his status as a heavenly figure:

Luke 9:29: τὸ εἶδος τοῦ προσώπου αὐτοῦ ἕτερον
Matt 17:2: ἔλαμψεν τὸ πρόσωπον αὐτοῦ ὡς ὁ ἥλιος
Dan 10:6: τὸ πρόσωπον αὐτοῦ ὡσεὶ ὅρασις ἀστραπῆς
Rev 1:16: ἡ ὄψις αὐτοῦ ὡς ὁ ἥλιος φαίνει ἐν τῇ δυνάμει αὐτοῦ
Rev 10:1: τὸ πρόσωπον αὐτοῦ ὡς ὁ ἥλιος

Daniel 10:6 is part of the description of the heavenly figure, the man/angel, that Daniel sees in a vision. As in Luke 9:29 and Matt 17:2 we have a reference to "his face" (τὸ πρόσωπον αὐτοῦ).[16] Similar to Matt 17:2, where the face of the transfigured Jesus shone "like the sun" (ὡς ὁ ἥλιος), the face of the angel in Dan 10:6 (LXX) was "like the appearance of lightning" (ὡσεὶ ὅρασις ἀστραπῆς). In Luke 9:29 the difference in the appearance of the face of the transfigured Jesus is paralleled by his clothing becoming white, "flashing like lightning" (ἐξαστράπτων).[17]

---

[15] NOLLAND, *Luke 9:21-18:34*, 498: "The sense we should give to the difference is only to be discerned from the parallel change to his garments (and from the resumption of v 29 in v 32 with 'they saw his glory')."

[16] The description of the angel's face is modeled on Ezek 1:13 where the four living creatures or cherubim are described, according to Di Lella in L.F. HARTMAN and A.A. DI LELLA, *The Book of Daniel* (AB 23; New York: Doubleday, 1978) 280; J.J. COLLINS, *Daniel: A Commentary on the Book of Daniel* (Hermeneia; Minneapolis: Fortress, 1993) 373.

[17] In Matt 28:3 the appearance of the angel of the Lord, who descended from heaven and rolled back the stone sealing the tomb of Jesus (28:2), "was like lightning (ὡς ἀστραπὴ)." In Luke 24:4 the women at the tomb of Jesus saw two men/angels in clothing that was "gleaming like lightning (ἀστραπτούσῃ)" (BAGD, 118). On these comparisons with "lightning" in the description of heavenly figures, see J. ZMIJEWSKI, "ἀστραπή," *EDNT* 1.175.

Revelation 1:16 climaxes the description of the "one like a Son of Man" (the risen Jesus in heaven) that John saw in a vision (1:13-16). Almost identical to Matt 17:2, where the "face" of the transfigured Jesus "shone like the sun (ὡς ὁ ἥλιος)," the "face" of the heavenly Son of Man in Rev 1:16 was "like the sun (ὡς ὁ ἥλιος) shining in its might."[18] The use of different words for "his face" (τὸ πρόσωπον αὐτοῦ in Matt 17:2; ἡ ὄψις αὐτοῦ in Rev 1:16) and "shine" (ἔλαμψεν in Matt 17:2; φαίνει in Rev 1:16) indicate that we are not dealing with the Book of Revelation's literary dependence upon Matthew (usually dated earlier); rather, both are dependent upon the OT and a common apocalyptic-eschatological milieu.

In Rev 10:1 we have John's vision of "another mighty angel coming down from heaven." That "his face was like the sun" (τὸ πρόσωπον αὐτοῦ ὡς ὁ ἥλιος) is identical to the depiction of the face of the transfigured Jesus in Matt 17:2, lacking only an explicit use of a verb for "shine."[19] Several other texts from the same general apocalyptic-eschatological milieu confirm that the description of the "face" of the transfigured Jesus as "shining like the sun" indicates that he has been transformed into a heavenly figure while still on earth:

Matt 17:2:   his face shone as the sun
4 Ezra 7:97: their face is to shine like the sun[20]

---

[18] There may be an allusion to Dan 10:6 here according to D.E. AUNE, *Revelation 1-5* (WBC 52A; Dallas: Word Books, 1997) 99. Aune goes on to say: "The face could be compared with the sun as a metaphor for beauty (Wis 7:29; *Jos. As.* 14:9; 18:9), but more frequently as a metaphor for sanctity, divinity, or transcendence, often in theophanies or angelophanies" (p. 99). See also P.R. CARRELL, *Jesus and the Angels: Angelology and the Christology of the Apocalypse of John* (SNTSMS 95; Cambridge: Cambridge University Press, 1997) 162-73. The actual wording of "like the sun shining in its might" in Rev 1:16 may derive from Judg 5:31 (LXX B) according to G.K. BEALE, *The Book of Revelation* (NIGTC; Grand Rapids: Eerdmans, 1999) 212.

[19] On the comparison of the face with the sun to describe the angel in Rev 10:1 and "to describe the transformed appearance of the righteous in the eschaton," see D.E. AUNE, *Revelation 6-16* (WBC 52B; Nashville: Nelson, 1998) 557. See also CARRELL, *Jesus and the Angels*, 132; BEALE, *Revelation*, 524.

[20] Translation of 4 Ezra (=2 Esdras) by B.M. METZGER, "The Fourth Book of Ezra," *OTP* 1.540. See also J.M. MYERS, *I and II Esdras: Introduction, Translation and Commentary* (AB 42; New York: Doubleday, 1974) 215, 239; M.E. STONE, *Fourth Ezra: A Commentary on the Book of Fourth Ezra* (Hermeneia; Minneapolis: Fortress, 1990) 237, 244-45. 4 Ezra is generally dated in the late first century C.E.

Apoc. Zeph. 6:11: his face shining like the rays of the sun in its glory[21]
2 Enoch 1:5:   their faces were like the shining sun[22]
2 Enoch 19:1:   their faces were more radiant than the radiance of the sun[23]

4 Ezra 7:97 occurs within an angelic description of the post-mortem state of the righteous (7:88-98). An angel promises the righteous that "their face is to shine like the sun, and how they are to be made like the light of the stars, being incorruptible from then on."[24] This means that after their death the righteous will be transformed into heavenly beings like angels (cf. *2 Apoc. Bar.* 51:10).[25] Thus, that Jesus was transfigured so that "his face shone like the sun" (Matt 17:2) indicates his temporary anticipation before death of this post-mortem state of the righteous as angel-like heavenly beings and points to his permanent acquisition of this status after his death.

In *Apoc. Zeph.* 6:11, *2 Enoch* 1:5 and 19:1 the "faces" that were "shining like the sun" all refer to angels as viewed in various visions. In *2 Enoch* 1:4 the introduction of the vision, "two huge men appeared to me, the like of which I had never seen on earth" (cf. Mark 9:3), underlines the *heavenly* nature of these angelic figures.

In all of the texts (except Dan 10:6) that we have associated with Matt 17:2 above the "faces" of heavenly beings have been compared with the "radiance" or "shining" of the "*sun.*" That the "face" of the transfigured Jesus "shone like the *sun*" thus indicates to the Gospel

---

[21] Translation by O.S. WINTERMUTE, "Apocalypse of Zephaniah," *OTP* 1.513. Wintermute dates the *Apocalypse of Zephaniah* between the first century B.C. and the first century C.E.

[22] Translation of both the A and J recensions of *2 Enoch* by F.I. ANDERSEN, "2 (Slavonic Apocalypse of) Enoch," *OTP* 1.106-7. Andersen dates *2 Enoch* in the late first century C.E.

[23] Translation of the J recension by ANDERSEN, "2 Enoch," 132.

[24] See also the closely related 4 Ezra 7:125 with the promise that "the faces of those who practiced self-control shall shine more than the stars." In reference to the heavenly Jerusalem personified as a woman, 4 Ezra 10:25 states that while Ezra was talking to her, "behold, her face suddenly shone exceedingly, and her countenance flashed like lightning." In his commentary on 4 Ezra 10:25 STONE (*Fourth Ezra*, 327) remarks: "The shining faces of heavenly and exalted persons are a common theme."

[25] STONE, *Fourth Ezra*, 245: "This situation suggests a direct correlation between the righteous and the stars. Indeed, in *2 Apoc Bar* 51:10 the righteous are said to be like angels and equal to stars."

audiences his temporary transformation like one of the righteous (4 Ezra 7:97; *2 Apoc. Bar.* 51:3, 10) into an angel-like, heavenly figure (Dan 10:6; Rev 1:16; 10:1; *Apoc. Zeph.* 6:11; *2 Enoch* 1:5; 19:1) before his death and while still on earth.[26]

C. White Clothing of the Transfigured Jesus

In all three accounts of Jesus' transfiguration his clothing became extremely white:

Mark 9:3: his clothes became very radiantly *white*, such as no bleacher on the earth could thus *whiten*
Matt 17:2: his clothes became *white* as the light
Luke 9:29: his clothing became dazzling *white*

As the transformation in the shining radiance of his face, so the transformation in the radiant whiteness of his clothing indicates that Jesus has been temporarily transformed into a heavenly figure.

The narrative context of each version of Jesus' transfiguration illustrates how his extremely white clothing indicates his transformation into an angel-like, heavenly figure. After the statement that Jesus' clothes became "very radiantly white" (στίλβοντα λευκὰ λίαν), Mark 9:3 adds that "no bleacher *on the earth* could thus whiten (λευκᾶναι)" them, implying a heavenly whiteness to the clothing that transcends anything possible on earth.[27] In Mark 16:5 when the women entered the tomb of Jesus they experience an angelophany in which "they saw a young man sitting on the right clothed in a white robe (στολὴν λευκήν)" indicative of his angel-like, heavenly nature.

---

[26] In comparing 4 Ezra 7:97 with Rev 1:16, *2 Enoch* 1:5 and 19:1, Stone (*Fourth Ezra*, 245) comments: "So the faces both of the angels and of the righteous shine and they are compared primarily with the sun." In the words of T. Holtz, "ἥλιος" *EDNT* 2.118: "The radiance of the sun is a sign of glory, which the redeemed righteous ones, the angels, and Christ share."

[27] This interpretation holds whether we take the phrase ἐπὶ τῆς γῆς to modify "bleacher" and translate "no bleacher on the earth" or to modify "whiten" and translate "no bleacher could thus whiten on the ground." For the latter interpretation see Gundry (*Mark*, 458), who adds that "the forward position of ἐπὶ τῆς γῆς will emphasize that divine whiteness exceeds what can be attained by bleaching on the ground." According to Öhler, "Verklärung," 204: "Die Erklärung, daß kein Walker auf Erden ein strahlenderes Weiß herstellen kann, sichert das Wissen der Lesenden: Hier ist von himmlischer Existenz die Rede."

In the angelophany that begins in Matt 28:2, after an "angel of the Lord" descended from heaven, rolled back the stone sealing the tomb of Jesus, and sat upon it, there occurs a description of this heavenly figure that bears a striking resemblance to the description of the transfigured Jesus:

> Matt 28:3: His appearance was like lightning and his clothing *white* as snow.[28]
>
> Matt 17:2: His face shone as the sun, while his clothes became *white* as the light.

Each epiphanic description contains comparisons for both the appearance/face (like lightning; as the sun) and the white clothing (as snow; as the light) of the angel and Jesus respectively. But whereas the appearance and white clothing describe the angel's permanent heavenly nature, Jesus was temporarily *transfigured*, so that his face shone like the sun and his clothes *became* white as the light. Whereas the "*white* as snow" (λευκὸν ὡς χιών) clothing of the angel signifies his permanent heavenly character, the "*white* as the light" (λευκὰ ὡς τὸ φῶς) clothes of the earthly Jesus indicates his temporary heavenly character.[29]

In the angelophany of Acts 1:10 while the disciples were watching the risen Jesus ascending into heaven, "suddenly two men in white (λευκαῖς) garments stood beside them" (cf. Luke 24:4). As for Matthew, noteworthy again are both the similarities and differences to the description of the transfigured Jesus in Luke 9:29: "his clothing became dazzling white (λευκὸς)." Whereas the *white* garments of the two angelic men describe their permanent heavenly status, Jesus' clothing *became* dazzling *white*, indicating to the audience his temporary transfiguration into a heavenly figure while on earth.[30]

---

[28] On Matt 28:2-3, see J.P. HEIL, *The Death and Resurrection of Jesus: A Narrative-Critical Reading of Matthew 26-28* (Minneapolis: Fortress, 1991) 98; IDEM, "The Narrative Structure of Matthew 27:55-28:20," *JBL* 110 (1991) 430. On the epiphanic significance of the comparison of the angel's white clothing with "snow" here, it is stated in "χιών," *EDNT* 3.468: "The NT uses imagery of snow for the divine radiance and purity in an epiphany."

[29] On the epiphanic significance of the comparison of Jesus' white clothes with "the light" here, H. RITT ("φῶς," *EDNT* 3.448) states: "The optical motif of 'light' is characteristic of epiphany narratives...The portrayal of heavenly figures of light with other-worldly radiance identifies such events as originating within God's transcendent realm."

[30] In the angelophany of John 20:12 Mary Magdalene "observed two angels in white (λευκοῖς) sitting there, one at the head and one at the feet, where the body of Jesus had been

Additional texts from the same general apocalyptic-eschatological milieu of the Gospel audiences further illustrate how the radiantly *white* clothing of the transfigured Jesus signifies his heavenly status:

1. *Dan 7:9: God's clothing was like snow, white*

In Dan 7:9, as part of his dream visions (cf. 7:1-2), Daniel watched God himself, as the "Ancient One," take his throne for judgment.[31] God's clothing was "like snow, *white*" (ὡσεὶ χιὼν λευκόν in the Theodotion recension) and the hair of his head like pure wool. Here, in a vision, God himself is dressed in *white* clothing indicative of his divine heavenly glory and splendor.[32]

2. *1 Enoch 14:20: God's gown whiter than any snow*

When Enoch had a heavenly vision (*1 Enoch* 14:8) of the "Great Glory," God himself, sitting on a throne, he described God's clothing: "as for his gown, which was shining more brightly than the sun, it was *whiter* than any snow" (14:20). Enoch goes on to mention the "face" of God: "None of the angels was able to come in and see the face of the Excellent and the Glorious One" (14:21).[33] The vocabulary of *1 Enoch* 14:20-21 recalls especially the Matthean description of the transfigured Jesus: "his *face shone* as the *sun*, while his *clothes* became *white* as the light" (Matt 17:2).[34] In *1 Enoch* 14:20 we have

---

lying." Here again white clothing in an epiphanic appearance signifies heavenly status; see J.P. HEIL, *Blood and Water: The Death and Resurrection of Jesus in John 18-21* (CBQMS 27; Washington: Catholic Biblical Association, 1995) 127.

[31] The "Ancient One" is "visually a human being, but he stands for God...Picturing him as an old man suggests someone august, venerable and respected, judicious and wise," according to J.E. GOLDINGAY, *Daniel* (WBC 30; Dallas: Word Books, 1989) 165.

[32] HARTMAN, *Daniel*, 218: "Not only does Yahweh have the white hair of an old man; his clothing is also 'as white as snow,' symbolizing unsullied majesty." On God's white clothing here, GOLDINGAY (*Daniel*, 165) states that it has the "basic meaning of brightness and luminosity, thus nobility and splendor." See also COLLINS, *Daniel*, 301.

[33] Translation by E. ISAAC, "1 (Ethiopic Apocalypse of) Enoch," *OTP* 1.21. Isaac dates *1 Enoch* between the second century B.C. and the first century C.E.

[34] On the correspondence between *1 Enoch* 14:20-21 and the description of the transfigured Jesus, see ROWLAND, *Open Heaven*, 367.

another example, in addition to Dan 7:9, of the *white* clothing of God himself indicating that *white* is the color of divine, heavenly clothing.

3. *2 Macc 11:8: An angelic horseman appeared in white clothing*

After Maccabeus, his men, and all the people prayed that God send a good angel (ἀγαθὸν ἄγγελον) to save Israel, Maccabeus went out with those willing to take up arms and fight for Israel (2 Macc 11:6-7). Then in 2 Macc 11:8 occurs an epiphany in answer to their prayer: While they were still near Jerusalem a horseman appeared (ἐφάνη) at their head in *white* clothing (ἐν λευκῇ ἐσθῆτι) and brandishing gold weapons. The *white* clothing of the horseman indicates that he is the good angel, the heavenly figure, for whom they prayed to save Israel.[35]

4. *1 Enoch 71:1: The white garments of angelic figures*

When Enoch ascended into the heavens, he "saw the sons of the holy angels walking upon the flame of fire; their garments were *white* — and their overcoats — and the light of their faces was like snow" (*1 Enoch* 71:1).[36] This text mentions not only the "garments" but the luminous "faces" of the angelic figures, similar to the description of the transfigured Jesus in Matt 17:2 and Luke 9:29. Here we have another example, in addition to 2 Macc 11:8, of the *white* clothing of angelic beings indicating that *white* is the color of divine, heavenly clothing.

5. *L.A.B. 64:6: The white robe of the resurrected Samuel*

In Pseudo-Philo's *Liber Antiquitatum Biblicarum* when Sedecla, the witch of Endor, raises up the dead Samuel at Saul's request, Saul asked her to describe his appearance. Sedecla said, "You are asking me about divine beings (*diis*; 1 Sam 28:14: אלהים; 1 Kgdms 28:14: θεοὺς). For behold his appearance is not that of a man. He is clothed

---

[35] The angelic horseman here is probably to be indentified with the angelic horseman that appears in the mandatory epiphany in 2 Macc 3:25; see GOLDSTEIN, *II Maccabees*, 405. For an analysis of the mandatory epiphany, see chap. 3.

[36] Translation by ISAAC, "1 Enoch," 49. On the relevance of *1 Enoch* 71:1 for the transfiguration, see NIEMAND, *Verklärungsperikopen*, 109.

in a *white* robe (*stolam albam*) with a mantle placed over it, and two angels are leading him" (*L.A.B.* 64:6).[37] It is often pointed out that Samuel's "*white* robe" refers simply to the white shroud in which he was buried.[38] But when the text goes on to say that Saul remembered the "mantle" that Samuel, when he was alive, had rent (*L.A.B.* 64:6), no mention is made of the "*white* robe." The resurrected Samuel's *white* robe may thus not only refer to his burial shroud but also, and most especially, correspond to his appearance as a "divine being." In addition to the above examples involving God and angels, here we have an example of a venerable human being, Samuel, whose *white* robe indicates his status as a "divine being."[39]

6. *Rev 3:5; 6:11; 7:9, 13-14; 19:14: The white garments of the right-eous in heaven*

Revelation 3:5, which occurs in the letter to Sardis (3:1-6), promises that the one who conquers will "thus" (οὕτως), that is, in accord with the promise in 3:4 that those who are worthy "will walk with me in *white* (ἐν λευκοῖς)," be clothed in *white* garments (ἐν ἱματίοις λευκοῖς). Here we have an eschatological promise that a group of righteous human beings, not just a venerable individual like Samuel, will be clothed in *white* garments as a heavenly reward (cf. 3:18).

In John's vision into heaven (Rev 4:1), when the Lamb opened the fifth seal of the scroll, he saw under the heavenly altar the souls of those slaughtered for the word of God and the testimony they had

---

[37] Text and translation in H. JACOBSON, *A Commentary on Pseudo-Philo's Liber Antiquitatum Biblicarum: With Latin Text and English Translation* (AGAJU 31; Leiden: Brill, 1996) 86, 193. See also D.J. HARRINGTON, "Pseudo-Philo," *OTP* 2.377; F.J. MURPHY, *Pseudo-Philo: Rewriting the Bible* (New York: Oxford University Press, 1993) 217-18. Pseudo-Philo is generally dated in the first century C.E. Jacobson's view of a second century C.E. date has been refuted in favor of a pre-70 C.E. date by D.D. BINDER, *Into the Temple Courts: The Place of the Synagogues in the Second Temple Period* (SBLDS 169; Atlanta: Society of Biblical Literature, 1999) 49-54.

[38] L.H. FELDMAN, "Prolegomenon," *The Biblical Antiquities of Philo* (M.R. James; New York: KTAV, 1971) cxliii; HARRINGTON, "Pseudo-Philo," 377; JACOBSON, *Commentary on Pseudo-Philo*, 1208.

[39] Although Josephus does not mention Samuel's white robe, he reports that when the witch of Endor saw Samuel "she saw someone arise in form like God (τῷ θεῷ τινα τὴν μορφὴν ὅμοιον)" (*A.J.* 6.14.2 §333).

(6:9). After they cried out for vindication (6:10), they were each given (ἐδόθη, divine passive) a *white* robe (στολὴ λευκή) and told to rest yet a little while, until the number is fulfilled of their fellow servants and brothers who are going to be killed as they had been (6:11). That each of the martyred souls is given a *white* robe begins to fulfill the promise in 3:5 that the one who conquers will be clothed in *white* garments as a heavenly reward.[40]

In Rev 7:9 John had a vision of a great crowd in heaven who stood before the throne of God and before the Lamb, wearing *white* robes (στολὰς λευκὰς) and holding palm branches in their hands, as they participated in the heavenly worship (7:10-12). After one of the elders asked John who are these wearing the *white* robes (τὰς στολὰς τὰς λευκὰς) and where did they come from (7:13), he answered his own question by announcing that they are the ones who have survived the time of the great distress and have washed their robes and made them *white* (ἐλεύκαναν) in the blood of the Lamb (7:14).[41] That each of the souls praying under the altar in heaven was given a *white* robe (στολὴ λευκή) in 6:11, in fulfillment of the promise in 3:5, equipped them to join in the heavenly worship of this large crowd clothed in *white* robes.[42]

In Rev 19:14, in another vision into the opened heaven (19:11), John saw a white horse with a rider followed by armies in heaven on white horses, dressed in pure *white* (λευκὸν) linen. The *white* garments worn by this heavenly army of the righteous are like those promised to the victors as a heavenly reward (3:5), given to the martyred souls under the altar in heaven (6:11), and worn by the crowd worshiping in heaven (7:9, 13-14).[43] Thus, the radiantly *white* clothing

---

[40] J.P. HEIL, "The Fifth Seal (Rev 6,9-11) as a Key to the Book of Revelation," *Bib* 74 (1993) 227-28. On the white robes as a recompense for the souls, see also H. ULFGARD, *Feast and Future: Revelation 7:9-17 and the Feast of Tabernacles* (ConBNT 22; Stockholm: Almqvist & Wiksell International, 1989) 81-85.

[41] On the background of this paradoxical metaphor of making the robes white by washing them in the blood, see AUNE, *Revelation 6-16*, 474; BEALE, *Revelation*, 436-38.

[42] On the relation between Rev 6:11 and 7:9, 13-14, see HEIL, "Fifth Seal," 231. AUNE, *Revelation 6-16*, 468: "In Revelation, white robes appear to symbolize heavenly existence or worthiness of heaven."

[43] The heavenly armies represent the bride which is the church, according to K.E. MILLER, "The Nuptial Eschatology of Revelation 19-22," *CBQ* 60 (1998) 315. See also D.E. AUNE, *Revelation 17-22* (WBC 52C; Nashville: Nelson, 1998) 1059-60; CARRELL, *Jesus and the Angels*, 206-7; BEALE, *Revelation*, 960-61.

of the transfigured Jesus while on earth anticipates the heavenly reward and victory over death promised to the righteous after judgment.[44]

7. *The glorious garments of the righteous in heaven*

The white clothing of the transfigured Jesus indicates his temporary heavenly "glory." This is explicit in Luke 9:32 where the disciples saw "his glory" (τὴν δόξαν αὐτοῦ), which he shared with the heavenly figures of Moses and Elijah, who likewise were appearing "in glory" (ἐν δόξῃ, 9:31). Thus, the dazzling white clothing of the transfigured Jesus is the *glorious* clothing of those in heaven, comparable to the *glorious* garments worn by the righteous in heaven:

a. 4 Ezra 2:39

Those who have departed from the shadow of this age have received *glorious* garments from the Lord.[45]

b. 1 Enoch 62:15

The righteous and elect ones shall rise from the earth and shall cease being of downcast face. They shall wear the garments of *glory*.[46]

c. 2 Enoch 22:8-10

The Lord said to Michael, "Take Enoch, and extract (him) from the earthly clothing. And anoint him with the delightful oil, and put (him) into the clothes of *glory*." And Michael extracted me from my clothes. He anointed me with the delightful oil; and the appearance of that oil is greater than the greatest light, its ointment is like sweet dew, and its fragrance like myrrh; and its shining is like the sun. And I gazed at all of myself, and I had become like one of the glorious ones, and there was no observable difference.[47]

---

[44] AUNE, *Revelation 1-5*, 223: "...the notion developed that white garments will be awarded to the righteous after judgment as a heavenly reward." J.-A. BÜHNER, "λευκός," *EDNT* 2.351: "...the righteous who also participate in the heavenly worship are, or will be at the resurrection — cult apocalyptic has a strong present eschatology and knows of the transfiguration of the righteous at the hour of death — clothed in heavenly-white garments." See also W. MICHAELIS, "λευκός," *TDNT* 4.249-50.

[45] Translation by METZGER, "Fourth Book of Ezra," 527. MYERS (*II Esdras*, 152) translates "dazzling garments" and refers to them as "accouterments of the saved and the heavenly messengers or servants." (4 Ezra[=2 Esdras] 1-2 is sometimes referred to as 5 Ezra.)

[46] Translation by ISAAC, "1 Enoch," 44.

[47] Translation of the A recension by ANDERSEN, "2 Enoch," 139.

D. Shining Radiance of the Transfigured Jesus

All three depictions of the transfigured Jesus include an overall shining radiance in his external appearance:

Mark 9:3: his clothes became very *radiantly* white
Matt 17:2: his face *shone* as the *sun,* while his clothes became white as the *light*
Luke 9:29: his clothing became *dazzling* white

The very radiantly or shining (στίλβοντα) white clothing of the transfigured Jesus in Mark 9:3 recalls the radiant or shining (στίλβοντος) bronze to which the appearance of a heavenly angelic figure is compared in both Ezekiel's vision in Ezek 40:3 (LXX) and Daniel's vision in the Theodotion recension of Dan 10:6.[48] Similarly, the dazzling or shining-like-lightning (ἐξαστράπτων) white clothing of the transfigured Jesus in Luke 9:29 recalls the dazzling or shining-like-lightning (ἐξαστράπτων) bronze to which the appearance of the heavenly angelic figure is compared in Dan 10:6 (LXX).

The shining radiance of the transfigured Jesus in Matt 17:2 recalls the previous promise in 13:43 that the "righteous" (δίκαιοι) will shine radiantly after the judgment (13:40-42) in the eschatological kingdom of heaven, which in turn recalls the promise in Dan 12:3 that the wise will shine radiantly:

Matt 13:43: The righteous will shine as the sun (ἐκλάμψουσιν ὡς ὁ ἥλιος) in the kingdom of their Father
Matt 17:2: his face shone (ἔλαμψεν) as the sun (ὡς ὁ ἥλιος)
Dan 12:3: The wise will shine (Theodotion: ἐκλάμψουσιν) like the brightness of the firmament[49].

Similarly, in *1 Enoch* 104:2 the righteous are promised that they will *shine* like the lights of heaven and that the windows of heaven will

---

[48] On the use of στίλβω ("shine, be radiant") here, G. Fitzer ("στίλβω," *TDNT* 7.666) states: "Shining white garments are a characteristic of epiphany stories."

[49] The brightness of the firmament should be equated with the stars, which are associated with the angels; see Collins, *Daniel*, 393-94.

be opened for them. And in the J recension of *2 Enoch* 66:7 the righteous will escape the Lord's great judgment and will be made to *shine*
seven times brighter than the sun.   Thus, the temporary shining
radiance of the face and clothes of the transfigured Jesus while still on
earth (Mark 9:2-3; Matt 17:2; Luke 9:29) expresses for the audience
his anticipation of the final and permanent shining radiance of the
righteous as heavenly beings in the transcendent kingdom of heaven.

E. Conclusion

Our investigation of the meaning and background of the literary
motif of the "transfiguration" of Jesus leads us to conclude that it
describes his external, proleptic, and temporary transformation by God
into a heavenly being while still on earth. It points the Gospel audiences to Jesus' future and permanent attainment of glory in heaven as
promised to the righteous after their death.

This result rules out several other suggested interpretations. Jesus'
transfiguration is not an internal self-transformation, but an external
transformation effected by God. It is not a "revelation" or "disclosure"
of his otherwise hidden eternal glory, but a temporary "transfiguration"
or "transformation" of his external appearance.   Although Jesus
ascends a mountain, which is close to the heavenly realm, to be transfigured, he does not ascend into heaven itself but remains on earth.

Jesus' transfiguration does not mean that he is a new, second, or greater Moses. The "glorification" of Moses on Mount Sinai did not occur in
an epiphany; it involved only his face; and it *followed* his speaking with
God. Jesus' transfiguration, on the other hand, occurred as an epiphanic
appearance; it involved not only his face but his clothing; and it *preceded* his conversation with the heavenly figures of Moses and Elijah.

Although the literary background to Jesus' transfiguration involves
similarities to the heavenly figures of God and angels, his transfiguration does not mean that he has become an actual angel or God, only
that his appearance has become temporarily angel-like or God-like.
Nor does his white clothing mean he has become a heavenly priestly
figure.[50] Rather, the background most relevant for the Gospel audien-

---

[50] Priests often wore white in the ancient world; see AUNE, *Revelation 1-5*, 223.

ces to understand the motif of the transfigured Jesus, a human being still on earth, is that involving the heavenly glory promised to the righteous in general after their death. The temporary transfiguration of Jesus into a heavenly figure enables the heavenly figures of Moses and Elijah to appear and speak with him. It is to the significance of this epiphanic appearance of Moses and Elijah with Jesus that we now turn.

CHAPTER 5

THE EPIPHANIC APPEARANCE OF MOSES
AND ELIJAH WITH JESUS

In all three versions of the transfiguration narrative the initial epiphanic transfiguration of Jesus is immediately followed by the additional epiphanic appearance to the three disciples of Moses and Elijah in conversation with the transfigured Jesus:

Mark 9:4: Then there appeared to them Elijah with Moses, and they were talking with Jesus.

Matt 17:3: Then behold there appeared to them Moses and Elijah talking with him.

Luke 9:30-31: Then behold two men were talking with him, who were Moses and Elijah, who, appearing in glory, were speaking about his exodus, which he was about to accomplish in Jerusalem.

The epiphanic transfiguration of Jesus into a heavenly figure has enabled the venerable figures of Moses and Elijah to appear from heaven with Jesus before the eyes of the three disciples. In each version Moses and Elijah "were talking" (συλλαλοῦντες in Mark 9:4 and Matt 17:3; συνελάλουν in Luke 9:30) with the transfigured Jesus, indicating his association with them as heavenly figures.[1] Only Luke gives the content of the conversation. They were speaking about his "exodus" or "departure" (ἔξοδον), that is, his "death"

---

[1] J. M. NÜTZEL, *Die Verklärungserzählung im Markusevangelium: Eine redaktionsgeschichtliche Untersuchung* (FB 6; Bamberg: Echter, 1973) 112. On the meaning of συλλαλεῖν here, Nützel states "daß das Wort eine Gemeinschaft zwischen Jesus und den beiden erschienenen himmlischen Gestalten zum Ausdruck bringen soll."

(and resurrection), which he was about to accomplish in Jerusalem (Luke 9:31; cf. 9:22).[2]

Whereas Matt 17:3 and Luke 9:30 mention Moses first and coordinate him with Elijah in the expression, "Moses and (καὶ) Elijah," Mark 9:4 mentions Elijah first and seems to subordinate Moses to him in the expression, "Elijah with (σὺν) Moses."[3] But a close examination of all the instances where Mark uses the preposition σύν indicates that this is not the case. On the contrary, the object of the preposition σύν in every instance represents the more notable party.

In Mark 2:26 the preposition σύν subordinates the members of David's army to him as their superior; they were allowed to eat the bread of the presence simply because they were "those who were *with him*" (τοῖς σὺν αὐτῷ οὖσιν), David, their leader. In 4:10 σύν subordinates "those around Jesus" to "the Twelve," the specially chosen elite sub-group of disciples (3:14). That "those around him" are "*with the Twelve*" (σὺν δώδεκα) enhances the stature of this grouping for the contrast to "those outside" (4:11).[4] In 8:34 σύν subordinates "the crowd" to "the disciples," the more prominent party. Jesus called "the crowd *with his disciples* (σὺν τοῖς μαθηταῖς αὐτοῦ)" in order to address his command to take up the cross and follow him especially to the disciples, who, despite already following him (8:33), do not understand the necessity for his suffering (8:31-32).[5] In 15:27 and 15:32 σύν subordinates the two robbers crucified "*with him*" (σὺν αὐτῷ) to Jesus, the chief character in the narrative.

Especially relevant here are Mark 4:10 and 8:34. They demonstrate how for Mark the party mentioned second and introduced with σύν actually enhances the grouping. The party added to a grouping with a σύν stands out for special emphasis: "those around him *with*

---

[2] R. PEPPERMÜLLER, "ἔξοδος," *EDNT* 2.8: "In Luke 9:31 and 2 Pet 1:15 ἔξοδος is used to mean *departure from life* (=death)." This meaning is also found in Wis 3:2; 7:6. In Josephus's *A.J.* 4.8.2 §189 Moses refers to his death as his "exit from life (ἐπ' ἐξόδῳ τοῦ ζῆν)."

[3] For past interpretations and detailed discussion, see NÜTZEL, *Verklärungserzählung*, 103-11.

[4] *Contra* GUNDRY, *Mark*, 478. On the significance of the Twelve here as the "kleinere und qualifiziertere Gruppe," see K. STOCK, *Boten aus dem Mit-Ihm-Sein: Das Verhältnis zwischen Jesus und den Zwölf nach Markus* (AnBib 70; Rome: Biblical Institute, 1975) 71 n. 206.

[5] GUNDRY's (*Mark*, 478-79) neglect of this point misleads him to the view that σύν subordinates the disciples to the crowd here.

(σύν), that is, including even and especially, the Twelve" (4:10) and "the crowd *with* (σύν), that is, including even and especially, his disciples" (8:34). Rather than subordinating Moses to Elijah, then, Mark 9:4 actually emphasizes the addition of Moses as enhancing their coupling. Thus, we might paraphrase this special use of σύν in Mark 9:4 as follows: "Then there appeared to them Elijah *with* (σύν), that is, including even, Moses" – not only Elijah but even Moses! Hence Mark says basically the same as Matthew and Luke here but with slightly more emphasis upon Moses as even more notable than Elijah.[6]

A. Past Interpretations of the Appearance of Moses and Elijah

There is certainly no current consensus on the meaning of Moses and Elijah appearing together and talking with the transfigured Jesus. Perhaps the most popular interpretation has been that together they represent the Jewish scriptures, the Law and the Prophets, now fulfilled and surpassed by Jesus. Although "Moses" can and often does stand for the Jewish Law/Torah, Elijah by himself does not normally represent all of the prophets to complement Moses in this way. Indeed, the scriptures consider both Moses and Elijah to be notable prophets, who together can represent the entire prophetic tradition.[7]

Many other possible interpretations for the meaning of Moses and Elijah appearing together have been suggested: Both encountered God

---

[6] Note that in referring to these two venerable figures again, Mark 9:5 follows the order, Moses — Elijah, as do Matt 17:4 and Luke 9:33. See also J.P. HEIL, "A Note on 'Elijah with Moses' in Mark 9,4," *Bib* 80 (1999) 115.

[7] On the juxtaposition of the two ideal figures, Moses and Elijah, in Mal 3:22-23, see A.E. HILL, *Malachi: A New Translation with Introduction and Commentary* (AB 25D; New York: Doubleday, 1998) 384. Hill points out: "The legacy of Moses as the *first* prophet preserved in the colophon to the Pentateuch (Deut 34:10-12) was blended with the legacy of Elijah as the *last* prophet in Malachi's colophon summarizing the message of the OT prophetic books" (p. 384 n. 4; his emphasis). In *Q.G.* 1.86 Philo refers to Moses as the "protoprophet." "Moses is as much a representative of the prophets as is Elijah: indeed, in Jewish thought Moses is the prophet *par excellence*," according to M.D. HOOKER, "'What Doest Thou Here, Elijah?': A Look at St Mark's Account of the Transfiguration," *The Glory of Christ in the New Testament* (eds. L.D. Hurst and N.T. Wright; Oxford: Clarendon, 1987) 63.

on Sinai/Horeb; both were connected to the Law; both were wonder-workers; both suffered rejection as prophets; both were transformed or transfigured in some way; both were eschatological figures associated with the ideas of restoration; both represent the old covenant; etc.[8]

Some have emphasized the individuality of Moses and Elijah and suggested that each represents something different: The role of Moses is typological, confirming the Exodus theme, while Elijah provides the scene an eschatological dimension;[9] Moses and Elijah are "respectively predecessor and precursor to Jesus;"[10] "Moses typifies the prophetic office that Jesus will occupy, while Elijah pictures the hope of the eschaton;"[11] etc.

Most of these past interpretations neglect the epiphanic nature of the appearance of Moses and Elijah. What does it mean that these two prophetic figures of old are now suddenly appearing *from heaven* and talking with the transfigured Jesus? Why do Moses and Elijah appear from heaven and not, e.g., Enoch, who like Elijah did not die but was taken by God to heaven (Gen 5:24), or perhaps the patriachs – Abraham, Isaac, and Jacob, who are now presumed to be living with God (cf. Matt 22:32; Mark 12:26-27; Luke 20:37-38)? What more precisely is the relationship between the epiphanic appearance of Moses and Elijah from heaven and the epiphanic transfiguration of Jesus into a heavenly figure?

B. NEW PROPOSAL FOR THE APPEARANCE OF MOSES AND ELIJAH

The key for the Gospel audiences to understand the significance of the appearance of Moses and Elijah is the way these prophets attained heavenly glory after their lives on earth in contrast to the way that

---

[8] For a survey and discussion of these and other past interpretations, see ÖHLER, "Verklärung," 205 n. 26; MOSES, *Matthew's Transfiguration Story*, 129-30; BOCK, *Luke 1:1-9:50*, 868-69; REID, *Transfiguration*, 121-24.

[9] W.L. LIEFELD, "Theological Motifs in the Transfiguration Narrative," *New Dimensions in New Testament Study* (eds. R.N. Longenecker and M.C. Tenney; Grand Rapids: Zondervan, 1974) 173.

[10] NOLLAND, *Luke 9:21-18:34*, 499.

[11] BOCK, *Luke 1:1-9:50*, 868.

Jesus will ultimately attain heavenly glory.[12] All three epiphanic figures in the transfiguration narrative – Moses, Elijah, and Jesus – were prophetic figures who experienced opposition, rejection, and suffering at the hands of their own people.[13] Although Elijah was rejected as a prophet, he was never put to death by his people. Indeed, Elijah escaped death altogether and rode a flaming chariot into heavenly glory (2 Kgs 2:11).

Likewise, the prophet Moses was never put to death by the people who opposed him. Moses attained heavenly glory either after dying peacefully at an old age (Deut 34:5) or according to some traditions by not dying at all but being translated to heaven like Elijah and Enoch.[14]

In contrast to Moses and Elijah Jesus will attain heavenly glory, not by forgoing death or after dying a natural death, but by being raised by God after being put to death by his own people as an innocent and righteous prophetic figure.[15] We propose that the point of the epiphanic appearance of Moses and Elijah in conversation with the transfigured Jesus is to indicate to the Gospel audiences that although Jesus

---

[12] In reply to GUNDRY (*Mark*, 458, 478), Moses and Elijah are not described as "arrayed in glistening white garments" like the transfigured Jesus, because their heavenly status as venerable prophets of the past has long been established and is largely presupposed. But Luke 9:31 does refer to them as "appearing in glory."

[13] This is recognized by M. PAMMENT, "Moses and Elijah in the Story of the Transfiguration," *ExpTim* 92 (1981) 338-39. But Pamment neglects the key difference that in the case of Jesus rejection included his being put to death by the people. For ÖHLER ("Verklärung," 207) Moses and Elijah are simply representatives of heaven without any further significance. He thus denigrates the uniqueness of Moses and Elijah as those heavenly figures who attained heavenly glory without being put to death as rejected prophets.

[14] Enoch, although he was translated into heaven without dying, does not appear in the transfiguration epiphany because he was a primeval figure preceding salvation history and not a prophet like Moses and Elijah.

[15] That Jesus will attain heavenly glory by being raised from death in contrast to Moses and Elijah is recognized by M.E. THRALL, "Elijah and Moses in Mark's Account of the Transfiguration," *NTS* 16 (1969-70) 314. But Thrall glosses over the tradition that Moses died and misses the more precise point that neither Elijah nor Moses died the death of a rejected prophet like Jesus. For REID (*Transfiguration*, 124-25), who recognizes the different way that Jesus will attain heavenly glory, Jesus' resurrection gives him a "status far superior" to Moses and Elijah. But this denigrates the heavenly glory of Moses and Elijah. As GREEN (*Luke*, 381) states: "That Jesus is engaged in conversation with these two figures of such high status makes it difficult to imagine that Luke wants to censure them...but rather implies a basic continuity between their work on God's behalf and his own."

will attain heavenly glory like Moses and Elijah, he, unlike them, will do so by being raised by God after suffering the unjust death of a rejected prophet.

To demonstrate our thesis we now need to review the literary traditions surrounding how Moses and Elijah attained heavenly glory at the end of their lives on earth, traditions familiar to the Gospel audiences of the transfiguration narratives.

C. The Heavenly Glory of the Prophet Elijah

After the prophet Elijah escaped Jezebel's attempt to murder the prophets of the Lord (1 Kgs 18:4), he stated, "I am the only surviving prophet of the Lord" (1 Kgs 18:22). But Jezebel vowed to kill Elijah, so that he had to flee for his life and prayed for death (1 Kgs 19:2-4). Elijah told God that the Israelites "put your prophets to the sword; I alone am left, and they seek my life" (1 Kgs 19:10, 14). Despite these attempts upon his life Elijah never died the death of a prophet. Instead, God took Elijah in a whirlwind "to the heavens" (הַשָּׁמַיִם in 2 Kgs 2:1) or "as into the heaven" (ὡς εἰς τὸν οὐρανὸν in 4 Kgdms 2:1). As Elijah and Elisha were walking and talking together, a chariot of fire and horses of fire came between them and Elijah "went" or "was taken" up in a whirlwind "to" or "as into" the heaven(s):

2 Kgs 2:11: וַיַּעַל אֵלִיָּהוּ בַּסְעָרָה הַשָּׁמָיִם

4 Kgdms 2:11: ἀνελήμφθη Ηλιου ἐν συσσεισμῷ ὡς εἰς τὸν οὐρανόν

With the introduction of "as" (ὡς) before "into the heaven" (εἰς τὸν οὐρανόν) the LXX expresses Elijah's destination in a bit more of an indirect fashion than the MT, which has simply "to the heavens" (הַשָּׁמַיִם). Whereas in the MT Elijah actively "went up" (וַיַּעַל) to heaven, in the LXX he "was taken up" (ἀνελήμφθη) to heaven by God (divine passive). But the MT of 2 Kgs 2:1, 3, 5, 9 (also 4 Kgdms 2:1, 3, 5, 9) indicates that *God* took up Elijah into heaven.

This ascent or assumption of Elijah into heavenly glory without dying seems to be a relatively stable tradition. It is mentioned also in 1 Macc 2:58, "Elijah, with his burning zeal for the law, was taken up into the heaven (ἀνελήμφθη εἰς τὸν οὐρανόν)," and Sir 48:9, "You were taken up (ἀναλημφθεὶς) in a whirlwind of fire, in a chariot of fiery horses."[16]   It undoubtedly contributed to the expectation that Elijah would return as a forerunner of the final age (Mal 3:23-24; Sir 48:9-10; Matt 17:10; Mark 9:11).[17] Thus, according to the biblical tradition Elijah attained heavenly glory without dying the death of a rejected prophet like Jesus.[18]

D. THE HEAVENLY GLORY OF THE PROPHET MOSES

1. Biblical Account

After Moses killed an Egyptian, he fled and thus escaped Pharaoh's attempt to put him to death (Exod 2:11-15). Although Moses, the preeminent and peerless prophet (Deut 34:10), experienced grumbling and various rebellions from his people (Exodus 15-16, 32; Numbers 16-17; 14:1-10), and although he would not enter the promised land but die because of the people's sin (Deut 1:37; 3:26-27; 4:21-22), he was never put to death by his people as a rejected prophet.[19] Indeed, according to

---

[16] See also *Apoc. Ezra* 7:6. On the assumption of Elijah into heaven, see G. LOHFINK, *Die Himmelfahrt Jesu: Untersuchungen zu den Himmelfahrts- und Erhöhungstexten bei Lukas* (SANT 26; Munich: Kösel, 1971) 57-59. On ἀναλαμβάνω as a common term for heavenly ascension and exaltation, see J. KREMER, "ἀναλαμβάνω," *EDNT* 1.83-84.

[17] For reservations in some traditions about Elijah's ascent into heaven, see M. COGAN and H. TADMOR, *II Kings: A New Translation with Introduction and Commentary* (AB 11; New York: Doubleday, 1988) 34. Josephus, for example, with his tendency to rationalize the miraculous, eliminates the whirlwind and ascent to heaven; he says that Elijah simply "disappeared from human beings" (ἐξ ἀνθρώπων ἠφανίσθη) and to this day no one knows his end. He goes on to link Elijah with Enoch, as those who "became invisible, and no one knows of their death (γεγόνασιν ἀφανεῖς, θάνατον δ᾽ αὐτῶν οὐδεὶς οἶδεν)" (*A.J.* 9.2.2 §28). On Elijah in Josephus, see L.H. FELDMAN, *Studies in Josephus' Rewritten Bible* (JSJSup 58; Leiden: Brill, 1998) 291-305.

[18] For the significance of Elijah in the biblical tradition, see J.T. WALSH, "Elijah," *ABD* 2.463-66; ÖHLER, *Elia*; D. ZELLER, "Elija und Elischa im Frühjudentum," *BK* 41 (1986) 154-60. On the parallelism between the conclusion of the prophetic careers of Elijah and Moses, WALSH ("Elijah," 465) notes: "Elijah's mysterious disappearance in Transjordan and the disciples' inability to recover his body parallel the death and divinely hidden burial of Moses (Deut 34:1-6)." See also J.W. OLLEY, "YHWH and His Zealous Prophet: The Presentation of Elijah in 1 and 2 Kings," *JSOT* 80 (1998) 45-46.

[19] S.E. LOEWENSTAMM, "The Death of Moses," *Studies on the Testament of Abraham* (SBLSCS 6; ed. G.W.E. Nickelsburg; Missoula: Scholars Press, 1972) 185-92; D.T. OLSON, *Deuteronomy and the Death of Moses: A Theological Reading* (OBT; Minneapolis: Fortress,

the biblical account Moses died at an old age and was buried on Mount Nebo after viewing the promised land:

Deuteronomy 34:5-8

5 Then Moses, the servant of the Lord, died there in the land of Moab at the Lord's command. 6 He buried him in a valley in the land of Moab opposite Beth-peor, but no one knows his burial place to this day. 7 Moses was one hundred twenty years old when he died; his sight was unimpaired and his vigor had not abated. 8 The Israelites wept for Moses in the plains of Moab thirty days; then the days of weeping and mourning for Moses ended.

Although the biblical account states that Moses died, the circumstances surrounding his death are rather extraordinary. God himself told him when and where he was to die (Deut 32:50), and so he died "at the Lord's command" (34:5).[20] Then *God himself* "buried him" (וֹיִקְבֹּר אֹתֹו) (34:6).[21] Although God buried him in a relatively speci-

---

1994) 165-67; J.-P. SONNET, *The Book Within the Book: Writing in Deuteronomy* (BIS 14; Leiden: Brill, 1997) 192-94, 223-26. On Moses as the first prophet and model for all other prophets, see J.W. WATTS, "The Legal Characterization of Moses in the Rhetoric of the Pentateuch," *JBL* 117 (1998) 419. Watts states: "In Deut 18:15-22, Moses presents himself as the first of a line of prophets who, by virtue of the authority delegated by the people ('you') as well as YHWH (vv. 16-17), will speak for God to Israel. Deuteronomy thus defines prophets by comparison with Moses, and so turns the statement 'Moses was a prophet' into a tautology." On Moses as a prophet, see also S. BEYERLE, *Der Mosesegen im Deuteronomium: Eine text-, kompositions- und formkritische Studie zu Deuteronomium 33* (BZAW 250; New York: De Gruyter, 1997) 288-90.

[20] Although Moses must die, God assures him of a heavenly afterlife in *Tg. Ps.-J.* Deut 31:16: "Lo, you are to sleep in the dust with your fathers, but your soul will be safeguarded in the treasury of eternal life with your fathers"; see E. LEVINE, *The Aramaic Version of the Bible: Contents and Context* (BZAW 174; Berlin: De Gruyter, 1988) 223.

[21] Despite the active verb form in the MT and the occurrence of the name of God as the last word in v. 5, both the NAB and the NRSV translate, "he was buried." J.W. WEVERS, *Notes on the Greek Text of Deuteronomy* (SBLSCS 39; Atlanta: Scholars Press, 1995) 559: "According to MT it was Yahweh who buried Moses. That this was the original account is clear from the next clause: 'no one knew his grave.' This was too much for LXX, so it used a plural verb ἔθαψαν so as to avoid the direct statement that the Lord buried him by using an indefinite plural. I would translate 'And Moses was buried.'" *Targum Neofiti 1* follows the LXX here with the indefinite plural, "they buried him"; see M. McNAMARA, *Targum Neofiti I: Deuteronomy: Translated, with Apparatus and Notes* (Aramaic Bible 5A; Collegeville: Liturgical Press, 1997) 174-75. But *Targum Onqelos* follows the MT, "he (God) buried him"; see B. GROSSFELD, *The Targum Onqelos to Deuteronomy: Translated, with Apparatus, and Notes* (Aramaic Bible 9; Wilmington: Glazier, 1988) 114. In *Targum Pseudo-Jonathan*, however, God and the ministering angels buried Moses; see E.G. CLARKE, *Targum Pseudo-Jonathan: Deuteronomy: Translated, with Notes* (Aramaic Bible 5B; Collegeville: Liturgical Press, 1998) 105.

fic place, "in a valley in the land of Moab opposite Beth-peor,"[22] the place of his burial remains forever unknown to human beings (34:6).[23] And although Moses died at the age of one hundred and twenty years, he amazingly still enjoyed an exceptionally youthful vision and vigor (34:7).[24] Rather than putting Moses to death as a rejected prophet, the people of Israel honored their revered prophet by weeping and mourning for him for a traditional thirty days (34:8).

The unique and mysterious circumstances surrounding the death of Moses gave it a very exceptional character. Indeed, no human being seems to have died and been buried quite like the great prophet Moses. This gave rise to some interesting interpretative elaborations upon the end of the earthly life of Moses in traditions prior to and/or roughly contemporaneous with the NT.

2. Josephus: Antiquitates Judaicae

To a much greater degree than the biblical account Josephus dramatically amplifies the murmuring and rebellion against the leadership of Moses.[25] Josephus reinforces the role of Moses as a prophet, "twice identifying him as a prophet when the biblical text does not."[26] Although the great prophet Moses repeatedly experiences opposition

---

[22] SONNET, *Deuteronomy*, 225: "These parameters are sufficient to rule out the construing of Moses' disappearance as an ascension; yet they are not sufficient to found a grave-site cult."

[23] WEVERS, *Deuteronomy*, 559: "That 'no one knew his grave (i.e. where he was buried) unto this day' accents the uniqueness of the Moses phenomenon, a uniqueness stressed even more by MT where it is said that the Lord buried him." On Deut 34:6 LOEWENSTAMM ("Death of Moses," 195) states: "The passage adumbrates that God in His glory — and He alone — attended to Moses' burial, and for this reason, his gravesite has remained forever a secret to men."

[24] OLSON, *Death of Moses*, 168: "These claims about Moses' extraordinary strength and youthfulness are common legendary motifs associated with heroes in ancient literature." See also G.W. COATS, "Legendary Motifs in the Moses Death Report," *CBQ* 39 (1977) 34-44.

[25] L.H. FELDMAN, "Josephus' Portrait of Moses," *JQR* 82 (1992) 316-17; IDEM, *Josephus's Interpretation of the Bible* (Berkeley: University of California Press, 1998) 388-93; P. SPILSBURY, *The Image of the Jew in Flavius Josephus' Paraphrase of the Bible* (TSAJ 69; Tübingen: Mohr Siebeck, 1998) 113-45.

[26] L.H. FELDMAN, "Josephus' Portrait of Moses: Part Two," *JQR* 83 (1993) 45. Compare *A.J.* 2.15.4 §327 with Exod 14:13 and *A.J.* 4.8.48 §320 with Deut 33:1. See also L.H. FELDMAN, "Prophets and Prophecy in Josephus," *JTS* 41 (1990) 386-422.

from various factions of the people, they never put him to death. Indeed, Josephus dramatically enhances the biblical account of the people's mourning for their revered prophet. It begins after Moses told the Israelites of his approaching death, but while he is still alive.[27]

Rather than repeating the biblical account that Moses died and was buried by God so that no one knows his burial place (Deut 34:5-6), Josephus dramatically develops it by reporting that Moses, instead of dying, simply disappeared and returned to God. Josephus begins to entertain this interpretation when he comments upon the Israelites' concern that Moses has been delayed on Mount Sinai for forty days (Exod 32:1):

a. Antiquitates Judaicae 3.5.7 §95-97

95 A fear seized the Hebrews that something had befallen Moses, and of all the horrors that they had encountered none so deeply distressed them as the thought that Moses had perished. 96 There was a conflict of opinions: some said that he had fallen a victim to wild beasts — it was principally those who were ill disposed towards him who voted for that view — others that he had been taken back to the divinity. 97 But the sober-minded, who found no private satisfaction in either statement — who held that to die under the fangs of beasts was a human accident, and that he should be translated by God to Himself by reason of his inherent virtue was likely enough — were moved by these reflections to retain their composure.[28]

Except for those opposed to Moses, the people cannot accept the thought that Moses may have died. The "sober-minded" or "wise" (σώφρονας) thought it quite appropriate in view of his virtue that Moses should be "translated by God to Himself" (τὸ ὑπὸ τοῦ θεοῦ πρὸς αὐτόν μεταστῆναι) instead of dying (3.5.7 §97). The opinion that, rather than dying Moses has been "taken back to the divinity" (πρὸς τὸ θεῖον ἀνακεχωρηκέναι, 3.5.7 §96) likens Moses to Enoch, who, according to Josephus, also "returned to the divinity" (ἀνεχώρησε πρὸς τὸ θεῖον, 1.3.4 §85) instead of dying.[29]

When Josephus reports on the end of the earthly life of Moses, he reinforces the above opinion by himself asserting that Moses never died but disappeared and returned to God:

---

[27] L.H. FELDMAN, "Josephus' Portrait of Moses: Part Three," *JQR* 83 (1993) 324-25.

[28] Translation from LCL.

[29] K. HAACKER and P. SCHÄFER, "Nachbiblische Traditionen vom Tod des Mose," *Josephus-Studien: Untersuchungen zu Josephus, dem antiken Judentum und dem Neuen Testament: Festschrift O. Michel* (ed. O. Betz, et al.; Göttingen: Vandenhoeck & Ruprecht, 1974) 148.

b. Antiquitates Judaicae 4.8.48 §326

And, while he bade farewell to Eleazar and Joshua and was yet communing with them, a cloud of a sudden descended upon him and he disappeared in a ravine. But he has written of himself in the sacred books that he died, for fear lest they should venture to say that by reason of his surpassing virtue he had gone back to the Deity.[30]

To some interpreters it appears that Josephus at this point is asserting that Moses actually died rather than simply disappeared and returned to God.[31] But this interpretation fails to distinguish between the assertion of Josephus himself and what Josephus reports about the concern of Moses. According to Josephus Moses "has written of himself" in the biblical account that he died (Deut 34:5). But Moses wrote this because of his modesty. He feared that the people would place too much emphasis upon his personal virtue (cf. *A.J.* 3.5.7 §97). Josephus frequently underlines the humility of Moses:

c. Antiquitates Judaicae 3.8.8 §212

Moses, for his part, having declined every honour which he saw that the people were ready to confer on him, devoted himself solely to the service of God....dressed like any ordinary person, in all else he bore himself as a simple commoner, who desired in nothing to appear different from the crowd, save only in being seen to have their interests at heart.[32]

Thus, in *A.J.* 4.8.48 §326 Josephus is further demonstrating the modesty of Moses. Moses "has written of himself" that he died because he did not want "to appear different from the crowd," as if he did not die like a "simple commoner." Although this is what *Moses* wrote, this is not what Josephus thinks. For Josephus Moses did not actually die, but disappeared in a cloud in a ravine and returned to God.[33]

---

[30] Translation from LCL.

[31] HAACKER and SCHÄFER, "Tod des Mose," 150: "der Tod Moses für Josephus außer Frage steht." See also FELDMAN, "Moses," 324; J. D. Tabor, "'Returning to the Divinity': Josephus's Portrayal of the Disappearance of Enoch, Elijah, and Moses," *JBL* 108 (1989) 237-38.

[32] Translation from LCL. On the modesty and humility of Moses, see also *A.J.* 2.12.2 §270; 3.4.2 §73; 4.6.13 §157-58; FELDMAN, "Moses: Part Two," 47.

[33] LOHFINK, *Himmelfahrt Jesu*, 61-62. The perceptive argument that the report of the death of Moses in *A.J.* 4.8.48 §326 alludes to his renowned modesty comes from C. BEGG, "'Josephus's Portrayal of the Disappearances of Enoch, Elijah, and Moses': Some Observations," *JBL* 109

That Moses "disappeared" (ἀφανίζεται, 4.8.48 §326) likens him to Elijah, who also "disappeared from human beings" (ἐξ ἀνθρώπων ἠφανίσθη), and to both Elijah and Enoch, as those who became "invisible" (ἀφανεῖς) so that no one knows of their death (9.2.2 §28).[34] That Moses "has gone back to the Deity" (πρὸς τὸ θεῖον αὐτὸν ἀναχωρῆσαι, 4.8.48 §326) at the end of his earthly life recalls the opinion of those who thought that he did not die on Mount Sinai, but had been "taken back to the Deity" (πρὸς τὸ θεῖον ἀνακεχωρηκέναι, 3.5.7 §96) like Enoch, who also did not die, but "returned to the Deity" (ἀνεχώρησε πρὸς τὸ θεῖον, 1.3.4 §85).[35] For Josephus, then, the great prophet Moses, like the prophet Elijah, did not suffer death at the hands of his people; in fact, Moses, like Elijah and Enoch, did not even die, but simply disappeared and returned to God in heaven.

3. *Pseudo-Philo: Liber Antiquitatum Biblicarum*

Pseudo-Philo's *Liber Antiquitatum Biblicarum* greatly expands upon the biblical account of the extraordinary character of the death of Moses:

Deuteronomy 34:5-6:

5 Then Moses, the servant of the Lord, *died* there in the land of Moab *at the Lord's command.* 6 *He buried him* in a valley in the land of Moab opposite Beth-peor, but *no one knows his burial place* to this day.

a. *Liber Antiquitatum Biblicarum 19:12, 16*

12 I will take you from here and lay you down to sleep with your fathers, and I will give you rest in your resting place and *bury* you in peace. All the angels will mourn over you, and

---

(1990) 691-93. SPILSBURY (*Image of the Jew*, 107 n. 48) declares that Begg's argument here is not convincing, but he offers no basis for this judgment. Begg's argument is well-founded, based on a close analysis of the text of *A.J.* 4.8.48 §326 that sees the distinction between what Moses wrote but what Josephus himself thinks about the death of Moses, as well as on Josephus's overall portrait of Moses.

[34] On ἀφανίζω/ἀφανὴς as characteristic terms for heavenly assumptions or translations, see LOHFINK, *Himmelfahrt Jesu*, 41; Begg, "Joshephus's Portrayal," 691-92. See also J. SIEVERS, "Josephus and the Afterlife," *Understanding Josephus: Seven Perspectives* (JSPSup 32; ed. S. Mason; Sheffield: Sheffield Academic Press, 1998) 24-25.

[35] See also *A.J.* 5.1.1 §1, which refers to Moses as "having in the aforesaid manner been rapt away from men (ἐξ ἀνθρώπων ἀπογεγονότος)" (LCL translation).

the heavenly hosts will grieve. But *no angel nor man will know your sepulchre* in which you will be buried. You will rest in it until I visit the world. I will raise up you and your fathers from the earth in which you sleep and you will come together and dwell in the immortal dwelling place that is not subject to time....

16 When Moses heard this, he was filled with understanding and his appearance was changed to a state of glory; and he *died* in glory *in accord with the word of the Lord*, and *he buried him* as he had promised him. The angels mourned his death and went before him all together with lightning bolts and torches and arrows. On that day the hymn of the heavenly hosts was not sung because of the passing of Moses, nor was there such a day from the time when the Lord made man upon the earth, nor shall there again be such forever, that the hymn of the angels should be humbled on account of men, because he loved him very much. *He buried him* with his own hands in a high place as a light for the entire world.[36]

Whereas the biblical account states succinctly that Moses "died" and God "buried him" (Deut 34:5-6), in *L.A.B.* 19:12 God promises not only that God himself "will take" Moses "from here" and euphemistically "lay you down to sleep," but that God himself will give him "rest" (*requiem*) and bury him "in peace" (*cum pace*). God further promises Moses a future resurrection from death and entrance into heaven, that is, "the immortal dwelling place that is not subject to time" (19:12). This promise of a dwelling in heaven is promptly reinforced when God promises further that "I will hasten to raise up you who are sleeping in order that all who will be restored to life will dwell in the place of sanctification that I showed you" (19:13).[37]

Pseudo-Philo greatly emphasizes the glorious circumstances and heavenly ramifications surrounding the death of Moses. Whereas the biblical account simply states that Moses "died" at the Lord's command (Deut 34:5), in *L.A.B.* 19:16, before Moses died, his appearance was changed "to a state of glory" (*in gloria*), and he died "in glory" (*in gloria*) in accord with the word of the Lord. As God promised (19:12), God himself buried Moses and the angels mourned his death and "went before him" in a kind of heavenly funeral procession (19:16).[38] That

---

[36] Translation of the Latin text of *L.A.B.* 19:12, 16 by JACOBSON, *Commentary on Pseudo-Philo*, 122-23; for the commentary, see pp. 641-43, 652-58.

[37] Since "place of sanctification" (*locum sanctificationis*) "recalls similar language used to refer to Jerusalem and the Temple," JACOBSON (*Commentary on Pseudo-Philo*, 645) states that *L.A.B.* 19:13 "follows the tradition that either identifies or strongly associates Paradise with the 'celestial' Jerusalem."

[38] JACOBSON, *Commentary on Pseudo-Philo*, 654: "This, so to speak, heavenly funeral procession is particularly interesting coming both after and before emphatic references to

no hymn was sung in heaven on the day Moses died, because God "loved him very much,"*and that God himself buried Moses "with his own hands" (19:16) further underscore the uniqueness of the death of Moses.[39]

Although Pseudo-Philo asserted that Moses was buried (19:16) and would remain in his grave until the future resurrection (19:12), there may be, nevertheless, especially in view of Pseudo-Philo's emphasis upon the glorious death of Moses, a suggestion that Moses already entered heaven when he died:

b. Liber Antiquitatum Biblicarum 32:9

When he was dying, God arranged the firmament for him and pointed out to him then what we now have as witnesses, saying, "Let there be as a witness between me and you and my people the heaven that you have entered and the earth on which you have walked until now."[40]

Although that "God arranged the firmament for him" may refer simply to God's revealing the heavens to Moses before he died (19:10), it could just as well refer to God's arrangement of the heavens for the entrance of Moses into them at his death.[41] And although "the heaven that you have entered" may allude to the past heavenly ascent of Moses on Mount Sinai, it also could refer to the entrance of Moses

---

Moses' burial. LAB gives us two sides of the death. On the one hand, Moses is buried. On the other, he is led forth to some unspecified other world." On this ambivalence surrounding the death of Moses in Pseudo-Philo, see also HAACKER and SCHÄFER, "Tod des Mose," 155-56; M. WADSWORTH, "The Death of Moses and the Riddle of the End of Time in Pseudo-Philo," *JJS* 28 (1977) 18-19. Wadsworth notes "the same author's insistence that Moses was glorified, but nevertheless that he died, that he was buried, but nevertheless not by men or by angels but by God himself" (p. 19).

[39] E. REINMUTH, *Pseudo-Philo und Lukas: Studien zum Liber Antiquitatum Biblicarum und seiner Bedeutung für die Interpretation des lukanischen Doppelwerks* (WUNT 74; Tübingen: Mohr Siebeck, 1994) 62: "Die Einmaligkeit des Sterbetages des Mose wird auf der metanarrativen Ebene herausgestellt." See also MURPHY, *Pseudo-Philo*, 94-95. JACOBSON, *Commentary on Pseudo-Philo*, 656: "One wonders whether the implication of Moses' uniqueness is somehow related to the Bible's statement at just this point (Deut 34:10) that there never arose a prophet in Israel like Moses."

[40] Translation by JACOBSON, *Commentary on Pseudo-Philo*, 150.

[41] HAACKER and SCHÄFER ("Tod des Mose," 156 n. 31) point out that Pseudo-Philo knows of the heavenly assumptions of both Enoch (*L.A.B.* 1:16) and Phinehas (48:1), who is identical to Elijah; see also MURPHY, *Pseudo-Philo*, 184-85; JACOBSON, *Commentary on Pseudo-Philo*, 1060, 1063.

into heaven now, "when he was dying."[42] At any rate, for Pseudo-Philo Moses did not suffer the ignominious death of a rejected prophet; on the contrary, he died "in glory" and entered heaven at the time of his death and/or will enter it in the future resurrection.

4. *Assumption of Moses*

The early first century C.E. document sometimes known as the *Testament of Moses* is more properly entitled the *Assumption of Moses*.[43] According to this document the prophet Moses, who "testified to us in his prophecies (*in profetis*)...suffered many things in Egypt, and in the Red Sea, and in the desert, during forty years" (3:11), but he did not suffer death at the hands of his people. Rather, as Moses himself euphemistically announces his upcoming death, that "I will go to the resting place of my fathers," he gives as the reason simply that "the time of the years of my life is fulfilled (*consummatum est tempus annorum vitae meae*)" (1:15).[44]

In *Ass. Mos.* 10:12 Moses describes his death as "my being taken away" or "my reception" (*receptione mea*). Although *receptio* can at times mean "taken" or "received" into heaven,[45] here it probably means "taken" or "received" into the realm of death.[46] This reference by Moses to his death as "my reception" provides a catch-word connection for Joshua's response:

Assumption of Moses 11:5-8

5 What place will receive you, 6 or what will be the monument on your grave, 7 or who, being human, will dare to carry your body from one place to another? 8 For all who die when

---

[42] JACOBSON, *Commentary on Pseudo-Philo*, 880-81: "I suspect that *disposuit ei firmamentum* means simply, 'God arranged the heavens for him,' i.e. God prepared the heavens for Moses' entry...This may refer to the present passage of Moses from life to 'death'...or to Moses' ascent at the time of Revelation."

[43] On the proper title and dating of this document, see J. TROMP, *The Assumption of Moses: A Critical Edition with Commentary* (SVTP 10; Leiden: Brill, 1993) 115-17.

[44] TROMP, *Assumption of Moses*, 143: "The reason for Moses' death is the 'completion' of his lifetime."

[45] For examples, see 4 Ezra 6:26 and the Vg of Sir 48:9 (Elijah); 49:16(14) (Enoch); 1 Macc 2:58 (Elijah). See also HAACKER and SCHÄFER, "Tod des Mose," 160.

[46] TROMP (*Assumption of Moses*, 239) argues against the view that *receptione mea* in 10:12 is a redactional gloss.

their time has come have a grave in the earth. But your grave extends from the East to the West, and from the North to the extreme South. The entire world is your grave.[47]

After Moses spoke of his death as "my reception" (*receptione mea*) in 10:12, Joshua's reply, "what place will receive (*recipit*) you?" in 11:5, raises the question of whether any specific place on earth can serve as a grave for Moses, and thus hints at the appropriateness of his assumption to heaven.[48] Joshua's emphasis upon the extraordinary character of the death of Moses further opens the way for the idea of his dwelling nowhere specifically on earth and therefore in heaven: no suitable earthly monument for his grave (11:6); no suitable human being (therefore only God and/or angels) to handle the body of Moses (11:7); all other human beings have a grave "in the earth" (*in terris*), but the grave of Moses encompasses "the entire world" (*omnis orbis terrarum*), which means that it cannot be localized in any one place, giving it really an other-worldly or heavenly character (11:8).

There may be an allusion to the lost ending of the *Assumption of Moses* in Jude 9: "But Michael the archangel, when he contended with the devil and disputed over the body of Moses, did not dare to bring a charge of blasphemy, but said, 'May the Lord rebuke you!'"[49] This may indicate that Michael buried the *body* of Moses (cf. 11:7), and thus leave open the possibility that his *soul or spirit* ascended to heaven. On the question of whether the lost ending contained an assumption of Moses to heaven:

...it is reasonable to conclude that As. Mos. considered Moses to have been taken up to heaven. But since the author of As. Mos. makes Moses allude to his own death (1:15; 10:14), an assumption must not in this case be conceived as a bodily assumption (which would imply that Moses did not die at all). If indeed Moses was thought to have been taken up, it is likely that the author of As. Mos. had only the assumption of a spiritual component of Moses' person (something like an ethereal, glorified, spiritual body, or perhaps his spirit or soul) in mind. An assumption of such a spiritual part of someone's person into heaven does not exclude death.

---

[47] Translation by TROMP, *Assumption of Moses*, 240.

[48] On the meaning of *recipit* here, TROMP (*Assumption of Moses*, 245) remarks: "*Recipere*, however, can be said of any displacement or removal to any place to which one is transferred, especially heaven, and it is possible that the ending of As. Mos. answered Joshua's question by having Moses' soul ascend into heaven."

[49] On the lost ending of the *Assumption of Moses* and its relation to Jude 9, see TROMP, *Assumption of Moses*, 270-85; R. BAUCKHAM, *Jude and the Relatives of Jesus in the Early Church* (Edinburgh: Clark, 1990) 235-80; S.J. JOUBERT, "Facing the Past: Transtextual Relationships and Historical Understanding in the Letter of Jude," *BZ* 42 (1998) 60-61.

All in all, As. Mos. is likely to have narrated the end of Moses' terrestial life as a death followed by the burial of his body by Michael and the ascent of a spiritual part of his person to heaven, possibly accompanied or transferred there by the archangel.[50]

Thus, for the *Assumption of Moses* the prophet Moses, although he suffered, did not suffer the usual infamous destiny of a prophet. Rather than being put to death by his people as a rejected prophet, he died when his life was brought to its completion (1:15). Indeed, he died and was buried in an extraordinary fashion that strongly suggests his assumption into heaven.

5. *Philo of Alexandria*

Philo of Alexandria (ca. 30 B.C.E.-50 C.E.) also greatly augments the biblical account of the extraordinary character of the death of the great prophet Moses.[51] According to Philo, Moses prophesied the story of his own death and burial, even while he was being taken by God to glorious exaltation in heaven:

a. De Vita Moysis 2.288, 291-292

288 Afterwards the time came when he had to make his pilgrimage from earth to heaven, and leave this mortal life for immortality, summoned thither by the Father Who resolved his twofold nature of soul and body into a single unity, transforming his whole being into mind, pure as the sunlight....291 for when he was already being exalted and stood at the very barrier, ready at the signal to direct his upward flight to heaven, the divine spirit fell upon him and he prophesied with discernment while still alive the story of his own death; told ere the end how the end came; told how he was buried with none present, surely by no mortal hands but by immortal powers; how also he was not laid to rest in the tomb of his forefathers but was given a monument of special dignity which no man has ever seen; how all the nation wept and mourned for him a whole month and made open display, private and public, of their sorrow, in memory of his vast benevolence and watchful care for each of them and for all.

292 Such, as recorded in the Holy Scriptures, was the life and such the end of Moses, king, lawgiver, high priest, prophet.[52]

Here Philo emphasizes the prophetic character of Moses, calling him a "prophet" (προφήτου, *Mos.* 2.292) who "prophesied" (προφητεύει)

---

[50] TROMP, *Assumption of Moses*, 285.

[51] On the background and significance of Philo, see E. BIRNBAUM, *The Place of Judaism in Philo's Thought: Israel, Jews, and Proselytes* (BJS 290; Atlanta: Scholars Press, 1996); P. BORGEN, *Philo of Alexandria: An Exegete for His Time* (NovTSup 86; Leiden: Brill, 1997).

[52] Translation from LCL.

the story of his own death and burial while still alive and on his way to heaven (2.291). Although a great prophet for Philo, Moses did not experience the usual humiliating and disgraceful death of a rejected prophet. On the contrary, Philo twice mentions that Moses at the end of his life was taken by God "to heaven" (εἰς οὐρανὸν, 2.288, 291). One of the words Philo employs to describe the heavenly ascent of Moses at the end of his life, his already "being exalted" (ἀναλαμ-βανόμενος, 2.291), a common term for ascension or translation into heaven, recalls the occurrences of this same verb (ἀναλαμβάνω) for the taking up by God of the prophet Elijah into heaven in 4 Kgdms 2:11; 1 Macc 2:58; Sir 48:9.

Although in *Mos.* 2.291-292 Philo seems to affirm the biblical account of the death of Moses, when he comments on the translation of Enoch into heaven in Gen 5:24, he denies the death of the "protoprophet" Moses:

b. Questiones et Solutiones in Genesin 1.86

What is the meaning of the words, "And he was not found, for God had translated him"?

First of all, the end of worthy and holy men is not death but translation and approaching another place. Second, something very marvellous took place. For he seemed to be rapt away and become invisible. For then he was not found....This gift the protoprophet also obtained, for no one knew his burial-place. And still another, Elijah, followed him on high from earth to heaven at the appearance of the divine countenance, or, it would be more proper and correct to say, he ascended.[53]

Since Moses was a worthy and holy man, indeed, the "protoprophet," he was not subject to death. Like Enoch and Elijah, Moses was translated or ascended "from earth to heaven."[54] For Philo both the

---

[53] Translation from LCL. On Philo's *Questiones et Solutiones in Genesin et in Exodum* BORGEN (*Philo*, 47) notes: "All but a small portion of the Greek original has been lost and for the bulk of the work we must depend upon the ancient Armenian version." "Philo also mentions the assumption of Moses to God in *Sacr.* 8-10, referring to Deut. 34.5-6: God 'drawing the perfect one from things earthly to Himself,'" according to P. BORGEN, "Heavenly Ascent in Philo: An Examination of Selected Passages," *The Pseudepigrapha and Early Biblical Interpretation* (JSPSup 14; eds. J.H. Charlesworth and C.A. Evans; Sheffield: JSOT, 1993) 251.

[54] In reference to Enoch, Moses, and Elijah, BORGEN ("Heavenly Ascent," 249) states: "...all three ended their earthly lives in an unusual and marvellous way by entering the heavenly form of existence directly by assumption. These three are among the most outstanding figures in Jewish ascent traditions. Moreover, here in *Quest. in Gen.* 1.86 Philo expresses the view that Moses was taken up to God by means of assumption without death and burial, in

"protoprophet" Moses and the prophet Elijah did not experience the death of rejected prophets. As worthy and holy men, they attained heavenly glory without suffering death at all.[55]

E. CONCLUSION

The prophets Moses and Elijah appear from heaven in conversation with the transfigured Jesus to contrast the way that he will ultimately attain the same heavenly glory they enjoy. According to the biblical account and later Jewish traditions familiar to the Gospel audiences Elijah, although he suffered persecution as a prophet, attained heavenly glory by ascending directly into heaven without dying the death of a rejected prophet. According to the biblical account Moses, although he suffered rebellion and opposition from his people, was never put to death as a rejected prophet. He died and was buried in a very extraordinary way, honored and revered by his people. Later Jewish traditions indicate that the great prophet Moses attained heavenly glory either at the time of his mysterious death and burial or, like the prophet Elijah, without dying at all.[56] The Gospel audiences know that Jesus, unlike Moses and Elijah, will suffer the destiny of the disgraceful death of a rejected prophet. The Gospel audiences know that Jesus, unlike Moses and Elijah, will attain heavenly glory only after being unjustly put to death by his people and raised from the dead by his heavenly Father.

---

conflict with Deut. 34.5 and the interpretation given by him in *Vit. Mos.* 2.291 where he states explicitly that Moses died and was buried. Thus Philo gives an early evidence for the two traditions that are found in other Jewish writings."

[55] BORGEN, "Heavenly Ascent," 267: "Philo gives an early documentation of traditions about the assumptions of Enoch, Moses and Elijah, meaning that they entered the heavenly realm without experiencing death. These traditions were widespread within Judaism, as evidenced by passages in Josephus's writings, apocalyptic writings, the New Testament and rabbinic writings."

[56] These traditions developed even further. See HAACKER and SCHÄFER, "Tod des Mose," 160-70; J. MacDONALD, "The Samaritan Doctrine of Moses," *SJT* 3 (1960) 149-62; IDEM, *The Theology of the Samaritans* (NTL; London: SCM, 1964) 215-22; J.E. FOSSUM, *The Name of God and the Angel of the Lord: Samaritan and Jewish Concepts of Intermediation and the Origin of Gnosticism* (WUNT 36; Tübingen: Mohr Siebeck, 1985) 129-44; L. GINZBERG, *The Legends of the Jews* (Philadelphia: Jewish Publication Society, 1909-38) 3.463-81, 6.158-68; J.Z. LAUTERBACH, *Mekilta de-Rabbi Ishmael* (Philadelphia: Jewish Publication Society, 1961) 2.224; A.J. SALDARINI, *The Fathers According to Rabbi Nathan: A Translation and Commentary* (SJLA 11; Leiden: Brill, 1975) 148-53.

CHAPTER 6

THE THREE TENTS

What would the Gospel audiences have understood as the meaning and significance of the three tents in the transfiguration narrative? After the three disciples see the epiphanic appearance of Moses and Elijah in conversation with the transfigured Jesus, Peter in all three versions suggests the building of a tent each for Jesus, Moses, and Elijah:

Mark 9:5-6: Then replying Peter said to Jesus, "Rabbi, it is good that we are here, so let us make three tents, for you one and for Moses one and for Elijah one." He did not know what to reply, for they had become terrified.

Matt 17:4: Replying Peter spoke to Jesus, "Lord, it is good that we are here. If you wish, I will make here three tents, for you one and for Moses one and for Elijah one."

Luke 9:33: As they were separating from him, Peter spoke to Jesus, "Master, it is good that we are here, so let us make three tents, one for you and one for Moses and one for Elijah," not knowing what he was saying.

In each version Peter tells Jesus that "it is good that we are here." He then suggests that either "I," Peter himself (Matt 17:4), or "we," Peter along with James and John (Mark 9:5; Luke 9:33) make three tents, one each for Jesus, Moses, and Elijah.[1] Each account indicates

---

[1] Despite the lack of grammatical indications for an interrogative sense, both Peter's statement and suggestion are to be understood as questions ("Is it good for us to be here?" and "Should I/we build...") according to R.E. OTTO, "The Fear Motivation in Peter's Offer to

in a different way Peter's uncertainty as to the appropriateness of his suggestion. In Mark 9:6 Peter really "did not know what to reply," as all three of the disciples "had become terrified." In Matt 17:4 Peter prefaces his suggestion with a deferential "if you wish," seeking Jesus' approval for the building of the three tents. And in Luke 9:33 Peter is described as "not knowing what he was saying" in offering to build a tent each for the three heavenly figures.

On an initial, surface level the making of three tents corresponds to the joyful enthusiasm of Peter's exclamation of how good it is for the three disciples to be present for this epiphanic appearance of heavenly glory. The three tents seem to function as temporary dwellings intended to honor each individual heavenly figure with the hospitality of a place to prolong the marvelous display of their heavenly glory for as long as they remain on the earthly mountain. But is there more to the meaning of the three individual tents provided for the Gospel audiences by the background of their scriptural traditions?

A. Past Interpretations of the Three Tents

It has been proposed that the three tents of the transfiguration narrative allude to the temporary dwellings constructed for the great Jewish pilgrimage Feast of Huts/Tents/Tabernacles/Booths/*Sukkoth*.[2] According to the biblical tradition the Israelites were to live in these temporary dwellings during the week long celebration of this joyous harvest festival as a commemoration of what God did for them in the Exodus event. They were to dwell "in tents" in order that their descendants may realize that when God led the Israelites out of the land of Egypt, he made them dwell "in tents" (Lev 23:42-43). At the resto-

---

Build Τρεῖς Σκηνάς," *WTJ* 59 (1997) 107. This accords with Otto's questionable interpretation that Peter's statements are motivated by fear, so that the three tents are meant as veils to protect the disciples from the display of divine glory in the transfiguration.

[2] G.H. Boobyer, *St. Mark and the Transfiguration Story* (Edinburgh: Clark, 1942) 76-79; H. Riesenfeld, *Jésus transfiguré: L'arrière-plan du récit évangélique de la transfiguration de Notre-Seigneur* (ASNU 16; Copenhagen: Munksgaard, 1947) 146-205; H. Baltensweiler, *Die Verklärung Jesu: Historisches Ereignis und synoptische Berichte* (ATANT 33; Zürich: Zwingli, 1959) 43-51; Fitzmyer, *Luke I-IX*, 801; Bock, *Luke 1:1-9:50*, 871; Green, *Luke*, 383.

ration of the feast after the Exile and during the time of Ezra, the people, the entire assembly of the returned exiles, made "tents" and dwelled "in tents" during the feast (Neh 8:16-17). The prophetically predicted future worldwide annual pilgrimage of all the nations to the temple in Jerusalem was to occur during this feast of "tents" (Zech 14:16-19).[3]

But there are problems with seeing a reference to the Feast of Tabernacles in the transfiguration narrative. Other than the mention of the "tents" there seem to be no clear textual indicators to the audience for a setting or background in the week long pilgrimage Feast of Tabernacles celebrated in Jerusalem. And as for the "tents," whereas the Israelites made tents for themselves to dwell in during the feast, Peter proposes to make a tent each for the three heavenly figures but not for the disciples.[4]

The Tent of Meeting operative while the Israelites were wandering in the wilderness (Exod 33:7-11; Num 11:16-17, 24-25; Deut 31:14-15) has been suggested as a possible background to the three tents in the transfiguration narrative. This "tent of meeting" (אהל מועד or σκηνὴ μαρτυρίου in Exod 33:7) was designed not only as a dwelling place for God, but preeminently as a place where God would appear in the form of a cloud and speak with Moses. There are two main objections to this proposal: First, although Jesus, Moses, and Elijah appear in the transfiguration narrative as heavenly beings, they are not God, and the Tent of Meeting was meant for God.[5] Second, the Tent of

---

[3] On the history, date, and origin of this greatest of the Jewish pilgrimage feasts, see J.J. CASTELOT and A. CODY, "Religious Institutions of Israel," *NJBC*, 1279-80. According to ULFGARD (*Feast and Future*, 121-22), in later Jewish literature, rabbinic texts, and targums the festal "tents" came to be understood as "clouds of glory": "God covered the people Israel with 'clouds of glory' during its wilderness wandering, and the festal booth is a reminder of this divine protection."

[4] For objections and arguments against a connection between the transfiguration narrative and the Feast of Tabernacles, see W. MICHAELIS, "σκηνή," *TDNT* 7.380; J.A. ZIESLER, "The Transfiguration Story and the Markan Soteriology," *ExpTim* 81 (1970) 263-68; NÜTZEL, *Verklärungserzählung*, 126-33; J. GNILKA, *Das Evangelium nach Markus: (Mk 8,27-16,20)* (EKKNT 2/2; Zürich: Benziger, 1979) 35; MARSHALL, *Luke*, 386; LUZ, *Matthäus*, 2.511; HAGNER, *Matthew 14-28*, 493; HOOKER, "Transfiguration," 65; OTTO, "Peter's Offer," 109; GUNDRY, *Mark*, 479: "...the suggestion to make them (the three tents/tabernacles) can scarcely have anything to do with the Festival of Tabernacles; for apart from the possibility of two persons per tabernacle, such a connection would require six tabernacles rather than three."

[5] MARSHALL, *Luke*, 386; NOLLAND, *Luke 9:21-18:34*, 500-501; HOOKER, "Transfiguration," 65.

Meeting involved only one tent, whereas Peter offers to build three tents.[6]

A third main suggestion for the background of the three tents is the tradition of eternal dwelling places for the righteous in heaven (*1 Enoch* 39:3-8; 71:16; *T. Abr.* A 20:14; Luke 16:9; John 14:2). According to this proposal the three tents that Peter offers to make on the mountain would be earthly counterparts to the heavenly dwellings reserved for Jesus, Moses, and Elijah as righteous heavenly beings.[7] One objection points to Peter's inability to construct on earth appropriate dwelling places for these heavenly figures.[8] Another objection insists that Peter would have wanted to build these dwellings for himself and the other two disciples as well.[9]

There have been various other unsatisfying suggestions for the background of the three tents, e.g., the alleged but unfounded tradition of an eschatological dwelling of the Messiah;[10] the "tent" that the prophet Jonah "made" for himself (Jonah 4:5);[11] God's promise to raise up the fallen "hut" or "tent" of David (Amos 9:11);[12] etc.

B. NEW PROPOSAL FOR THE THREE TENTS

Although serious objections have been raised regarding the three main proposals above for the background of the three tents, each of them nevertheless offers meaningful possibilities for what the Gospel audiences might think Peter intended by his suggestion for the making

---

[6] MICHAELIS, "σκηνή," 379; DAVIES and ALLISON, *Matthew*, 2.700; REID, *Transfiguration*, 134; GUNDRY, *Mark*, 479.

[7] MARSHALL, *Luke*, 386-87; DAVIES and ALLISON, *Matthew*, 2.700; ÖHLER, "Verklärung," 208-9.

[8] GUNDRY, *Mark*, 479; LUZ, *Matthäus*, 2.511: "Dann will Petrus ganz unpassend die Himmlischen nach der Art der Irdischen empfangen. Daß die Himmlischen in Zelten auf Bergen wohnen, ist ein unmöglicher Gedanke!"

[9] GUNDRY, *Mark*, 479; OTTO, "Peter's Offer," 110: "Peter and the disciples would have suggested building six σκηνάς, three for their glorious visitors and three for themselves, which is not in fact what occurred."

[10] Against the existence of this tradition see MICHAELIS, "σκηνή," 380; REID, *Transfiguration*, 135.

[11] J.D.M. DERRETT, "Peter and the Tabernacles (Mark 9,5-7)," *DRev* 108 (1990) 37-48.

[12] MACH, "Christus Mutans," 196; MOSES, *Matthew's Transfiguration Story*, 133.

of the three tents.[13]   Although Peter is uncertain and confused, he evidently thinks there is something appropriate in making a tent for each heavenly figure. What were the most likely possible meanings available for the Gospel audiences, who would be very familiar with the various functions of "tents" or "dwellings" in the biblical tradition, to connect with the three tents in the transfiguration narrative?[14] If we do not insist upon a direct correspondence of all the elements of each main proposal, but concentrate on the respective connections with the function of the tents, we can glean some analogous meanings for the three transfiguration tents, meanings readily available to the Gospel audiences.

We suggest that each of the three main past proposals contributes a distinctive possibility to be heard by the audience in Peter's uncertain and confused offer to make three tents: 1) From their recall of the role of the tents during the annual Feast of Tabernacles the audience may think that Peter intends that the tents, in an analogous, temporary and festive way, celebrate and commemorate God's salvific activity evident in the appearance of the three heavenly figures. 2) From their knowledge that the tent made for the Tent of Meeting serves as a place where a heavenly being appears in glory and communicates with human beings, the audience may think that Peter intends the tents as an analo-

---

[13] In commenting upon the tents in Mark 9:5, NÜTZEL (*Verklärungserzählung*, 133) underlines the importance of what the tents mean not just for Peter but for the reader or audience: "Hier wird nämlich nicht danach gefragt, welches Verständnis die Erzählung dem P e t r u s zuschreibe; vielmehr wird hier die Funktion von V.5f innerhalb der Erzählung in den Blick genommen. Was soll der L e s e r aus diesen Versen erkennen?" In other words, the important question is what function(s) the *audience* thinks Peter intends for the three tents.

[14] The Greek word used for the tents, σκηνή, occurs in the LXX 434 times with a variety of uses. J.-A. BÜHNER, "σκηνή," *EDNT* 3.251: "In the LXX it translates words for several types of shelter that (from a cultural-historical perspective) fall 'beneath' that provided by a house." According to MICHAELIS ("σκηνή," 369): "In Israel, too, the use of tents was common in every age. With the help of the σκηνή passages one might almost follow the whole story of Israel." In the words of HOOKER ("Transfiguration," 64-65): "The term σκηνή is used in the LXX in a variety of ways. Its most common use is as a translation of the Hebrew אהל, meaning 'tent' – usually referring to an ordinary dwelling, but occasionally to the 'tent of meeting'. This latter structure is also termed משכן in Hebrew – literally 'dwelling place' – once again translated by σκηνή in the LXX, and usually referred to in English as the 'tabernacle'. Thirdly, σκηνή is used to translate the Hebrew סכה, which means some kind of matted construction. The plural was regularly used of the structures erected at the Feast of Tabernacles or Booths....the term σκηναί can be assumed to evoke a whole range of ideas."

gous place from which each heavenly figure may address the disciples. 3) From their familiarity with the tradition of eternal heavenly dwellings for the righteous, the audience may conjecture that Peter intends the tents to be temporary, hospitable dwelling places for each of the heavenly beings while they are on earth. The audience could link any one, two, or all three of these possibilities to the three tents.

But it soon becomes evident to the audience that Peter's uncertain offer to make a tent each for Jesus, Moses, and Elijah was inappropriate for two reasons: 1) Although Peter names Jesus in the honorary first position in his offer to make each a tent, he nevertheless places Jesus on the same level as Moses and Elijah, giving each a tent in which to dwell and/or from which to speak. But the heavenly voice from the cloud, which functions as the climactic command of the mandatory epiphany, makes clear to Peter, the disciples, and the audience that Jesus is the one to whom they are to listen (Mark 9:7; Matt 17:5; Luke 9:35). 2) Although the tents Peter offers to make are only temporary dwellings, the appearance of the three heavenly beings is even more temporary – it is but a momentary glimpse. The appearance of the transfigured Jesus is but a fleeting anticipation of the permanent heavenly glory he will attain only after his suffering, death and resurrection, which he has just predicted – the prediction the heavenly voice from the cloud bids the disciples and audience to heed.

C. THE TENTS FROM THE FEAST OF TABERNACLES

Although it would be going too far to say that in offering to make the three tents Peter wants to celebrate the Feast of Tabernacles, there are nevertheless resonances for the audience with some of the key elements of that celebration.[15]   Peter's initial response, "it is good (καλόν) that we are here," voices an enthusiastic joy congruent with the great joy that was one of the hallmarks of that festival.[16]   Accord-

---

[15] A direct relation between the transfiguration and the Feast of Tabernacles has been discussed and denied recently by H. ULFGARD, *The Story of Sukkot: The Setting, Shaping, and Sequel of the Biblical Feast of Tabernacles* (BGBE 34; Tübingen: Mohr Siebeck, 1998) 263-65.

[16] Peter's enthusiastic joy has led some to surmise that he wants to celebrate the actual feast; see FITZMYER, *Luke I-IX*, 801; BOCK, *Luke 1:1-9:50*, 870-71.

ing to Neh 8:17 (=2 Esdr 18:17), when the assembly of returned exiles celebrated the Feast of Tabernacles, there was "very great rejoicing" (MT: שִׂמְחָה גְדוֹלָה מְאֹד; LXX: εὐφροσύνη μεγάλη). And according to Lev 23:40, when the Israelites celebrated the week long Feast of Tabernacles, they were "to rejoice before the Lord your God" (MT: וּשְׂמַחְתֶּם לִפְנֵי יהוה אֱלֹהֵיכֶם; LXX: εὐφρανθῆναι ἔναντι κυρίου τοῦ θεοῦ ὑμῶν).

The reason for the great joy of the feast was to celebrate what God has done for his people. Similarly, Peter presumably wants to celebrate what God has done in this transfiguration epiphany. Peter's joyful response of how good it is that "we," that is, the disciples, are present has a twofold meaning. It is good for the disciples that they are present to experience what God has done in bringing about this marvelous manifestation of heavenly glory. And it is good for the heavenly figures that the disciples are present so that they can make the three tents to celebrate and commemorate what God has done in this spectacular epiphany of heavenly glory.[17]

The key point of connection between the transfiguration epiphany and the Feast of Tabernacles lies in the motif of "making tents" as temporary dwellings to commemorate what God has done for the people. Peter's offer to "make" (ποιήσω/ποιήσωμεν) three "tents" (σκηνάς) reminds the audience that for the celebration of the Feast of Tabernacles after the return from the Exile the Israelites were told to "make tents" (ποιῆσαι σκηνάς) according to what is written in the Law (2 Esdr 18:15). So the people went out and brought in branches and "made" (ἐποίησαν) for themselves "tents" (σκηνάς) (2 Esdr 18:16). Indeed, the whole assembly of those who had returned from the captiv-

---

[17] MARSHALL (*Luke*, 386) excludes the second meaning, stating that "there is no reason why the heavenly beings should want booths if it were not for the benefit of the disciples who wish to prolong the experience." The tents, however, are intended not to fulfill a desire of the heavenly beings, but to celebrate and commemorate what God has done in allowing them to appear. GUNDRY (*Mark*, 479) excludes the first meaning, stating that "'good' does not mean enjoyable or advantageous to the three disciples. That meaning would require the dative of advantage ἡμῖν to produce 'it is good for us to be here'....As it is, the accusative ἡμᾶς produces 'it is good [that] we are here.'" Gundry may be grammatically correct, but the accusative with the infinitive can substitute for the dative (see BDF §409 [3]). Furthermore, the context implies that it is "good" both for the disciples and for the heavenly beings that the disciples are present to make the tents to commemorate what God has done.

ity "made tents" (ἐποίησαν...σκηνὰς) and they dwelled "in tents" (ἐν σκηναῖς) during the festival (2 Esdr 18:17).

But the reason why the people were to dwell in the tents they made was to commemorate what God had done for them in the Exodus event. Through Moses God told the people: "You shall live in tents (ἐν σκηναῖς) for seven days; every native in Israel shall dwell in tents (ἐν σκηναῖς), so that your generations may realize that in tents (ἐν σκηναῖς) I made the sons of Israel dwell when I brought them out of the land of Egypt. I am the Lord your God" (LXX Lev 23:42-43).[18] Similarly, Peter may be offering to build three "tents" (σκηνάς), one each for the three heavenly figures to dwell in, for the purpose of prolonging, celebrating, and commemorating what God has done in allowing them to manifest their heavenly glory on earth. Since the emphasis is upon celebrating and commemorating what God has done in allowing *each* of these heavenly individuals to appear in heavenly glory, Peter offers to make tents only for each of them and not for the disciples.

D. THE TENT FROM THE TENT OF MEETING

The Tent of Meeting provides another possibility for the meaning the audience may associate with each of the tents Peter wants to construct.[19] The Tent of Meeting, a place where God could continually

---

[18] J.W. WEVERS, *Notes on the Greek Text of Leviticus* (SBLSCS 44; Atlanta: Scholars Press, 1997) 386-87: "The feast will then serve to remind the Israelites of the great redemptive act of the Exodus by reliving their manner of dwelling at the time of deliverance from the land of bondage." J.E. HARTLEY, *Leviticus* (WBC 4; Dallas: Word Books, 1992) 389-90: "...these booths came to symbolize the temporary shelters the people lived in during the wilderness journey....These shelters, however, are not to recall the hardship of the wilderness, but the grace of God in providing for his people in so many ways....These booths are a symbol of the people's gratefulness to their caring God during this joyful feast."

[19] On the Tent of Meeting, see M. GÖRG, *Das Zelt der Begegnung: Untersuchung zur Gestalt der sakralen Zelttraditionen Altisraels* (BBB 27; Bonn: Hanstein, 1967); B.S. CHILDS, *The Book of Exodus: A Critical, Theological Commentary* (OTL; Philadelphia: Westminster, 1974) 589-93; R.W.L. MOBERLY, *At the Mountain of God: Story and Theology in Exodus 32-34* (JSOTSup 22; Sheffield: JSOT, 1983) 63-66; J.I. DURHAM, *Exodus* (WBC 3; Waco: Word Books, 1987) 439-43; A.H.J. GUNNEWEG, "Das Gesetz und die Propheten: Eine Auslegung von Ex 33,7-11; Num 11,4-12,8; Dtn 31,14f.; 34,10," *ZAW* 102 (1990) 171-73; J. JOOSTEN, *People and Land in the Holiness Code: An Exegetical Study of the Ideational Framework of the Law in Leviticus 17-26* (VTSup 67; Leiden: Brill, 1996) 141-45.

appear and meet with the people, was a single, unique tent, meant for only one heavenly, divine being, God himself. Each of the heavenly figures in the transfiguration epiphany, however, is analogous to God, inasmuch as each appears in divine heavenly glory. Since each of the three heavenly figures has his own distinct personal identity, the audience may think it appropriate for Peter to want to make three tents, one for the glorious appearance of each heavenly individual.

The key point of contact between the Tent of Meeting and the three tents of the transfiguration epiphany lies in the theme of the communication of the heavenly with the earthly. The purpose of God's appearance from heaven at the Tent of Meeting was to communicate with Moses and his people on earth.[20] Divine or heavenly communication is likewise the major theme of the transfiguration narrative. After Moses and Elijah appear from heaven and engage in conversation with the transfigured Jesus on earth, the voice of God from the cloud, the climactic moment in this mandatory epiphany, directs the disciples to listen to what Jesus has to communicate. Furthermore, the theme of divine communication coincides with the prophetic character of each of the three heavenly figures. Each was known as a "prophet," that is, one who communicates God's word to the people. The audience, then, may think that Peter wants to make for each of the three prophetic, heavenly figures a tent, analogous to the Tent of Meeting, as a place on earth to continue to appear in heavenly glory and address their divine communications to the three disciples.

According to the LXX of Exod 33:7, Moses used to take his tent (σκηνὴν), called "tent of testimony" (σκηνὴ μαρτυρίου), and pitch it outside the camp. And everyone who sought the Lord would go out to this tent (σκηνὴν) outside the camp.[21] The Targumic traditions underline how this tent was considered a place for the people to seek instruction from God:

---

[20] J. MILGROM, *Leviticus 1-16: A New Translation with Introduction and Commentary* (AB 3; New York: Doubleday, 1991) 140: "...the basic purpose of the Tent was to provide a 'meeting' between God and Israel (through the mediation of Moses)." According to K. KOCH ("אהל," *TDOT* 1.124), the Tent of Meeting was "the place where God reveals himself in order that communication with the God of Sinai might continue after the people leave this region."

[21] J.W. WEVERS, *Notes on the Greek Text of Exodus* (SBLSCS 30; Atlanta: Scholars Press, 1990) 544-45. "The clause then shows customary action, and the sense might be given as 'when anyone was seeking (i.e. an oracle from) the Lord he would go out into the tent outside the camp.'"

Tg. Neof. Exod 33:7: And everyone who sought *instruction from before* the Lord went out to the tent of meeting.[22]

Tg. Ps.-J. Exod 33:7: He called it the tent *of the house of instruction.*[23]

Tg. Onq. Exod 33:7: ...called it the *Tent of the Place of Instruction.* Now, anyone *seeking instruction from before the Lord* would go out to the *Tent of the Place of Instruction...*[24]

Analogously, Peter wants to make three tents (σκηνάς), one for each of the heavenly prophetic figures, as places where each could receive and deliver divine instructions.

Whenever Moses entered the tent, God would come down from heaven in the form of a "pillar of cloud" and stand at the entrance of the tent, and God spoke (ἐλάλει) with Moses (LXX Exod 33:9). Indeed, the Lord spoke (ἐλάλησεν) with Moses in a very intimate and personal way, "face to face" (MT: פָּנִים אֶל־פָּנִים; LXX: ἐνώπιος ἐνωπίῳ), just as one would speak (λαλήσει) with his own friend (Exod 33:11; see also Exod 29:42-43; Num 11:16-17, 24-25; Deut 31:14-15).[25]

The Tent of Meeting was a place where God could meet and speak not just with Moses but with the entire people of Israel. God told Moses that "at the entrance of the tent of meeting before the Lord, where I will meet with you, to speak there to you. There I will meet with the people of Israel, and it shall be sanctified by my glory" (Exod 29:42-43).[26] Whenever Moses went out to the tent, *all the people* would rise and stand, each of them, at the entrance of their tents, watching Moses until he entered the tent (Exod 33:8). And when *all the people* saw the pillar of cloud standing at the entrance of the tent,

---

[22] M. MCNAMARA and R. HAYWORD, *Targum Neofiti I: Exodus: Translated, with Introduction and Apparatus and Notes* (Aramaic Bible 2; Collegeville: Liturgical Press, 1994) 134.

[23] M. MAHER, *Targum Pseudo-Jonathan: Exodus: Translated, with Notes* (Aramaic Bible 2; Collegeville: Liturgical Press, 1994) 256.

[24] B. GROSSFELD, *The Targum Onqelos to Exodus: Translated, with Apparatus and Notes* (Aramaic Bible 7; Wilmington: Glazier, 1988) 92.

[25] DURHAM, *Exodus*, 443: "...'face to face' is here to be understood as an idiom of intimacy."

[26] On this "explicit priestly definition of the function of the tent of meeting," see JOOSTEN, *People and Land*, 143.

all the people would stand and worship, each of them, from the entrance of their tents (Exod 33:10). Indeed, as we have already noted, "everyone" who sought instruction from God would go out to the Tent of Meeting (Exod 33:7).

Similar to the Tent of Meeting, where God appeared from heaven and spoke with Moses, in the transfiguration epiphany Moses and Elijah appeared to the disciples from heaven and "were speaking with" (συλλαλοῦντες, Mark 9:4; Matt 17:3; συνελάλουν, Luke 9:30) Jesus, who has been transfigured into a heavenly being while on earth. As the appearance of God at the Tent of Meeting was an occasion for God to converse not only with Moses but potentially with each of the people of Israel, so Peter would seemingly make the appearance of the three heavenly figures an occasion for them not just to converse with themselves but for each of these prophetic individuals to potentially communicate with the disciples as well. The audience, then, by way of analogy with the Tent of Meeting, may think that Peter wants to make a tent for each of the three heavenly, prophetic figures to provide a place where each of them can continue their appearance in heavenly glory and communicate heavenly instruction to the disciples.[27]

E. The Tents and the Heavenly Dwelling Places

Also available to the audiences of the transfiguration accounts was a tradition of dwelling places or "tents" for the righteous in heaven. In Luke 16:9 Jesus tells the disciples to make friends for themselves by means of dishonest wealth so that when it is gone, they may be welcomed into "eternal tents" (αἰωνίους σκηνάς), presumably "tents" located in heaven. In John 14:2 Jesus tells the disciples of the heavenly "dwelling places" he is going to prepare for them: "In my Father's house there are many dwelling places (μοναὶ). If it were not so, would I have told you that I go to prepare a place for you?" In *T. Abr.* A 20:14, at the time of Abraham's death, God tells the angels: "Take,

---

[27] Note that in Luke 9:30-32 the disciples fall asleep so that they do not hear the content of the conversation that Moses and Elijah have with Jesus. They are aware of the fact of the conversation, however, as they awaken to see the glory of Jesus and the two men standing with him (9:32), the two men who were speaking with him (9:30).

then, my friend Abraham into Paradise, where there are the tents (σκηναὶ) of my righteous ones and (where) the mansions (μοναὶ) of my holy ones, Isaac and Jacob, are in his bosom..."[28]. The *Testament of Abraham* thus refers to both the "tents" (cf. Luke 16:9) and the "mansions" or "dwelling places" (cf. John 14:2) of the righteous in heaven.

In *1 Enoch* 39:3-5, 8 Enoch recounts his vision of the heavenly "dwelling places" and "resting places" for the righteous that he desires for himself: "In those days, whirlwinds carried me off from the earth, and set me down into the ultimate ends of the heavens. There I saw other dwelling places of the holy ones and their resting places too. So there my eyes saw their dwelling places with the holy angels, and their resting places with the holy ones...There (underneath his wings) I wanted to dwell; and my soul desired that dwelling place."[29] And in *1 Enoch* 71:16 an angel promises Enoch that those who follow his path of righteousness will likewise share in his heavenly dwelling place: "Everyone that will come to exist and walk shall (follow) your path, since righteousness never forsakes you. Together with you shall be their dwelling places; and together with you shall be their portion."[30]

From their familiarity with traditions of "tents" and "dwelling places" for the righteous in heaven the audience may think that Peter wants to make for each of the three heavenly figures a "tent" to serve as a temporary, earthly counterpart to their eternal, heavenly "tents" or "dwelling places." Since they presumably dwell in "tents" in heaven, Peter would be offering them the hospitality of a similar dwelling place for their sojourn on earth. Peter, then, wants to make not *heavenly* "tents" on earth, but *earthly* "tents" for the heavenly figures to dwell in while on earth.[31] Since the "tents" are intended as the temporary dwelling places only for the heavenly figures while they are on earth, there is no need for Peter to make tents for the disciples as well.[32]

---

[28] Greek text from M.E. STONE, trans., *The Testament of Abraham: The Greek Recensions* (SBLTT 2; Missoula: Society of Biblical Literature, 1972) 56. Translation by E.P. SANDERS, "Testament of Abraham," *OTP* 1.895. On the date Sanders (p. 875) states: "It seems best to assume a date for the original of c. A.D. 100, plus or minus twenty-five years."

[29] Translation by ISAAC, "1 Enoch," 30-31.

[30] IBID., 50.

[31] Since Peter does not want to make "paradisic tabernacles" on earth, there is no need for him to be "adept in heavenly architecture," as GUNDRY (*Mark*, 479) would require.

[32] *Contra* GUNDRY, Mark, 479; OTTO, "Peter's Offer," 110.

F. Conclusion

Since Peter himself appears rather uncertain as to the appropriateness of making a tent for each of the three heavenly visitors, the audiences of the transfiguration narratives cannot be sure what exactly Peter has in mind for the tents. After all, "tents" and "dwelling places" play various and yet very important roles in the biblical traditions. From their knowledge and familiarity with these various "tent" traditions the audience may think that Peter wants to make three tents as temporary dwelling places (1) to honor each individual heavenly figure and commemorate what God has done in bringing about this marvelous manifestation of each of the three heavenly figures, analogous to the commemorative role of the tents at the Feast of Tabernacles; (2) to provide fitting locations for each of the heavenly, prophetic figures to continue his glorious appearance and communicate divine instructions to the disciples on earth, analogous to the role of the tent as a place for divine communication in the Tent of Meeting; (3) to furnish on earth appropriate hospitable habitations for their sojourn similar to the habitations that Abraham, the patriarchs, and all the righteous enjoy in heaven.

But the audience soon realizes that whatever Peter meant by the making of three tents, his offer was inappropriate for two main reasons. 1) Although Peter mentions Jesus in the most important first position in his offer to make three tents, he nevertheless places Jesus on the same level and in the same category as Moses and Elijah. That this is wrong becomes evident as God's voice from the overshadowing cloud directs the disciples and the audience to listen only to Jesus, God's own Son. 2) Although tents are temporary dwellings, the epiphanic manifestation of the three heavenly figures turns out to be an extremely ephemeral event, negating any need for even the temporary dwelling of a tent. The appearance of the transfigured Jesus is but a momentary anticipation of the permanent heavenly glory he will attain only after the suffering, death and resurrection that he has predicted for himself. It is this prophetic prediction by God's own beloved/chosen Son that the heavenly voice from the cloud commands the disciples and audience to heed. And so we now turn to the significance and background of the divine voice from the overshadowing cloud, as a second epiphanic action which interrupts Peter's offer to make three tents.

CHAPTER 7

THE EPIPHANIC APPEARANCE
OF THE OVERSHADOWING CLOUD

A further epiphanic action interrupts Peter's offer to make three tents in each account of the transfiguration narrative. An overshadowing cloud suddenly and unexpectedly appears. From this epiphanic cloud the commanding voice of God speaks to the disciples about Jesus:

> Mark 9:7: Then there came a cloud overshadowing them, then there came a voice from the cloud, "This is my beloved Son; listen to him!"
>
> Matt 17:5-7: While he was speaking, behold a bright cloud overshadowed them, and behold a voice from the cloud saying, "This is my beloved Son, with whom I am well pleased; listen to him!" Hearing this the disciples fell upon their face and were greatly frightened. But Jesus came forward, and touching them, said, "Arise and do not be afraid."
>
> Luke 9:34-35: While he was saying these things, a cloud came and was overshadowing them. They were frightened as they entered into the cloud. Then a voice came from the cloud saying, "This is my chosen Son; to him listen!"

A. PAST INTERPRETATIONS OF THE OVERSHADOWING CLOUD

There is no scholarly consensus as to whom precisely the cloud overshadows. Several possibilities have been proposed: The cloud overshadows (1) all six characters in the scene – Jesus, Moses, Elijah, and the three disciples;[1] (2) only the three heavenly figures – Jesus, Moses, and Elijah;[2] (3) only the three disciples;[3] (4) only Moses and Elijah.[4]

Many have rightly pointed to the cloud as symbolic of God's presence or glory based on its OT background, especially in the Sinai and Exodus traditions, but are often not very specific and do not agree as to how this divine presence functions or how it relates to the various characters. The cloud obviously serves as the medium out of which the "voice" of God speaks. But the appearance of a cloud is not a necessary prerequisite for the utterance of God's voice. After the baptism of Jesus in each Synoptic Gospel the "voice" of God comes simply and directly "from heaven" (Mark 1:11; Matt 3:17; Luke 3:22).[5] So what is the point of the "voice" coming "from the *cloud*" here? In addition, some have pointed to the cloud as also the means of transporting Moses and Elijah back to heaven at least in Luke's version.[6]

---

[1] GUNDRY, *Mark*, 460-61; NOLLAND, *Luke 9:21-18:34*, 501; BOCK, *Luke 1:1-9:50*, 872-73; NÜTZEL, *Verklärungserzählung*, 143, 246.

[2] ÖHLER, "Verklärung," 210-11; LUZ, *Matthäus*, 2.510-12; GNILKA, *Markus*, 2.35; DAVIES and ALLISON, *Matthew*, 2.701; MARSHALL, *Luke*, 387; A. OEPKE, "νεφέλη," *TDNT* 4.908; M.D. HOOKER, *The Gospel According to Saint Mark* (Peabody, MA: Hendrickson, 1991) 217-18.

[3] HAGNER, *Matthew 14-28*, 494; GREEN, *Luke*, 383-84; REID, *Transfiguration*, 137. For FITZMYER (*Luke I-IX*, 802) it is unclear whether the cloud overshadows only the three heavenly figures or also the three disciples.

[4] This has been suggested for Luke's account by LOHFINK, *Himmelfahrt Jesu*, 190; J. LUZARRAGA, *Las tradiciones de la nube en la Biblia y en el Judaismo primitivo* (AnBib 54; Rome: Biblical Institute, 1973) 219; L. SABOURIN, "The Biblical Cloud: Terminology and Traditions," *BTB* 4 (1974) 307.

[5] This is pointed out for Mark by NÜTZEL, *Verklärungserzählung*, 143. For an extensive study of the variety of ways that God's revelational "voice" is heard in ancient Judaism see P. KUHN, *Offenbarungsstimmen im Antiken Judentum: Untersuchungen zur Bat Qol und verwandten Phänomenen* (TSAJ 20; Tübingen: Mohr Siebeck, 1989).

[6] LOHFINK, *Himmelfahrt Jesu*, 191; A.W. ZWIEP, *The Ascension of the Messiah in Lukan Christology* (NovTSup 87; Leiden: Brill, 1997) 105: "...the cloud at the transfiguration prevented the by-standers from seeing what happened and at the same time provided Moses and Elijah with access to the heavenly realm."

B. New Proposal for the Overshadowing Cloud

Although it is at first grammatically ambiguous to the audience as to whom the cloud overshadows, we propose that a close reading of the immediate context and a careful consideration for the dynamics of how the cloud functions within the epiphany lead the audience eventually to realize that the cloud has overshadowed *only Moses and Elijah* in each version of the transfiguration narrative. Furthermore, we propose that the audience of each version recognizes a double function of the epiphanic cloud:

1) Based on the background provided primarily by the cloud that overshadowed the Tent of Meeting, the overshadowing cloud of the transfiguration epiphany functions as an *oracular cloud*. As such, it not only interrupts, in an ironic fashion for the audience, Peter's suggestion to make three tents. It also climactically concludes, by providing the oracular mandate of this pivotal mandatory epiphany, the theme of divine or heavenly communication initiated by the conversation that the transfigured Jesus has with Moses and Elijah.

2) Based on the background provided by a variety of apocalyptic-eschatological traditions, the overshadowing cloud of the transfiguration epiphany also and at the same time functions as a *vehicular cloud*. As such, it not only brings the epiphanic appearance of Moses and Elijah as heavenly figures to an end by beginning to transport them back to heaven. It also, in separating them from Jesus, climactically concludes the epiphanic transfiguration of Jesus into a heavenly figure by leaving him with the disciples on earth, restored to his pre-transfigured state.[7]

---

[7] Lohfink (*Himmelfahrt Jesu*, 191) recognizes this double function of the cloud in Luke when he states that the cloud "ist erstens *Wolke der Epiphanie*, in der sich die Herrlichkeit Gottes verbirgt. Das zeigt die Stimme, die aus der Wolke kommt (9,35); das zeigt die numinose Furcht der Apostel, als Moses und Elias in die Wolke hineingehen (9,34); das zeigt schließlich der alttestamentliche Hintergrund, wo sich mit der Wolke die δόξα τοῦ θεοῦ auf den Berg niederläßt (Ex 24,16). Sie ist zweitens *Wolke der Himmelfahrt*. Denn sie erscheint, als Moses und Elias im Begriff sind, wieder in den Himmel zurückzukehren (9,33f.). Die beiden Propheten gehen in die Wolke hinein (9,34), und als diese entschwunden ist, sind sie nicht mehr zu

C. THE ORACULAR FUNCTION OF THE OVERSHADOWING CLOUD

1. *Exod 16:10-11: The glory of the Lord appeared in a cloud and the Lord spoke*

During Israel's wandering in the wilderness, Moses directed Aaron to tell the whole Israelite community to present themselves before the Lord, who has heard their grumbling about lack of food (Exod 16:9).[8] After Aaron announced this, the whole Israelite community turned toward the wilderness, "and behold the glory of the Lord appeared in a cloud! The Lord spoke to Moses and said..." (Exod 16:10-11). The Lord goes on to tell Moses from the cloud that the Israelites will have food (Exod 16:12).

Here we have an epiphanic oracular cloud very much like the one in the transfiguration narrative. The introduction of the epiphanic appearance of the cloud with "and behold" (וְהִנֵּה) in Exod 16:10 reminds the audience of the introduction of the epiphanic appearance of the cloud in Matt 17:5: "behold (ἰδού) a bright cloud overshadowed them."[9] "And behold" (καὶ ἰδού) likewise introduced the prior epiphanic appearance of Moses and Elijah in the transfiguration narratives in Matt 17:3 and Luke 9:30. In addition, that the glory (δόξα) of the Lord appeared (ὤφθη) in a cloud (Exod 16:10) resembles the epiphanic appearance (ὤφθη) of Moses and Elijah (Matt 17:3; Mark 9:4), "who appeared in glory" (οἳ ὀφθέντες ἐν δόξῃ) (Luke 9:31).

The oracle that the Lord spoke to Moses from the appearance of his glory "in a cloud" (ἐν νεφέλῃ) (Exod 16:10-11) parallels the way the

---

sehen (9,36). Sie sind also in der Wolke entrückt worden." We go beyond Lohfink in applying this double function of the cloud also to Mark and Matthew. In addition, we shall supply a detailed presentation of the relevant background, as well as a more precise determination of how both functions of the cloud operate as part of the transfiguration epiphany.

[8] According to CHILDS (*Exodus*, 287), the term "to present yourselves before the Lord" or "to approach before the Lord" (קְרֹב לִפְנֵי יהוה) "is a technical one and refers to an encounter at a sanctuary (27.21; Num. 16.17, etc.) Here the tent of meeting is undoubtedly meant (Num. 14.10; 16.19)."

[9] As noted by WEVERS (*Exodus*, 248), the LXX of Exod 16:10 lacks the word "behold."

voice of God comes "from the cloud" (ἐκ τῆς νεφέλης) in the transfiguration narratives (Matt 17:5; Mark 9:7; Luke 9:35). In both Exod 16:10-11 and the transfiguration narratives the epiphanic appearance of a cloud indicates God's revelatory presence.[10] In Exod 16:10-11 the oracle from the cloud of God's glorious presence functions as the decisive divine utterance that responds to the Israelites' grumbling uncertainty about procuring food for themselves in the wilderness. Similarly, the oracle from the cloud in the transfiguration narratives functions as the decisive divine intervention that responds to Peter's uncertainty regarding the building of three tents.[11]

2. *Exod 19:9: God will come in a cloud so that the people may hear him*

In the transfiguration narratives the voice of God from the epiphanic oracular cloud directs the disciples and the audiences to hear Jesus, God's beloved/chosen Son (Matt 17:5; Mark 9:7; Luke 9:35). This reminds the audiences of Exod 19:9, where God foretells the Sinai event in which he will come in a cloud so that the people may hear him as well as Moses (cf. Exod 19:16-19): "Behold I am about to come to you in a pillar of cloud, so that when the people hear me speaking with you, they may always believe in you also." That God will come in a pillar of cloud (ἐν στύλῳ νεφέλης) for the people of Israel to hear (ἀκούσῃ) him speaking with Moses implies that in the future they will also hear and believe in Moses as an authentic and authoritative revealer of God's word.[12] Similarly, the oracle that the disciples and the

---

[10] CHILDS (*Exodus*, 288) expresses the epiphanic nature of the cloud in Exod 16:10, when he states: "The real point of the verse is the sudden divine manifestation." And according to WEVERS (*Exodus*, 248): "The appearance of the Lord's glory refers to his actual presence in a revelatory sense."

[11] On the function of the oracle from the cloud in Exod 16:10-11 CHILDS (*Exodus*, 288) states: "In all the wilderness stories the people complain, men dispute, but finally God himself appears and brings the matter to a halt with a decisive judgment." Similarly, in the transfiguration narratives God himself appears in the form of an epiphanic cloud and brings the matter of making three tents as well as the epiphanic appearances of Jesus, Moses, and Elijah to a halt with a decisive oracle, the decisive mandate of this pivotal mandatory epiphany — listen to Jesus as God's Son!

[12] For another example of God speaking "in a pillar of cloud" (ἐν στύλῳ νεφέλης), see LXX Ps 98:7.

audiences hear God speaking from the cloud (ἐκ τῆς νεφέλης) directs them to hear (ἀκούετε) God's own Son as *the* authentic and authoritative revealer of God's word.[13]

3. *Exod 24:15-18: The Lord called Moses from the midst of the cloud on the mountain*

In the transfiguration narratives the voice of God comes from the epiphanic oracular cloud that appears after Jesus led the three disciples up to a high mountain (εἰς ὄρος ὑψηλὸν, Matt 17:1; Mark 9:2) or after Jesus with the three disciples went up to the mountain (ἀνέβη εἰς τὸ ὄρος, Luke 9:28). This recalls for the audiences Exod 24:15-18, where Moses and Joshua went up (ἀνέβη) to the mountain (εἰς τὸ ὄρος) (v. 15), before "the glory of God came down on Mount Sinai, and the cloud covered it for six days, and the Lord called Moses on the seventh day from the midst of the cloud" (v. 16). Just as God called to Moses from the midst of the cloud (ἐκ μέσου τῆς νεφέλης), so the voice of God calls to the disciples from the cloud (ἐκ τῆς νεφέλης) in the transfiguration narratives (Matt 17:5; Mark 9:7; Luke 9:35).

Only in Matt 17:5 does the epiphanic cloud appear as "bright" or "luminous" (φωτεινή). This reminds the audience of Exod 24:17, where the form of the glory of the Lord, which came down on the mountain in the cloud (cf. v. 16), appeared very bright or luminous, like a "flaming fire" (πῦρ φλέγον) on the top of the mountain.[14]

Since Moses is on the mountain that is covered by the cloud when God called him "from the midst of the cloud," some scholars appeal to Exod 24:15-18 for evidence that, like Moses, the disciples are overshadowed by the cloud when they hear the voice of God coming "from

---

[13] According to WEVERS (*Exodus*, 297) the "pillar of cloud" makes the divine presence concrete and fulfills "two necessary conditions: it hides God's presence so that no one can see him, and it permits the people to hear him when he speaks to Moses." Similarly, the cloud in the transfiguration narratives on the one hand hides God's presence so that the disciples do not see him, but on the other hand permits the disciples and the audiences to hear the voice of God.

[14] WEVERS, *Exodus*, 389: "If the divine glory was in the cloud or appeared in cloudy form (see v.16) it was luminous indeed, since it is likened to a πῦρ φλέγον on the crest of the mountain, i.e. 'a flaming fire.'"

the cloud."[15]   But a close reading of the passage indicates otherwise. Although Moses and Joshua went up to the mountain and the cloud covered the mountain (Exod 24:15), Moses has not yet entered into the cloud at this point, because, as becomes clear, the cloud has not covered the entire mountain.   "Moses entered into the midst of the cloud and went (further) up to the mountain" (Exod 24:18) only *after* the Lord called him from the midst of the cloud (Exod 24:16), which represents "the form of the glory of the Lord" that was "like a flaming fire" not upon the entire mountain but only "upon the summit (MT בְרֹאשׁ; LXX: ἐπὶ τῆς κορυφῆς) of the mountain" (Exod 24:17). Hence, Moses was outside the cloud when God called him from the midst of the cloud and then he entered into the midst of the cloud as he went further up to the very top of the mountain (cf. Exod 19:20).[16]

Similarly, the disciples are outside the overshadowing cloud when they hear the voice of God coming "from the cloud" (Matt 17:5; Mark 9:7; Luke 9:35). Furthermore, since the disciples are outside the overshadowing cloud, that the voice from out of the cloud directs them to listen to Jesus by employing the demonstrative, "this is" (οὗτός ἐστιν) my beloved/chosen Son, strongly suggests that Jesus is also outside the overshadowing cloud.[17]   In addition, at the conclusion of each transfiguration narrative (Mark 9:8; Matt 17:8; Luke 9:36) there is no explicit notice that the overshadowing cloud has as yet disappeared from the scene. That the disciples see *only* Jesus, while the overshadowing cloud may still be there concealing Moses and Elijah, further suggests that both the disciples and Jesus have remained outside of the cloud.

In Luke 9:34 the disciples were frightened as "they," that is, Moses and Elijah, "entered into the cloud." There is somewhat of a precedent

---

[15] For examples of those who hold this view, see GUNDRY, *Mark*, 460-61; REID, *Transfiguration*, 137. For examples of those who hold that the voice coming "from the cloud" indicates that the disciples are outside the cloud, see DAVIES and ALLISON, *Matthew*, 2.701; MARSHALL, *Luke*, 387; OEPKE, "νεφέλη," 4.908; HOOKER, *Mark*, 217-18.

[16] On the meaning of κορυφή as "summit," "top," "crown," "extremity," "tip," or "head," see J. LUST, E. EYNIKEL and K. HAUSPIE, *A Greek-English Lexicon of the Septuagint* (Stuttgart: Deutsche Bibelgesellschaft, 1992, 1996) 2.264.

[17] LOHFINK, *Himmelfahrt Jesu*, 190: "Das demonstrative οὗτός ἐστιν legt nahe, daß auch Jesus außerhalb der Wolke bleibt." For an additional reason why Jesus remains outside the cloud, see below on the vehicular function of the cloud.

for this for the audience who remembers how likewise only "Moses entered into the midst of the cloud":

LXX Exod 24:18: καὶ εἰσῆλθεν Μωυσῆς εἰς τὸ μέσον τῆς νεφέλης

Luke 9:34: ἐν τῷ εἰσελθεῖν αὐτοὺς εἰς τὴν νεφέλην

Joshua, who went up the mountain with Moses (Exod 24:13, 15), as well as "the children of Israel," before whom the form of the glory of the Lord in the cloud appeared as a flaming fire on the top of the mountain (Exod 24:17), remained outside the cloud. Likewise, Jesus and the disciples remained outside the overshadowing cloud that Moses and Elijah entered.

4. *Exod 33:9: The cloud came down to the Tent of Meeting and spoke with Moses*

The voice of God which speaks to the disciples from the epiphanic cloud (ἐκ τῆς νεφέλης) in the transfiguration narratives recalls for the audiences how, when Moses entered into the Tent (σκηνήν) of Meeting, the pillar of cloud (τῆς νεφέλης) would come down and stand at the entrance of the tent (σκηνῆς), and speak to Moses (Exod 33:9).[18] This creates irony for the audiences who hear in Peter's offer to make three tents (σκηνὰς) for Jesus, Moses, and Elijah (Matt 17:4; Mark 9:5; Luke 9:33) the possibility of an analogy to the Tent of Meeting.[19] Whereas Peter would make a tent like the Tent of Meeting for each of the three heavenly figures, so that each can continue to receive and deliver divine communications to the disciples, God himself interrupts Peter's offer by coming down in the form of an epiphanic cloud and speaking directly to the disciples, just as he used to come down to the Tent of Meeting in a cloud and speak directly to Moses (Exod 33:11).

5. *Exod 40:35: The cloud was overshadowing the Tent of Meeting*

In each transfiguration narrative the epiphanic oracular cloud (νεφέλη), although the verbal form is different in each case, was an

---

[18] On Exod 33:9 WEVERS (*Exodus*, 545) states: "The pillar of cloud is then the manifestation of deity and its speaking was the voice of God."

[19] On this possibility, see chap. 6.

"overshadowing" (ἐπισκιάζουσα in Mark 9:7; ἐπεσκίασεν in Matt 17:5; ἐπεσκίαζεν in Luke 9:34) cloud. This reminds the audiences of how "Moses could not enter into the Tent of Meeting, because the cloud (νεφέλη) was overshadowing (ἐπεσκίαζεν) it as the Tent was filled with the glory of the Lord" (Exod 40:35).[20] The close intertextual and linguistic connections between "overshadow" (ἐπισκιάζω) and "tent" (σκηνή) reinforce for the audiences the irony of the epiphanic appearance of the overshadowing cloud in response to Peter's offer to make a tent for each of the three heavenly figures in the transfiguration narratives.

The Greek verbal forms for "overshadow" in the transfiguration narratives, ἐπισκιάζουσα-ἐπεσκίασεν-ἐπεσκίαζεν, are linked to the Greek noun for "tents," σκηνάς, in Peter's offer to make three tents by way of alliteration, as both words share the sk-as/z sound sequence. In addition, both words are linked in a conceptual and connotative way by their association with the Tent of Meeting. In the LXX of Exod 40:35 both the Greek verb ἐπεσκίαζεν and the noun ἡ σκηνή have their respective counterparts in the MT in the Hebrew verb and noun for "dwelling," ‏שׁכן/משׁכן‎:

MT Exod 40:35: ‏עליו הענן וכבוד יהוה מלא את־ה משׁכן כי־שׁכן‎

LXX Exod 40:35: ὅτι ἐπεσκίαζεν ἐπ’ αὐτὴν ἡ νεφέλη καὶ δόξης κυρίου ἐπλήσθη ἡ σκηνή

While the noun ‏ה משׁכן‎, "the tent" or "the dwelling place," has its parallel in ἡ σκηνή, "the tent" or "the dwelling place,"[21] the verb ‏שׁכן‎, "to dwell," "to make a dwelling place" or "to make a tent," has its parallel in ἐπεσκίαζεν, "to overshadow" or "to cover."[22]

---

[20] On the "glory of the Lord" (δόξης κυρίου), which is synonymous with "the cloud" here, WEVERS (*Exodus*, 651) notes that it "should be taken as a subjective genitive phrase in the sense of the splendor which the deity shows as a revelatory presence."

[21] MICHAELIS, "σκηνή," 371-72: "If the rendering of ‏משׁכן‎ by σκηνή impressed itself on the translators as the natural one, this was not because σκηνή had of itself the sense of 'dwelling.'...Rather, it seemed to the translators that σκηνή was the predestined word for ‏משׁכן‎ because the two terms contain the same three consonants skn in the same sequence....the principle of transl. by similarity of sound, which may be noted elsewhere in the LXX, was normative in the case of ‏משׁכן‎ and σκηνή too."

[22] On the meaning of ‏משׁכן/שׁכן‎, see BDB, 1014-15; D. KELLERMANN, "‏משׁכן‎," *TWAT* 5.62-69; M. GÖRG, "‏שׁכן‎," *TWAT* 7.1137-47. On the meaning of ἐπισκιάζω, see BAGD, 298;

In the MT of Exod 40:35 Moses could not enter into the Tent of Meeting, because the cloud that contained the glory of the Lord was dwelling over it in the sense of making a dwelling place or, to express the word play, "making a tent" (שָׁכַן) over the Tent (הַמִּשְׁכָּן). For the LXX the cloud was overshadowing in the sense of completely covering or enveloping (ἐπεσκίαζεν) the Tent (ἡ σκηνή).[23] As a counterpart to שָׁכַן in the MT, then, ἐπεσκίαζεν in the LXX of Exod 40:35 carries a connotation of "dwell over" or "make a tent over."[24]

Based on their recall of Exod 40:35, the audiences of the transfiguration narratives experience an added irony in the overshadowing cloud. Whereas Peter would make three tents for the three heavenly figures to serve as dwelling places or coverings, the epiphanic cloud of God's revelatory presence made its "dwelling place" or "tent" over Moses and Elijah by overshadowing or completely covering them. Whereas Peter wanted to make a tent for each of the heavenly figures, thus placing Jesus on the same level as Moses and Elijah, the over-shadowing cloud corrects this error of Peter's by overshadowing or "making a tent" over Moses and Elijah only, separating them from Jesus as God's beloved/chosen Son, whom the voice from the cloud bids the disciples to heed.

NIEMAND, *Verklärungsperikopen*, 239-40; G. SCHNEIDER, "ἐπισκιάζω," *EDNT* 2.34-35. Whether ἐπισκιάζω means overshadow in the sense of completely cover or envelop, or in the sense of cast a shadow over or hover over, depends on the context. The context, OT background, and functions of the cloud in the transfiguration narratives call for the sense of com-pletely cover or envelop. In Acts 5:15 ἐπισκιάζω has the sense of cast a shadow over in ref-erence to the healing effect of Peter's shadow. And in Luke 1:35, the only other use in the NT of ἐπισκιάζω outside the transfiguration narratives, it is used figuratively in reference to the divine power of the Holy Spirit coming upon Mary.

[23] Although the LXX does not preserve the same conceptual word play as the Hebrew, there is an alliterative word play between ἐπεσκίαζεν and σκηνή provided by the s-k-n sequence.

[24] In the MT of Exod 24:16 the glory of the Lord in the form of the cloud "dwelled" or "made a dwelling" (וַיִּשְׁכֹּן) over Mount Sinai. Whereas this is the only place where the LXX uses κατέβη, "came down," for this Hebrew verb, the Aquila version at this point uses ἐσκήνωσεν, "settled down, tented," as noted by WEVERS, *Exodus*, 388. For a discussion of the Hebrew and Targumic Aramaic counterparts of ἐπισκιάζω, see D. DAUBE, *The New Testa-ment and Rabbinic Judaism* (New York: Arno, 1973) 32.

6. *Num 9:18-23: The voice of the Lord comes from the cloud overshadowing the Tent*

The voice (φωνή) of God comes out of the overshadowing cloud and directs the disciples to listen to Jesus as God's Son in each transfiguration narrative.[25] This reminds the audience of Num 9:18-23, where the voice of the Lord is very closely associated, if not actually synonymous, with the cloud that overshadows the Tent of Meeting and directs the Israelites when to continue their journey and when to remain in camp.[26]

As long as the cloud overshadowed the Tent, the Israelites remained in camp and did not set out (Num 9:18, 22).[27] For "overshadow" the LXX here employs the simple verb form σκιάζω, which is synonymous with the compound form ἐπισκιάζω employed by the transfiguration accounts.[28] Since the LXX utilizes the preposition ἐπί with σκιάζω, it offers an almost identical parallel with the overshadowing of the cloud in the transfiguration narratives:

Num 9:18: σκιάζει ἡ νεφέλη ἐπὶ τῆς σκηνῆς
Num 9:22: νεφέλης σκιαζούσης ἐπ᾽ αὐτῆς
Mark 9:7: νεφέλη ἐπισκιάζουσα αὐτοῖς
Matt 17:5: νεφέλη φωτεινὴ ἐπεσκίασεν αὐτούς
Luke 9:34: νεφέλη καὶ ἐπεσκίαζεν αὐτούς

That the LXX of Num 9:18, 22 uses σκιάζω and the LXX of Exod 40:35 uses ἐπισκιάζω for the same verb, שׁכן, in the MT confirms their synonymy here.

---

[25] W. RADL "φωνή," *EDNT* 3.447: "Φωνή has great theological significance first because its bearers are primarily God, Christ, spiritually gifted persons, and spiritual beings. Except in Acts 7:31 God is not named directly; rather, the φωνή sounds 'from heaven' (ἐκ τοῦ οὐρανοῦ and similar phrases: Mark 1:11 par.; John 12:28; Acts 11:9; Rev 10:4, 8; 11:12; 14:2a, 13, 14; 18:4), 'out of the cloud' (Mark 9:7 par.), or 'from the temple' (Rev 16:1, 17)."

[26] On Num 9:18-23, see ASHLEY, *Numbers*, 184-86; J. DE VAULX, *Les Nombres* (SB; Paris: Gabalda, 1972) 127-29; P.J. BUDD, *Numbers* (WBC 5; Waco: Word Books, 1984) 101-4; B.A. LEVINE, *Numbers 1-20: A New Translation with Introduction and Commentary* (AB 4A; New York: Doubleday, 1993) 298-300.

[27] J.W. WEVERS, *Notes on the Greek Text of Numbers* (SBLSCS 46; Atlanta: Scholars Press, 1998) 142: "The cloud denotes the presence of deity, a deity who reveals himself."

[28] LUST, EYNIKEL, and HAUSPIE, *Septuagint*, 174, 428-29; S. Schulz, "σκιά," TDNT 7.394-400.

A comparison of the LXX of Num 9:18 with 9:20 indicates how closely associated, if not virtually identical, the overshadowing cloud is with "the voice of the Lord." In 9:18, "all the days on which the cloud overshadowed the Tent, the Israelites remained in camp." And in 9:20, "whenever the cloud covered the Tent for a few days, through the voice of the Lord (διὰ φωνῆς κυρίου) they remained in camp..." Similarly, whenever the cloud lifted, through the command of the Lord (διὰ προστάγματος κυρίου) they departed (9:23).[29]

Numbers 9:20 exhibits the only instance within 9:18-23 where διὰ φωνῆς κυρίου, "through the voice of the Lord," appears for the MT עַל־פִּי יְהֹוָה, "through the mouth of Yahweh." In all other instances (9:18 [twice], 20, 23 [twice]) the LXX employs διὰ προστάγματος κυρίου, "through the command of the Lord."[30] The parallelism with πρόσταγμα, "command," in 9:20, as well as the context, give φωνή, "voice," the connotation of "command" here. That the "voice" represents the command of God from the cloud enhances its value as background for the transfiguration narratives, in which the "voice" from the cloud issues the command of God that serves as the climactic mandate of the pivotal mandatory epiphany. Whereas the overshadowing cloud in Num 9:18-23 merely represents or indicates the "voice" of God that commands the Israelites to remain in camp, in the transfiguration narratives the "voice" of God actually comes from the overshadowing cloud and commands the disciples to listen to Jesus as God's Son.[31]

7. *LXX Num 10:36: The cloud was overshadowing the Israelites themselves*

In the transfiguration narratives the cloud was overshadowing not a tent but persons, "them" (αὐτούς in Matt 17:5; Luke 9:34; αὐτοῖς in

---

[29] DE VAULX, *Nombres*, 129: "la Nuée est comme la 'bouche de Yahweh' (v. 18, 23), qui lui permet de manifester sa volonté, que Moïse doit interpréter et faire exécuter (v. 23)."

[30] On the change WEVERS (*Numbers*, 143) states: "No lexical difference was intended; the change simply avoided the monotony of constant repetition." Note that the LXX renders only two of the three occurrences of עַל־פִּי יְהֹוָה in MT Num 9:23.

[31] For further examples of the oracular cloud out of which God speaks at the Tent of Meeting, see Num 11:25; 12:5-6; 17:7-10; Deut 31:15-16. In the LXX of Num 7:89, when Moses entered into the Tent of Meeting to speak with God, he heard "the voice of the Lord" (τὴν φωνὴν κυρίου) speaking to him, but not from the cloud, rather, from the mercy seat or cover that was on the ark of the covenant.

Mark 9:7). This reminds the audiences of the LXX of Num 10:36, where "the cloud came overshadowing them (αὐτοῖς) by day when they set out from the camp."[32] Indeed, the cloud that overshadows the Israelites in the LXX of Num 10:36 bears a striking resemblance to Mark 9:7:

LXX Num 10:36: καὶ ἡ νεφέλη ἐγένετο σκιάζουσα ἐπ' αὐτοῖς
Mark 9:7: καὶ ἐγένετο νεφέλη ἐπισκιάζουσα αὐτοῖς

8. *Num 17:7-10: Moses and Aaron fell upon their face at the voice of God from the cloud*

In the Matthean version of the transfiguration narrative the disciples "fell upon their face" and became frightened when they heard the voice of God speaking to them from the overshadowing cloud (Matt 17:5-6). This reminds the audience of how Moses and Aaron similarly fell upon their face when they heard the voice of God speaking to them from the cloud at the Tent of Meeting in Num 17:7-10: When the congregation had assembled against Moses and Aaron, they turned toward the Tent of Meeting. The cloud (ἡ νεφέλη, v. 7) covered it and the glory of the Lord appeared. Then Moses and Aaron went to the front of the Tent of Meeting and the Lord spoke to them, saying, "Depart from the midst of this congregation, that I may consume them at once." Then Moses and Aaron "fell upon their face" (see also Num 16:4, 22), a gesture of submission offering a remarkable linguistic resemblance to Matt 17:6:[33]

LXX Num 17:10: ἔπεσον ἐπὶ πρόσωπον αὐτῶν
Matt 17:6: ἔπεσαν ἐπὶ πρόσωπον αὐτῶν

---

[32] The LXX of Num 10:36 corresponds to the MT of Num 10:34, which lacks a reference to the overshadowing of the cloud and reads simply: "The cloud of Yahweh was over them by day when they set out from the camp." For a discussion of the role of the cloud here and its relation to the cloud in Num 9:15-23, see ASHLEY, *Numbers*, 199. In the LXX of Num 14:14 the cloud "stands over" the Israelites (ἡ νεφέλη σου ἐφέστηκεν ἐπ' αὐτῶν).

[33] LEVINE, *Numbers*, 363: "Falling prostrate has differing symbolic significance in varying contexts, but it invariably connotes submission." On the further meaning of the gesture, see ASHLEY (*Numbers*, 327) and BUDD (*Numbers*, 156), who suggest a motive of intercession here.

9. *Job 38:1; T. Job 42:1-3; Ezek 1:4, 28; 2:1: The voice of God speaks through a cloud*

Examples of oracular clouds are not limited to the traditions surrounding the Tent of Meeting. In the LXX of Job 38:1 the Lord spoke to Job "through a storm and clouds" (διὰ λαίλαπος καὶ νεφῶν). And in *T. Job* 42:1-3, "After Elihu ended his arrogant speech, the Lord – having appeared to me (Job) through a hurricane and clouds (διὰ λαίλαπος καὶ νεφῶν) – spoke and censured Elihu, showing me that the one who spoke in him was not a human but a beast. And when the Lord spoke to me through the cloud (διὰ τῆς νεφέλης), the four kings also heard the voice (τῆς φωνῆς) of him who spoke."[34]

Shortly after Ezekiel saw a "great cloud" (νεφέλη μεγάλη, Ezek 1:4), he states that "I fell upon my face (cf. Matt 17:6) and heard the voice (φωνὴν) of one speaking" (Ezek 1:28). The voice of God then said to Ezekiel, "Son of man, stand upon your feet, and I will speak with you" (Ezek 2:1). This example of an oracular cloud not only reports that the "voice" (φωνή) of God was heard from a cloud like in the previous examples, but actually narrates what the voice says. The transfiguration narratives likewise not only report that a voice came from the overshadowing cloud but actually narrate what the voice of God says to the disciples.

10. *Resulting interpretation of the overshadowing oracular cloud*

Through their knowledge and recall of the above literary traditions the implied audiences of the transfiguration narratives interpret the function of the overshadowing oracular cloud as follows: The overshadowing cloud represents a further epiphanic appearance of God's glorious revelatory presence itself, in addition to the epiphanic transformation of Jesus into a heavenly figure and the epiphanic appearance of Moses and Elijah from heaven. The overshadowing cloud and the voice of God that comes from it interrupts and corrects

---

[34] The Greek text is taken from R.A. KRAFT, ed., *The Testament of Job According to the SV Text: Greek Text and English Translation* (SBLTT 5; Missoula: Scholars Press, 1974) 74. The translation is from R.P. SPITTLER, ("Testament of Job," *OTP* 1.861), who dates the *Testament of Job* to the first century B.C. or C.E. (p. 833).

Peter's uncertain offer to make a tent for each of the three heavenly figures.

One of the possible reasons why Peter wants to make a tent – a covering or dwelling place – for each epiphanic, heavenly figure is to allow each, by analogy with the Tent of Meeting, to continue to receive and deliver divine or heavenly communications. In other words, Peter would prolong and extend to the disciples the conversation taking place among these three heavenly figures. But, ironically, God himself in the form of a cloud "overshadows," with the connotation of "dwells over" or "makes a tent or covering over," Moses and Elijah, who have been conversing with Jesus. As God in the form of a cloud spoke directly to Moses at the Tent of Meeting, so God's voice from the cloud speaks directly to the disciples, who remain outside of the cloud. God's voice directs them to listen to the divine communication of Jesus as God's Son, who likewise remains outside of the overshadowing cloud, which by the end of the narrative has separated Moses and Elijah from Jesus and concealed them from the disciples, so that the disciples see *only* Jesus.

Although not strictly necessary as a medium for the utterance of the heavenly voice of God, the overshadowing cloud serves to correct Peter's offer to make three tents. By offering to make a tent each for Jesus, Moses, and Elijah, Peter would place each of these three heavenly figures in the same category, with the same prophetic ability and authority to deliver divine oracles. But by "overshadowing" with the subtle, ironical connotation of "tenting over" Moses and Elijah, God himself in the form of the cloud indicates to the audiences that Peter is mistaken. The overshadowing cloud is thus necessary in order dramatically to separate Moses and Elijah not only from Jesus but also from the disciples, with God's voice from the cloud commanding the disciples to listen at this point not to the venerable, prophetic figures of Moses and Elijah, who have disappeared into the cloud, but to Jesus who now stands there alone authorized by God as his own beloved/chosen Son.

D. THE VEHICULAR FUNCTION OF THE OVERSHADOWING CLOUD

Although it is not explicitly narrated that the overshadowing cloud has transported Moses and Elijah back to heaven, by the end of each transfiguration account it has certainly concealed them from the eyes of the disciples. The implication for the audiences is that the overshadowing cloud either has already or is in the process of taking Moses and Elijah back to heaven from where they have made an epiphanic appearance on earth. By the end of each transfiguration narrative only Jesus, restored to his pre-transfigured state, remains on earth with the disciples:

> Mark 9:8: Then suddenly, looking around, they no longer saw anyone but Jesus alone with them.
>
> Matt 17:8: Raising their eyes they saw no one but him, Jesus alone.
>
> Luke 9:36: When the voice came there was found Jesus alone. And they kept silent and reported to no one in those days any of the things they had seen.

In Mark 9:8 and Matt 17:8 the overshadowing cloud has clearly concealed Moses and Elijah from the eyes of the disciples, as they "saw" no one but Jesus alone, that is, the pre-transfigured Jesus no longer in an epiphanic appearance with the heavenly figures of Moses and Elijah. Similarly, in Luke 9:36 the voice from the overshadowing cloud has signaled to the audience that the epiphanic appearances have ended. Jesus alone was found there without Moses and Elijah, who have entered into the overshadowing cloud (Luke 9:34) and disappeared, returning from earth to heaven. Thus, the overshadowing cloud functions as a vehicular cloud, which brings the epiphanic appearances of Jesus, Moses, and Elijah to an end by transporting Moses and Elijah back to heaven but leaving Jesus on earth.

1. *2 Kgs 2:11; 1 Enoch 39:3: Elijah and Enoch go from earth to heaven in a whirlwind*

The implied audiences of the transfiguration narratives would be familiar with the tradition of a vehicular cloud that transports selected individuals or groups from earth to heaven from literary sources preceding and contemporaneous with the NT.[35] In 2 Kgs 2:11, as we have already observed (see chap. 5 above), Elijah at the end of his life on earth, instead of dying, went up "in a whirlwind to the

---

[35] On the various other functions of vehicular clouds, see AUNE, *Revelation 6-16*, 625.

heavens" (בסערה השמים). The "whirlwind" or "storm-wind"
(סערה; cf. ἐν συσσεισμῷ in 4 Kgdms 2:11) is closely related to a
cloud, as indicated in Ezek 1:4, where "whirlwind" (סערה) is equated with "a great cloud" (ענן גדול).[36] Similarly, in *1 Enoch* 39:3
(cf. 14:8) Enoch describes his journey from earth to heaven by
means of "whirlwinds": "In those days, whirlwinds carried me off
from the earth, and set me down into the ultimate ends of the heavens."[37]

2. *Testament of Abraham: Michael brought Abraham from earth to heaven on a cloud*

In *T. Abr.* B 8:1-3, after the archangel Michael went up "in the
heavens" (ἐν τοῖς οὐρανοῖς) and spoke to God about Abraham, God
told Michael, "Go and take up Abraham in the body and show him
everything..." Then Michael took Abraham up "on a cloud" (ἐπὶ
νεφέλης) in the body and bore him up to the river Oceanus, a heavenly
river. From there Abraham has a vision of heaven (8:4ff.).

In *T. Abr.* B 10:1-2, after Abraham asked God to lead him to the
place of judgment so that he may see how people are judged, Michael
took Abraham "on a cloud" (ἐπὶ νεφέλης) and brought him into Paradise. In *T. Abr.* B 12:1, after Abraham saw the place of judgment, "the
cloud" (ἡ νεφέλη) itself took him down to the firmament below. And
in *T. Abr.* B 12:9 "the cloud" (ἡ νεφέλη) again took Abraham to another place within the heavenly realm. Thus, the vehicular cloud not
only transports Abraham from earth to heaven but from one area of
heaven to another. These last two examples are particularly relevant,
since in them "the cloud" alone, without the agency of an angel, transports Abraham. Similarly, in the transfiguration narratives the overshadowing cloud (νεφέλη) of God's presence takes Moses and Elijah
back to heaven.[38]

---

[36] BEALE, *Revelation*, 600. This equation is lacking in the LXX of Ezek 1:4.

[37] Translation by ISAAC, "1 Enoch," 30.

[38] Greek text is from STONE, *Testament of Abraham*, 72, 76, 80. In *T. Abr.* A 10:1 Michael
lifted Abraham up into the air of heaven and led him on a cloud, but for the purpose of viewing
the inhabited world rather than entering heaven; see SANDERS, "Testament of Abraham," 887.

3. *A.J.* 4.8.48 *§326: A cloud suddenly descended on Moses and he disappeared*

As we have already observed (see chap. 5 above), when Josephus reports on the end of the earthly life of Moses in *A.J.* 4.8.48 §326, he narrates that when a cloud (νέφους) suddenly descended upon Moses, he disappeared in a ravine. Although it is not explicitly stated that the cloud took Moses from earth to heaven, it is certainly implied as his disappearance into the cloud is equivalent to his having "gone back to the Deity" (πρὸς τὸ θεῖον αὐτὸν ἀναχωρῆσαι, 4.8.48 §326; cf. 3.5.7 §96). That Moses "disappeared" (ἀφανίζεται) in a cloud likens him to Elijah, who also "disappeared from human beings" (ἐξ ἀνθρώπων ἠφανίσθη, 9.2.2 §28) at the end of his earthly life.[39] Similarly, in the transfiguration narratives Moses and Elijah disappear into the over-shadowing cloud, leaving the audiences to conclude that the cloud has taken them back to heaven.

4. *1 Thess 4:17: The living and the dead will be caught up in the clouds to meet the Lord*

Paul assured his Thessalonian audience that at the second coming of Christ they would all be reunited with their fellow believers who have already died. The Lord Jesus himself will come down "from heaven" (ἀπ' οὐρανοῦ), and the dead in Christ will rise first (1 Thess 4:16). Then those who are still alive together with those who have died will be caught up "in the clouds" (ἐν νεφέλαις) to meet the Lord in the air, "and thus we shall be with the Lord forever" (1 Thess 4:17). Here "the clouds" function as a vehicle for transporting the dead and the living into the heavenly realm to be with the Lord Jesus forever in heaven. Similarly, in the transfiguration narratives Moses and Elijah are overshadowed by a cloud that not only conceals but also transports them back to heaven.[40]

---

[39] On ἀφανίζω as a characteristic term for heavenly translations, see LOHFINK, *Himmel-fahrt Jesu*, 41; BEGG, "Josephus's Portrayal," 691-92.

[40] F.F. BRUCE, *1 & 2 Thessalonians* (WBC 45; Waco: Word Books, 1982) 102; C.A. WANAMAKER, *The Epistles to the Thessalonians* (NIGTC; Grand Rapids: Eerdmans, 1990) 175; E.J. RICHARD, *First and Second Thessalonians* (SacPag 11; Collegeville: Liturgical

5. *Acts 1:9-10: A cloud took the risen Jesus to heaven*

In Acts 1:9, while the disciples were looking on, Jesus was lifted up and "a cloud took him from their eyes" (νεφέλη ὑπέλαβεν αὐτὸν ἀπὸ τῶν ὀφθαλμῶν).[41] The fourfold refrain of the phrase "into heaven" (εἰς τὸν οὐρανόν) in Acts 1:10-11, climaxed by the statement of "his going into heaven" (αὐτὸν πορευόμενον εἰς τὸν οὐρανόν), reinforces the fact that the cloud transported Jesus from earth to heaven.[42] Just as a cloud took Moses and Elijah from the eyes of the disciples and transported them back to heaven in the transfiguration narratives, so a cloud took the risen Jesus from the eyes of the disciples and transported him to heaven in Acts 1:9-10. But the two angelic figures promise that Jesus will return in the same way as they saw him going into heaven, namely on a cloud (Acts 1:10-11; cf. Luke 21:27; Mark 13:26; Matt 24:30).[43]

Press, 1995) 246: "While clouds were a frequent motif in OT theophanies (Exod 16:10; 19:16f.) they were also a divine and heavenly vehicle (Isa 19:1; Dan 7:13) suggesting divine power and presence...the Pauline text [is] unclear as to whether the elect are borne heavenward on the clouds as vehicle or are enveloped in the clouds as symbols of divine power and the heavenly sphere."

[41] ZWIEP, *Ascension*, 104-5: "The phrase νεφέλη ὑπέλαβεν αὐτόν may accordingly be translated as 'a cloud suddenly came upon him' or 'a cloud enveloped him'. The cloud, then, covers the event from the eyes of the disciples. In the light of Luke's treatment of prepositions in combination with *verba composita* elsewhere — he has a preference for unbalanced constructions — ὑπέλαβεν...ἀπὸ τῶν ὀφθαλμῶν αὐτῶν should be taken as a single construction, in which ἀπὸ τῶν ὀφθαλμῶν αὐτῶν ('away from their eyes') explicates what is already in ὑπολαμβάνω: take up (movement) secretly (concealment): a cloud enveloped him and took him away from their eyes."

[42] LOHFINK, *Himmelfahrt Jesu*, 195; C.K. BARRETT, *The Acts of the Apostles: Volume I: Preliminary Introduction and Commentary on Acts I-XIV* (ICC; Edinburgh: Clark, 1994) 83: "Luke believed that the risen body of Jesus was withdrawn from human sight by motion into a heaven that was 'up there'." J.A. FITZMYER, *The Acts of the Apostles: A New Translation with Introduction and Commentary* (AB 31; New York: Doubleday, 1998) 210: "Borne up by God's cloud, Christ is seen no more and thus returns to glory at his Father's right hand (2:33). The cloud is used in the OT sense of an apocalyptic stage prop, an instrument of God's presence, power, or glory."

[43] ZWIEP, *Ascension*, 105: "Luke speaks of a cloud in the singular (ἐν νεφέλῃ) thereby suggesting that the parousia cloud (Lk 21:27), the Transfiguration cloud (Lk 9:34-35), and the ascension cloud (Acts 1:9) are the same."

6. *Rev 11:12: The two prophetic witnesses went up to heaven in a cloud*

The two witnesses who were commissioned to prophesy (Rev 11:3) were killed by the beast (11:7). But after three and a half days a breath of life from God entered them (11:11). Then, in Rev 11:12, they heard a loud voice from heaven saying to them, "Come up here!" So they went up to heaven in a cloud (ἀνέβησαν εἰς τὸν οὐρανὸν ἐν τῇ νεφέλῃ), while their enemies watched them. Here we have another example of a vehicular cloud that transports selected individuals from earth to heaven, as the cloud in the transfiguration narratives transports Moses and Elijah back to heaven.[44]

7. *Gr. Apoc. Ezra 5:7: A cloud came and took Ezra up again to the heavens*

In *Gr. Apoc. Ezra* 5:7 Ezra reports how "a cloud (νεφέλη) came and seized me and took me up again to the heavens (εἰς τοὺς οὐρανούς)." Although this example is from a time later than the NT, it expresses explicitly the vehicular function of the cloud that is implicit in the transfiguration narratives – that the overshadowing cloud took Moses and Elijah back to heaven.[45]

E. Conclusion

By the end of each transfiguration narrative the audience realizes that the epiphanic cloud has overshadowed *only Moses and Elijah.*

---

[44] AUNE, *Revelation 6-16*, 625: "The ascension of the two witnesses narrated in vv 11-12 is essentially a *rapture story*, as distinguished from stories of the heavenly journey of the soul; that is, the two witnesses are physically taken up alive into heaven as the final conclusion of their earthly lives." BEALE, *Revelation*, 599-600: "The acceptance of the witnesses into the cloud shows the divine approval, since the cloud in 10:1 and in the OT was representative of God's presence either in judgment or in commissioning his prophetic servants. The validity of Elijah's prophetic authority was confirmed by God at the end of his ministry in the same manner."

[45] Greek text is from O. WAHL, *Apocalypsis Esdrae, Apocalypsis Sedrach, Visio Beati Esdrae* (PVTG 4; Leiden: Brill, 1977) 31. Translation is from M.E. STONE ("Greek Apocalypse of Ezra," *OTP* 1.576), who states that "a date sometime between A.D. 150 and 850 is probable" (p. 563).

The cloud, representative of God's presence, has not only concealed Moses and Elijah from the eyes of the disciples but has also separated them from Jesus, so that the disciples no longer see Moses and Elijah, but only Jesus. This is confirmed by the *oracular* function of the cloud, in which the voice of God speaks "from the cloud" to the disciples, who are thus outside the cloud, and directs them to listen to Jesus, the only one left standing there, who is also thus outside of the cloud.

Although a cloud is not necessary as a medium for the voice of God, the overshadowing cloud and the voice work together as an ironic interruption of Peter's uncertain offer to make a tent each for Jesus, Moses, and Elijah. By way of analogy with the Tent of Meeting, Peter plausibly wants to make a tent in honor of each heavenly figure at which each can continue to deliver divine communication, thus prolonging and extending to the disciples the conversation they see but do not hear taking place among the three heavenly figures. By making a tent for each, Peter would thus place each on the same level, honoring each with an equal opportunity to speak and thus prolong the epiphanic event. But the overshadowing cloud ironically interrupts Peter's offer to make a "tent," "dwelling place," or "covering" for each as it "covers over" or "tents over" Moses and Elijah. Then, adding to the irony, the voice of God himself utters a dramatic divine communication to the disciples, the mandate of this pivotal mandatory epiphany, directing them and the audiences to listen not to Moses and Elijah at tents but to Jesus left standing there alone, authorized as God's Son.

The *vehicular* function of the overshadowing cloud complements its oracular function. Since the disciples see only Jesus after the voice of God speaks from the overshadowing cloud, the audience, from their knowledge of the vehicular function of clouds, is naturally to deduce that the overshadowing cloud has not only concealed Moses and Elijah but is in the process of or has already transported these heavenly figures back to heaven from which they appeared in conversation with the transfigured Jesus. By enveloping and transporting Moses and Elijah back to heaven, the epiphanic overshadowing cloud has brought this entire epiphanic event to an abrupt conclusion, as the disciples see Jesus left there alone, restored to his pre-transfigured, earthly state.

CHAPTER 8

MARK 9:2-8 AND THE ANTECEDENT NARRATIVE

We have been treating all three versions of the transfiguration narrative together, concentrating on the basic motifs that they share as examples of the same literary genre. We will now demonstrate how each individual version functions as a "pivotal mandatory epiphany" in its respective narrative context. Two chapters will be devoted to each version. In the first we will consider how the implied audience responds to the transfiguration narrative as a "mandatory epiphany" based on its intertextual knowledge of biblical traditions and on what it has heard in the antecedent narrative. Then, in a second chapter for each version we will consider how the transfiguration narrative as a "mandatory epiphany" prepares the implied audience for the subsequent narrative, thus confirming its "pivotal" nature. We begin with Mark, which offers the most concise account of the transfiguration epiphany.

A. MARK 9:2A

And after six days Jesus took along Peter and James and John, and led them up to a high mountain privately, alone.

"And after six days" (9:2) expresses an interval of time which leads the audience both to connect and to separate what is about to happen from what they have just heard in 8:27-9:1.[1] On the one hand, what is

---

[1] M.A. TOLBERT, *Sowing the Gospel: Mark's World in Literary-Rhetorical Perspective* (Minneapolis: Fortress, 1989) 205: "The specific time reference in Mark 9:2, 'after six days,' both connects the transfiguration with the immediately preceding teaching session and separates it somewhat from it."

about to happen is closely connected to the preceding, occurring within a week of Peter's confession of Jesus as the Christ (8:29), of Jesus' first prediction of his suffering, death and resurrection (8:31), of his call for the crowd and the disciples to follow him in that suffering and death in order to share in the glory that follows it (8:34-38), and of his solemn promise that "there are some standing here who will not taste death until they see that the kingdom of God has come in power" (9:1).

On the other hand, what is about to happen occurs nearly a week later, indicating the initiation of a new and separate event. This means that what is about to happen is not limited to a relationship only with the immediately preceding events and predictions, so that the transfiguration narrative would be simply the fulfillment of the promise given in 9:1.[2]

The explicit naming of Jesus (ὁ 'Ιησοῦς) for the first time since the beginning of the previous pericope in 8:27 further indicates to the audience the beginning of a new and separate unit in 9:2.[3] In the previous scene Peter "took aside" (προσλαβόμενος) Jesus and began to rebuke him for speaking openly the word (8:32) about the divine necessity that he suffer and die before being raised (8:31). After rebuking Peter (8:33), Jesus then "summoned" (προσκαλεσάμενος) to himself the crowd with his disciples (8:34), calling them to follow him in his passion and death (8:34-38). That Jesus now "took along" (παραλαμβάνει) Peter and James and John (9:2) prepares the audience

---

[2] That the audience at this point would hear an echo of the "six days" in Exod 24:16 appears rather doubtful despite the opinion of many, e.g., NÜTZEL, *Verklärungserzählung*, 161; GNILKA, *Markus*, 2.32; W.L. LANE, *The Gospel According to Mark: The English Text with Introduction, Exposition and Notes* (NICNT; Grand Rapids: Eerdmans, 1974) 317; J. ERNST, *Das Evangelium nach Markus* (RNT; Regensburg: Pustet, 1981) 256; B.M.F. VAN IERSEL, *Mark: A Reader-Response Commentary* (JSNTSup 164; Sheffield: Sheffield Academic Press, 1998) 294. In Mark 9:2 the "six days" refers to an *interval* of time between events, whereas in Exod 24:16 the cloud covered Mount Sinai for a *duration* of six days within the same event, so that "on the seventh day" God called to Moses from the cloud. Based on Markan usage, GUNDRY (*Mark*, 474) suggests that "after six days" in Mark 9:2 means "on the sixth day." Despite the problem of the different functions, some still hold for an allusion to Exod 24:16 because of other perceived Exodus allusions in the transfiguration narrative. For a further objection to an Exodus allusion for the "six days," see ÖHLER, "Verklärung," 203. For a discussion and critique of further possible symbolic allusions in the "six days," see GUNDRY, *Mark*, 474.

[3] On the Markan usage of ὁ 'Ιησοῦς and 'Ιησοῦς, see J.K. ELLIOTT, *The Language and Style of the Gospel of Mark* (NovTSup 71; Leiden: Brill, 1993) 137.

for a new and further private revelation regarding Jesus' suffering and death as well as the participation of others in it.[4] This is confirmed for the audience by the fact that the disciples' "taking along" (παρα-λαμβάνουσιν) of Jesus in the boat (4:36) led to the new and private revelation of his power to still a stormy sea (4:35-41). And Jesus' previous "taking along" (παραλαμβάνει) of the parents and those with him (5:40) led to the new and private revelation of his power to raise a dead child back to life (5:35-43).[5]

That Jesus took along "Peter and James and John," the elite sub-group of three within the special group of the Twelve, whom Jesus chose to be with him and to have the authority to preach and expel demons (3:13-19), separating them from the crowd and the rest of the disciples (8:34), begins to prepare the audience for a unique, private revelation of Jesus to these chosen three disciples.[6] The audience recalls that Jesus did not allow anyone to accompany him to witness the revelation of his power to raise the daughter of Jairus from the dead except this same elite three, "Peter and James and John the brother of James" (5:37). That these three were among "some of those standing here" (9:1) alerts the audience to the possibility that these three, as well as the audience, may experience something in the special, private event that is about to take place that will enable them to "see that the kingdom of God has come in power" (9:1).

As the audience has already heard, when Jesus previously "went up to the mountain" (3:13) and summoned those disciples whom he wanted-ed, the mountain functioned as an elevated place for the separation of the special group of the Twelve from the crowd.[7] After Jesus alone "went to the mountain to pray" (6:46), the mountain, as a secluded area

---

[4] On Jesus' "taking along" in Mark 9:2 as an expression of "the movement in the crisis time in the Gospel as Jesus journeys forward," see B.D. SCHILDGEN, *Crisis and Continuity: Time in the Gospel of Mark* (JSNTSup 159; Sheffield: Sheffield Academic Press, 1998) 21.

[5] A. KRETZER, "παραλαμβάνω," *EDNT* 3.30: "As a community-building term in the broader sense, παραλαμβάνω is applied to the disciple-Jesus relationship (Mark 4:36) and includes both the sphere of glorification (Mark 5:40; 9:2 par.: Jesus takes three disciples along with him) and the experience of the crucifixion (Mark 10:32 par. Matt 17:1/Luke 9:28: Jesus takes the disciples aside and speaks to them of his suffering; cf. Mark 14:33 par. Matt 26:27: the scene on the Mount of Olives)."

[6] On Peter, James, and John as an elite sub-group within the Twelve, see STOCK, *Boten*, 34.

[7] On the role of the mountain in Mark 3:13, see STOCK, *Boten*, 10-11.

close to the heavenly realm, functioned as a place suitable for Jesus to pray and from which to see the distress of the disciples below, who were crossing the stormy sea in a boat. From a position of communion with God in prayer on the mountain with its celestial implications Jesus appropriately made an epiphanic appearance, revealing to his disciples his divine power to walk on the sea (6:48).[8] That Jesus now leads Peter, James, and John up to a "high mountain" (9:2) thus prepares the audience for some sort of privileged revelatory or heavenly encounter.[9] That Jesus led them up "privately" and "alone" (9:2) underscores their separation from both the crowd and the rest of the disciples (8:34) for this special secretive event.[10]

The audience's recall of special encounters that select individuals have had with God on mountains in the past adds to their expectation of a divine encounter here. After the angel of the Lord called to Abraham from heaven and commanded him not to proceed with the sacrifice of his son Isaac, since Abraham has demonstrated his devotion to God (Gen 22:12), "Abraham called the name of that place 'the Lord has seen,' so that they say today, 'the Lord appeared on this mountain'" (LXX Gen 22:14).[11] After Elijah walked forty days and forty nights to the mountain of God, Horeb (1 Kgs 19:8), God told him to stand on the

---

[8] HEIL, *Jesus Walking on the Sea*, 68-69. H. KLEINE, "ὄρος," *EDNT* 2.534: "The use of final προσεύξασθαι (Mark 6:46 par. Matt 14:23; Luke 6:12; 9:28) as well as the fact that the *mountain* is often the locus of extraordinary events can also function, however, to single out the mountain as the place of special proximity to God." On the role of the mountain in Mark, see also E.S. MALBON, *Narrative Space and Mythic Meaning in Mark* (San Francisco: Harper & Row, 1986) 84-89.

[9] That the moutain is "high" (ὑψηλὸν) emphasizes its closeness to the heavenly realm; see KLEINE, "ὄρος," 534. E. MANICARDI, *Il cammino di Gesù nel Vangelo di Marco: Schema narrativo e tema cristologico* (AnBib 96; Rome: Biblical Institute, 1981) 101: "La salita su un 'monte altissimo' (v. 2a), compiuta assieme ai tre discepoli più intimi (cfr. 5,37.40b-43), insiste sulla eccezionalità della manifestazione sequente (vv. 2b-8)." Although the "high mountain" is not named or located, the very high Mount Hermon was near the villages of Caesarea Philippi (8:27). Traditionally Jesus' transfiguration has been located on Mount Tabor in Galilee.

[10] GUNDRY, *Mark*, 458: "'Privately' (κατ' ἰδίαν) modifies the verb and therefore refers to a private taking away from the crowd that Jesus summoned in 8:34. 'Alone' (μόνους) modifies Peter, James, and John and therefore stresses separation from the other disciples, also mentioned in 8:34."

[11] On the meaning of the LXX of Gen 22:14 and its difference from the MT, see J.W. WEVERS, *Notes on the Greek Text of Genesis* (SBLSCS 35; Atlanta: Scholars Press, 1993) 324-25.

mountain before the Lord, for the Lord will be passing by (1 Kgs 19:11).

After Moses "went up the mountain to God" (Exod 19:3), he and all the people of Israel (Exod 19:11) had a dramatic encounter with God in the form of a theophany on Mount Sinai (Exod 19:16-20). After Moses went up to the mountain with Aaron, Nadab, Abihu, and seventy elders of Israel, they beheld the God of Israel (Exod 24:9-10). And after Moses along with Joshua "went up to the mountain of God" (Exod 24:13), the Israelites saw the glory of God as a consuming fire on the mountaintop (Exod 24:17). And so, when the audience hears that "Jesus took along Peter and James and John, and led them up to a high mountain privately, alone" (Mark 9:2), they have been prepared for the possibility of another dramatic encounter with God.[12]

B. MARK 9:2B-3

And he was transfigured before them, that is, his clothes became very radiantly white, such as no bleacher on the earth could thus whiten.

Although the audience has been prepared for some sort of heavenly encounter or event, they have not been prepared for what happens next, a rather unique epiphanic appearance. Jesus was suddenly "transfigured" or "transformed" (μετεμορφώθη) by God (divine passive) into a heavenly figure before the three disciples (9:2).[13] Jesus' "transfiguration" indicates to the audience his external, temporary transformation

---

[12] On the mountain of the transfiguration not being limited to simply a Moses or Sinai typology, see ÖHLER ("Verklärung," 202-4), who concludes, "Der Berg ist jener Ort, an dem der Mensch nach antikem Weltbild dem Himmel und damit der Gottheit besonders nahe ist. Daher geschehen Visionen und Entrückungen gerne an solch erhöhten Plätzen, da hier der Kontakt mit der himmlischen Welt leicht herstellbar ist" (p. 204). GUNDRY (*Mark*, 475-76) states pertinently that "ancient Jewish literature does not limit God's mountainous and cloud-cloaked revelations to Sinai" (p. 476). Also against a Moses typology here is Zeller, "Verwandlung Jesu," 312-13. On Exodus echoes to the transfiguration narrative in Mark, see R.E. WATTS, *Isaiah's New Exodus and Mark* (WUNT 88; Tübingen: Mohr Siebeck, 1997) 126-27.

[13] On the significance and background of the epiphanic motif of the "transfiguration" of Jesus, see chap. 4. VAN IERSEL, *Mark*, 294: "God makes visible who Jesus is by giving him, for a moment, the appearance of a figure that belongs to heaven. God is not mentioned, but the passive 'he was transfigured' (μετεμορφώθη) is a divine passive."

by God into a heavenly being while still on earth. It points to his future and permanent attainment of glory in heaven as promised to the righteous after their death.

That "his clothes became very radiantly white" (9:3) further defines for the audience what is meant by the "transfiguration."[14] It is a physical transformation of his external appearance visible in his clothing. The clothing that transmitted healing power to the sick who touched it (5:27-30; 6:56) now radiates (στίλβοντα) the extreme (λίαν) *whiteness* characteristic of the clothing of those who dwell in heaven. That no bleacher *on the earth* could whiten to this degree (9:3) confirms for the audience the heavenly rather than earthly nature of Jesus' transformed clothing.[15] Jesus has thus been temporarily transfigured before the eyes of the three select disciples into a heavenly figure, although he remains on the earth.

C. MARK 9:4

Then there appeared to them Elijah with Moses, and they were talking with Jesus.

The initial epiphanic appearance of the transfigured Jesus "before them" (ἔμπροσθεν αὐτῶν, 9:2), the three disciples, is immediately followed by an additional epiphanic appearance of Elijah with Moses "to them" (αὐτοῖς, 9:4), referring again to Peter, James, and John. That Elijah with Moses "appeared" (ὤφθη) to them reminds the audience of the way that God and the angel of the Lord made epiphanic "appearances" from heaven to chosen individuals in the OT.[16] Hence the entire composite epiphanic event of the transfigured Jesus in conversation

---

[14] The καὶ that introduces v. 3 is epexegetical; see chap. 1, p. 26 n. 17.

[15] A "bleacher" or "fuller" (γναφεύς, which occurs only here in the NT) was "one who cleans woolen cloth" (BAGD, 162).

[16] Note the use of ὤφθη for the appearance of God to Abraham (LXX Gen 12:7; 17:1) and for the appearance of the angel of the Lord to Moses (LXX Exod 3:2) and to Gideon (LXX Judg 6:12). It is thus a technical term for the appearances of heavenly figures in the LXX and the NT; see J. KREMER, "ὁράω," *EDNT* 2.528. On the use of ὤφθη, BAGD, 578: "Mostly of beings that make their appearance in a supernatural manner, almost always w. dat. of the pers. to whom they appear."

with Moses and Elijah is for the benefit of these three chosen disciples, as well as the audience who identifies with them.[17]

In 4:10 the audience heard how "those around Jesus" were subordinated to "the Twelve," the specially chosen elite sub-group of disciples (3:14), by the preposition "with." That "those around him" were "with" (σὺν) the Twelve enhanced the stature of this grouping for the contrast to "those outside" (4:11). In 8:34 the audience heard how "the crowd" was subordinated to "the disciples," the more prominent party, likewise by the preposition "with." Jesus called the crowd "with" (σὺν) his disciples in order to address his command to take up the cross and follow him especially to the disciples, who, despite already following him (8:33), do not understand the necessity for his suffering (8:31-32). Similarly, in 9:4 the audience hears how the preposition "with" subordinates Elijah to Moses as an even more prominent figure, thus embellishing their coupling: "Then there appeared to them Elijah *with* (σὺν), that is, including even, Moses" — not only Elijah but even Moses![18]

The audience has heard Moses and Elijah mentioned individually in the previous narrative. Jesus alluded to Moses as the representative of the Law (1:44) and giver of "the commandment of God" (7:9-10). Some have identified Jesus as the wonder-working prophet Elijah (6:15; 8:28), who was taken up to heaven without dying (2 Kgs 2:11) and was expected to return to earth as a forerunner to the eschatological age (Mal 3:23-24; Sir 48:9-10).[19] But now Moses and Elijah appear together from heaven in conversation with the transfigured Jesus. The preposition "with" that associates Elijah "with" (σὺν) Moses also associates both of them in conversation "with" (συλλαλοῦντες) Jesus (9:4). This reminds the audience of how Moses, whose face was glorified from his encounters with God on earth, used to "talk with" (συλλαλεῖν) the Lord (LXX Exod 34:35).[20]

---

[17] W. MICHAELIS, "ὁράω" *TDNT* 5.354: "The transfiguration was obviously not necessary for Jesus' own sake. Nor did Moses and Elijah appear on His account....the disciples alone need to be taught by this revelation." See also GNILKA, *Markus*, 2.34.

[18] This was explained in detail above in chap. 5. See also HEIL, "Elijah with Moses," 115.

[19] On the identification of Jesus with Elijah in Mark 6:14-16 and 8:27-30, see ÖHLER, *Elia*, 111-18.

[20] On the LXX of Exod 34:35 WEVERS (*Exodus*, 573) states: "The purposive infinitive chosen by Exod to translate לדבר is particularly fine, the present infinitive συλλαλεῖν. The root itself is unique in the Pentateuch, and it interprets the situation perfectly; the action involved is a talking together, a conversation."

Is Jesus on earth receiving a new revelation from the heavenly Moses and Elijah by "talking with" them, as Moses on earth received new revelations from God by "talking with" the Lord? Or is the Jesus who was just "speaking" (ἐλάλει) openly the word (8:32) about the divine necessity that he suffer and die before being raised (8:31) now "speaking" that same word "with" (συλλαλοῦντες) the heavenly figures of Moses and Elijah (9:4)?

The audience knows that Elijah, although he suffered persecution as a prophet, attained heavenly glory by ascending into heaven without dying (2 Kgs 2:11). And the great prophet Moses (Deut 34:10), although he suffered rebellion and opposition from his people, was never put to death as a rejected prophet. He died and was buried in a very extraordinary way, revered by his people. Later traditions familiar to the audience indicate that Moses attained heavenly glory either at the time of his mysterious but honorable death and burial or without dying at all.[21]

Does the appearance of the heavenly Moses and Elijah in close association with the transfigured Jesus mean that he also will attain heavenly glory like them, without dying the death of a rejected prophet? Does the conversation of these two great prophetic and heavenly figures with the transfigured Jesus represent a new revelation from God that now reverses Jesus' previous prediction that he "must suffer greatly and be rejected by the elders, the chief priests, and the scribes, and be killed" (8:31)? Further, does it annul Jesus' previous appeal for the crowd, the disciples, and the audience who want to follow him to deny themselves, take up their cross, and lose their lives in order to save them (8:34-35)?

D. MARK 9:5-6

Then replying, Peter said to Jesus, "Rabbi, it is good that we are here, so let us make three tents, for you one and for Moses one and for Elijah one." He did not know what to reply, for they had become terrified.

Peter has not been addressed by Jesus, and so his "replying" (ἀποκριθεὶς, 9:5) to him expresses his response, as spokesman for the

---

[21] For a full discussion of the significance of Moses and Elijah in the transfiguration narratives, see chap. 5.

group of the three chosen disciples (9:2), to this private epiphanic appearance of the transfigured Jesus in conversation with the heavenly Moses and Elijah (9:2-5).[22] Peter's address of Jesus as "Rabbi" stands in notable contrast to his similarly introduced previous confession of him as "the Christ":

8:29: ἀποκριθεὶς ὁ Πέτρος λέγει αὐτῷ, Σὺ εἶ ὁ Χριστός
9:5: καὶ ἀποκριθεὶς ὁ Πέτρος λέγει τῷ Ἰησοῦ, Ῥαββί...

After Peter, as spokesman for the disciples, confessed Jesus to be the Christ, the audience heard how Jesus immediately "rebuked" (ἐπετίμησεν) them not to tell anyone about him (8:30), since his status as the Christ includes the divine necessity that he suffer, die, and rise (8:31). After Peter began "to rebuke" (ἐπιτιμᾶν) Jesus for saying this (8:32), Jesus in turn "rebuked" (ἐπετίμησεν) Peter, calling him "Satan" and accusing him of thinking "the things of human beings" rather than "the things of God" (8:33).[23]

While Peter's address of Jesus as "Rabbi," that is, "my master," or more literally, "my great one" (9:5),[24] is certainly very appropriate and does not necessarily nullify his previous confession of Jesus as "the Christ" (8:29), it does serve to separate Jesus from what the audience has just heard – that Jesus is "the Christ" who must suffer and be put to death by the leaders of his people (8:31).[25]

---

[22] On ἀποκριθεὶς in Mark 9:5 GUNDRY (*Mark*, 459) states: "Strictly speaking, Peter does not answer a question, for no one has asked him one (contrast 8:29, which the present phraseology echoes). But he is responding to what he and his fellow disciples have seen and heard; in that sense ἀποκριθεὶς is more than a meaningless appendage (see v 6a; 11:14; 12:35; 14:40, 48)." Although Peter and his fellow disciples have *seen* (implied by ὤφθη) Moses and Elijah in conversation with Jesus (9:4), there is no explicit indication that they have *heard* the conversation or anything else. Peter's role in the transfiguration narrative would be better described as "outspoken member of the group" rather than "spokesman" according to T. WIARDA, "Peter as Peter in the Gospel of Mark," *NTS* 45 (1999) 34. But Peter is surely both.

[23] On the "rebukes" of Peter and Jesus here, see S.R. GARRETT, *The Temptations of Jesus in Mark's Gospel* (Grand Rapids: Eerdmans, 1998) 76-82.

[24] On the title "rabbi" G. SCHNEIDER ("ῥαββί," *EDNT* 3.205-6) states that although it "was the form of address for scholars or the learned...Judaism of Jesus' time did not yet restrict the address "rabbi" to educated and ordained scholars...In Mark ῥαββί is used of Jesus by Peter (9:5; 11:21) and Judas (14:45)." In Mark 9:5 ῥαββί means "lord" (cf. Matt 17:4) rather than "teacher," according to B.T. VIVIANO, "Rabbouni and Mark 9:5," *RB* 97 (1990) 207-18.

[25] HOOKER, *Mark*, 217: "Peter's use of Rabbi to address Jesus seems strange so soon after Caesarea Philippi, especially in a scene of this nature." See also LANE, *Mark*, 320 n. 24.

By addressing Jesus as "Rabbi," Peter thus associates Jesus more closely with Moses and Elijah, great prophets of the past who entered heavenly glory without suffering and being put to death by their own people. This is immediately confirmed for the audience, as Peter, by suggesting that the disciples build a tent for each (9:5), places the transfigured Jesus into the same category as the heavenly Moses and Elijah.

The audience has heard Jesus tell the Syrophoenician woman, who begged Jesus to expel a demon from her daughter (7:26), that "it is not good (οὐ γάρ ἐστιν καλὸν) to take the bread of the children and throw it to the dogs" (7:27). This means that it would not be "good," that is, appropriate to God's plan of salvation, according to which "the children" (the people of Israel) should be "fed first" (7:27) from the bread (salvific benefits) Jesus brings, nor would it be beneficial for the children, if Jesus were to throw the bread that belongs first to them to "the dogs" (Gentiles, such as the Syrophoenician woman).[26] Now the audience hears Peter tell Jesus, "Rabbi, it is good (καλόν ἐστιν) that we are here" (9:5).[27] In other words, it is "good," that is, appropriate to God's salvific plan and beneficial for Peter, James, and John to be present to witness this spectacular epiphanic appearance of the heavenly Moses and Elijah in conversation with the transfigured Jesus, and also beneficial for the three heavenly figures that the disciples are here to build a tent for each (9:5).[28]

Peter's statement that "it is good that we are *here*" (9:5) reminds the audience of Jesus' previous prediction that "there are some standing *here* who will not taste death until they see that the kingdom of

---

[26] For a discussion of Mark 7:24-30, see HEIL, *Mark*, 159-63.

[27] For the interpretation that "we" (ἡμᾶς) in 9:5 refers to the three disciples and does not include either Jesus or Moses and Elijah, see NÜTZEL, *Verklärungserzählung*, 123-26; GUNDRY, *Mark*, 460.

[28] J. WANKE, "καλός," *EDNT* 2.245: "In a wider sense καλός can connote the (physical) perfection, suitability, or usefulness of an object, usually in metaphorical speech, and can be translated *useful, profitable, precious, flawless*, etc....To be noted separately is the formulaic use of καλός (ἐστιν) (e.g., Mark 9:5: 'it is *good* that we are here'). Yet this can be understood to indicate that which is salutary and good before God (cf. 7:27..." The interpretation that it is good that Peter, James and John are present to build tents is denied by WIARDA, "Peter as Peter," 30 n. 25.

God has come in power" (9:1). But by "here" Jesus and Peter are referring to two quite different locations. Whereas "here" (ὧδε) in 9:5 refers to the mountain of the transfiguration epiphany, "here" (ὧδε) in 9:1 refers to Caesarea Philippi (8:27), the location of Jesus' prediction. Although Peter, James, and John were among "some standing here," they were not the only ones present for Jesus' prediction. There may be others, besides these three, who will likewise fulfill Jesus' prediction. Indeed, it is not yet clear in what sense the three disciples' involvement in the transfiguration epiphany will enable them (and the audience) "to see that the kingdom of God has come in power" (9:1).[29]

By suggesting that the three disciples make a tent each for Jesus, Moses, and Elijah (9:5), Peter, even though he mentions Jesus first, would place each heavenly figure on the same level and in the same category, as well as prepare a place for each to prolong his glorious epiphanic appearance. Although the three "tents" may remind the audience of the commemorative tents used for the Feast of Tabernacles and/or the dwelling places appropriate for the righteous in heaven, the primary allusion is to the Tent of Meeting. Since the three epiphanic figures are in conversation among themselves (9:4), and there is no indication that the three disciples hear the conversation, Peter wants to provide a tent, analogous to the Tent of Meeting, for each to continue his divine communication for the benefit of the three disciples.[30]

---

[29] *Pace* GUNDRY (*Mark*, 459-60), who maintains that the verbal link between "here" in the prediction at 9:1 and in Peter's statement in 9:5 furthers the interpretation of that prediction being fulfilled in the transfiguration epiphany. As we will see, the fulfillment of the prediction at 9:1 is certainly very closely related, but not limited, to what the disciples experience in the transfiguration epiphany. For another interpretation of the connection between the transfiguration narrative and 9:1 by way of Moses and Elijah as deathless witnesses that the kingdom of God is forceful, see B.D. CHILTON, "The Transfiguration: Dominical Assurance and Apostolic Vision," *NTS* 27 (1981) 115-24.

[30] For a full discussion of the background and meaning of the tents, see chap. 6. According to GUNDRY (*Mark*, 459): "Elijah and Moses appear to the disciples but are talking with Jesus, not to the disciples. 'Talking with Jesus' does not reveal what Elijah and Moses say to him. Rather, it prepares for Peter's wanting to make three tabernacles in order that he and his fellow disciples may keep listening to what Elijah and Moses are saying to Jesus." But Peter envisions a tent for *each* heavenly figure. The three individual tents would thus provide each heavenly figure with a place (like the Tent of Meeting) from which to address his own divine communication to the three disciples.

The narrator's aside that Peter "did not know what to reply" (9:6) indicates to the audience Peter's uncertainty regarding the appropriateness of his suggestion to build three tents in response to the epiphanic appearance of the transfigured Jesus in conversation with the heavenly Moses and Elijah.[31] Peter's lack of understanding, as the representative of the disciples ("for *they* had become terrified," 9:6), reminds the audience of the disciples' lack of understanding in response to the previous epiphany of Jesus walking on the sea:

6:52: οὐ γὰρ συνῆκαν ἐπὶ τοῖς ἄρτοις
9:6: οὐ γὰρ ᾔδει τί ἀποκριθῇ

That the disciples "did not understand on the basis of the loaves" (6:52) means that they did not understand the true significance of Jesus as revealed by the epiphany of his walking on the sea (6:45-52), since they have not understood his significance as revealed in the miraculously overabundant multiplication of the loaves (6:30-44).[32] Similarly, Peter apparently does not understand the true significance of Jesus in relation to Moses and Elijah, as revealed by the epiphany of his transfiguration. In wanting to build a tent for each heavenly figure, the question arises for the audience: Is Peter still "thinking the things of human beings" rather than "the things of God" (8:33), as he was when he rejected Jesus' announcement of the necessity of his suffering and death (8:31-32)?

Not just Peter, the spokesman, but all three disciples "had become terrified" (9:6) in response to these spectacular epiphanic appearances.[33] This reminds the audience of the disciples' response to the previous epiphany of Jesus stilling the storm at sea:

---

[31] On the literary device of the "narrative aside," see S.M. SHEELEY, *Narrative Asides in Luke-Acts* (JSNTSup 72; Sheffield: JSOT, 1992). GUNDRY, *Mark*, 460: "Since Peter's suggestion overexalts Moses and Elijah, more of whose words Peter and his fellow disciples want to hear, Mark designs his editorial comment, 'for he [Peter] did not know what [or "how"] he should answer' (cf. 14:40), to keep the audience of the gospel from overlooking Peter's error." WIARDA ("Peter as Peter," 35) describes Peter here as "an individual disciple floundering between devotion and mistaken thinking."

[32] For a full discussion of Mark 6:52, see HEIL, *Jesus Walking on the Sea*, 73-75.

[33] GUNDRY (*Mark*, 460) points out the emphatic position and "the perfective preposition in ἔκφοβοι, 'terrified.'" In the NT ἔκφοβος occurs only in Mark 9:6 and Heb 12:21, while ἐκφοβέω occurs only in 2 Cor 10:9. GNILKA (*Markus*, 2.35) misinterprets the fear motif as the disciples' lack of courage (menschlicher Kleinmut) in the face of the necessity for suffering (8:31-38).

4:41: καὶ ἐφοβήθησαν φόβον μέγαν
9:6: ἔκφοβοι γὰρ ἐγένοντο

That the disciples "feared a great fear" led to their question regarding the more profound identity of Jesus based on the storm-stilling epiphany: "Who then is this that even the wind and the sea obey him?" (4:41). Similarly, that the three disciples "had become terrified" at the epiphany of the transfigured Jesus in conversation with Moses and Elijah was the reason Peter "did not know what to reply" (9:6), when he attempted to respond to this revelation of the more profound identity of Jesus in relation to Moses and Elijah by suggesting the making of a tent for each (9:5).[34]

E. MARK 9:7

Then there came a cloud overshadowing them, then there came a voice from the cloud, "This is my beloved Son; listen to him!"

Yet another sudden and unexpected epiphanic appearance occurs as "there came a cloud overshadowing them" (9:7).[35] At this point the audience is not sure as to whom precisely the cloud overshadows. Does it overshadow all six characters in the scene – the three disciples as well as Jesus, Moses, and Elijah? Does "overshadowing them (αὐτοῖς)" refer only to the three disciples, the previous referent of "them" (αὐτοῖς), as the recipients of the epiphanic appearance of Moses and Elijah in conversation with the transfigured Jesus (9:4)?

---

[34] Note also the use of φοβέομαι in reactions of "fear" to the manifestations of Jesus' divine healing power in Mark 5:15, 33; cf. 6:50. H. BALZ, "φοβέομαι," *EDNT* 3.430: "In the Gospels the motif of fear in the presence of an epiphany carries particular theological weight...The revelation of God's power in extraordinary occurrences (Matt 27:54; Luke 2:9) and in Jesus' own deeds evokes astonishment, fear, and terror in witnesses....The transfiguration and Easter stories, however, associate this fear motif in a special way with the person and destiny of Christ. The distance between the yet uncomprehending disciples and their Lord becomes apparent over against the immediacy between the Son and the Father (Mark 9:6: ἔκφοβοι γὰρ ἐγένοντο; cf. Luke 9:34; Matt 17:6)."

[35] For a full discussion of the background and meaning of the overshadowing cloud, see chap. 7.

Does the heavenly cloud overshadow only the three heavenly, epiphanic figures, or only Moses and Elijah?

That "then there came a voice *from* the cloud" (9:7) indicates to the audience that the three disciples, whom the divine voice addresses, have remained outside of the cloud, representative of God's presence. The voice comes "from" or "out of" (ἐκ) the cloud and speaks to the disciples.[36] Furthermore, that the voice emphatically directs the disciples to listen to Jesus (9:7) indicates to the audience that Jesus also is outside of the cloud. The cloud appropriately overshadows only the heavenly figures of Moses and Elijah, concealing them from the eyes of the disciples, as it implicitly transports them back to heaven, which is confirmed at the end of the scene when the disciples see only Jesus with them after the voice has spoken from the cloud (9:8).[37]

The overshadowing cloud of God's presence interrupts, ironically for the audience, Peter's uncertain and fearful offer to make a tent each for Jesus, Moses, and Elijah (9:5). The audience recognizes an analogy with the traditions surrounding the Tent of Meeting, the privileged place of divine communication, when Peter wants to make a tent in honor of each heavenly figure at which each can continue to deliver divine communication.[38] Peter would thus prolong this epiphany of heavenly glory and extend to the three disciples the heavenly conversation they witness but do not hear taking place among the three epiphanic figures.

With an alliterative Greek word play the epiphanic cloud ironically interrupts Peter's offer to make three "tents" (σκηνάς, 9:5) for the three epiphanic figures, as it "covers over" or "tents over" (ἐπισκιάζουσα, 9:7) Moses and Elijah, thus separating them from the Jesus Peter wanted to make equal to them.[39] Adding to the irony, the voice of God himself, without the provision of a tent like the Tent of Meeting and without speaking through such preeminent prophetic intermediaries as Moses and Elijah, proclaims a dramatic divine communication directly to the disciples, "This is my beloved Son; listen to

---

[36] See BAGD, 234, on ἐκ as denoting the direction from which something comes.

[37] For the background of the vehicular function of the cloud, see chap. 7.

[38] On the Tent of Meeting as background for the transfiguration, see chap. 6.

[39] GUNDRY (*Mark*, 460) points out "that ἐπισκιάζουσα includes complete envelopment, not just shade overhead."

him!" (9:7). This climactic command serves as the mandate of this pivotal mandatory epiphany, directing the three disciples and the audience to listen at this point not to Moses and Elijah for divine communication at tents but to Jesus, God's beloved Son, the only one that the overshadowing cloud has left standing there with the three disciples (9:8).

God's command to the disciples from the overshadowing cloud develops for the audience God's pronouncement to Jesus after his baptism by John:

1:11: καὶ φωνὴ ἐγένετο ἐκ τῶν οὐρανῶν, Σὺ εἶ ὁ υἱός μου ὁ ἀγαπητός, ἐν σοὶ εὐδόκησα

9:7: καὶ ἐγένετο φωνὴ ἐκ τῆς νεφέλης, Οὗτός ἐστιν ὁ υἱός μου ὁ ἀγαπητός, ἀκούετε αὐτοῦ

After Jesus' baptism the divine voice came "from the heavens" (1:11), God's dwelling place. Now the divine voice comes "from the cloud" (9:7), symbolic of God's presence. After the baptism God told Jesus, "You are my beloved Son; with you I am well pleased!" (1:11). But now God tells the three disciples, "This is my beloved Son; listen to him!" (9:7).

What the audience (1:1, 11) and the demonic world have already known (3:11: "You are the Son of God!"; 5:7: "Jesus, Son of the most high God"), namely, the more profound identity of Jesus as God's unique, beloved Son, God now finally reveals directly to the three disciples (9:7).[40] God's voice from the overshadowing cloud corrects Peter's misinterpretation of the epiphanic appearance of Jesus (9:6). Peter would place the transfigured Jesus on the same level as the heavenly Moses and Elijah by building a tent for each (9:5). But with an emphatic "*this* one" (οὗτός), God points out that Jesus is not equal to Moses or Elijah, since he is "my beloved Son" (9:7). The disciples and the audience are to realize then that Jesus, as God's unique, "beloved Son," is much more than the mere "Rabbi" of Peter's address (9:5), and more even than "the Christ" of Peter's previous confession (8:29).

---

[40] On the identification of Jesus by the demons as "Son of the most high God," see J. GNILKA, *Das Evangelium nach Markus: (Mk 1,1-8,26)* (EKKNT 2/1; Zürich: Benziger, 1978) 204.

God's urgent command to "listen to him!," the mandate of this pivotal mandatory epiphany, "pivots" the audience back to and thus reinforces Jesus' own urgent appeals to "listen to" and understand his teaching:

4:2-3: he said to them in his teaching, "Listen (Ακούετε)!"

4:9: "Whoever has ears to listen, let him listen (ἀκούειν ἀκουέτω)!"

4:23: "If anyone has ears to listen, let him listen (ἀκούειν ἀκουέτω)!"

4:24: "Attend to what you are listening (ἀκούετε)!"[41]

7:14: "Listen (ἀκούσατε) to me, all of you, and understand!"

8:18: "having ears do you not listen (ἀκούετε)?"

9:7: "Listen (ἀκούετε) to him!"

God's mandate for the disciples to "listen to him" (ἀκούετε αὐτοῦ, 9:7) reminds the audience of Moses's promise that God would raise up from and for the people of Israel a prophet like Moses, so that "you shall listen to him" (αὐτοῦ ἀκούσεσθε, LXX Deut 18:15). God himself reinforced the promise of a prophet like Moses, and added: "I will place my word in his mouth, and he will speak to them as I command him" (LXX Deut 18:18).[42] But now the disciples and the audience are to listen to Jesus not just as a prophet like Moses (or Elijah) but as God's own beloved Son, who speaks as God, his Father, commands him. Peter and his fellow disciples, who would build the three tents to prolong the divine communication taking place among Jesus, Moses, and Elijah (9:4-5), should not be so much concerned with what Moses and Elijah might have to say as with what Jesus, as God's beloved Son, has had and will have to say to them.[43] The audience's recall of Deut 18:15-18, then, reinforces for them that what

---

[41] On the significance of "hearing" for Jesus' teaching in parables, see J.P. HEIL, "Reader-Response and the Narrative Context of the Parables About Growing Seed in Mark 4:1-34," *CBQ* 54 (1992) 271-86.

[42] WEVERS, *Deuteronomy*, 303: "The prophet is thus the one who transmits what God tells him to the people; he is the intermediary between God and man."

[43] GUNDRY, *Mark*, 461: "The command to hear Jesus contrasts with the three disciples' interest in hearing Elijah and Moses talk with him (v 5: 'it's good that we [three disciples] are here')."

they have already heard and what they will hear from Jesus is the very word of God himself.

The divine mandate to listen to Jesus as God's beloved Son especially refers the disciples and the audience back to what Jesus has just spoken in the preceding scene (8:31-9:1). Attentively listening to "the word he was speaking openly" (παρρησίᾳ τὸν λόγον ἐλάλει, 8:32a) would enable the disciples and the audience to grasp the more profound identity of the transfigured Jesus as God's beloved Son in contrast to the heavenly figures of Moses and Elijah.[44] As Jesus has been teaching, it is divinely necessary for him, the Son of Man, to be rejected by the leaders of his people and killed before rising from the dead after three days (8:31). His temporary transfiguration into a heavenly figure indicates that he will ultimately attain heavenly glory like Moses and Elijah. But unlike them Jesus will do so only after being rejected and put to death by his own people.

By the time of the transfiguration scene there has been no indication that Peter, although he rebuked (8:32) and was rebuked by Jesus (8:33), or the crowds and the disciples have really heard and understood what Jesus has said. Attentively listening to what Jesus told the crowd together with the disciples would enable Peter, James, and John, as well as the audience, to realize that they must follow Jesus on his way of suffering and death, by denying themselves and taking up their cross (8:34), if they are to join him in the ultimate and permanent heavenly glory that his transfiguration prefigures. They must lose their lives for the sake of Jesus and the gospel in order to save them (8:35).[45] They must not be ashamed of Jesus and "my words" (ἐμοὺς λόγους, 8:38), especially his "word" (λόγον, 8:32a) about the necessity for his suffering and death before resurrection (8:31) and his word about the necessity to follow him in that suffering and death (8:34-37), in order to join him in heavenly glory. That Jesus, as the Son of Man,

---

[44] Comparing Mark 2:2b with 8:32a, GUNDRY (*Mark*, 431) notes: "The addition of παρρησίᾳ, its placement in first position after the conjunction, and the advance of τὸν λόγον to second position, ahead of the verb, put great weight on the point that Jesus really did teach the disciples beforehand about his passion and resurrection. Mark's audience can be absolutely sure that Jesus was not taken by surprise, that those events happened by design."

[45] For an enlightening analysis of the antithetical aphorism in Mark 8:35, see R.C. TANNEHILL, *The Sword of His Mouth* (Philadelphia: Fortress, 1975) 99-100.

is still to "come in the glory of his Father with the holy angels" (8:38) confirms that his transfiguration into a heavenly figure is but a temporary anticipation of his final glory yet to come as God's beloved Son (9:7).[46]

Attentively listening to Jesus' words about the necessity to follow him on his way to suffering and death would enable the three disciples and the audience to realize how the transfiguration epiphany prepares them to fulfill Jesus' promise that "there are some standing here who will not taste death until they see that the kingdom of God has come in power" (9:1). The temporary transfiguration of Jesus into a heavenly figure assures the three disciples and the audience that he will ultimately and permanently achieve the heavenly glory of God's kingdom after his necessary suffering, rejection, and death. The transfiguration epiphany will thus enable them to see that "the kingdom of God has come in power" already and paradoxically in the apparent weakness of Jesus' suffering, rejection, and death, which some of them will witness before they "taste"[47] the bitterness of their own death as followers of Jesus.[48]

F. MARK 9:8

Then suddenly, looking around, they no longer saw anyone but Jesus alone with them.

God's powerful voice from the cloud (9:7) has brought this pivotal mandatory epiphany to its climactic conclusion. "Suddenly," that

---

[46] Note the implication that as the Son of Man Jesus is also the Son of God, his Father; see also 1:1, 11; 3:11; 5:7. On Mark 8:38, GUNDRY (*Mark*, 439) comments: "'Of his Father' shows that God is not ashamed of his Son even though others may be. Inserting 'of his Father' establishes this point at the linguistically odd expense of making the Son of man the Son of God and prepares for God's pronouncement of Jesus as his beloved Son in 9:7."

[47] On the significance of "taste" (γεύομαι) in the frequently occurring phrase, "taste death," H.-J. VAN DER MINDE ("γεύομαι," *EDNT* 1.246) states that "γεύομαι implies the moment of suffering."

[48] K. BROWER, "Mark 9:1: Seeing the Kingdom in Power," *JSNT* 6 (1980) 41: "These shall see the kingdom in power, albeit power in weakness, and it may not be perceived as power. Nevertheless, in the cross of Jesus, God's rule has been decisively established, shown by the darkness at noon and the rending of the veil, and witnessed to by the Roman centurion." This does not rule out that they will also see that the kingdom of God has come in power when they see Jesus risen from the dead (16:6-7).

is, simultaneously with the voice uttering the mandate, the three disciples looked around and "no longer saw anyone but Jesus alone with them" (9:8). This confirms for the audience that the cloud, which overshadowed Moses and Elijah, has taken them back to heaven.[49]

That Jesus alone is *with* the three disciples means that he is no longer in conversation *with* the heavenly figures of Moses and Elijah. His epiphanic transfiguration into a heavenly being has ended; he has returned to his earthly status and is again "alone" (μόνον, 9:8) with the disciples whom he took along with him to the high mountain privately, "alone" (μόνους, 9:2). That the disciples see only Jesus eliminates for them and the audience any doubt as to whom the mandate refers. They are to listen for the divinely authoritative communication that comes not from Moses and Elijah but from Jesus, whom God himself has just declared "my beloved Son" (9:7).

That Jesus was alone "with themselves" (μεθ' ἑαυτῶν, 9:8) reminds the audience of how the disciples previously had only one loaf "with themselves" (μεθ' ἑαυτῶν) in the boat (8:14). On the cryptic, metaphorical level the "one loaf" symbolizes Jesus himself who can reveal his more profound character by satisfying his disciples with the "one loaf" of his self-revelation (8:13-21; see also 7:27). Although the disciples have only "one loaf" (Jesus) with them in the boat, the audience knows that, because of Jesus' previous miraculously overabundant feedings (6:30-44; 8:1-9), this "one loaf" (Jesus) is sufficient to satisfy both physically with food and metaphorically with his self-revelation.[50] That Jesus is again alone "with themselves" (9:8) means that he can reveal his more profound character to the disciples and the audience, if they obey the mandate and listen to him.

Although God's voice from the cloud has commanded the three disciples to listen to Jesus as his beloved Son, there is as yet no indication that they will obey it. The pivotal mandate of the epiphany has thus created a dramatic suspense for the rest of Mark's narrative. Will the disciples (and audience) listen to what Jesus has already said (8:31-38)

---

[49] For the vehicular function of the cloud, see chap. 7. VAN IERSEL, *Mark*, 297: "When the voice had died away, the cloud has dissolved too. The disciples can freely look around again. Along with the cloud, Elijah and Moses have also vanished from sight. The reader presumes that they have returned to the heavenly world to which they belong."

[50] For this interpretation of Mark 8:13-21, see HEIL, *Mark*, 170-73.

and what he still has to say about the necessity for suffering and death before entering into the heavenly glory of God's kingdom anticipated by his transfiguration?

G. Conclusion

When the audience hears that "Jesus took along Peter and James and John, and led them up to a high mountain privately, alone" (Mark 9:2), they are prepared for the possibility of a dramatic revelatory encounter with God. The initial epiphanic action of this pivotal mandatory epiphany occurs as Jesus was suddenly and unexpectedly "transfigured" by God into a heavenly figure before the three disciples (9:2). That no bleacher *on the earth* could thus whiten his clothes that became very radiantly white (9:3) confirms for the audience the heavenly nature of Jesus' transformed clothing. Jesus' transfiguration, his external, proleptic, and temporary transformation by God into a heavenly being while still on earth, indicates to the audience his future and permanent attainment of glory in heaven as promised to the righteous after their death.

The epiphanic transfiguration of Jesus is immediately followed by an additional epiphanic appearance of the heavenly figures of Elijah with Moses in conversation with Jesus before the eyes of the three disciples (9:4). The audience knows that neither Moses nor Elijah, although great prophets who experienced opposition, were put to death by their people. Does the appearance of the heavenly Moses and Elijah in close association with the transfigured Jesus mean that he also will attain heavenly glory like them, without dying the death of a rejected prophet?

That the three disciples became terrified at the epiphany of the transfigured Jesus in conversation with Moses and Elijah was the reason Peter did not know what to reply (9:6), when he responded to the revelation of the more profound identity of Jesus in relation to Moses and Elijah by suggesting the making of a tent for each (9:5). Peter would place each heavenly figure on the same level by making a tent for each to prolong his glorious epiphanic appearance and to continue the divine communication for the benefit of the disciples.

But Peter is interrupted by yet another sudden and unexpected epiphanic appearance as a cloud overshadowed Moses and Elijah, implicitly transporting them back to heaven. After Jesus' baptism God's voice from the heavens told Jesus, "You are my beloved Son; with you I am well pleased!" (1:11). But now God's voice from the cloud tells the three disciples, "This is my beloved Son; listen to him!" (9:7). What the audience (1:1, 11) and the demonic world have already known (3:11; 5:7) God now reveals directly to the three disciples (9:7).

God's voice from the cloud (9:7) serves as the pivotal mandate that distinguishes Jesus from Moses and Elijah as God's beloved Son and commands the disciples and the audience to listen to Jesus. The mandate thus "pivots" them back to the previous teaching of Jesus (4:2-3, 9, 23-24; 7:14; 8:18), especially his teaching about the necessity for him and his followers to suffer and to lose their lives (8:31-38) before entering into the heavenly glory of God's kingdom anticipated by Jesus' transfiguration. As the pivotal mandatory epiphany concludes with Jesus again alone with the disciples (9:8), the burning question remains: Will the disciples and the audience heed the pivotal epiphanic mandate and listen to Jesus in order to understand the way that he and they will attain the heavenly glory anticipated by his transfiguration?

CHAPTER 9

MARK 9:2-8 AND THE SUBSEQUENT NARRATIVE

In the preceding chapter we considered how the Markan transfiguration narrative functions as a pivotal mandatory epiphany in relation to the antecedent Markan narrative. More specifically, we saw how the mandate, "Listen to him!" (9:7), pivoted the audience back especially to Jesus' pronouncement of the necessity for his disciples to follow him on his way to suffering and death before being raised to heavenly glory (8:31-38) as a key to understanding the significance of the transfiguration epiphany. In this chapter we will consider how the Markan transfiguration epiphany, especially its pivotal mandate, relates to and prepares the audience for the subsequent Markan narrative.

A. MARK 9:9-13: ELIJAH HAS ALREADY COME

1. *Mark 9:9: Jesus orders the disciples to silence until he has arisen from the dead*

When Jesus and the three disciples came down from the mountain of the transfiguration, he "ordered them" (διεστείλατο αὐτοῖς) to tell no one (ἵνα μηδενὶ) what they had seen, until the Son of Man had risen from the dead (9:9). This "order" of Jesus serves as the first instance of what the disciples and audience are to listen to, as enjoined by the pivotal mandate of God's voice from the overshadowing cloud (9:7). It reminds the audience that after Jesus took these same three disciples – Peter, James, and John (5:37) – along with the parents (5:40) of a little girl to witness his resuscitation of her from death, he strictly "ordered them" (διεστείλατο αὐτοῖς) that no one (ἵνα μηδεὶς) should know this (5:43).

The audience further remembers how Jesus similarly "ordered them" (διεστείλατο αὐτοῖς), in this case, the crowd (7:33), to tell no one (ἵνα μηδενὶ), after he miraculously opened the ears and mouth of a deaf man with a speech impediment. But the more he ordered them, all the more did they proclaim it (7:36).

After Peter confessed Jesus to be the Christ (8:29), Jesus immediately "rebuked them" (ἐπετίμησεν αὐτοῖς) to tell no one (ἵνα μηδενὶ) about him (8:30). These commands to silence impress upon the audience that the more profound character of Jesus, as glimpsed in his miraculous healings (5:21-43; 7:31-37), in Peter's confession (8:29), and in Jesus' glorious transfiguration (9:2-8), cannot be fully understood until he has risen from the dead (9:9).[1]

The emphasis upon "*from the dead*" in a forward position in the statement, "until the Son of Man from the dead has risen (ἐκ νεκρῶν ἀναστῇ)" (9:9), makes explicit what Jesus' first passion prediction implies (8:31), namely, that he will rise *from the dead* three days after the Jewish leaders kill him. This emphasis upon Jesus' resurrection *from the dead* provides the disciples and the audience a key for understanding the significance of Jesus' transfiguration. Unlike the great prophetic figures of Moses and Elijah, who attained heavenly glory without being put to death by their people, Jesus will attain the heavenly glory anticipated by his transfiguration only after his resurrection *from the dead*, from a death perpetrated by the leaders of his own people. Elijah ascended directly to heaven without entering the realm of the dead (2 Kgs 2:11). The unknown burial place of Moses (Deut 34:6) stimulated speculations that perhaps he did not really enter the realm of the dead but was translated to heavenly glory at the time of his death as a venerable prophet (Deut 34:5-12).[2] Unlike them, Jesus,

---

[1] *Pace* GUNDRY (*Mark*, 482) who states: "Nor does the text of the command to secrecy give any reason to discover a deep theological meaning to the effect that only the Cross and the Resurrection will enable people to understand Jesus truly." Although, as Gundry continues, "Jesus himself has already taught the others as well as the three about his death and resurrection (8:31)," the point is that they do not yet fully understand this key teaching (cf. 8:32-33; 9:30-32). As LANE (*Mark*, 323) notes: "The reality of his exaltation as the transfigured Son, however, can be appreciated only when the significance of his sufferings has been grasped."

[2] For the various traditions surrounding the mysterious death of Moses, see chap. 5.

the beloved Son of God (9:7) and the Son of Man, will rise to heavenly glory *from the dead*.

The audience has heard previously the opinion of some, including King Herod (6:16), that Jesus is John the Baptist, whom Herod beheaded, raised from the dead (ἐκ νεκρῶν 6:14). As John raised from the dead, Jesus would thus represent God's vindication for the brutal murder of this "just and holy man" (6:20). Although the audience knows that Jesus is not John raised from the dead, they are to realize that Jesus' resurrection from the dead (ἐκ νεκρῶν, 9:9), anticipated by his transfiguration, represents God's vindication of both John and Jesus as prophetic figures put to death by their own people.

Although there is a definite emphasis upon "from the dead" in 9:9, the ultimate focus is upon Jesus' triumphant *resurrection* over death.[3] Indeed, Jesus' statement expresses the inseparable connection between his death and resurrection. When Jesus first predicted his suffering, death and resurrection, Peter's rebuke of Jesus indicated to the audience that he heard the words about suffering and death but not about the triumphant resurrection after three days (8:31-33). Jesus' transfiguration gave the disciples a glimpse of his future resurrection to heavenly glory. But they have yet to make the connection between the necessity of his suffering and death before his resurrection to heavenly glory. Therefore, God's mandate to listen to Jesus (9:7) directs the disciples and the audience to hear the connection Jesus makes between his necessary death but subsequent resurrection when he demands silence about the transfiguration until he has "*from the dead been raised*" (9:9).

2. Mark 9:10: The disciples question what the rising from the dead means

The disciples respond to Jesus' command for silence by keeping his word to themselves, questioning what "the rising from the dead" means (9:10).[4] Rather than questioning what resurrection from the dead

---

[3] GUNDRY, *Mark*, 462: "Attention focuses on his resurrection from the dead, not on his death, as shown especially by the addition of ἐκ νεκρῶν, 'from [the] dead,' in a forward position."

[4] According to TOLBERT (*Sowing the Gospel*, 207), "Peter, James, and John had better reason than anyone else to know 'what the rising from the dead meant' (9:10)," since they were the only three disciples to witness Jesus' raising of the daughter of Jairus from death (5:37-42). But Jesus' raising of the daughter of Jairus was a resuscitation from death; she will

means in general, they are questioning what it means for Jesus as the Son of Man (9:9) in view of their experience of the transfiguration e-piphany.[5] They have just witnessed the heavenly glory that Moses and Elijah have attained without having arisen from the dead. And they have just seen the earthly Jesus transfigured, without first dying and rising from the dead, into a glorious heavenly figure in conversation with Moses and Elijah (9:3-4). So why is it necessary for Jesus as the Son of Man "to rise from the dead" in order to attain heavenly glory?[6]

3. *Mark 9:11: The disciples object that Elijah must come first*

The disciples then ask Jesus why the scribes say that Elijah must come first (9:11).[7] They thus relativize the divine necessity that Jesus as the Son of Man "must" (δεῖ) suffer, be killed, and rise (8:31) with the divine necessity that Elijah "must" (δεῖ) come beforehand.[8] Ironically the disciples appeal to the teaching of the scribes, one of the groups of Jewish leaders who will put Jesus to death (8:31; cf. 2:6, 16; 3:22; 7:1, 5). This appeal to scribal authority is especially ironic for the audience who recalls the response of those whom Jesus taught in the synagogue at Capernaum: "They were astounded at his teaching, for he was teaching them as one having authority and not as the scribes" (1:22). The disciples' appeal to scribal teaching thus underlines their continued lack of understanding regarding the more profound character and authority of Jesus.

---

eventually die again. "The rising from the dead" refers to the eschatological resurrection after which one – in this case Jesus as the Son of Man (9:9) – will never die again. See also GUNDRY, *Mark*, 463.

[5] *Contra* M. ÖHLER, "The Expectation of Elijah and the Presence of the Kingdom of God," *JBL* 118 (1999) 464 n. 12. VAN IERSEL, *Mark*, 298: "At the time of the story, belief in the resurrection is so common among Jewish people that those who deny it have to be explicitly mentioned (12:18)." GUNDRY, *Mark*, 463: "As such, rising from the dead would not be meaningless to first century Jews. But the definite article is anaphoric: '*the* rising from the dead' refers back to *the Son of man's* rising from the dead" (his emphasis).

[6] LANE, *Mark*, 324: "The disciples' real question is, What have death and resurrection to do with the Son of Man?"

[7] For a highly speculative reconstruction of an alleged Aramaic source behind Mark 9:11-13, see M. CASEY, *Aramaic Sources of Mark's Gospel* (SNTSMS 102; Cambridge: Cambridge University Press, 1998) 111-37.

[8] On δεῖ as an expression of divine necessity, see W. POPKES, "δεῖ," *EDNT* 1.279-80.

That Elijah must come first reminds the audience of the scriptural expectation that Elijah, who ascended to heaven without dying (2 Kgs 2:11), would return before the great and manifest "Day of the Lord" comes (Mal 3:23; Sir 48:10).[9] This eschatological "Day of the Lord" is closely associated with the time of the eschatological resurrection of the dead to be inaugurated by the resurrection from the dead of Jesus as the Son of Man (9:9).[10] The disciples' objection that Elijah must come first implies that indeed Elijah has already returned in the transfiguration epiphany. The disciples are thus insinuating that if Elijah, the expected forerunner of the eschatological age, has returned as a heavenly figure rather than as an earthly mortal to undergo the death he escaped at his first coming, then why must Jesus, who was just transfigured into a heavenly figure like Elijah, die and rise as the Son of Man to inaugurate the eschatological age?[11]

4. *Mark 9:12: Jesus reaffirms the necessity of his suffering*

Jesus affirms the idea that Elijah will come first,[12] but he adds that he comes to "restore all things (ἀποκαθιστάνει πάντα)"

---

[9] Mal 3:23 and Sir 48:10 state that Elijah will come before the Day of the Lord. For a debate on whether there was a tradition that Elijah would come before the *Messiah*, see M.M. FAIERSTEIN, "Why Do the Scribes Say That Elijah Must Come First?" *JBL* 100 (1981) 75-86; D.C. ALLISON, "Elijah Must Come First," *JBL* 103 (1984) 256-58; J.A. FITZMYER, "More About Elijah Coming First," *JBL* 104 (1985) 295-96; MARCUS, *Way of the Lord*, 110; GUNDRY, *Mark*, 483-84.

[10] GUNDRY, *Mark*, 463, 484: "The disciples ask why the scribes say it is necessary for Elijah to come first, i.e. to come before the Day of the Lord and therefore in the disciples' view – since resurrection is associated with that day – before the Son of man's resurrection....The disciples appear to assume that the Son of man's resurrection will accompany or trigger the resurrection of others and thus occur on arrival of the Day of the Lord after Elijah's return....Given the eschatological nature of that day, the disciples would make this assumption quite naturally." See also ÖHLER, "Expectation of Elijah," 464.

[11] For a tradition that Elijah came again in the person of Phinehas to "taste death," see *L.A.B.* 48:1; ÖHLER, *Elia*, 24-27, 45-46; MURPHY, *Pseudo-Philo*, 184-85. JACOBSON (*Commentary on Pseudo-Philo*, 1063) states that *L.A.B.* 48:1 seems to be suggesting that those people who were translated to heaven without dying, such as Enoch, Elijah (Phinehas), and possibly Moses, "need to die before they can gain eternal life through resurrection."

[12] Some interpret Jesus' statement here as a sceptical question: "Coming first, does Elijah indeed restore all things?" or "Elijah, when he comes first, restores all things?" (see MARCUS, *Way of the Lord*, 94). But GUNDRY (*Mark*, 485) objects that "militating against this interpretation

(9:12).[13] This already begins to dispel the disciples' implicit notion that perhaps Elijah's appearance in the transfiguration epiphany fulfills the expectation that he must come first. The brief appearance of the heavenly Elijah with Moses to converse with the transfigured Jesus (9:4) can scarcely be understood as his "restoring all things."

Having affirmed the disciples' question about Elijah coming first, Jesus counters it with a question of his own: "But how is it written of the Son of Man that he should suffer greatly and be treated with contempt?" (9:12).[14] To the scriptural divine necessity that Elijah "must" (δεῖ) come first (9:11) Jesus adds the scriptural divine necessity that "it is written" (γέγραπται) that he suffer greatly (9:12), thus complementing the necessity of his resurrection from the dead (9:9).[15] By obeying God's command to listen (9:7) to what Jesus is saying here (9:9-12), the disciples and the audience are to realize that both Elijah's coming first and Jesus' suffering, death and resurrection are part of the necessity of the divine plan.

What Jesus says about the divine necessity of his suffering greatly before rising from the dead in 9:9-12 reinforces the first prediction of his resurrection after a necessary suffering and death:

> 8:31: "The Son of Man must suffer greatly (πολλὰ παθεῖν) and be rejected by the elders, the chief priests, and the scribes, and be killed, but after three days rise."
> 9:12: "Yet how is it written of the Son of Man that he should suffer greatly (πολλὰ πάθῃ) and be treated with contempt?"
> 9:9: "...until the Son of Man has risen from the dead."

---

is the declarative thrust of μέν, 'indeed, it's true,' which even in a question would assume an affirmative answer in the mind of the questioner."

[13] Jesus thus broadens and generalizes the scriptural expectations regarding Elijah. According to the LXX of Mal 3:23 Elijah will come before the Day of the Lord and "restore (ἀποκαταστήσει) the heart of a father to his son and the heart of a man to his neighbor." According to Sir 48:10 Elijah will come "to turn the heart of father to son and to restore (καταστῆσαι) the tribes of Jacob." In the words of GUNDRY (Mark, 464), "'Restores all things' enlarges Malachi's prophecy to include everything needed for the consummation." See also ÖHLER, "Expectation of Elijah," 465 n. 15.

[14] On the formula "it is written" as an exegetical conclusion based on a number of passages and for the possible passages in question, see MARCUS, Way of the Lord, 95-97; GUNDRY, Mark, 485-86; VAN IERSEL, Mark, 300.

[15] POPKES, "δεῖ," 279-80: "As an eschatological statement, δεῖ would point to a particular eschatological necessity....At least since Mark the interpretation of δεῖ as allusion from Scripture has been dominant."

The pivotal mandate of the transfiguration epiphany, "Listen to him!" (9:7), thus points the disciples and the audience not only back to heed Jesus' first passion prediction in 8:31-38 but also forward to heed Jesus' additional passion prediction in 9:9-12. By listening carefully and completely to these predictions of Jesus, the disciples and the audience are to realize that the necessity for Elijah to come first (9:11-12) does not nullify the necessity for Jesus to suffer and die before rising to the heavenly glory he anticipated in his transfiguration (9:2-4).

5. Mark 9:13: The Elijah who has already come also had to suffer and die

Jesus' concluding authoritative assertion, "But I say to you that indeed Elijah has come, yet they did to him whatever they wished, as it is written of him" (9:13), confirms the disciples' implication that Elijah has already come.[16] But Elijah has come not as the heavenly figure the disciples witnessed in the transfiguration epiphany, since Elijah has already come in the person of John the Baptist. From the beginning of Mark's narrative the audience has known that John the Baptist, who wore the clothing of a prophet (Zech 13:4) like Elijah (2 Kgs 1:8), represents the expected Elijah figure sent by God to be the "messenger" (Mal 3:1, 23) who prepares the way of Jesus (1:2-6).[17] That "they did to him whatever they wished (ἤθελον)" refers to the death of John

---

[16] Note how the emphatic καὶ ("indeed") before the name of Elijah in 9:13 serves to confirm the implication that Elijah has already come. The assertion "that indeed Elijah has already come" forms the midpoint of a concentric structure in 9:12-13 in which it is framed by expressions of the scriptural necessity for both Elijah and the Son of Man to suffer rejection and death:

a Yet how is it written of the Son of Man
b that he should suffer greatly and be treated with contempt?
c But I say to you that indeed Elijah has already come,
b' yet they did to him whatever they wished,
a' as it is written of him.

On this concentric structure, see GUNDRY, *Mark*, 465-66; C. MYERS, *Binding the Strong Man: A Political Reading of Mark's Story of Jesus* (Maryknoll, NY: Orbis, 1988) 253.

[17] On John the Baptist as Elijah in Mark 1:2-6, see HEIL, *Mark*, 30-32; ÖHLER, *Elia*, 31-37; IDEM, "Expectation of Elijah," 465.

through the cunning manipulation of Herod by Herodias, who "wished (ἤθελεν) to kill him" (6:19).

That John, as the Elijah who has already come, suffered and died in accord with the scriptural divine necessity "written" (γέγραπται) about him (9:13) reinforces for the disciples and the audience that Jesus as the Son of Man likewise must suffer as "written" (γέγραπται) about him (9:12) before rising from the dead (9:9) to the heavenly glory glimpsed at his transfiguration.[18] This is what the pivotal mandate (9:7) directs the disciples and the audience to heed. But by the end of Jesus' discourse after his transfiguration (9:9-13) there is no indication that the disciples as yet have really heard and understood what Jesus has said.

B. MARK 9:14-29: JESUS CAN HEAL HIS DEAF AND MUTE DISCIPLES THROUGH THEIR FAITH-FILLED PRAYER

Jesus' lamentful questions to the "faithless generation" represented by the crowd, the scribes (9:14) and the father who brought his son to Jesus after the disciples failed to heal him (9:17-18) – "How long am I to be with you? How long am I to bear with you?" (9:19; cf. Num 14:27) – express an ironic double meaning.[19] On

---

[18] On the scriptural necessity for Elijah to suffer as "an exegetical conclusion drawn from several passages," see MARCUS, *Way of the Lord*, 97-107. GUNDRY, *Mark*, 465: "Since neither Malachi nor any other OT prophet speaks about maltreatment of the coming Elijah, perhaps the clause, 'according as (καθώς) it is written about him' refers to the written record of the historical Elijah's maltreatment, considered a pattern for the maltreatment of Elijah returned as John...the very wording of the statement that 'they did as many things as they wanted' to the returned Elijah seems to carry the implication that what the enemies of Elijah wanted but failed to do in the OT the enemies of John have succeeded in doing." VAN IERSEL, *Mark*, 300: "Thus, the reader sees fulfilled in John the baptist what Jezebel had told Elijah she would do to him: 'So may the gods do to me, and more also, if I do not make your life like the life of one of the [killed] prophets by this time tomorrow' (1 Kgs 19.2)."

[19] GUNDRY, *Mark*, 489: "Thus the unbelieving generation takes in the father and the crowd. But it does not take in the disciples; for they stand opposite the crowd in the foregoing dispute, and Jesus will not mention unbelief on their part when they ask him why they failed at exorcising the spirit...It looks as though Jesus is condemning the crowd, including the father and the scribes in it, for making the disciples' failure a reason to dispute the power of Jesus himself, whom the disciples represent and whose shared exorcistic ability they have demonstrated in the past (6:13)."

the one hand, they express the extreme length of time Jesus has had to endure their lack of faith. On the other hand, they warn of the short period Jesus will still be with them before his approaching death, as anticipated by his absence from them during his transfiguration.

The mute (9:17) and, as it turns out, deaf (9:25) son that the distraught father brought to Jesus symbolically characterizes the disciples, who have remained metaphorically deaf and mute to the transfiguration's pivotal mandate directing them to listen (9:7) to Jesus' pronouncement regarding the necessity of his suffering (9:12) before rising from the dead (9:9). Jesus' pronouncement to the father that "all things are possible for one who believes!" (9:23) invites the father to acknowledge his faith in the divine healing power at work in Jesus.[20] It also indicates to the audience that faith in God will enable both Jesus and his followers to accept the divine necessity of suffering and death before rising to the heavenly glory foreshadowed by Jesus' transfiguration (8:31-9:13).

The father's remarkable display of humble faith, "I do believe; help my unbelief!" (9:24), not only extricates him from the "faithless generation" (9:19), but models the kind of faith the disciples and the audience need both to expel difficult demons and to follow Jesus' difficult way of suffering and death before resurrection to heavenly glory. In raising the boy who appeared to be dead (9:26), so that "he stood up" or "arose" (ἀνέστη, 9:27), Jesus symbolically alluded to his own death and resurrection (cf. ἀναστῆναι in 8:31; ἀναστῇ in 9:9). Only with a humble, faith-filled prayer for God's powerful help will the disciples and the audience be able, not only to expel "this kind" of mute and deaf demon from others (9:28-29), but to be healed of their own metaphorical deafness and muteness to the divine necessity of following Jesus' way of suffering and death before the resurrection to heavenly glory indicated by his transfiguration.[21]

---

[20] C.D. MARSHALL, *Faith as a Theme in Mark's Narrative* (SNTSMS 64; Cambridge: Cambridge University Press, 1989) 118-20.

[21] For a full discussion of Mark 9:14-29, see HEIL, *Mark*, 191-96. On the role of prayer here, see S.E. DOWD, *Prayer, Power, and the Problem of Suffering: Mark 11:22-25 in the Context of Markan Theology* (SBLDS 105; Atlanta: Scholars Press, 1988) 117-19.

C. MARK 9:31-32: THE DISCIPLES STILL DO NOT UNDERSTAND THAT
JESUS WILL BE KILLED BEFORE RISING

Jesus' next announcement to his disciples privately of his resurrection after death places a noteworthy emphasis upon his violent death: "The Son of Man is to be delivered into the hands of men, and they will kill him, and having been killed, after three days he will rise" (9:31; cf. 8:31; 9:9).[22] The addition of the passive participle, "having been killed" (ἀποκτανθείς), immediately after the active verb, "they will kill" (ἀποκτενοῦσιν) him underlines what the pivotal mandate (9:7) is urging the disciples and audience to hear in order to understand the significance of Jesus' transfiguration. Unlike Moses and Elijah, who were not delivered into the hands of men and killed before attaining heavenly glory, Jesus will be violently killed, but after three days rise to heavenly glory.

As after Jesus' first announcement that he would be killed before rising, when he rebuked Peter for thinking not "the things of God" but "the things of human beings" (8:31-33), and when the three disciples questioned what "rising from the dead" meant (9:9-10), so now the disciples still "did not understand the saying, and they were afraid to question him" (9:32). Their failure both to heed God's command to listen to Jesus (9:7) in order to understand and to question him demonstrates further their metaphorical deafness and muteness. As they were unable to expel the mute and deaf demon from the possessed boy because of their lack of prayer and faith (9:14-29), so now they are unable to eliminate their own muteness and deafness to the divine necessity of Jesus' violent death before rising to the heavenly glory prefigured by his transfiguration.

---

[22] MYERS, *Binding the Strong Man*, 260: "In case the reader is entertaining any doubts, Mark stresses twice that Jesus will be *killed*" (his emphasis). In comparing 9:31 with 8:31, GUNDRY (*Mark*, 503-4) notes: "Killing carries over, but changes from the passive voice to the active for additional stress on merciless violence. The passive is retained, however, in a second, participial reference to killing. That there is no need for this second reference shows the extent to which stress continues to fall on merciless violence."

D. MARK 10:32-34: JESUS TELLS THE TWELVE OF HIS DEATH BEFORE RESURRECTION

That Jesus "took along" (παραλαβὼν) the Twelve (10:32), underlining the special role of the Twelve to receive revelation from Jesus, reminds the audience how he "took along" (παραλαμβάνει) an elite subgroup of the Twelve – Peter, James and John – to witness the special private revelation of his transfiguration (9:2).[23] Jesus' authoritative prediction to the Twelve again emphasizes the necessity of his death before resurrection.[24] The chief priests and the scribes will condemn him "to death" (θανάτῳ) and deliver him to the Gentiles (10:33). The Gentiles in turn will mock him, spit upon him, scourge him, and "kill" (ἀποκτενοῦσιν) (him), but after three days he will rise (10:34).[25] Despite the transfiguration's pivotal mandate that the disciples listen to Jesus (9:7), there is no indication at this point that they have heard and understood him with regard to the necessity of his death before resurrection to heavenly glory. Indeed, in contrast to the previous announcements of his death and resurrection (8:31-33; 9:9-10, 31-32), there is now no immediate reaction whatsoever, adding to the suspense of their deafness and muteness.

E. MARK 10:35-45: HEAVENLY GLORY WITH JESUS COMES ONLY AFTER SUFFERING AND DEATH

Complementing Peter, who responded to Jesus as spokesman for the three disciples at the transfiguration (9:5-6), the other two disci-

---

[23] The Twelve were last called by Jesus to receive a special revelation in 9:35; see STOCK, *Boten*, 133-34.

[24] Jesus previously "taught" that he will die and rise (8:31; 9:31). That he now simply "tells" what is going to happen to him (10:32) underlines his authoritiatvie power to predict his resurrection after death, which is becoming more imminent; see MANICARDI, *Il cammino di Gesù*, 106-7. GUNDRY (*Mark*, 571) notes how the addition of "the things that were going to happen to him" (10:32) "lends greater weight to Jesus' power of prediction by pointing to the nearness and certainty of fulfilment."

[25] The ellipsis of a fourth "him" in 10:34 places even more emphasis upon the verb "kill." See GUNDRY, *Mark*, 572-73.

ples, James and John, together make their own request of Jesus (9:35).[26] Their request serves as an indirect response to the previous passion prediction (10:32-34), to which there was no immediate reaction, and indicates to the audience their continuing lack of understanding about the suffering and death that precedes heavenly glory. Whereas Peter erred in suggesting the placing of Moses and Elijah in the same category of heavenly glory as Jesus by building a tent for each, James and John err by wanting for themselves the places of preeminence – seats at the right and left – with Jesus in his glory (10:37). In response to Jesus' first prediction of his death and resurrection Peter focused only on the suffering and death and failed to hear the promise of the resurrection (8:31-32). In response to Jesus' last prediction of his death and resurrection (10:32-34) James and John, who have heard Jesus speak of his coming in the glory of his Father (8:38) and have witnessed Jesus' temporary transfiguration into heavenly glory (9:2-3), focus only on the glory while neglecting the suffering and death (10:37).[27]

In asking for the most prominent places next to Jesus, the brothers James and John, after experiencing the glory of the transfigured Jesus, have modified Jesus' coming "in the glory (δόξῃ) of his Father" (8:38) to a coming "in your glory (δόξῃ)" (10:37). The request of James and John makes no mention of the necessity for followers of Jesus to take up the cross and lose their lives for the sake of Jesus and the gospel in order to save them and join Jesus in glory (8:34-38). After underscoring the need for James and John to "drink of" and "be baptized in" the same suffering and death he will undergo (10:38-39), Jesus reminds them that his glory is ultimately the glory of his Father, who has prepared (ἡτοίμασται, divine passive) the requested places of heavenly honor (10:40).[28] Jesus con-

---

[26] Since the transfiguration John alone (9:38) and Peter again (10:28) have addressed Jesus as spokesmen for the rest of the disciples.

[27] VAN IERSEL, *Mark*, 333: "Where Peter seemed to have heard only what Jesus had said about the execution of the Son of Man Jesus, James and John give the impression that they have heard only what he has said about his resurrection."

[28] GUNDRY, *Mark*, 578: "...in all probability the passive obliquely refers to God as the preparer – cf. Matt 20:23 ['prepared by my Father']." This does not necessarily mean, as VAN IERSEL (*Mark*, 335) suggests, that the places at the right and left of Jesus have already been prepared for Moses and Elijah.

cludes with a further revelation about the significance of his death as freely accepted humble service for others before he enters into and comes again in glory: "For the Son of Man did not come to be served but to serve and to give his life as a ransom for many" (10:45).[29] Will not only James and John but the other ten disciples (10:41) and the audience heed the transfiguration's pivotal mandate and listen to Jesus (9:7)?

F. MARK 12:1-12: AS THE BELOVED SON OF GOD JESUS WILL BE KILLED BUT VINDICATED

In a parable he addresses to the Jewish leaders in the temple (12:1-12), Jesus tells how the owner (God) of the vineyard finally sends to the tenants (Jewish leadership), who have already killed or mistreated all of his servants (prophets) (12:2-5), his beloved son (υἱὸν ἀγαπητόν), thinking, "They will respect my son (τὸν υἱόν μου)" (12:6). This reminds the audience of the transfiguration's pivotal mandate uttered by God's voice from the cloud: "This is my Son, the beloved (ὁ υἱός μου ὁ ἀγαπητός); listen to him!" (9:7; cf. 1:11). That the tenants killed (ἀπέκτειναν, 12:8) the beloved son, after saying to one another, "Come, let us kill (ἀποκτείνωμεν) him, and the inheritance will be ours" (12:7), recalls Jesus' predictions that he will be killed (ἀποκτανθῆναι, 8:31; ἀποκτενοῦσιν…ἀποκτανθείς, 9:31; ἀποκτενοῦσιν, 10:34) by both the Jewish leaders and the Gentiles. That Jesus, the beloved Son, represents "the stone which the builders rejected (ἀπεδοκίμασαν)" (12:10) in his quotation of Ps 117:22-23 (LXX) echoes his prediction that he must "be rejected (ἀποδοκιμασθῆναι) by the elders, the chief priests, and the scribes" (8:31).

Although Jesus, "the stone," will be rejected and killed, God will marvelously vindicate him by transforming him into the "cornerstone" or "head of the corner" (12:10-11), which implies his resurrection from

---

[29] On the significance of "ransom" (λύτρον) in 10:45 as a metaphorical reference to a ritual expiation for the offenses of many, see A. YARBRO COLLINS, "The Signification of Mark 10:45 Among Gentile Christians," *HTR* 90 (1997) 371-82. On Mark 10:41-45, see O. WISCHMEYER, "Herrschen als Dienen – Mk 10,41-45," *ZNW* 90 (1999) 28-44.

the dead.[30] This reinforces what the transfiguration's pivotal mandate (9:7) wants the disciples and the audience to hear and understand. Jesus will attain the heavenly glory prefigured by his transfiguration only after he is rejected and killed as God's beloved Son.

G. MARK 12:18-27: JESUS TEACHES THAT GOD WILL RAISE THE DEAD TO LIFE

In his refutation of the attempt by the Sadducees to discredit a belief in the resurrection of the dead (12:18-27) Jesus asserts that when people rise from the dead, they become "like angels in heaven" (12:25). When he was transfigured, Jesus' "clothes became very radiantly white, such as no bleacher on the earth could thus whiten" (9:3), indicating that he has temporarily become like an angel in heaven.[31] Jesus' transfiguration into an angel-like heavenly figure, which foreshadows his future resurrection from the dead, bolsters for the audience his pronouncement that when the dead are raised they enter into a heavenly existence that transcends earthly categories such as marriage.

Jesus concludes that when God revealed himself to Moses as "the God of Abraham, the God of Isaac, and the God of Jacob" (Exod 3:6), he indicated that "he is not the God of the dead but of the living!" (12:26-27). Since the three patriarchs were already dead when God uttered this to Moses, it implies "the power of God" (12:24) to raise them from the dead.[32] In other words, since God in his covenantal

---

[30] GUNDRY, *Mark*, 663: "The marvel of the Lord's making the rejected stone head of a corner agrees with Jesus' having predicted that he will rise from the dead three days after being killed (8:31; 9:31; 10:33-34)...becoming head of a corner refers to rulership following resurrection, not to resurrection itself." VAN IERSEL, *Mark*, 369: "The contrast between the rejection of the stone and its privileged place as the cornerstone of the building suggests that the murder of the son by the tenants will be followed by his rehabilitation, or, to put it in terms of the total story, by his resurrection from the dead." See also J.P. HEIL, "The Narrative Strategy and Pragmatics of the Temple Theme in Mark," *CBQ* 59 (1997) 81-83.

[31] On the transfigured Jesus as an angel-like heavenly figure, see chap. 4.

[32] GUNDRY, *Mark*, 708-9: "It is not enough to say that Jesus plays on Jewish belief that the patriarchs and martyrs are even now living to God (4 Macc 7:19; 16:25). If they are already living to God without having been resurrected, where lies the necessity of a future resurrection? Jesus would be saying nothing to answer the Sadducees' question."

fidelity to the people of Israel promises to be the saving God not of those who are "dead" but of those who are "living," the patriarchs of Israel – Abraham, Isaac, and Jacob – cannot remain dead but are still living through the power of God, so that there is a resurrection of the dead.[33] If the disciples and the audience heed the transfiguration's pivotal mandate to listen to Jesus (9:7), they will hear in this pronouncement that although Jesus, unlike Moses and Elijah, will be put to death, he will surely be raised from the dead like the patriarchs, since God is "not the God of the dead but of the living!" (12:27).[34] This gives them hope in God's power also to raise them to new life after they have given their lives to God for the sake of Jesus and the gospel (8:33-35).[35]

H. MARK 13:26: JESUS IS STILL TO COME IN CLOUDS WITH MUCH POWER AND GLORY

The three disciples who witnessed Jesus' transfiguration – Peter, James, and John (9:2) – are joined by Andrew (cf. 1:16-20) for another special private revelation from Jesus sitting on the Mount of Olives opposite the temple (13:3). Jesus discloses to them that at the end of the world (13:24-25) people will see him as "the Son of Man coming in clouds with much power and glory" (13:26; cf. Dan 7:13-14). Whereas Moses and Elijah were transported by the divine overshadowing cloud (νεφέλη) back to heaven after their appearance in glory with the transfigured Jesus on earth (9:7-8), Jesus, after his death and resurrection to heavenly glory, will be transported in clouds (ἐν νεφέλαις) from heaven to earth, where he will send out the angels to

---

[33] HEIL, *Mark*, 243-44. GUNDRY, *Mark*, 703: "Since the Sadducees have raised a question about resurrection, Jesus transfers God's statement to a new temporal frame, viz., the future. Just as that statement, when pointed backward, demands past physical life for Abraham, Isaac, and Jacob even though they are now dead, so also the statement, when pointed forward, demands future physical life for Abraham, Isaac, and Jacob even though they are now dead."

[34] Although the disciples are not explicitly present for the scene with the Sadducees in Mark 12:18-27, they are implicitly present during Jesus' acitivity in the temple; see 11:1, 14, 20-25; 12:43; 13:1.

[35] HEIL, "Temple Theme in Mark," 84.

gather together his elect from wherever they have been scattered (13:26-27).[36]

That Jesus as the Son of Man is still to come "in clouds with much power and glory (δόξης)" (13:26) reminds the audience of Jesus' previous prediction that as the Son of Man he is still to come "in his Father's glory (δόξῃ) with the holy angels" (8:38).[37] The transfiguration's pivotal mandate to listen to Jesus (9:7) thus directs the disciples and the audience backward (8:38) and forward (13:26) to these two pronouncements about Jesus' future coming in glory, so that they will realize that the transfigured glory of Jesus before his suffering and death is only a preliminary glimpse of his final coming in glory after his suffering, death and resurrection (8:31; 9:9, 12, 31; 10:33-34).

I. MARK 14:8: A WOMAN ANOINTS JESUS FOR BURIAL

An anonymous woman honors Jesus, who is soon to be killed (14:1-2), with an extravagant gesture of hospitality. She "came with an alabaster flask of perfumed ointment, costly genuine spikenard," and after breaking the flask, she poured out the perfumed ointment on Jesus' head, while he was reclining at table in the house of Simon the leper at Bethany (14:3). Jesus interprets her lavishly hospitable anointing as a prophetic gesture anticipating his upcoming burial (14:8).[38] Because she acknowledges and esteems the death of Jesus, this woman stands in sharp contrast to the disciples, who have not heeded the transfiguration's mandate to listen to Jesus (9:7) in order to understand and accept the necessity of his death as a prerequisite to the heavenly glory anticipated by his transfiguration.[39]

---

[36] On the vehicular function of clouds, see chap. 7.

[37] GUNDRY, Mark, 786: "The correspondence between 'with the holy angels' (8:38) and 'with much power' (13:26) favors that 'much power' (δυνάμεως πολλῆς) means a large army of angels (cf. the sending of angels in the next clause, and the LXX of 2 Chr 24:24; Ezek 38:15)."

[38] On Mark 14:8 GUNDRY (Mark, 804) states that "Jesus is making a passion prediction. His being in the prime of life rules out an implication of normal death. The indirectness of the prediction — burial only implies death — suits the presence of the woman and perhaps of others in addition to the Twelve."

[39] J.P. HEIL, "Mark 14,1-52: Narrative Structure and Reader-Response," Bib 71 (1990) 310-11.

J. MARK 14:22-25: JESUS INTERPRETS HIS FINAL MEAL
AS SYMBOLIC OF HIS DEATH

After Jesus again predicts that as the Son of Man he will be delivered/betrayed (παραδίδοται) to death (14:21; cf. 9:31; 10:33), he interprets his final Passover meal with his disciples (14:12-16) as a symbolic anticipation of the sacrificial death he must undergo before he partakes of the eschatological banquet in the kingdom of God. As they were eating, Jesus offered the disciples bread he designated as "my body" (τὸ σῶμά μου, 14:22), the "body" (τὸ σῶμά μου, 14:8) already anointed for death and burial.[40] After they all drank from the cup Jesus gave them (14:23), he designated it as "my blood of the covenant, which will be poured out for many" (14:24), thus interpreting his death as the sacrifice that establishes *the* (new) covenant which atones for the sins of all people.[41] Although this is Jesus' last meal on earth, he looks forward to partaking of the heavenly banquet in the kingdom of God (14:25) after his triumph over death through his resurrection. The transfiguration's pivotal mandate (9:7) thus enjoins the disciples and the audience to listen to these words of Jesus in order to understand that his transfiguration into a heavenly figure portends his future partaking of the heavenly banquet in the kingdom of God that will occur only after his sacrificial death.

K. MARK 14:27-31: JESUS AGAIN PREDICTS HIS RESURRECTION
AFTER DEATH TO UNHEEDING DISCIPLES

In the course of predicting that all of his disciples will abandon him, Jesus again predicts his resurrection after death. In an adaptation

---

[40] GUNDRY, *Mark*, 830: "Taken together, Jesus' breaking the bread, giving a piece of it to each of the Twelve, telling them to take it, and saying that it represents his body make yet another passion prediction, this one taking the form of an object lesson acted out and accompanied by interpretation." See also HEIL, *Mark*, 288-89.

[41] HEIL, *Mark*, 290-92; IDEM, "Mark 14,1-52," 317-20; L.C. BOUGHTON, "'Being Shed for You/Many': Time-Sense and Consequences in the Synoptic Cup Citations," *TynBul* 48 (1997) 249-70. GUNDRY, *Mark*, 832: "For it is in Jesus' shed blood that Mark finds a passion prediction...'Of the covenant' and 'being poured out for many' (cf. Isa 53:12 MT) indicate the sacrificial character of Jesus' approaching death, its violence and atoning value for others..."

of Zech 13:7 Jesus accentuates how his suffering and death are ultimately the doing of God himself: "I" (God) "will strike" (with suffering and death) "the shepherd" (Jesus), and "the sheep" (disciples) will
be scattered (14:27).[42] But after being struck by God with death Jesus
will be raised up by God and go before the disciples to Galilee (14:28).
Although Peter insists that he will be the exception to this abandonment by all (14:29), Jesus predicts that Peter will deny him three times
(14:30). Peter then vehemently objects: "Even if I must die with you,
I will not deny you!" And the rest of the disciples similarly disclaim
Jesus' prediction (14:31).

Although Peter's objection seems to indicate that he has heard the
prediction of Jesus' death, there is no indication that he and the rest of
the disciples have heard the promised assurance of resurrection after
the necessity of death.[43] Indeed, Peter's objection that he will not deny
(ἀπαρνήσομαι) Jesus, even if he must die with him (14:31), rings
ironic for the audience who has heard Jesus tell Peter and the disciples
that they must deny (ἀπαρνησάσθω, 8:34) themselves, take up their
cross, and lose their lives for his sake in order to save them (8:35).[44]
The disciples still have not heeded what the transfiguration's pivotal
mandate has urged them to hear (9:7), namely, the necessity for them
to suffer and die with Jesus in order to share in the resurrection to
heavenly glory (8:31-38) prefigured by his transfiguration.

---

[42] S.L. COOK, "The Metamorphosis of a Shepherd: The Tradition History of Zechariah
11:17 + 13:7-9," *CBQ* 55 (1993) 464: "By using Zechariah, Mark places the passion within
the context of the eschatological time of fulfillment. Mark's use of the first person future
πατάξω ('I will strike') is significant in this regard. The change to 'I [God] will smite'
emphasizes that it is God who is performing his eschatological work in Jesus' passion. It is
God who appoints Jesus to die on the cross, and Jesus' suffering is to be understood as an act
of obedience." See also HEIL, *Mark*, 294-95; VAN IERSEL, *Mark*, 429-30. GUNDRY (*Mark*,
845), on the other hand, thinks that the striker remains unidentified and thus "keeps God from
blame."

[43] TOLBERT, *Sowing the Gospel*, 212-13: "Lost in Peter's eagerness to repel any reproach
on his future actions is Jesus' promise, 'But after I am raised up, I will go before you to Galilee' (14:28). Not only does Peter ignore the remark but the earlier confusion of the disciples
concerning 'what the rising from the dead meant' (9:10) bodes ill for their ability to share in
this assurance."

[44] GUNDRY (*Mark*, 846) notes how the use of the subjunctive mood in the protasis of
Peter's objection (14:31) suggests that Peter "thinks the necessity of his suffering with Jesus a
remoter possibility than that of his fellow disciples' being tripped up (contrast v 29)."

L. MARK 14:32-42: JESUS ACCEPTS DEATH THROUGH PRAYER WHILE HIS DISCIPLES SLEEP

Peter, James, and John are the three Jesus "takes along" (παρα-λαμβάνει) not only to witness his transfiguration (9:2), but also to participate in the scene of his prayer at Gethsemane (14:33). In and through his praying, Jesus, although tested by his distress and sorrow over his imminent death (14:34), and voicing his quite human desire to avoid the "cup" of suffering and death, nevertheless submitted his own will to God's will that he suffer and die (14:35-36). That Jesus "finds" the three disciples "sleeping" (14:37) is precisely what he warned them against in his discourse preparing them for the time before his final coming: "Watch, therefore; for you do not know when the lord of the house will come...and *find you sleeping*" (13:35-36). The disciples' sleeping, then, not only indicates their inability to stay awake and "watch" (14:34) during this critical time while Jesus prays before his suffering and death, but also points to their and the audience's potential failure to be prepared for Jesus' final coming in the glory anticipated by his transfiguration.

After Jesus finds the disciples sleeping, he commands them to "watch and pray" (14:38). The addition of "pray" to his earlier command to "watch" (v. 34) indicates the significance and power of Jesus' own praying. Now that he has prayed, he can command and empower his disciples likewise to pray. That Jesus prays precisely while the disciples sleep and are unable to watch indicates to the audience that the prayer of Jesus is not only a model to be emulated but the basis, source, and empowerment of prayer. The sleeping disciples and the audience can "watch and pray" only because Jesus watched and prayed. They pray on the strength of Jesus' powerful prayer.

Jesus commands the disciples to watch and pray, "so that you may not come into testing (πειρασμόν).[45] The spirit is willing but the flesh

---

[45] On πειρασμός (test, trial, temptation) SPICQ (*Theological Lexicon*, 3.86) notes that it "is not an incitation to evil, a wicked solicitation – which is what 'temptation' suggests in modern English – but a difficult or painful trial. This test permits an assessment of the strength, the faithfulness, the love of the believer (which is a good thing), but it is dangerous, and that explains the humble request to be excused from it."

is weak" (14:38). By his praying Jesus has demonstrated how the disciples and the audience can escape the testing of their calling to deny themselves, take up their cross, and follow Jesus (8:34) on his way to suffering and death by submitting their own wills to God's will. The disciples, whose "spirit" is ready to die with Jesus (14:31), but whose "flesh" prevents them from staying alert and watching (14:37), illustrate the tension between the willing spirit and the weak flesh. Jesus exemplifies how to overcome this tension in and through prayer. He voiced his own concerns of the "flesh" as he begged God to take away his cup of suffering and death. But in and through his prayer his "willing spirit" predominated over the "weak flesh" as he submitted his own will to that of God (14:36).[46]

When Jesus returns after praying a second time (14:39), he finds the disciples again sleeping (14:40). Their inability to answer him reminds the audience of Peter's perplexed incomprehension of Jesus' transfiguration:

9:6: He did not (οὐ) know what to reply (ἤδει τί ἀποκριθῇ), for they had become terrified.
14:40: They did not know what to reply (οὐκ ᾔδεισαν τί ἀποκριθῶσιν) to him.

This illustration of the disciples' continuing misunderstanding underscores the importance and power of Jesus' praying for them.[47]

After Jesus returns a third and final time and finds the disciples still sleeping (14:41), his exhortation, "Get up, let us go!" (14:42), indicates to the audience the powerful effect Jesus' prayer has on him and his disciples. Before he withdrew to pray, Jesus commanded his disciples to "sit here" (v. 32) and "remain here" (v. 34) while he prayed (v. 35). But after he has prayed, Jesus empowers his disciples to "get up" or

---

[46] On Mark 14:38 GARRETT (*Temptations of Jesus*, 93) comments: "Jesus is here admonishing his followers to *do as he has done*. In other words, Jesus' just-concluded petitions that the hour may pass and that God remove the cup were likewise prayers to escape πειρασμός. Jesus has beseeched God in order that he might himself avoid entry into the time of trial; now he exhorts the disciples to do likewise" (Garrett's emphasis).

[47] The parallel between Mark 9:6 and 14:40 "suggests that in Mark 14:40 the human frailty and misunderstanding of the disciples is being highlighted," according to R.E. BROWN, *The Death of the Messiah: From Gethsemane to the Grave: A Commentary on the Passion Narratives in the Four Gospels* (ABRL; New York: Doubleday, 1994) 206.

"rise" (ἐγείρεσθε) from their inert, sleeping position and enables them to go with him – "let *us* go (ἄγωμεν)!" Now that Jesus has been strengthened through his prayer, he and his disciples can go together to play their respective roles in God's plan – the disciples to be scattered (14:27) and Jesus to be betrayed (14:41-42).[48]

The disciples and the audience must heed the transfiguration's mandate to listen (9:7) to Jesus' command for them to watch and pray (14:38; cf. 13:35-37). By praying the Gethsemane prayer of Jesus they can likewise submit their wills to God's will and follow Jesus' way of suffering and death, in order to share in the heavenly glory anticipated by his transfiguration. The Gethsemane prayer of Jesus empowers the audience to play their role in God's plan by watching and praying as they await Jesus' final coming in the glory prefigured by his transfiguration.

M. MARK 14:62: JESUS WILL BE SEEN SEATED AT GOD'S RIGHT AND COMING WITH THE CLOUDS OF HEAVEN

Jesus further demonstrates the fortitude he gained through his Gethsemane prayer, when he stands before the high priest and the assembly of Jewish leaders seeking to put him to death (14:1, 55). By directly responding to the high priest's question, "Are you the Christ, the Son of the Blessed One?" (14:61), with the words, "I am" (14:62), Jesus not only boldly affirms his true messianic identity but courageously accepts the death to which his confession leads.

But he goes on to valiantly proclaim his ultimate vindication and triumph over death to the assembly of Jewish leaders and to the audience by promising that "you will see the Son of Man seated at the right hand of the Power (Ps 110:1) and coming with the clouds of heaven (Dan 7:13; cf. Mark 13:26)!" (14:62). As the Son of Man, Jesus must suffer, die, and rise in accord with God's scriptural will (8:31; 9:9, 12, 31; 10:33, 45; 14:21, 41). But as the Son of Man, Jesus, after the resurrection following his death, will be exalted by God ("the Power") and vindicated over his enemies (cf. Ps 110:1 in Mark 12:36)

---

[48] For a full discussion of Mark 14:32-42, see HEIL, *Mark*, 297-304.

before his final coming in glory "with the clouds (νεφελῶν; cf. 13:26; 9:7-8) of heaven" (14:62).[49]

The transfiguration's mandate (9:7) bids the disciples (Peter is still present, 14:54) and the audience to listen to this courageous confession of Jesus. Just as Jesus gained courage by his prayer and by faith in his ultimate triumph over death, so the disciples and the audience can gain courage to endure possible suffering and death (13:11-13), in order to share in the heavenly glory presaged by the transfiguration of Jesus.

N. MARK 15:34-36: WILL ELIJAH COME TO TAKE JESUS DOWN FROM THE CROSS?

The attempt of some of the bystanders at Jesus' crucifixion to prevent his death by twisting his prayer of lament from Ps 22:2, "My God (Ελωι), My God (Ελωι), why have you abandoned me?" (15:34), into a mocked plea, "Look, he is calling Elijah!" (15:35), in order to see his rescue, "Let us see if Elijah comes to take him down!" (15:36), illustrates their stubborn blindness to the divine necessity of Jesus' death.[50] The irony for the audience is that not even Elijah can rescue Jesus, because as Jesus himself stated, "Elijah already has come and they did to him whatever they pleased, as it is written of him" (9:13). In the person of John the Baptist (1:6; 6:14-29) Elijah has already come and suffered the same fate Jesus is now suffering in accord with God's will.[51] Furthermore, the transfiguration's mandate has urged the audience to listen (9:7) to Jesus' passion predictions, in order to understand that unlike the Elijah in the transfiguration epiphany, who attained heavenly glory without being put to death, Jesus must suffer a death perpetrated by the leaders of his people before attaining the heavenly glory foreshadowed by his transfiguration.

---

[49] GUNDRY (*Mark*, 886) notes how "the Power" in 14:62 "substitutes for an expected 'God' in the preceding reference to heavenly session."

[50] On Elijah as a helper of those in distress, see ÖHLER, *Elia*, 139-53.

[51] GUNDRY, *Mark*, 968; J.P. HEIL, "The Progressive Narrative Pattern of Mark 14,53-16,8," *Bib* 73 (1992) 349.

O. MARK 15:39: THE CENTURION CONFESSES THAT THE CRUCIFIED JESUS WAS SON OF GOD

From the overshadowing cloud at Jesus' transfiguration the voice of God declared: "This is my beloved Son; listen to him!" (9:7). But the disciples failed to listen to Jesus' pronouncements of the divine necessity of his suffering, death, and resurrection, in order to understand his unique relation of sonship to God. The audience experiences a shocking irony, then, when the Roman centurion who witnessed Jesus' death is the only human being to confess this sonship: "Truly this man was Son of God!" (15:39).[52] The gentile centurion utters this climactic confession after "seeing how he expired" (15:39), a reference to Jesus' letting out a loud cry (φωνὴν μεγάλην) as he expired (15:37), which in turn refers to the loud cry (φωνῇ μεγάλη) of Jesus' quotation of Ps 22:2, "My God, my God, why have you abandoned me?" (15:34).[53]

Having endured God's silent abandonment, symbolized by the supernatural darkness God has caused (15:33) instead of rescuing him from death at the hands of reviling accusers (15:29-32), Jesus begs for the reason "why" or "for what purpose" (εἰς τί) God has abandoned him (15:34). Although indicative of his intense anguish as he dies alone and without divine intervention, Jesus' loud scream is not a cry of despair but the lamentful prayer of "the suffering just one," uttered with complete confidence that his God has a purpose for abandoning him at this crucial moment. By witnessing the way Jesus expired, which implies the hearing of his final loud "voice" (φωνῇ in v. 34; φωνὴν in v. 37), the centurion ironically obeys the "voice" (φωνὴ) of God in the

---

[52] K. STOCK, "Das Bekenntnis des Centurio: Mk 15,39 im Rahmen des Markusevangeliums," *ZKT* 100 (1978) 289-301.

[53] GUNDRY, *Mark*, 969: "Mark's noting the loudness in both v 34 and v 37, providing no different words for the shout in v 37, and subordinating that shout to the new element of expiration all favor a back reference to the previously quoted shout." BROWN, *Death of the Messiah*, 1144 n. 3: "In discussing the relationship of the vocalized loud cry in 15:34 and the unvocalized loud cry in 15:37, I found it more likely that Mark did not think of two cries but in 15:37 was simply resuming his storyline (after interruption in 15:35-36) by recalling the loud cry he had mentioned in 15:34."

transfiguration's mandate to listen to Jesus (9:7). He is able to acknowledge that Jesus was truly Son of God, thus confirming God's own voice at the transfiguration, only because he witnessed how Jesus revealed himself to be Son of God by dying on the cross with a loud voice of total trust in God's plan that he suffer and die (cf. 12:6; 14:36) before rising to the heavenly glory prefigured by his transfiguration.[54]

P. MARK 16:5-8: A WHITE ROBED MAN DECLARES
THAT THE CRUCIFIED JESUS HAS BEEN RAISED

The Gospel of Mark concludes with a mandatory epiphany (16:5-8) exhibiting allusions for the audience to the pivotal mandatory epiphany of the transfiguration (9:2-8).[55] The audience associates the epiphanic, angelic "young man" clothed in a white (λευκήν) robe (16:5) with the epiphanic, transfigured Jesus, whose "clothes became very radiantly white (λευκὰ), such as no bleacher on the earth could thus whiten (λευκᾶναι)" (9:3). Whereas the whiteness of Jesus' clothing indicates his temporary transformation into a heavenly figure, the white robe of the young man indicates the heavenly origin of this angelic figure who brings a divine revelation and mandate to the women who see him after they enter Jesus' tomb (16:5).[56]

The angelic young man tells the women that although they "seek Jesus of Nazareth, the crucified. He has been raised! He is not here;

---

[54] Although it is implied that the rending of the veil in the temple sanctuary (15:38) is the result of Jesus' expiration with a loud voice (15:37), what the centurion "saw" (ἰδὼν, 15:39) is not limited to the rending of the veil (cf. GUNDRY, *Mark*, 950; H.M. JACKSON, "The Death of Jesus in Mark and the Miracle from the Cross," *NTS* 33 [1987] 28.), but includes everything the centurion saw (and heard) in 15:33-38 (BROWN, *Death of the Messiah*, 1144-45; C. BURCHARD, "Markus 15:34," *ZNW* 74 [1983] 1-11.).

[55] For a treatment of Mark 16:5-8 as an angelophany, see HEIL, *Mark*, 346-50. For a comparison of 9:2-9 with 16:1-8, see J.L. MAGNESS, *Sense and Absence: Structure and Suspension in the Ending of Mark's Gospel* (Atlanta: Scholars Press, 1986) 102-3.

[56] On white clothing as indicative of heavenly figures, see chap. 4. For other examples of "young men" or "men" as the equivalent of angels appearing in epiphanies, see Acts 1:10; 2 Macc 3:26, 33. In Acts 10:30 Cornelius refers to the "angel" who appeared to him earlier in 10:3 as a "man." GUNDRY, *Mark*, 991: "The whiteness of the robe associates the young man with Jesus, whose garments turned an unearthly white at the Transfiguration (9:3), and begins to identify the young man as a heavenly figure."

behold, the place where they laid him!" (16:6). The divine revelation that the Jesus who was crucified and whom the women still expect to find crucified (ἐσταυρωμένον, perfect tense) has now been raised (ἠγέρθη, aorist tense) by God (divine passive) confirms Jesus' previous predictions of the resurrection following the divine necessity of his suffering and death (8:31; 9:9, 12, 31; 10:34; 14:28). The heavenly young man thus reinforces the divine authority of these predictions, which the transfiguration's mandate urged the disciples and the audience to heed (9:7).

The young man then utters to the women the mandate of this mandatory epiphany: "But go and tell his disciples and Peter, 'He is going before you to Galilee; there you will see him, as he told you'" (16:7). Peter is singled out not only because he distinguished himself from the other disciples as the one who said he would not abandon Jesus (14:29), although he later denied him three times (14:30-31, 66-72), but also because he was the disciple who "did not know what to reply" (9:6), when he suggested the building of three tents in response to the transfiguration that anticipated Jesus' resurrection after death (9:5). That the risen Jesus is going before his disciples to Galilee fulfills his previous prediction to them that "after I have been raised up, I will go before you to Galilee" (14:28). In seeing that the crucified one has been raised by the power of God the disciples will "see that the kingdom of God has come in power" (9:1). The words, "as he told you" (16:7), reminding the disciples that Jesus himself told them of his resurrection after death, complements the transfiguration's mandate, which urged the disciples to hear Jesus' predictions of his resurrection after death (9:7).

Just as the disciples repeatedly failed to obey the transfiguration's mandate to listen to Jesus' predictions of his resurrection after death, so the women at the tomb fail to obey the angelophany's mandate to communicate the revelation of Jesus' resurrection to the disciples. The women ran away from the tomb in astonishment and said nothing to anyone because of their fear (16:8). The women's silence thus prevents the disciples from telling others of the transfiguration that can now be properly understood because Jesus has risen from the dead (9:9).[57] Although the audience presumes that the revelation of Jesus'

---

[57] P. DANOVE, "The Characterization and Narrative Function of the Women at the Tomb (Mark 15,40-41.47; 16,1-8)," *Bib* 77 (1996) 391: "The women through their silence remove the possibility for these disciples to fulfill their mandate to narrate the events of the transfiguration."

resurrection eventually reaches the disciples, the women's silence brings the narrative to an open-ended conclusion.[58]

It is left to the audience to make known the message of Jesus' resurrection which the fearful women are too amazed to utter. By pointing back to the beginning of the gospel in Galilee, the open end of the narrative invites the audience to continue the task of proclaiming the gospel of Jesus Christ, Son of God (1:1), not just in Galilee but beyond it to all peoples of the world (13:10; 14:9), with the risen Jesus going before them and leading the way.[59] Following the lead of the risen Jesus calls for the audience to obey the transfiguration's mandate (9:7) to listen to Jesus' challenge for them to deny themselves, take up their cross, follow Jesus, and save their lives by losing them for the sake of Jesus and the gospel (8:34-38), in order to share in the heavenly glory foreshadowed by his transfiguration. By heeding the revelatory mandates of both the transfiguration (9:7) and the angelophany (16:6-7), the audience can tell others of the significance of Jesus' transfiguration (9:9) as the assurance that resurrection to heavenly glory follows suffering and death for the gospel of Jesus.[60]

Q. CONCLUSION

The mandate of the Markan transfiguration epiphany, "Listen to him!" (9:7), has pivoted the disciples and the audience back to Jesus' first pronouncement for them to follow him on his way to suffering

---

[58] E.S. MALBON, "Fallible Followers: Women and Men in the Gospel of Mark," *The Bible and Feminist Hermeneutics* (*Semeia* 28; ed. M.A. Tolbert; Chico: Scholars Press, 1983) 45; GUNDRY, *Mark*, 1009: "Mark's audience still expect the prediction that the disciples will see Jesus in Galilee to reach fulfilment despite the women's present failure to tell the disciples according to the instructions given them. Too many other predictions of Jesus have reached fulfilment in Mark to leave any doubt that this one will likewise reach fulfilment."

[59] MANICARDI, Il cammino di Gesù, 171-93; C.H. GIBLIN, "The Beginning of the Ongoing Gospel (Mk 1,2-16,8)," *The Four Gospels 1992: Festschrift Frans Neirynck* (BETL 100; ed. F. Van Segbroeck, et al; Leuven: Leuven University, 1992) 975-85.

[60] On the role of the audience in bringing closure to the narrative, see MAGNESS, *Sense and Absence*; R. VIGNOLO, "Una finale reticente: interpretazione narrativa di Mc 16,8," *RivB* 38 (1990) 129-89; P. DANOVE, *The End of Mark's Story: A Methodological Study* (BIS 3; Leiden: Brill, 1993); J.D. HESTER, "Dramatic Inconclusion: Irony and the Narrative Rhetoric of the Ending of Mark," *JSNT* 57 (1995) 61-86.

and death before being resurrected to heavenly glory (8:31-38). It has also pivoted them forward to the subsequent predictions of the necessity for him (9:12, 31-32; 10:32-34; 12:1-12; 14:8, 22-25, 27-31, 32-42) as well as them (10:35-45) to give their lives in humble, suffering service for others with the assurance of being raised from the dead (9:9; 12:18-27; 16:5-8) and seeing his final coming in the heavenly glory (13:26; 14:62) prefigured by his transfiguration.

Elijah has already come in the person of John the Baptist (1:2-6), and "they did to him whatever they wished" (9:13), that is, put him to death (6:19), as Jesus will be put to death. Therefore, the audience is to realize that Elijah has not come (9:11) as the heavenly figure the disciples witnessed in the transfiguration epiphany (9:4). And Elijah will not come to take Jesus down from the cross (15:35-36), because unlike the Elijah in the transfiguration epiphany, who attained heavenly glory without being put to death, Jesus must suffer death before attaining the heavenly glory foreshadowed by his transfiguration.

The audience experienced a shocking irony when the Roman centurion who witnessed Jesus' death is the only human being to confess his divine sonship: "Truly this man was Son of God!" (15:39). Because he listened to how Jesus revealed himself to be Son of God by dying on the cross with a loud voice of total trust in God's plan that he suffer and die (cf. 12:6; 14:36), the centurion confirmed for the audience God's own voice from the overshadowing cloud at the transfiguration: "This is my beloved Son; listen to him!" (9:7; cf. 1:11).

Only with a humble, faith-filled prayer for God's powerful help will the disciples and the audience be healed of their metaphorical deafness and muteness (9:14-29) to the divine necessity of following Jesus' way of suffering and death. The powerful Gethsemane prayer of Jesus empowers the audience to play their role in God's plan by watching and praying. By praying in imitation and on the strength of Jesus' prayer, they can submit their wills to God's will and follow Jesus' way of suffering and death, as they await Jesus' final coming in the glory prefigured by his transfiguration (14:32-42, 62).

The Markan narrative challenges the audience to tell others of the significance of Jesus' transfiguration (9:9) as the assurance that resurrection to heavenly glory follows suffering and death for the gospel of Jesus (16:5-8).

CHAPTER 10

MATTHEW 17:1-8 AND THE ANTECEDENT NARRATIVE

We will now demonstrate how the Matthean version of the transfiguration narrative functions as a "pivotal mandatory epiphany" in its narrative context. In this chapter we will consider how the Matthean implied audience responds to the transfiguration narrative as a "mandatory epiphany" based on its intertextual knowledge of biblical traditions and on what it has heard in the antecedent narrative. In the next chapter we will consider how the Matthean transfiguration narrative as a "mandatory epiphany" prepares the implied audience for the subsequent Matthean narrative, thus confirming its "pivotal" nature.

A. MATT 17:1

And after six days Jesus took along Peter and James and John his brother, and led them up to a high mountain privately.

"And after six days" (17:1) expresses an interval of time which leads the audience both to connect and to separate what is about to happen from what they have just heard in 16:13-28.[1] On the one hand,

---

[1] The "six days" of Matt 17:1 do not present an exact parallel with Exod 24:16; they refer to an *interval* of time between events, whereas in Exod 24:16 the cloud covered Mount Sinai for a *duration* of six days within the same event. "In Ex 24.15-18, in contrast to the Transfiguration Narrative, the six day period was the length of time during which Moses was on the cloud-covered mountain before he heard the voice of God," according to T.L. DONALDSON, *Jesus on the Mountain: A Study in Matthean Theology* (JSNTSup 8; Sheffield: JSOT, 1985) 143.

what is about to happen is closely connected to the preceding, occurring within a week of Peter's confession of Jesus as "the Christ, the Son of the living God" (16:16), of Peter's being designated the "rock" of Jesus' church and given the keys of the kingdom of heaven (16:18-20), of Jesus' first prediction of his suffering, death and resurrection (16:21), of his challenge for the disciples to follow him in that suffering in order to share in the glory that follows it (16:24-27), and of his solemn promise that "there are some standing here who will not taste death until they see the Son of Man coming in his kingdom" (16:28).[2]

On the other hand, what is about to happen occurs nearly a week later, indicating the initiation of a new and separate event. This means that what is about to happen is not limited to a relationship only with the immediately preceding events and predictions, so that, for example, the transfiguration narrative would be simply the fulfillment of the promise given in 16:28.

Jesus took along "Peter and James and John his brother" (17:1), three of the first four disciples Jesus called to follow him (4:18-22), and three of the first four in the list of the specially chosen twelve disciples (10:1-2), with Peter again mentioned first as their leader and spokesman.[3] This begins to prepare the audience for a special, private revelation of Jesus to these three disciples, who have been separated from the group of disciples Jesus has just called to follow him in his suffering and death (16:24-27). That these three were among "some of those standing here" (16:28) alerts the audience to the possibility that these three, as well as the audience, may experience something in the event that is about to take place that will prepare them to "see the Son of Man coming in his kingdom" (16:28).

That Jesus took along (παραλαμβάνει) the three disciples and led them up to a high mountain privately (εἰς ὄρος ὑψηλὸν κατ᾽ ἰδίαν) (17:1) reminds the audience of how the devil similarly took along (παραλαμβάνει) Jesus to a very high mountain (εἰς ὄρος ὑψηλὸν

---

[2] Moses (*Matthew's Transfiguration Story*, 114-15) lists a "network of ideas" which bind Matt 16:13-17:13 together as a structural unit.

[3] John is again designated as "his brother" in relation to James, as in 4:21 and 10:2, but this time without any mention of their father Zebedee. On the primacy and leadership role of Peter in Matthew, see J.C. Anderson, *Matthew's Narrative Web: Over, and Over, and Over Again* (JSNTSup 91; Sheffield: JSOT, 1994) 92-94; D.C. Sim, *The Gospel of Matthew and Christian Judaism: The History and Social Setting of the Matthean Community* (Edinburgh: Clark, 1998) 196-99.

λίαν) in order to tempt him (4:8). After the voice of God from heaven had declared of Jesus, "This is my beloved Son, with whom I am well pleased!" (3:17), the devil thrice tested that divine sonship (4:3, 6). Jesus withstood the third test, the one on the very high mountain, by commanding, "Go ("Υπαγε), Satan!" (4:10).

After Peter, who confessed Jesus to be "the Christ, the Son of the living God" (16:16), rebuked Jesus for his pronouncement of the necessity of his suffering and death before resurrection (16:21-22) as incompatible with his messianic divine sonship, Jesus withstood Peter's diabolical test by commanding, "Go ("Υπαγε) behind me (ὀπίσω μου), Satan!" (16:23; cf. 4:10). Jesus then indicates that suffering and death are an essential part not only of his messianic divine sonship but of Peter's discipleship. When Jesus called Peter and his brother Andrew to be his first disciples, he said, "Come behind me (ὀπίσω μου), and I will make you fishers of people" (4:19). Jesus now tells Peter and the rest of his disciples, "If anyone wishes to come behind me (ὀπίσω μου), let him deny himself and take up his cross and follow me" (16:24; cf. 10:38). By telling Peter to go "behind me" (ὀπίσω μου, 16:23), Jesus is not only dismissing Peter's diabolical temptation to his divine sonship by telling him not to stand in the way of his suffering and death. He is also calling Peter to a kind of discipleship that involves following "behind me" (ὀπίσω μου, 4:19; 10:38; 16:24), that is, following Jesus' way of suffering and death.[4]

That Jesus led Peter and the two other disciples up to a high mountain "privately" (κατ' ἰδίαν) underscores their separation from the rest of the disciples (16:24) for this special secluded event. The audience has thus been prepared for a further private revelation on a "high mountain," a place close to the heavenly realm, regarding the nature not only of Jesus' divine sonship but also of discipleship in relation to that sonship (cf. 17:5) for the benefit of Peter and his two fellow disciples (17:1).[5]

---

[4] DAVIES and ALLISON, *Matthew*, 2.663: "But it is possible that Jesus is telling Peter...to become a follower so that he might once more learn what discipleship is all about." HAGNER, *Matthew 14-28*, 480: "The command to get 'behind me' (ὀπίσω μου) refers to the clearing of Jesus' path by the removal of an obstacle (and perhaps hints at the proper place for a disciple following Jesus; cf. esp. v 24; and 4:19; 10:38)."

[5] Matt 4:8 and 17:1 are the only occurrences of a "high" (ὑψηλός) mountain in Matthew; for previous occurrences of a "mountain" (ὄρος), see 5:1, 14; 8:1; 14:23; 15:29. "In each case ὄρος is the setting for a momentous event in Jesus' ministry," according to D.D. KUPP,

B. Matt 17:2

And he was transfigured before them, that is, his face shone as the sun, while his clothes became white as the light.

While the audience has been prepared for a special revelation involving Jesus, they have not been prepared for the spectacular event that occurs, an extraordinary epiphanic appearance. Jesus was suddenly "transfigured" or "transformed" (μετεμορφώθη) by God (divine passive) into a heavenly figure before the three disciples (17:2).[6] Jesus' "transfiguration" indicates to the audience his external, temporary transformation by God into a heavenly being while still on earth. It anticipates his future and permanent attainment of glory in heaven as promised to the righteous after their death.

That "his face shone as the sun, while his clothes became white as the light" (17:2) further defines for the audience what is meant by the "transfiguration."[7] It is a physical transformation of Jesus' external appearance visible in his face and clothing.

That "his face shone as the sun" (ἔλαμψεν τὸ πρόσωπον αὐτοῦ ὡς ὁ ἥλιος) indicates to the audience that Jesus is anticipating the heavenly state of the righteous after the last judgment.[8] In the climactic conclusion to the allegorical explanation of the parable of the weeds (13:36-43) the audience heard how, after the punishment of the wicked in the final judgment (13:41-42), the righteous "will shine like the sun (ἐκλάμψουσιν ὡς ὁ ἥλιος) in the kingdom of their Father" (13:43).[9]

Matthew's Emmanuel: Divine Presence and God's People in the First Gospel (SNTSMS 90; Cambridge: Cambridge University Press, 1996) 103. For a discussion of the mountain of the transfiguration in Matthew, see DONALDSON, *Jesus on the Mountain*, 136-56. Ezekiel's vision of heavenly phenomena takes place "on a very high mountain" (ἐπ' ὄρους ὑψηλοῦ σφόδρα, LXX Ezek 40:2); see MOSES, *Matthew's Transfiguration Story*, 117 n. 9.

[6] On the significance and background of the epiphanic motif of the "transfiguration" of Jesus, see chap. 4.

[7] The καὶ (translated "that is") before ἔλαμψεν is epexegetical.

[8] For background and parallels to the motif of the transfigured face of Jesus, see chap. 4.

[9] On Matt 13:43 as the encouraging climax of the allegory, see HEIL, *Matthew's Parables*, 85-86. MOSES, *Matthew's Transfiguration Story*, 126: "I conclude that the radiance of Jesus in 17.2 (ὡς ὁ ἥλιος) is a probable prolepsis of the reward of the 'righteous' at their resurrection."

That his clothes became white "as the light" (ὡς τὸ φῶς) complements the comparison of his face shining "as the sun" (ὡς ὁ ἥλιος). The clothing that transmitted healing power to the sick who touched it (9:20-21; 14:36) has now attained the extreme whiteness characteristic of the clothing of those who dwell in heaven.[10] It underscores for the audience how Jesus has momentarily, through this unique epiphanic appearance, achieved the glory of a heavenly status. Jesus has thus been temporarily transfigured before the eyes of the three select disciples into a heavenly figure, although he remains on the earth.

C. MATT 17:3

Then behold there appeared to them Moses and Elijah talking with him.

The initial epiphanic appearance of the transfigured Jesus "before them" (ἔμπροσθεν αὐτῶν, 17:2), the three disciples, is immediately followed by an additional epiphanic appearance. It is introduced by Matthew's characteristic "behold" (ἰδού).[11] Moses and Elijah suddenly appeared "to them" (αὐτοῖς, 17:3), referring again to Peter, James, and John. That Moses and Elijah "appeared" (ὤφθη) to them reminds the audience of the way that God and the angel of the Lord made epiphanic "appearances" from heaven to chosen individuals in the OT (LXX Gen 12:7; 17:1; Exod 3:2; Judg 6:12).[12] Hence the entire composite epiphanic event of the transfigured Jesus in conversation with Moses and Elijah is for the benefit of these three chosen disciples, as well as the audience who identifies with them.[13]

---

[10] For the background of the extremely white clothing as indicative of heavenly glory, see chap. 4.

[11] MOSES, *Matthew's Transfiguration Story*, 127-28: "Here, the use of ἰδού is particularly characteristic of Matthew (cf. 1.20; 2.1, 13, 19; 9.10, 18, 32; 12.46; 17.5; 26.47; 28.11), and points to something unexpected. ἰδού and its semitic equivalents are often associated with angelic appearances or theophanies...It may be that by adding the word here Matthew heightens the idea that Moses and Elijah are 'heavenly' beings." See also W.D. DAVIES and D.C. ALLISON, *The Gospel According to Saint Matthew: Volume I: Introduction and Commentary on Matthew I-VII* (ICC; Edinburgh: Clark, 1988) 206.

[12] On ὤφθη as a technical term for the appearances of heavenly figures in the LXX and the NT, see chap. 4.

[13] MICHAELIS, "ὁράω" 5.354.

The audience has heard Moses and Elijah mentioned individually in the previous narrative. Jesus alluded to Moses as the representative of the Law (8:4). Elijah, as the audience knows, was the wonder-working prophet who was taken up to heaven without dying (2 Kgs 2:11) and was expected to return to earth as a forerunner to the eschatological age (Mal 3:23-24; Sir 48:9-10). Jesus designated John the Baptist as this "Elijah who is to come" (11:14). Some have identified Jesus himself as Elijah (16:14). But now Moses and Elijah appear together from heaven in conversation with the transfigured Jesus.

That the heavenly Moses and Elijah were "talking with" (συλλα-λοῦντες) the transfigured Jesus reminds the audience of how Moses, whose face was glorified from his encounters with God on earth, used to "talk with" (συλλαλεῖν) the Lord (LXX Exod 34:35).[14] Is Jesus on earth receiving a new revelation from the heavenly Moses and Elijah by "talking with" them, as Moses on earth received new revelations from God by "talking with" the Lord? Or is the Jesus who has begun to show his disciples that he must suffer and die before being raised (16:21), and told them that they are to follow him in that suffering (16:24-27), now speaking about that divine necessity with the heavenly figures of Moses and Elijah (17:3)?

The audience knows that Elijah, although he suffered persecution as a prophet, attained heavenly glory by ascending into heaven without dying (2 Kgs 2:11). And the great prophet Moses (Deut 34:10), although he suffered rebellion and opposition from his people, was never put to death as a rejected prophet. He died and was buried in a very extraordinary way, revered by his people. Later traditions familiar to the audience indicate that Moses attained heavenly glory either at the time of his mysterious but honorable death and burial or without dying at all.[15]

Does the appearance of the heavenly Moses and Elijah in close association with the transfigured Jesus mean that he also will attain heavenly glory like them, without dying the death of a rejected prophet? Does the conversation of these two great prophetic and heavenly

---

[14] DAVIES and ALLISON, *Matthew*, 2.697: "συλλαλοῦντες would seem to indicate that Jesus belongs to the same world as Moses and Elijah (cf. Apoc. Zeph. 9.5)."

[15] For a full discussion of the significance of Moses and Elijah in the transfiguration narratives, see chap. 5.

figures with the transfigured Jesus represent a new revelation from God that now reverses Jesus' previous prediction that he "must suffer greatly from the elders, the chief priests, and the scribes, and be killed" (16:21)? Further, does it annul Jesus' previous challenge for the disciples and the audience to deny themselves, take up their cross, and lose their lives in order to save them (16:24-27)?

D. Matt 17:4

Replying, Peter spoke to Jesus, "Lord, it is good that we are here. If you wish, I will make here three tents, for you one and for Moses one and for Elijah one."

Since Peter has not been addressed by Jesus, his "replying" (ἀποκριθεὶς, 17:4) to him expresses his response, as spokesman for the group of the three chosen disciples (17:1), to this private epiphanic appearance of the transfigured Jesus in conversation with the heavenly Moses and Elijah (17:2-3). Peter's reply continues the repeated pattern of his replying to Jesus as the representative individual disciple and spokesman for the rest of the disciples (cf. ἀποκριθεὶς in 14:28; 15:15; 16:16; see also 16:22)[16]. But whereas Peter previously replied to the words of Jesus directed toward the group of disciples, here Peter and the other disciples are not part of the conversation of Jesus with Moses and Elijah, so that Peter is responding not to the words of Jesus but to the entire epiphanic event.

Peter's reply to Jesus, "Lord (κύριε), it is good that we are here" (17:4), stands in striking contrast to his previous reply to Jesus in the preceding scene, after Jesus' pronouncement of the necessity of his suffering and death before resurrection (16:21), "Far be it from you, Lord (κύριε), this will never happen to you!" (16:22).[17] Jesus then

---

[16] On this repeated pattern ANDERSON (*Matthew's Narrative Web*, 93) notes: "With each repetition the predictability of the pattern is increased. In a form of assent, the reader assumes more and more that Peter will speak for the disciples...Indeed, through the repeated pattern, for the reader, Peter *is* the spokesman."

[17] We translate ἵλεώς σοι as a Septuagintism meaning "far be it from you," following BDF §128(5); DAVIES and ALLISON, *Matthew*, 2.662; HAGNER, *Matthew 14-28*, 480. Others translate as "[God be] gracious to you." See *EDNT* 2.186-87; BAGD, 376.

shockingly addressed Peter as "Satan," dismissing his response as a diabolical temptation, "Go behind me, Satan! You are a stumbling block to me, for you are not thinking the things of God but the things of human beings" (16:23).[18] He then exhorted Peter and the rest of the disciples to follow his way of suffering and death in order to share in the heavenly glory of his kingdom (16:24-28). Whereas Peter's response to Jesus as "Lord" in 16:22 ignored his prediction that he will be raised on the third day after his death (16:21), his response to Jesus as "Lord" in 17:4 seems to ignore the predicted necessity for Jesus and his disciples to suffer and die before attaining the heavenly glory prefigured by Jesus' transfiguration into a heavenly figure like Moses and Elijah.

The audience has heard Jesus tell the Canaanite woman, who begged Jesus to expel a demon from her daughter (15:22), that "it is not good (οὐκ ἔστιν καλὸν) to take the bread of the children and throw it to the dogs" (15:26). This means that it would not be "good," that is, appropriate to God's plan of salvation, according to which "the children," that is, "the lost sheep of the house of Israel" (15:24), are entitled to the bread (salvific benefits) Jesus brings, nor would it be beneficial for the children, if Jesus were to throw the bread that belongs to them to "the dogs" (Gentiles, such as the Canaanite woman). Now the audience hears Peter tell Jesus, "Lord, it is good (καλὸν ἔστιν) that we are here" (17:4). In other words, it is "good," that is, appropriate to God's salvific plan and beneficial for Peter, James, and John to be present to witness this spectacular epiphanic appearance of the heavenly Moses and Elijah in conversation with the transfigured Jesus.[19]

Peter's statements that "it is good that we are *here*" and "if you wish, I will make *here* three tents" (17:4) reminds the audience of Jesus' previous prediction that "there are some standing *here* who will not taste death until they see the Son of Man coming in his kingdom" (16:28). But by "here" Jesus and Peter are referring to two quite differ-

---

[18] On Peter as a negative example of discipleship in 16:22-23 in contrast to his positive example in 16:16-19, see M.J. WILKINS, *The Concept of Disciple in Matthew's Gospel* (NovTSup 59; Leiden: Brill, 1988) 202-3. As Wilkins notes, "No one else is ever called 'Σατανάς,' as Peter is here" (p. 203 n. 128).

[19] WANKE ("καλός," 2.245) notes that the formulaic use of "it is good" (καλός ἐστιν) "can be understood to indicate that which is salutary and good before God."

ent locations. Whereas the double occurrence of "here" (ὧδε) in 17:4 refers to the mountain of the transfiguration epiphany, "here" (ὧδε) in 16:28 refers to Caesarea Philippi (16:13), the location of Jesus' prediction. Although Peter, James, and John were among "some standing here," they were not the only ones present for Jesus' prediction. There may be others, besides these three, who will likewise fulfill Jesus' prediction. Indeed, it is not yet clear in what sense the three disciples' involvement in the transfiguration epiphany will enable them (and the audience) "to see the Son of Man coming in his kingdom" (16:28).

By suggesting that he make a tent each for Jesus, Moses, and Elijah (17:4), Peter, even though he prefaces his offer with a deferential, "If you wish," and mentions Jesus first, would place each heavenly figure on the same level and in the same category.[20] Peter apparently wants to prepare a place for each heavenly figure to prolong his glorious epiphanic appearance. Although the three "tents" may remind the audience of the commemorative tents used for the Feast of Tabernacles and/or the dwelling places appropriate for the righteous in heaven, the primary allusion is to the Tent of Meeting. Since the three epiphanic figures are in conversation among themselves (17:3), and there is no indication that the three disciples hear the conversation, Peter seemingly wants to provide a tent, analogous to the Tent of Meeting, for each to continue his divine communication for the benefit of the three disciples. The three individual tents would thus provide each heavenly figure with a place from which to address his own divine communication to the three disciples.[21]

Peter's offer to place the transfigured Jesus on the same level and in the same category as the heavenly figures of Moses and Elijah insinuates that perhaps Jesus, despite his previous prediction about the necessity of his suffering and death before resurrection on the third day (16:21), has already or will attain heavenly glory like Moses and Eli-

---

[20] On Peter's "if you wish" DAVIES and ALLISON (*Matthew*, 2.699) note: "Its purpose is to make Peter act with due deference." MOSES (*Matthew's Transfiguration Story*, 131-35) suggests a connection between Peter's offer to make a tent each for Jesus, Moses, and Elijah and Jesus' promise to build his church on the "rock" of Peter (16:18). But Jesus' promise employs the word "build" (οἰκοδομήσω) and is metaphorical; whereas Peter's offer employs the word "make" (ποιήσω) and is literal.

[21] For a full discussion of the background and meaning of the tents, see chap. 6.

jah, that is, without being put to death by his people. Standing in tension with Jesus' previous passion prediction, Peter's offer to make three tents rings rather inappropriate to the audience.[22]

E. MATT 17:5

While he was still speaking, behold a bright cloud overshadowed them, and behold a voice from the cloud saying, "This is my beloved Son, with whom I am well pleased; listen to him!"

While Peter was still speaking, that is, incongruously offering to make three tents (17:4), he is dramatically interrupted as yet another sudden and unexpected epiphanic appearance occurs.[23] Recalling the "behold" (ἰδού) that introduced the previous epiphanic appearance of the heavenly Moses and Elijah in conversation with the transfigured Jesus (17:3), the epiphanic appearance of the cloud is similarly introduced: "Behold (ἰδού) a bright cloud overshadowed them" (17:5).[24] That the epiphanic cloud was "bright" or "luminous" (φωτεινὴ) underscores its heavenly character, assimilating it to the bright and luminous features of Jesus transfigured into a heavenly figure – "his face shone as the sun, while his clothes became white as the light (φῶς)" (17:2). The epiphanic luminous cloud represents God's glorious presence, reminding the audience of Exod 24:17, where the form of the glory of the Lord, which came down on the mountain in the cloud (cf. v. 16), appeared very bright or luminous, like a "flaming fire" on the top of the mountain.[25]

---

[22] According to WILKINS (*Disciple*, 203-4), Peter is "making a basically foolish request. Whether Peter thought that this was the new center of the coming kingdom, wanted to care for these honorific personages, wanted to prolong this scene of glory, or wanted to establish new 'tabernacles' for the center of communication with God, he is still overlooking that Jesus must move on to the cross (cf. 16:21)."

[23] Jesus is interrupted "while he was still speaking" (ἔτι αὐτοῦ λαλοῦντος) in Matt 12:46 and 26:47; cf. 17:5.

[24] For a full discussion of the background and meaning of the overshadowing bright cloud, see chap. 7.

[25] Only in the Matthean transfiguration epiphany does the cloud of God's presence appear as "bright" or "luminous" (φωτεινὴ); see also chap. 7.

At this point the audience is not sure as to whom precisely the bright cloud has overshadowed. Has it overshadowed all six characters in the scene – the three disciples as well as Jesus, Moses, and Elijah? Does "overshadowed them (αὐτούς)" refer only to the three disciples, the previous referent of "them" (αὐτοῖς), as the recipients of the epiphanic appearance of Moses and Elijah in conversation with the transfigured Jesus (17:3)? Has the bright heavenly cloud overshadowed only the three heavenly, epiphanic figures, or only Moses and Elijah?

Yet another "behold" (ἰδοὺ) points to a further epiphanic event – "behold a voice from the cloud" (17:5), indicating to the audience that the three disciples, whom the divine voice addresses, have remained outside of the cloud of God's presence. The voice comes "from" or "out of" (ἐκ) the cloud and speaks to the disciples.[26] Furthermore, that the voice emphatically directs the disciples to listen to Jesus (17:5) indicates to the audience that Jesus also is outside of the cloud. The cloud appropriately overshadows only the heavenly figures of Moses and Elijah, concealing them from the eyes of the disciples, as it implicitly transports them back to heaven.[27] This is confirmed when Jesus comes and touches the fearful disciples, who then see no one except Jesus alone (17:6-8).

When Peter wants to make a tent in honor of each heavenly figure at which each can continue to deliver divine communication, the audience recognizes an analogy with the traditions surrounding the Tent of Meeting as the privileged place of divine communication.[28] Peter would thus prolong this marvelous epiphany of heavenly glory and extend to the three disciples the heavenly conversation they witness but do not hear taking place among the three epiphanic figures.

With an alliterative Greek word play the epiphanic bright cloud ironically interrupts Peter's offer to make three "tents" (σκηνάς, 17:4) for the three epiphanic figures, as it "covered over" or "tented over" (ἐπεσκίασεν, 17:5) Moses and Elijah, thus separating them from the Jesus Peter wanted to make equal to them. Adding to the irony, the voice of God himself, without the provision of a tent like the Tent of Meeting and without speaking through such preeminent prophetic

---

[26] See BAGD, 234, on ἐκ as denoting the direction from which something comes.

[27] For the background of the vehicular function of the cloud, see chap. 7.

[28] On the Tent of Meeting as background for the transfiguration, see chap. 6.

intermediaries as Moses and Elijah, proclaims a dramatic divine communication directly to the disciples, "This is my beloved Son, with whom I am well pleased; listen to him!" (17:5). This climactic command serves as the mandate of this pivotal mandatory epiphany, directing the three disciples and the audience to listen at this point not to Moses and Elijah for divine communication at tents but to Jesus, God's beloved, favored Son, the only one the overshadowing bright cloud has left standing there with the three disciples (17:8).

The voice of God "from the cloud" recalls for the audience the proclamation of the voice of God "from the heavens" after Jesus was baptized by John, but adds the command, "Listen to him!":

3:17: καὶ ἰδοὺ φωνὴ ἐκ τῶν οὐρανῶν λέγουσα, Οὗτός ἐστιν ὁ υἱός μου ὁ ἀγαπητός, ἐν ᾧ εὐδόκησα

17:5: καὶ ἰδοὺ φωνὴ ἐκ τῆς νεφέλης λέγουσα, Οὗτός ἐστιν ὁ υἱός μου ὁ ἀγαπητός, ἐν ᾧ εὐδόκησα· ἀκούετε αὐτοῦ

After Jesus' baptism God's declaration that he is God's beloved Son, with whom God is well pleased (3:17) indicated to the audience God's approval and favor of Jesus as the one uniquely equipped with God's Spirit (3:16) to be able to fulfill "all righteousness" (3:15), that is, God's salvific will.[29] Once the Pharisees decided to destroy Jesus (12:14), who then withdrew to a less public ministry (12:15-16), God's voice from a fulfillment quote from the prophet Isaiah (12:17) reaffirmed for the audience God's continuing approval and favor of Jesus: "Behold my servant whom I have chosen, my beloved (ὁ ἀγαπητός μου) in whom my soul is well pleased (εὐδόκησεν)" (Isa 42:1 in 12:18).[30]Now that Jesus himself has for the first time predicted his suffering, death and resurrection at the hands of the Jewish leaders (16:21) God's voice from the cloud confirms that Jesus is still "my beloved Son, with whom I am well pleased" and enjoins the disciples and the audience to listen to him (17:5).

---

[29] For the significance of Jesus' baptism in Matt 3:13-17, see LENTZEN-DEIS, *Taufe Jesu*, 282-84.

[30] For a detailed discussion of the use of Isa 42:1-4 in 12:18-21, see R.H. GUNDRY, *The Use of the Old Testament in St. Matthew's Gospel* (NovTSup 18; Leiden: Brill, 1967) 110-16; M.J.J. MENKEN, "The Quotation from Isaiah 42,1-4 in Matthew 12,18-21: Its Textual Form," *ETL* 75 (1999) 32-52. See also LENTZEN-DEIS, *Taufe Jesu*, 187-93; G. SCHNEIDER, "ἀγάπη," *EDNT* 1.12; S. LÉGASSE, "εὐδοκέω," *EDNT* 2.75.

God's voice from the overshadowing bright cloud corrects Peter's misinterpretation of the epiphanic appearance of Jesus. Peter would place the transfigured Jesus on the same level as the heavenly Moses and Elijah by building a tent for each (17:4). But with an emphatic "*this* one" (οὗτός), God points out that Jesus is not equal to Moses or Elijah, since he is "my beloved Son, with whom I am well pleased" (17:5).[31]

After the disciples experienced the epiphanic manifestation of Jesus' divine power to save them from a sea storm by walking over the chaotic waves (14:22-27), they confessed, "Truly you are the Son of God!" (14:33).[32] At Caesarea Philippi Peter, through divine revelation (16:17), confessed to Jesus, "You are the Christ, the Son of the living God!" (16:16). Now God's voice from the cloud confirms the disciples' and Peter's confessions of Jesus' divine sonship. But the disciples, Peter, and the audience must listen to Jesus (17:5) in order to fully understand the nature of this divine sonship and the role they are to play in it as followers of Jesus.

God's urgent command to "listen to him!" (ἀκούετε αὐτοῦ, 17:5), the mandate of this pivotal mandatory epiphany, "pivots" the audience back to and thus reinforces Jesus' own urgent appeals to "listen to" and obey his teaching about the reign of the heavens.[33] God's mandate reminds the audience of Moses's promise that God would raise up from and for the people of Israel a prophet like Moses, so that "you shall listen to him" (αὐτοῦ ἀκούσεσθε, LXX Deut 18:15). God himself reinforced the promise of a prophet like Moses, and added: "I will place my word in his mouth, and he will speak to them as I command him" (LXX Deut 18:18). But now the disciples and the audience are to listen to Jesus not just as a prophet like Moses (or Elijah) but as God's own beloved and favored Son, who speaks as God, his Father, commands him. Peter, who would build the three tents to prolong the divine communication taking place among Jesus, Moses, and Elijah (17:4), should not be so much concerned with what Moses and Elijah

---

[31] HAGNER, *Matthew 14-28*, 494: "The divine voice thus identifies Jesus as the unique Son of God who possesses unique authority. Moses and Elijah are but his attendants."

[32] On the significance of this confession of Jesus' divine sonship, see HEIL, *Jesus Walking on the Sea*, 66-67.

[33] Matt 5:21-22, 27-28, 31-32, 33-34, 38-39, 43-44; 7:24, 26; 11:15; 13:9, 18-23, 43; 15:10.

might have to say as with what Jesus, as God's beloved and favored Son, has had and will have to say to them.[34] The audience's recall of Deut 18:15-18, then, reinforces for them that what they have already heard and what they will hear from Jesus is the very word of God himself.

Attentively listening to what Jesus has just spoken in the previous scene (16:21-28) would enable the disciples and the audience to grasp the more profound identity of the transfigured Jesus as God's beloved and favored Son in contrast to the heavenly figures of Moses and Elijah. As Jesus has been teaching, it is divinely necessary for him, "the Christ, the Son of the living God" (16:16), to be rejected by the leaders of his people and killed before rising from the dead on the third day (16:21). His temporary transfiguration into a heavenly figure indicates that he will ultimately attain heavenly glory. But unlike Moses and Elijah Jesus will be permanently glorified only after being rejected and put to death by his own people.

When the audience hears the transfiguration epiphany, there has been no indication that Peter, although he rebuked (16:22) and was in turn admonished by Jesus (16:23), or the other disciples have really heard and understood what Jesus has said. Attentively listening to what Jesus just told them would enable Peter, James, and John, as well as the audience, to realize that they must follow Jesus on his way of suffering and death, by denying themselves and taking up their cross (16:24), if they are to join him in the ultimate and permanent heavenly glory that his transfiguration prefigures. They must lose their lives for the sake of Jesus in order to save them (16:25). That Jesus, as the Son of Man, is still to "come in the glory of his Father with his angels" (16:27) confirms that his transfiguration into a heavenly figure is but a temporary anticipation of his final glory yet to come as God's beloved and favored Son (17:5).

Attentively listening to Jesus' words about the necessity to follow him on his way to suffering and death would enable the three disciples and the audience to realize how the transfiguration epiphany pre-

---

[34] DAVIES and ALLISON, *Matthew*, 2.703: "The command to hear or obey Jesus — directed to the disciples, not Moses and Elijah — probably pertains not solely to the future ('listen to him from now on') but also looks back to the episode at Caesarea Philippi, where Jesus' words about suffering were not easily digested."

pares them to fulfill Jesus' promise that "there are some standing here who will not taste death until they see the Son of Man coming in his kingdom" (16:28). The temporary transfiguration of Jesus into a heavenly figure assures the three disciples and the audience that he will ultimately and permanently achieve the heavenly glory of God's kingdom after his necessary suffering, rejection, and death. The transfiguration epiphany thus prepares them to be able to see "the Son of Man coming in his kingdom" already and paradoxically in Jesus' suffering, death and resurrection, which some of them will witness before they "taste" the bitterness of their own death as followers of Jesus.[35]

F. MATT 17:6-7

Hearing this the disciples fell upon their face and were greatly frightened. But Jesus approached, and touching them, said, "Arise and do not be afraid."

When the disciples heard (ἀκούσαντες) the voice of God from the overshadowing cloud (17:5), they "fell upon their face" (ἔπεσαν ἐπὶ πρόσωπον αὐτῶν) in a gesture of submission, indicating the overwhelming effect of the epiphanic mandate (17:6). This reminds the audience of how, when Moses heard (ἀκούσας) the disturbing voice of the rebellious assembly, he immediately "fell on his face" (ἔπεσεν ἐπὶ πρόσωπον) (LXX Num 16:1-4). And when Moses and Aaron heard the epiphanic mandate that issued from the appearance of the glory of the Lord to the entire assembly, they "fell upon their face" (ἔπεσαν ἐπὶ πρόσωπον αὐτῶν) (vv. 20-22). But even more pertinent, the audience recalls how Moses and Aaron similarly "fell upon their face" (ἔπεσαν ἐπὶ πρόσωπον αὐτῶν) when they heard the epiphanic mandate after the cloud (ἡ νεφέλη) covered the Tent of Meeting and the glory of the Lord appeared (LXX Num 17:7-10).[36]

---

[35] "Taste" (γεύομαι) in the frequently occurring phrase, "taste death," connotes the bitterness of suffering; see VAN DER MINDE, "γεύομαι," 1.246.

[36] On Num 17:7-10, see also chap. 7. K. BERGER, "πρόσωπον," *EDNT* 3.180: "The fixed phrase 'fall on one's *face*' is used of reaction to epiphanies...it is in a person's face that the relationship between two parties expresses itself in a decisive way."

That the disciples fell upon their face and were greatly frightened (17:6) at God's voice from the overshadowing cloud at the transfiguration contrasts sharply with the total lack of response to God's similar voice from heaven at the baptism of Jesus (3:17). This underscores for the audience how it is the epiphanic mandate to listen to Jesus (17:5), an addition to the heavenly voice at the baptism, that has so overwhelmed the disciples with fear.[37]

A reaction of fear is a common occurrence in epiphanies.[38] As the audience recalls, when Jesus made his epiphanic appearance of walking on the sea, the disciples "were frightened (ἐταράχθησαν), saying, 'It is a ghost!' and they cried out from fear (ἀπὸ τοῦ φόβου)" (14:26). But then Jesus immediately allayed their fear, as he told them, "Take courage, it is I; do not be afraid (μὴ φοβεῖσθε)" (14:27).[39] Now, similarly, when the disciples "were greatly frightened" (ἐφοβήθησαν σφόδρα, 17:6) in reaction to the epiphanic mandate of God from the overshadowing cloud, "Jesus approached, and touching them, said, 'Arise and do not be afraid (μὴ φοβεῖσθε)'" (17:7).[40]

That Jesus approached and touched the disciples to reassure them after they fell upon their face in fear at hearing the voice of God (17:6-7) reminds the audience of how Daniel was similarly touched and reassured after falling upon his face in a panic upon hearing the divine voice following his visions. First of all, after Daniel heard

---

[37] HAGNER's (*Matthew 14-28*, 494) suggestion that "in 3:17 the voice was probably heard only by Jesus" contradicts the third person address ("This is...") directed toward all present in contrast to the second person address ("You are...") directed specifically to Jesus in Mark 1:11 and Luke 3:22. Hagner further suggests that the disciples fell upon their face "probably partly in fear...and partly in worship." But the falling down here is not accompanied by the explicit word for "worship" (προσκυνέω) as in 2:11, 4:9 and 18:26. WILKINS (*Disciple*, 135) notes that "Matthew does not connect fear with reverence." On the theme of worship in Matthew, see M.A. POWELL, "A Typology of Worship in the Gospel of Matthew," *JSNT* 57 (1995) 3-17.

[38] On the fear motif in epiphanies, see HEIL, *Jesus Walking on the Sea*, 11-12. Note again that the fear motif occurs at different places in the various versions of the transfiguration — at the epiphanic appearance of Moses and Elijah with the transfigured Jesus in Mark 9:6, at the entrance into the epiphanic cloud in Luke 9:34, and at the epiphanic mandate of God from the overshadowing cloud in Matt 17:6.

[39] On Matt 14:26-27, see HEIL, *Jesus Walking on the Sea*, 56-59.

[40] Note that it is only in the Matthean version of the transfiguration episode that Jesus speaks.

(ἤκουσα) the voice (φωνὴν) of a man, which is actually an angelic or divine voice (LXX Dan 8:16),[41] and the angel Gabriel came near, Daniel recounts how "I was overcome with panic (ἐθορυβήθην) and fell upon my face (ἔπεσα ἐπὶ πρόσωπόν μου)" (v. 17).[42] When Gabriel spoke with him, Daniel recounts how he "touched (ἀψάμενός) me" and "raised (ἤγειρέ) me upright" (v. 18). Similarly, the disciples, upon hearing (ἀκούσαντες) the divine voice (φωνὴ, 17:5), fell upon their face (ἔπεσαν ἐπὶ πρόσωπον αὐτῶν) and were greatly frightened (ἐφοβήθησαν σφόδρα) (17:6). But then Jesus came and touched (ἀψάμενος) them and told them to "arise" (ἐγέρθητε) and not to be afraid (17:7).

Later, after Daniel had another vision of a heavenly figure (Dan 10:5-8), he heard (ἤκουσα) the voice (φωνὴν) of his speech and, as Daniel recounts, "I fell upon my face (πεπτωκὼς ἐπὶ πρόσωπόν μου) to the ground" (v. 9). Then a hand approached ("touched" [ἀπτομένη] in the Theodotion version) Daniel and raised (ἤγειρέ) him (v. 10), thus strengthening him to hear the divine communication (v. 11; see also v. 18). After Daniel stood up trembling (v. 11), he was told, "Do not be afraid" (μὴ φοφοῦ) (v. 12; see also v. 19). Similarly, after the disciples heard (ἀκούσαντες) the divine epiphanic voice (φωνὴ) and fell upon their face (ἔπεσαν ἐπὶ πρόσωπον αὐτῶν) in great fear, Jesus, touching (ἀψάμενος) them, said, "Arise and do not be afraid (ἐγέρθητε καὶ μὴ φοβεῖσθε)," thus strengthening them to hear the divine communication from the epiphanic cloud (17:5-7).[43]

The audience has heard how Jesus touched (ἥψατο) a man with leprosy before uttering the powerful words that cleansed and re-

---

[41] GOLDINGAY (*Daniel*, 214) identifies this "human voice" as actually "the voice of God." And on the "human voice" here COLLINS (*Daniel*, 336) states: "In the context of the vision, this represents an angelic voice. Compare the voices in Ezek 1:28; Isa 40:3."

[42] According to COLLINS (*Daniel*, 337), the motif of falling upon one's face in fear is "the standard, appropriate response to an epiphany. Compare Dan 10:9; Josh 5:14; Ezek 1:28; 3:23; Rev 1:17; *1 En* 14:14; 4 Ezra 10:29-30; *Apoc. Abr.* 10:2."

[43] Cf. Ezek 1:28-2:1. On the comparison with Daniel here, see also MOSES, *Matthew's Transfiguration Story*, 149-50. COLLINS (*Daniel*, 374) notes that the formula, "do not be afraid," is "a standard reassurance given by heavenly visitors: Gen 15:1; 26:24; Jdg 6:23; and others; also Luke 1:13, 30." DAVIES and ALLISON (*Matthew*, 2.703) state: "Like touching, the expression is common in epiphanies."

stored him to health (8:3). After Jesus touched (ἥψατο) the hand of Peter's mother-in-law, the fever left her so that she arose (ἠγέρθη) and served him (8:15). Jesus touched (ἥψατο) the eyes of two blind men before pronouncing the restoration of their sight in accord with their faith (9:29).[44]   Similarly, Jesus now touches (ἁψάμενος) his disciples who have fallen on their face in great fear before enjoining them to arise (ἐγέρθητε) and not to be afraid (17:6-7), thus restoring their courage and reassuring them to hear God's epiphanic mandate from the overshadowing cloud, "Listen to him!" (17:5).

That Jesus approached and touched the disciples further separates him from the heavenly figures of Moses and Elijah, whom Peter wanted to put in the same category as Jesus by offering to make a tent for each of the three epiphanic figures (17:4). It further confirms for the audience that the bright, epiphanic cloud has overshadowed only Moses and Elijah and (implicitly) transported them back to heaven. As this entire composite epiphany comes to an end, Jesus now reestablishes physical contact with the disciples by "touching" them, indicating that he is no longer transfigured into a heavenly figure, but has rejoined his disciples in the earthly, physical realm.[45]   By compassionately touching the disciples and telling them to arise and not to be afraid (17:7), Jesus has thus reassured and empowered them to hear and obey the epiphanic mandate.[46] By listening to Jesus (17:5) the disciples and the audience will realize that they are to follow Jesus in his suffering and death (16:21-28) before following him to the heavenly glory prefigured by his transfiguration.

---

[44] In 9:20-21 and 14:36 individuals "touch" (ἅπτω) Jesus in order to be restored to physical health.

[45] HAGNER, *Matthew 14-18*, 495: "The recording of the touch of Jesus here may well have the purpose of showing that it was the real Jesus they had seen transfigured and talking to Moses and Elijah and that they therefore had not simply experienced an illusion. The Jesus of transcendent glory remains the compassionate Master who led them into discipleship."

[46] KUPP (*Matthew's Emmanuel*, 206) calls the gestures and words of Jesus here "a specific movement of reassurance and utterances to quell their uncertainty." WILKINS (*Disciple*, 135) claims that "the mention of the 'touch' of Jesus carries overtones of commissioning and empowering." Cf. Dan 10:9-20.

G. MATT 17:8

Raising their eyes they saw no one but him, Jesus alone.

The dramatic gesture of the disciples falling upon their face when they "heard" (ἀκούσαντες) the voice of God from the overshadowing cloud (17:5-6) is now complemented by the raising of their eyes to "see" (εἶδον) no one but Jesus (17:8). They see no one but the Jesus who has compassionately touched and reassured them (17:7). This completes the confirmation for the audience that the overshadowing cloud has taken Moses and Elijah back to heaven.[47] The grammatical emphasis in the statement that the disciples "saw no one but *him*, Jesus alone" eliminates any doubt as to whom the voice of God is directing them to heed.[48] Only Jesus, the beloved Son of God with whom God is well pleased (17:5) remains with them. The extraordinary, complex epiphany of the transfiguration has concluded. The earthly Jesus who was with the disciples before he was transfigured into a heavenly figure is the only one they now see. They are to listen at this point not to the heavenly Moses and Elijah for divine communication but to Jesus alone.

Although God's voice from the overshadowing cloud has commanded the three disciples to listen to Jesus, there is as yet no indication that they will obey it. The pivotal mandate of the transfiguration epiphany has thus created a dramatic suspense for the rest of Matthew's narrative. Will the disciples (and audience) listen to what Jesus has already said (16:21-28) and what he still has to say about the necessity for suffering and death before entering into the glory of the kingdom of heaven anticipated by his transfiguration?

---

[47] DAVIES and ALLISON, *Matthew*, 2.704: "Evidently Moses and Elijah have been taken away to heaven by the cloud."

[48] HAGNER, *Matthew 14-28*, 495: "This final verse serves not only to bring the account of the experience to an end but to emphasize the exclusive focus upon Jesus. The repetition involved in the syntax effectively makes this point: when they looked up 'they saw no one [οὐδένα] except' αὐτόν 'Ιησοῦν μόνον, 'him [emphatic], Jesus alone.'"

H. Conclusion

When the audience hears that "Jesus took along Peter and James and John his brother, and led them up to a high mountain privately" (Matt 17:1), they are prepared for the possibility of some sort of a dramatic revelatory encounter with God. The initial epiphanic action of this pivotal mandatory epiphany occurs as Jesus was suddenly and unexpectedly "transfigured" by God into a heavenly figure before the three disciples. That "his face shone as the sun, while his clothes became white as the light" (17:2) confirms for the audience the heavenly nature of Jesus' transformed face and clothing. Jesus' metamorphosis, his external, proleptic, and temporary transformation by God into a heavenly being while still on earth, indicates to the audience his future and permanent attainment of glory in heaven as promised to the righteous after their death.

The epiphanic transfiguration of Jesus is immediately followed by an additional epiphanic appearance of the heavenly figures of Moses and Elijah in conversation with Jesus before the eyes of the three disciples (17:3). The audience knows that although Moses and Elijah were great prophets who experienced opposition and rejection, they were never put to death by their own people. Does the appearance of the heavenly Moses and Elijah in close association with the transfigured Jesus mean that he also will attain heavenly glory like them, without dying the death of a rejected prophet?

Peter would place each heavenly figure in the same category by offering to make a tent for each to prolong his glorious epiphanic appearance and to continue the divine communication for the benefit of the disciples (17:4). But Peter is interrupted by yet another sudden and unexpected epiphanic appearance as a bright cloud overshadowed the heavenly Moses and Elijah, implicitly taking them back to heaven. God's voice from the cloud not only confirms the disciples' (14:33) and Peter's (16:16) confessions of Jesus' divine sonship. It reinforces God's declaration from the heavens at Jesus' baptism (3:17) and God's voice from a fulfillment quote (12:17-18) that Jesus, now on his way to suffering and death (16:21), is still "my beloved Son, with whom I am well pleased" (17:5).

God's voice from the cloud (17:5) serves as the pivotal mandate that distinguishes Jesus from Moses and Elijah as God's beloved, favored Son and commands the disciples and the audience to listen to Jesus. The mandate thus "pivots" them back to Jesus' previous teaching about the kingdom of heaven, especially his teaching about the necessity for him and his followers to suffer and be put to death (16:21-27) before entering into the glory of the kingdom of heaven anticipated by Jesus' transfiguration.

Upon hearing God's voice from the bright, overshadowing cloud, the disciples react in a way typical in epiphanies. They fell upon their face and were greatly frightened, overwhelmed into a fearful submission (17:6). After Jesus, returned to his pre-transfiguration, earthly status, approached the disciples and compassionately touched them, he strengthened and reassured them with a formula common to epiphanies, "Arise and do not be afraid" (17:7). Only in Matthew does Jesus utter words that complement the voice of God from the cloud by encouraging the disciples and the audience to heed the divine mandate.

The pivotal mandatory epiphany concludes with the earthly Jesus as the only one of the epiphanic figures remaining with the disciples (17:8). A dramatic suspense has been established for the remainder of the narrative: Will the disciples and the audience heed the pivotal epiphanic mandate and listen to Jesus in order to understand the way that he and they will attain the heavenly glory anticipated by his transfiguration?

CHAPTER 11

MATTHEW 17:1-8 AND THE SUBSEQUENT NARRATIVE

In the preceding chapter we considered how the Matthean transfiguration narrative functions as a pivotal mandatory epiphany in relation to the antecedent Matthean narrative. We saw how the mandate, "Listen to him!" (17:5), pivoted the audience back especially to Jesus' pronouncement of the necessity for his disciples to follow him in suffering and death before being raised to heavenly glory (16:21-27) as a key to understanding the significance of the transfiguration epiphany. In this chapter we will consider how the Matthean transfiguration epiphany, especially its pivotal mandate, relates to and prepares the audience for the subsequent Matthean narrative.

A. MATT 17:9-13: ELIJAH HAS ALREADY COME

1. Matt 17:9: Jesus commands the disciples to silence until he has been raised from the dead

When they came down from the mountain of the transfiguration, Jesus, who had just touched the three disciples and told them not to be afraid (17:6-7), "commanded them" (ἐνετείλατο αὐτοῖς) to tell no one (μηδενὶ εἴπητε) the vision until the Son of Man has been raised from the dead (17:9).[1] This "command" of Jesus serves as the first

---

[1] HAGNER (Matthew 14-28, 498) expresses the "epiphanic" as opposed to "visionary" connotation of ὅραμα, when he comments: "The word here means a supernatural 'vision,' not in the sense of something imagined but in the sense of something seen." *Contra* MOSES (*Mat-*

example of what the disciples and audience are to listen to, as enjoined by the pivotal mandate, the "command" of God's voice from the bright, overshadowing cloud (17:5). With the authority of God the Father, who "commands" (ἐντελεῖται, 4:6) and speaks the "command-ment" (ἐντολὴν, 15:3-4), Jesus, his beloved and favored Son (17:5), "commands" the disciples.[2] The command of Jesus reminds the audience that after Peter confessed Jesus to be the Christ, the Son of the living God (16:16), Jesus "ordered" (διεστείλατο) the disciples to tell no one (μηδενὶ εἴπωσιν) that he is the Christ (16:20). These two commands to silence impress upon the audience that the more pro-found character of Jesus as the Christ (16:16, 20) and Son of God (16:16; 17:5) cannot be fully understood until God has raised him from the dead (17:9).[3]

The emphasis upon "*from the dead*" in a forward position in the statement, "until the Son of Man from the dead has been raised (ἐκ νεκρῶν ἐγερθῇ)" (17:9), makes explicit what Jesus' first passion pre-diction implies (16:21), namely, that he will be raised (ἐγερθῆναι) *from the dead* on the third day after the Jewish leaders have killed him. This emphasis upon Jesus' resurrection *from the dead* provides the dis-ciples and the audience a key for understanding the significance of Jesus' transfiguration. Unlike the great prophetic figures of Moses and Elijah, who attained heavenly glory without being put to death by their people, Jesus will attain the heavenly glory anticipated by his transfig-uration only after God raises him *from the dead*, from a death perpetra-ted by the leaders of his own people.[4] Unlike Moses and Elijah, Jesus, the beloved and favored Son of God (17:5) and the Son of Man, will be raised to heavenly glory *from the dead*.

---

thew's Transfiguration Story, 151), who states: "Matthew's description of the transfiguration as τὸ ὅραμα suggests that Matthew sees it as theophanic vision akin to those found in Old Testament and New Testament apocalyptic." For the distinction between theophanies, visions, and epiphanies, see chap. 2.

[2] L. MORRIS, *The Gospel According to Matthew* (Grand Rapids: Eerdmans, 1992) 441 n. 21: "ἐνετείλατο signifies 'commanded'; Jesus was not making a request."

[3] MOSES (*Matthew's Transfiguration Story*, 151) states that "this is the fifth and last occa-sion the disciples are commanded to be silent, the earlier occasions being 8.4; 9.30; 12.16; 16.20." But in 8:4, 9:30, and 12:16 Jesus' command to silence is issued to recipients of his healing power rather than to the disciples.

[4] For the various traditions about how Moses and Elijah achieved heavenly glory, see chap. 5.

As the audience has heard, Herod the tetrarch thought that the reason mighty powers were at work in Jesus was that he was John the Baptist, whom Herod had beheaded, "raised from the dead" (ἠγέρθη ἀπὸ τῶν νεκρῶν) (14:1-2). As John raised from the dead, Jesus would thus represent God's vindication for the brutal murder of one whom the crowd held to be a prophet (14:5). Although the audience knows that Jesus is not John raised from the dead, they are to realize that Jesus' being "raised from the dead" (ἐκ νεκρῶν ἐγερθῇ, 17:9), anticipated by his transfiguration, represents God's vindication of both John and Jesus as prophetic figures put to death by their own people.

Although the phrase, "from the dead," is emphasized in 17:9, the ultimate focus is, of course, upon Jesus' being *raised* by God in triumph over death.[5] Indeed, Jesus' statement expresses the inseparable connection between his death and resurrection. When Jesus first predicted his suffering, death and resurrection, Peter's rebuke of Jesus indicated to the audience that he heard the words about suffering and death but not about the triumphant resurrection on the third day (16:21-23). Jesus' transfiguration gave the disciples a glimpse of his future resurrection to heavenly glory. But they have yet to make the connection between the necessity of his suffering and death before his resurrection to heavenly glory. Therefore, God's command to listen to Jesus (17:5) directs the disciples and the audience to hear the connection Jesus makes between his necessary death but subsequent resurrection when he commands silence about the transfiguration until he has "*from the dead been raised*" (17:9).

2. Matt 17:10: The disciples object that Elijah must come first

The disciples then ask Jesus why therefore do the scribes say that Elijah must come first (17:10). The word "therefore" (οὖν) connects the disciples' question not only with Jesus' command for their silence about the transfiguration until he has been raised from the dead (17:9),

---

[5] MORRIS, *Matthew*, 442: "The passive *raised* looks to the action of the Father in bringing his Son back from the dead. Jesus looks through death to the certainty of the resurrection (which, of course, implies that his death will take place along the way). By referring to the resurrection he concentrates on the ultimate triumph."

but also with their seeing of Moses and Elijah together with Jesus in heavenly glory (without having been raised from the dead) in the trans-figuration epiphany (17:3).[6]

The disciples' question relativizes the divine necessity that Jesus as the Son of Man "must" (δεῖ) suffer, be killed, and raised (16:21) with the divine necessity that Elijah "must" (δεῖ) come first.[7] Ironically the disciples appeal to the teaching of the scribes, one of the groups of Jewish leaders who will put Jesus to death (16:21; cf. 20:18; 26:57; 27:41). This appeal to scribal authority is especially ironic for the audience who recalls the response of the crowds whom Jesus taught in his sermon on the mount (5:1-7:27): "The crowds were astounded at his teaching, for he was teaching them as one having authority and not as their scribes" (7:28-29). The disciples' appeal to scribal teaching thus underlines their lack of understanding regarding the more pro-found character and authority of Jesus.

That Elijah must come first reminds the audience of the scriptural expectation that Elijah, who ascended to heaven without dying (2 Kgs 2:11), would return before the great and manifest "Day of the Lord" comes (Mal 3:23; Sir 48:10). This eschatological "Day of the Lord" is closely associated with the time of the eschatological resurrection of the dead to be inaugurated by the resurrection from the dead of Jesus as the Son of Man (17:9). The disciples' objection that Elijah must come first implies that indeed Elijah has already returned in the trans-figuration epiphany. The disciples are thus insinuating that if Elijah, the expected forerunner of the eschatological age, has returned as a heavenly figure rather than as an earthly mortal to undergo the death he escaped at his first coming, then why must Jesus, who was just trans-figured into a heavenly figure like Elijah, be put to death and raised as the Son of Man to inaugurate the eschatological age?[8]

---

[6] MOSES, *Matthew's Transfiguration Story*, 153: "Matthew's use of οὖν is significant; it makes for a closer connection with the preceding v. 9, with its (i) 'vision' motif, which includes their seeing Elijah on the mountain, and (ii) statement on the resurrection (and therefore death)."

[7] On δεῖ as an expression of divine necessity, see POPKES, "δεῖ," 1.279-80. MORRIS, *Matthew*, 442: "Their word *must* indicates a compelling divine necessity."

[8] MOSES, *Matthew's Transfiguration Story*, 153: "How do we fit the resurrection motif (17.9, and therefore death), with the Elijah motif?" For a tradition that Elijah came again in the person of Phinehas to "taste death," see *L.A.B.* 48:1; ÖHLER, *Elia*, 24-27, 45-46; MURPHY,

3. Matt 17:11: Jesus affirms the expectation of Elijah's return and restoration of everything

Jesus affirms the scribal expectation that Elijah will indeed come first, but he adds that "he will restore all things (ἀποκα-ταστήσει πάντα)" (17:11).[9] Jesus' addition further affirms the scriptural expectation regarding Elijah, rather than introduces his own new expectation of Elijah's future coming for the restoration of everything.[10] This already begins to dispel the disciples' implication that perhaps Elijah's appearance in the transfiguration epiphany fulfills the expectation that he must come first. The brief appearance of the heavenly Elijah with Moses to converse with the transfigured Jesus (17:3) can hardly be understood as his restoration of all things.

4. Matt 17:12: Jesus asserts that he will suffer like the Elijah who has already come

After affirming the scribal expectation that Elijah will come again to restore everything (17:11), Jesus asserts, "But I say to you that Elijah has already come, yet they did not recognize him but did to him whatever they wished" (17:12). This confirms the disciples' implica-

---

Pseudo-Philo, 184-85. JACOBSON (Commentary on Pseudo-Philo, 1063) states that L.A.B. 48:1 seems to be suggesting that those people who were translated to heaven without dying, such as Enoch, Elijah (Phinehas), and possibly Moses, "need to die before they can gain eternal life through resurrection."

[9] Jesus thus broadens and generalizes the scriptural expectations regarding Elijah. According to the LXX of Mal 3:23 Elijah will come before the Day of the Lord and "he will restore (ἀποκαταστήσει) the heart of a father to his son and the heart of a man to his neighbor." According to Sir 48:10 Elijah will come "to turn the heart of father to son and to restore (καταστήσαι) the tribes of Jacob." As DAVIES and ALLISON (Matthew, 2.715) note: "The precise nature of Elijah's task of apokatastasis is left unstated and we cannot tell what Matthew had in mind, for there were differing notions."

[10] On Elijah's "restoration" here, DAVIES and ALLISON (Matthew, 2.714) state that "the passage in Malachi gave the word an eschatological connotation (cf. Acts 1.6; 3.21). In its present context, the future tense, ἀποκαταστήσει, is not likely to mean that Elijah is still to come or will come again. 'Will restore' simply agrees with what the OT and the scribes say." See also LUZ, Matthäus, 2.512-13; HAGNER, Matthew 14-28, 499; contra GUNDRY, Matthew, 347.

tion that Elijah has already come, but not as the heavenly figure they witnessed in the transfiguration epiphany. As the audience has previously heard from the mouth of Jesus, Elijah has already come in the person of John the Baptist (11:14).[11] But John the Baptist was not recognized either by the scribes or in general as the Elijah to come.[12] That "they did to him whatever they wished (ἠθέλησαν)" refers to the death of John by Herod the tetrarch, who was "wishing (θέλων) to kill him," even though the crowd held John to be a prophet (14:5).[13]

Jesus then announces that like John he too will suffer at the hands of the Jewish leadership: "So also the Son of Man is going to suffer at their hands" (17:12). To the divine necessity that Elijah "must" (δεῖ) come first (17:10) Jesus adds that he "is going" or "is destined" (μέλλει) to suffer at the hands of his own people like John.[14] That Jesus is destined to suffer complements the divine necessity of his resurrection from the dead (17:9). By obeying God's command to listen (17:5) to what Jesus is saying here (17:9-12), the disciples and the audience are to realize that both Elijah's coming first to suffer death as John the Baptist as well as Jesus' suffering, death and resurrection are part of the necessity of the divine plan.

---

[11] DAVIES and ALLISON, *Matthew*, 2.715: "The reader of the gospel immediately equates Elijah with John the Baptist, for the equation has already been made."

[12] MOSES, *Matthew's Transfiguration Story*, 156-57: "Matthew's καὶ οὐκ ἐπέγνωσαν αὐτὸν is emphatic, for it makes the point that though the scribes were right in their expectation (17.11) the reality within which it was being worked out (in relation to the coming of John the Baptist, and also in the light of the Jesus-Baptist relationship) was so very different from their view of things that 'they did not know him'." MORRIS, *Matthew*, 443: "Jesus does not say who *they* were, but evidently it is people at large who are in mind, perhaps particularly the Jewish leaders; there was no general recognition of Elijah."

[13] On the significance of the suffering and death of the Baptist as Elijah in Matthew, see M. KNOWLES, *Jeremiah in Matthew's Gospel: The Rejected-Prophet Motif in Matthaean Redaction* (JSNTSup 68; Sheffield: JSOT, 1993) 231.

[14] That Jesus "is going to suffer" (μέλλει πάσχειν) "is not a simple future, but a compound that expresses the certainty of the outworking of a divine purpose," according to MORRIS, *Matthew*, 444. According to BAGD (501), μέλλει in 17:12 denotes "an action that necessarily follows a divine decree." W. RADL, "μέλλω" *EDNT* 2.404: "μέλλω can express the necessity of an event that is based on the divine will and thus is certain to occur, e.g., Matt 17:12: 'he *must* suffer'."

What Jesus says about the divine necessity of his suffering at the hands of his own people before rising from the dead in 17:9-12 reinforces the first prediction of his resurrection after a necessary suffering and death:

16:21: "From that time on Jesus began to show his disciples that he must (δεῖ) go to Jerusalem and suffer greatly (πολλὰ παθεῖν) from the elders, the chief priests, and the scribes, and be killed, but on the third day be raised (ἐγερθῆναι)."

17:12: "So also the Son of Man is going to suffer (μέλλει πάσχειν) at their hands"

17:9: "...until the Son of Man has been raised (ἐγερθῇ) from the dead."

The pivotal mandate of the transfiguration epiphany, "Listen to him!" (17:5), thus points the disciples and the audience not only back to heed Jesus' first passion prediction in 16:21-27 but also forward to heed Jesus' additional passion prediction in 17:9-12. By listening attentively to these predictions of Jesus, the disciples and the audience are to realize that just as John the Baptist was put to death by Jewish leadership, so it is divinely necessary for Jesus to suffer and die at the hands of the Jewish leaders before rising to the heavenly glory he anticipated in his transfiguration.[15]

5. Matt 17:13: The disciples understood that Jesus was speaking about John the Baptist

That "then (τότε) the disciples understood (συνῆκαν) that (ὅτι) he was telling (εἶπεν) them about John the Baptist" (17:13) reminds the audience of a similar statement about the understanding of the disciples in 16:12: "Then (τότε) they understood (συνῆκαν) that (ὅτι) he was not telling (εἶπεν) them to beware of the leaven of bread but of the teaching of the Pharisees and Sadducees." In both cases the disciples' understanding is only partial and creates a deeper suspense regarding what they still do not understand.

---

[15] MORRIS, Matthew, 444: "There is glory on the mountain of transfiguration, but it is a glory that meant suffering for the Baptist and would mean suffering for Jesus."

After Jesus warned the disciples to beware of the "leaven" of the Pharisees and Sadducees (16:6), the disciples misunderstood, thinking he was referring to the fact that they had forgotten to bring bread with them (16:5, 7). In explaining that he was not referring to bread, Jesus' questions revealed that the disciples still have not understood the more profound character of Jesus based on his miraculously overabundant feedings.[16]   In reply to Jesus' questions, "Do you not remember the five loaves for the five thousand, and how many baskets you took up? Or the seven loaves for the four thousand, and how many baskets you took up?" (16:9-10), the disciples remain surprisingly silent (cf. Mark 8:19-20). Although the disciples understood that Jesus was telling them to beware of the teaching of the Pharisees and Sadducees (16:12), they still did not understand the significance of his miraculously overabundant feedings.[17] Similarly, although the disciples understood that Jesus was telling them that Elijah has already come in the person of John the Baptist (17:13), there is no indication that they understand that Jesus must suffer and die before being raised to the heavenly glory they saw in the transfigured Jesus.[18]

B. MATT 17:14-20: JESUS ASSURES HIS DISCIPLES THAT WITH FAITH NOTHING WILL BE IMPOSSIBLE

Jesus' lamentful questions to the "faithless and perverse generation" (cf. Deut 32:5, 20) represented by the crowd (17:14) and the father who brought his son to Jesus after the disciples failed to heal him (17:15-16) – "How long am I to be with you? How long am I to

---

[16] Note the suspense created by the fact that there was no acknowledgment of these miracles by either the crowds or the disciples who witnessed them; see 14:13-21; 15:32-39.

[17] HAGNER, *Matthew 14-28*, 461: "The disciples had not yet learned that they could trust in God's provision for their needs."

[18] G. YAMASAKI, *John the Baptist in Life and Death: Audience-Oriented Criticism of Matthew's Narrative* (JSNTSup 167; Sheffield: Sheffield Academic Press, 1998) 136: "…although this statement indicates that the disciples grasp Jesus' explanation on John as set out in vv. 11-12, it does not indicate that they grasp his concluding statement on the Son of Man. Therefore, just as the disciples' question of v. 10 suggests that they miss Jesus' allusion in v. 9 to his coming suffering, so also this statement by the narrator in v. 13 suggests that the disciples also miss Jesus' reference in v. 12 to his coming suffering."

bear with you?" (17:17; cf. Num 14:27) – express an ironic double meaning. On the one hand, they express the extreme length of time Jesus has had to endure their lack of faith. On the other hand, they warn of the short period Jesus will still be with them before his approaching death, as anticipated by his absence from them during his transfiguration.

After Jesus exorcized the demon from the suffering boy (17:18), the disciples asked why they were not able to exorcize it (17:19).[19] Jesus replied that it was because of their "little faith" and that if they had faith the size of a grain of mustard, nothing would be impossible for them (17:20).[20] The failure of the disciples to exorcize the child stands in continuity with their failure to understand the necessity for Jesus to suffer and die before being raised.[21] Only with faith will they be able not only to heal as Jesus, but to follow him on his way to suffering, death and resurrection (16:21, 24-27; 17:9, 12) in order to join him in the heavenly glory anticipated by his transfiguration.

C. MATT 17:22-23: THE DISCIPLES WERE GREATLY SADDENED BY JESUS' PREDICTION OF HIS PASSION

To his disciples gathered together in Galilee Jesus develops the predictions of his resurrection after suffering and death. That Jesus as the Son of Man is going (μέλλει) to suffer under those who did not recognize John the Baptist as Elijah (17:12) progresses to "the Son of Man is going (μέλλει) to be delivered into the hands of men" (17:22). This

---

[19] If the variant reading, "suffers severely" (κακῶς πάσχει), is accepted in 17:15, then the boy's suffering is linguistically linked to the predicted suffering (πάσχειν) of Jesus in 17:12. On the preference for the reading κακῶς πάσχει in 17:15, see B.M. METZGER, *A Textual Commentary on the Greek New Testament* (New York: United Bible Societies, 1971) 43.

[20] This is the final, climactic reference to the "little faith" of the disciples in Matthew; the previous references are in 6:30; 8:26; 14:31; 16:8. On the Matthean theme of "little faith," see HEIL, *Jesus Walking on the Sea*, 63; G. BARTH, "ὀλιγοπιστία," *EDNT* 2.506; WILKENS, *Disciple*, 182: "In Matthew's use the expression should not be understood so much as indicating having a 'little' faith, as referring to one who has in the past exercised faith and now no longer uses it; it is rather a faith which has failed or is bankrupt."

[21] Note how the theme of the disciples' "little faith" in 16:8 is linked with their failure to understand the significance of Jesus' miraculously overabundant feedings in 16:9-11.

expresses divine agency because Jesus' suffering and death has already been assigned to divine necessity (16:21) and "delivered" (παραδίδοσθαι) can be understood as a divine passive.[22] The divine necessity, expressed in the passive voice and aorist tense, that Jesus "be killed" (ἀποκτανθῆναι, 16:21) progresses to the human agency embraced by that divine necessity, expressed in the active voice and more imminent future tense. The men into whose hands the Son of Man is going to be delivered "will kill" (ἀποκτενοῦσιν) him (17:23). That Jesus "be raised" (ἐγερθῆναι, 16:21; ἐγερθῇ 17:9) on the third day as part of God's plan progresses to "he will be raised" (ἐγερθήσεται) on the third day by God in triumphant vindication over the men who "will kill" him (17:23), as they fail to recognize his role in God's plan (17:12).

The gathered disciples' response to this prediction, "and they were greatly saddened" (17:23), indicates to the audience more acceptance of the divine necessity and inevitability of Jesus' death than Peter's vehement protest after the first prediction (16:21-23). Whereas the disciples who saw the transfiguration did not react to Jesus' prediction of his own suffering (17:12), but only understood that he was speaking to them about John the Baptist (17:13), while the rest of the disciples were unable to exorcize because of their "little faith" (17:20), now the whole group of disciples was greatly saddened.[23] Their great sadness is due to the divine necessity that the Jesus whose glorious transfiguration Peter wanted to preserve and prolong (17:4), the Jesus who lamented, "How much longer will I be with you?" (17:17), will not be with them much longer but will suffer and die.

Yet the disciples' great sadness indicates that Jesus' prediction that he "will be raised on the third day" (17:23) has not properly registered with them.[24] Like Peter (16:21-22) the group of gathered disciples hear the prediction only of the death but not of the triumphant resurrec-

---

[22] J. GNILKA, *Das Matthäusevangelium: Kommentar zu Kap. 14,1 - 28,20 und Einleitungsfragen* (HTKNT 1/2; Freiburg: Herder, 1988) 2.112.

[23] ANDERSON, *Matthew's Narrative Web*, 163: "Preceded by the failure to exorcise due to little-faith, 17.22-23a is followed by a sign that the disciples are beginning to grasp the seriousness of Jesus' end: after this prediction, 'they were grieved exceedingly' (17.23b)."

[24] MORRIS, *Matthew*, 451: "But at that time the disciples were more impressed by the words about death than by those about resurrection."

tion.[25] The disciples' great sadness at Jesus' prediction of his death and resurrection (17:23) further confirms their "little faith" (17:20), their failure to share the firm faith of Jesus himself in God's power to raise him from the dead. Thus, the disciples and the audience need to heed the pivotal mandate (17:5) to listen attentively to Jesus' predictions and hear of his *resurrection* from the dead, in order to understand that his temporary transfiguration into a heavenly figure with Moses and Elijah (17:2-3) indicates that he will ultimately achieve heavenly glory by being raised from the dead.

D. MATT 20:17-19: JESUS TELLS THE TWELVE OF HIS RESURRECTION AFTER DEATH

That Jesus on his way to Jerusalem "took along" (παρέλαβεν) the Twelve disciples "privately" (κατ' ἰδίαν) (20:17) reminds the audience how he "took along" (παραλαμβάνει) an elite subgroup of the Twelve – Peter, James and John – and led them up to a high mountain "privately" (κατ' ἰδίαν) to witness his transfiguration (17:1). Introducing yet another passion prediction, Jesus draws the disciples more closely to himself, "Behold, *we* are going up to Jerusalem" (20:18).[26]

In further specifying that "the Son of Man is going to be delivered into the hands of men" (17:22), Jesus' prediction that "the Son of Man will be delivered to the chief priests and scribes, and they will condemn him to death and deliver him to the Gentiles to be mocked and scourged and crucified" (20:18-19) reminds the audience of what Jesus predicted for the Twelve disciples (10:1-2, 5; 11:1) in the missionary discourse (9:35-11:1). Just as the Jewish leaders will deliver (παραδώσουσιν) Jesus to be mocked and scourged (μαστιγῶσαι), so Jews will deliver (παραδώσουσιν) the Twelve disciples to councils

---

[25] HAGNER, *Matthew*, 508: "Matthew thus records the emotion of the disciples. Though quite beyond their understanding at this time, because the resurrection is beyond their mental horizon, these words fill them with trouble."

[26] W. CARTER, *Households and Discipleship: A Study of Matthew 19-20* (JSNTSup 103; Sheffield: JSOT, 1994) 164: "Jesus includes the disciples by his use of a first person plural verb, 'we are going up' (ἀναβαίνομεν). This inclusiveness contrasts with the use of singular verb forms in the two predictions of 16.21 and 17.22-23, which maintained a focus on Jesus' special destiny to the exclusion of the disciples."

and scourge (μαστιγώσουσιν) them in their synagogues (10:17).[27]
Just as Jesus will be delivered to the Gentiles (τοῖς ἔθνεσιν), so the
disciples will be led before rulers as well as kings on account of Jesus
as a witness to them and to the Gentiles (τοῖς ἔθνεσιν) (10:18). Just
as the Jewish leaders will condemn Jesus to death (θανάτῳ), so among
the disciples brother will deliver brother to death (εἰς θάνατον) and
children will rise up against their parents and put them to death
(θανατώσουσιν) (10:21).[28]

If disciples are destined to share in the suffering and death of
Jesus, their master (10:24-25, 38-39; 16:24-26), they can also share in
his triumph over death. Jesus once again climactically concludes his
passion prediction with the promise, "but on the third day he will be
raised" (20:19; cf. 16:21; 17:9, 23). Jesus' triumphant resurrection
over death is the basis for his promise that persecuted disciples (and
audience) who persevere to the end will be saved (10:22). The transfiguration's pivotal mandate to listen to Jesus (17:5) has directed the
disciples to listen to this passion prediction (20:17-19) in order to
understand that although they will share in his suffering and death,
they will also share in his triumph over death, as prefigured in his
transfiguration. But, in contrast to previous predictions of his resurrection from the dead (16:21-22; 17:10, 23), the disciples do not respond,
increasing the suspense for the audience.

E. MATT 20:20-28: HEAVENLY GLORY WITH JESUS COMES ONLY AFTER SUFFERING AND DEATH

Peter responded to Jesus as spokesman for himself as well as James
and John at the transfiguration (17:4). Now the mother of "the sons of
Zebedee" – James and John (cf. 4:21; 10:2) – complements Peter by
speaking to Jesus on behalf of her sons (20:20).[29] Her request serves

---

[27] H. BALZ, "μαστιγόω," *EDNT* 2.396: "According to Matt 10:17...23:23, those whom Jesus
sent out will be threatened with scourging, which is to be understood against the background of
the Jewish punishment of thirty-nine stripes." See also D.J. WEAVER, *Matthew's Missionary Discourse: A Literary Critical Analysis* (JSNTSup 38; Sheffield: JSOT, 1990) 199 n. 116.

[28] For an analysis of 10:17-21, see WEAVER, *Matthew's Missionary Discourse*, 93-100.

[29] Peter addressed Jesus as spokesman for the disciples again in 17:26; 18:21; and 19:28.

as an indirect response to the previous passion prediction (20:17-19), to which there was no immediate reaction, and indicates to the audience a continuing lack of understanding about the suffering and death that must precede heavenly glory.[30] Whereas Peter erred in suggesting the placing of Moses and Elijah in the same category of heavenly glory as Jesus by building a tent for each, the mother of James and John errs by wanting for her sons the places of preeminence – seats at the right and left – with Jesus in his kingdom (20:21). Previous responses by Peter and the disciples to Jesus' predictions of his death and resurrection focused only on the suffering and death and failed to hear the promise of the resurrection (16:21-22; 17:22-23). In indirect response to Jesus' most recent prediction of his death and resurrection (20:17-19) the mother of James and John, who have heard Jesus speak of his coming in the glory of his Father (16:27) and have witnessed Jesus' temporary transfiguration into heavenly glory (17:2), focuses only on the glory without mention of the suffering and death (20:21).

Jesus' promise that he is going to come "in the glory of his Father" (ἐν τῇ δόξῃ τοῦ πατρὸς αὐτοῦ) to execute judgment (16:27) was paralleled by his promise that there are some standing there who will not taste death until they see him as the Son of Man coming "in his kingdom" (ἐν τῇ βασιλείᾳ αὐτοῦ) (16:28). Jesus also promised Peter and the disciples (19:27) that whenever the Son of Man sits "upon his throne of glory" (ἐπὶ θρόνου δόξης αὐτοῦ), they also will sit upon twelve thrones judging the twelve tribes of Israel (19:28). In asking for the most prominent places for her sons to sit "in your kingdom" (ἐν τῇ βασιλείᾳ σου, 20:21), the mother of James and John is thus asking for exalted positions of glory for her two sons.[31]

The request of the mother of James and John makes no mention of the necessity for followers of Jesus to take up the cross and lose their

---

[30] On the request of the mother of James and John, see CARTER, *Households and Discipleship*, 165-68.

[31] P. LUOMANEN, *Entering the Kingdom of Heaven: A Study on the Structure of Matthew's View of Salvation* (WUNT 101; Tübingen: Mohr Siebeck, 1998) 136: "To be sure, the mother talks only about 'your kingdom,' but the passage is intimately connected to the preceding passion prediction where Jesus has talked about himself as the Son of Man. The term may refer to final salvation in general, but in the light of Matthew's addition in 19:28 it may also be connected to Jesus' and his disciples' role as judges."

lives in order to save them and thus join Jesus in the glory of his kingdom (10:38-39; 16:24-27). Jesus then underscores the need for James and John to "drink of the cup" and thus share in the same suffering and death he will undergo (20:22).[32] He reminds all three – the mother and her two sons – that his glory is ultimately the glory of his Father, who has prepared the requested places of heavenly honor (20:23).[33] Jesus concludes with a further revelation about the significance of his death as freely accepted humble service for others before he enters into and comes again in the glory of his kingdom: "For the Son of Man did not come to be served but to serve and to give his life as a ransom for many" (20:28). But once again no one responds, adding to the suspense for the audience as to whether they will heed the pivotal mandate (17:5) to listen to what Jesus is saying about the necessity to share in his suffering and death in order to share in the heavenly glory presaged by his transfiguration.

F. Matt 21:33-46: As God's Son Jesus will be killed like a prophet but vindicated

Jesus addresses a parable to the Jewish leaders in the temple (21:33-46) in which he tells how the tenants (Jewish leadership) of the vineyard killed or mistreated all of the servants (prophets) the owner (God) sent them (21:33-36).[34] Finally, the owner (God) sent his son (τὸν υἱὸν αὐτοῦ), thinking, "They will respect my son (τὸν υἱὸν

---

[32] H. Patsch, "ποτήριον," *EDNT* 3.142: "The logion concerning the cup of death...is comprehensible only against the background of OT and Jewish cup metaphors: The cup in or out of Yahweh's hand is an enduring image of judgment (e.g., Ps 75:9; Jer 25:15ff.; Hab 2:16); a cup can also acquire in a general fashion the meaning 'fate, destiny' (Pss 11:6; 16:5; 4QpNah 4:6). This justifies the interpretation: 'Are you able to accept the *fate of death* that God has determined for me?'"

[33] Carter (*Households and Discipleship*, 167) notes how Jesus' use of the plural in addressing the mother (20:22) "draws her two sons into the exchange, indicating for the audience that her question and rebuke are also their request and rebuke."

[34] Carter, *Matthew's Parables*, 161: "The audience knows the prophetic tradition in which prophets are frequently identified as God's 'servants' (Jer 7:25; Amos 3:7). Though sent by God they experience conflict with and rejection by the people's leaders (cf. Jer 7:25-26; 25:4; 26:5; 29:19; 35:15; 2 Chr 36:15-16; Neh 9:26; Dan 9:6: 'we have not listened to your servants the prophets'; *Jub.* 1:12-13)."

μου)" (21:37). But when the tenants saw the son (τὸν υἱὸν), who represents Jesus, they decided to kill him (21:38).[35] This triple reference to "the son" reminds the audience of the last time Jesus was referred to as God's Son, the transfiguration's pivotal mandate uttered by God's voice from the cloud: "This is my Son (ὁ υἱός μου), the beloved, in whom I am well pleased; listen to him!" (17:5). That the tenants killed (ἀπέκτειναν, 21:39) the son, after saying to one another, "Come, let us kill (ἀποκτείνωμεν) him and have his inheritance" (21:38), recalls Jesus' predictions that he will be killed (ἀποκτανθῆναι, 16:21; ἀποκτενοῦσιν, 17:23) by both the Jewish leaders, who "will condemn him to death" (20:18), and the Gentiles (20:19).

Realizing that the parable was directed against them, the chief priests and the Pharisees were seeking to arrest Jesus, but they feared the crowds, who held him to be a prophet (21:45-46; cf. 21:11). But the audience knows that this will not prevent the Jewish leaders from killing Jesus. Just as the tenants of the parable killed the servants, who represent the prophets (21:33-36), and just as Herod killed John the Baptist, although he was held to be a prophet (14:5; 21:26), so they will kill Jesus. Even though Jesus, as God's beloved and favored Son, is more than a prophet, he is destined to the same fate as the prophet John (17:12).[36] Unlike the prophets Moses and Elijah, who attained heavenly glory (17:3) without being killed by their people, Jesus will attain the heavenly glory prefigured by his transfiguration only after being killed by his own people.

Jesus represents "the stone" which the builders (Jewish leaders) rejected, but which God marvelously transformed into the "cornerstone" or "head of the corner" in the quotation of Ps 117:22-23 (LXX) in the parable (21:42). Although Jesus will be rejected and killed, God

---

[35] As CARTER (*Matthew's Parables*, 162) notes, the audience knows that "the son" of the parable represents Jesus, because "Jesus has been identified as God's son previously in the narrative (2:15; 3:17; 4:3, 6; 11:27; 14:33; 16:16; 17:5)" and "the audience knows from the passion predictions (16:21; 17:12, 22; 20:17-19) that Jesus must die at the hands of the religious leaders."

[36] ANDERSON, *Matthew's Narrative Web*, 174: "Jesus and John have preached the same message, been misunderstood, angered the same enemies. Inevitably they will meet the same fate. John has been delivered up and executed. Jesus will soon be delivered up and crucified. John is the foreshadower as well as the forerunner of Jesus."

will vindicate him through resurrection from the dead.[37] The transfiguration's pivotal mandate (17:5) bids the disciples and audience to hear and understand that although Jesus will be rejected and killed like a prophet, as God's beloved and favored Son, he will be vindicated and ultimately attain the heavenly glory anticipated by his transfiguration.

G. MATT 22:23-33: JESUS TEACHES THAT GOD WILL RAISE THE DEAD TO LIFE

In his refutation of the attempt by the Sadducees to discredit a belief in the resurrection of the dead (22:23-33) Jesus asserts that when people rise from the dead, they become "like angels in heaven" (22:30). When he was transfigured, Jesus' "face shone as the sun, while his clothes became white as the light" (17:2), indicating that he has temporarily become like an angel in heaven.[38] Jesus' transfiguration into an angel-like heavenly figure, which foreshadows his future resurrection from the dead, bolsters for the audience his pronouncement that when the dead are raised they enter into a heavenly existence that transcends earthly categories such as marriage.

Jesus concludes that when God revealed himself to Moses as "the God of Abraham, the God of Isaac, and the God of Jacob" (Exod 3:6), he indicated that "he is not the God of the dead but of the living!" (22:32). Since the three patriarchs were already dead when God pronounced this to Moses, it implies "the power of God" (22:29) to raise them from the dead. In other words, since God in his covenantal fidelity to the people of Israel promises to be the saving God not of those who are "dead" but of those who are "living," the patriarchs of Israel – Abraham, Isaac, and Jacob – cannot remain dead but are still living through the power of God (cf. 8:11), so that there is a resurrection of the dead.[39] If the disciples and the audience heed the transfiguration's

---

[37] CARTER, *Matthew's Parables*, 163: "As with other citations in the gospel this use of Psalm 118 makes sense only in relation to Jesus. He is rejected by people but vindicated by God."

[38] On the transfigured Jesus as an angel-like heavenly figure, see chap. 4.

[39] HAGNER, *Matthew 14-28*, 642: "The point that Abraham, Isaac, and Jacob, although having died, 'are alive in God' ($\zeta\tilde{\omega}\sigma\iota\nu$ $\tau\tilde{\omega}$ $\theta\epsilon\tilde{\omega}$) is also made in 4 Macc 7:19; 16:25. If God is the God of the patriarchs, they are by implication alive after their death...and thus the ground is prepared for the reality of the future resurrection."

pivotal mandate to listen to Jesus (17:5), they will hear in this pronouncement that although Jesus, unlike Moses and Elijah, will be put to death, he will surely be raised from the dead like the patriarchs, since God is "not the God of the dead but of the living!" (22:32).[40] This gives them hope in God's power also to raise them to new life after they have given their lives to God for the sake of Jesus (10:39; 16:24-28).

H. MATT 24:30; 25:31: JESUS IS STILL TO COME ON THE CLOUDS OF HEAVEN AND WITH GLORY

Jesus took the three disciples up a high mountain "privately" (κατ' ἰδίαν, 17:1) for the special revelation of his transfiguration into a heavenly figure. When Jesus sits upon the Mount of Olives after leaving the temple, the disciples approach him "privately" (κατ' ἰδίαν, 24:3; cf. 17:19; 20:17) for a special revelation about his parousia and the end of the world. Jesus tells them that people will see him as "the Son of Man coming on the clouds of heaven with much power and glory" (24:30; cf. Dan 7:13-14). Whereas Moses and Elijah were transported by the bright overshadowing cloud (νεφέλη) back to heaven after their appearance in glory with the transfigured Jesus on earth (17:5, 8), Jesus, after his death and resurrection to heavenly glory, will be transported on the clouds (ἐπὶ τῶν νεφέλαις) of heaven to earth, where he will send out the angels to gather together his elect from wherever they have been scattered (24:30-31).[41]

As the Son of Man Jesus is still to come "on the clouds of heaven with much power and glory (δόξης)" (24:30) and will "come in his glory (δόξῃ) and all the angels with him" before he sits "upon his throne of glory (δόξης)" for the final, universal judgment (25:31).[42] This reminds the audience of Jesus' previous predictions that as the

---

[40] Although the disciples are not explicitly present for the scene with the Sadducees in Matt 22:23-33, they are implicitly present during Jesus' acitivity in the temple; see 21:1, 6, 20-22; 23:1; 24:1.

[41] On the vehicular function of clouds, see chap. 7.

[42] On Matt 25:31, see J.P. HEIL, "The Double Meaning of the Narrative of Universal Judgment in Matthew 25.31-46," JSNT 69 (1998) 5; IDEM, Matthew's Parables, 200-201.

Son of Man he is still to come "in his Father's glory (δόξη) with his angels" for judgment (16:27) and will sit "upon his throne of glory (δόξης)" (19:28). The transfiguration's pivotal mandate to listen to Jesus (17:5) thus directs the disciples and the audience backward (16:27) and forward (19:28; 24:30; 25:31) to these pronouncements about Jesus' future coming in glory, so that they will realize that the transfigured glory of Jesus before his suffering and death is only a preliminary glimpse of his final coming in glory after his suffering, death and resurrection (16:21; 17:9, 12, 22-23; 20:18-19).

I. Matt 26:2, 12: A woman anoints Jesus, who will be crucified, for burial

After Jesus predicts his imminent death to the disciples, "You know that after two days will be the Passover, and the Son of Man will be delivered to be crucified" (26:2; cf. 16:21; 17:9, 12; 22-23; 20:17-19), they once again fail to respond with any indication of understanding. But shortly thereafter an anonymous woman honors him with an extravagant gesture of hospitality. With an alabaster flask of costly perfumed ointment she approached Jesus and poured out the perfumed ointment on his head, while he was reclining at table in the house of Simon the leper at Bethany (26:6-7). Jesus interprets her lavishly hospitable anointing as a prophetic gesture anticipating his upcoming burial (26:12).[43] Because she acknowledges and esteems the death of Jesus, this woman stands in sharp contrast to the disciples, who have not heeded the transfiguration's mandate to listen to Jesus (17:5) in order to understand and accept the necessity of his death as a prerequisite to the heavenly glory anticipated by his transfiguration.

J. Matt 26:26-29: Jesus interprets his final meal as symbolic of his death .

After Jesus again predicts that as the Son of Man he will be delivered/betrayed (παραδίδοται) to death (26:24; cf. 17:22; 20:18-19;

---

[43] On the woman's prophetic gesture, see Heil, *Death and Resurrection*, 27.

26:2), he interprets his final Passover meal with his disciples (26:26-29) as a symbolic anticipation of the sacrificial death he must undergo before he partakes of the eschatological banquet in the kingdom of his Father. As they were eating, Jesus offered the disciples bread he designated as "my body" (τὸ σῶμά μου, 26:26), the "body" (τοῦ σώματός μου, 26:12) already anointed for death and burial. Then he offered them all a cup of wine, which he designated as "my blood of the covenant, which will be poured out for many for the forgiveness of sins" (26:28), thus interpreting his death as the sacrifice that establishes the (new) covenant which atones for the sins of all people.[44] Although this is Jesus' last meal on earth, he looks forward to partaking of the heavenly banquet in the kingdom of his Father (26:29) after his triumph over death through his resurrection. The transfiguration's pivotal mandate (17:5) thus enjoins the disciples and the audience to listen to these words of Jesus in order to understand that his transfiguration into a heavenly figure portends his future partaking of the heavenly banquet in the kingdom of his Father that will occur only after his sacrificial death.

K. MATT 26:31-35: JESUS AGAIN PREDICTS HIS RESURRECTION AFTER DEATH TO UNHEEDING DISCIPLES

While predicting that all of his disciples will abandon him, Jesus again predicts his resurrection after death. In an adaptation of Zech 13:7 Jesus accentuates how his suffering and death are ultimately part of God's plan of salvation: "I" (God) "will strike" (with suffering and death) "the shepherd" (Jesus), and "the sheep" (disciples) of the flock will be scattered (26:31).[45] But after being struck by God with death Jesus will be raised up by God and go before the disciples to Galilee (26:32). Although Peter insists that he will be the exception to this abandonment by all (26:33), Jesus predicts that Peter will deny him three times (26:34). Peter then vehemently objects: "Even if I must

---

[44] HEIL, *Death and Resurrection*, 36-37; O. HOFIUS, "'Für euch gegeben zur Vergebung der Sünden': Vom Sinn des Heiligen Abendmahls," *ZTK* 95 (1998) 313-37.

[45] J.P. HEIL, "Ezekiel 34 and the Narrative Strategy of the Shepherd and Sheep Metaphor in Matthew," *CBQ* 55 (1993) 706-7.

die with you, I will not deny you!" And all of the disciples similarly disclaim Jesus' prediction (26:35).

Although Peter's objection seems to indicate that he has heard the prediction of Jesus' death, there is no indication that he and the rest of the disciples have heard the promised assurance of resurrection after the necessity of death. Indeed, Peter's objection that he will not deny (ἀπαρνήσομαι) Jesus, even if he must die with him (26:35), rings ironic for the audience who has heard Jesus tell Peter and the disciples that they must deny (ἀπαρνησάσθω, 16:24) themselves, take up their cross, and lose their lives for his sake in order to save them (16:25). The disciples still have not heeded what the transfiguration's pivotal mandate has urged them to hear (17:5), namely, the necessity for them to suffer and die with Jesus in order to share in the resurrection to heavenly glory (16:24-27) prefigured by his transfiguration.

L. MATT 26:36-46: JESUS ACCEPTS DEATH THROUGH PRAYER WHILE HIS DISCIPLES SLEEP

Jesus "took along" (παραλαμβάνει) Peter and James and John his brother to witness his transfiguration (17:1). Now he similarly "took along" (παραλαβὼν) Peter and "the two sons of Zebedee" (cf. 20:22) to participate in the scene of his prayer at Gethsemane (26:37). In and through his praying, Jesus, although tested by his distress and sorrow over his imminent death (26:37-38), and voicing his quite human desire to avoid the "cup" of suffering and death (26:39, 42), nevertheless submitted his own will to God's will that he suffer and die – "not as I will but as you will!" (26:39) and "your will be done!" (26:42; cf. 6:10).[46]

That Jesus repeatedly finds the three disciples sleeping (26:40, 43, 45) is precisely what he warned them against in his discourse preparing them for the time before his final coming: "Watch, therefore; for you

---

[46] GUNDRY, *Matthew*, 534: "'Let your will come to pass' reflects the thought of the last two clauses in Jesus' first prayer (v 39), but takes its phraseology from the Lord's Prayer in Matthew's version." W.D. DAVIES and D.C. ALLISON, *The Gospel According to Saint Matthew: Volume III: Commentary on Matthew XIX-XXVIII* (ICC; Edinburgh: Clark, 1997) 500: "The citation of the Lord's Prayer makes Jesus embody his own imperative."

do not know on which day your Lord will come...you also must be prepared, for at an hour you do not expect the Son of Man will come" (24:42, 44). After the parable contrasting the wise with the foolish maidens, who fell asleep waiting for the bridegroom (25:1-12), Jesus exhorted the disciples, "Watch, therefore, for you know neither the day nor the hour!" (25:13).[47] The disciples' sleeping, then, not only indicates their inability to stay awake and "watch" with Jesus (26:38, 41) during this critical time while he prays before his suffering and death, but also points to their and the audience's potential failure to be prepared for Jesus' final coming in the glory anticipated by his transfiguration.

The first time Jesus finds the disciples sleeping he commands them to "watch and pray" (26:41). The addition of "pray" to his earlier command to "watch with me" (v. 38) indicates the significance and power of Jesus' own praying. Now that he has prayed, he can command and empower his disciples likewise to pray. That Jesus prays precisely while the disciples sleep and are unable to watch indicates to the audience that the prayer of Jesus is not only a model to be emulated but the basis, source, and empowerment of prayer. The sleeping disciples and the audience can "watch and pray" only because Jesus watched and prayed. They pray on the strength of Jesus' powerful prayer.[48]

Jesus commands the disciples to watch and pray, "so that you may not come into testing.[49] The spirit is willing but the flesh is weak" (26:41). By his praying Jesus has demonstrated how the disciples and the audience can overcome the testing of their calling to deny themselves, take up their cross, and follow Jesus (16:24) on his way to suffering and death by submitting their own wills to God's will. The disciples, whose "spirit" is ready to die with Jesus (26:35), but whose "flesh" prevents them from staying alert and watching (26:40, 43, 45),

---

[47] For an analysis of this parable, see HEIL, *Matthew's Parables*, 193-96.

[48] HAGNER, *Matthew 14-28*, 783: "For a second time the command to 'watch' (γρηγορεῖτε) is given, but here it is linked with προσεύχεσθε, 'pray.' Now the focus is not upon watching μετ' ἐμοῦ, 'with me,' but upon the need for vigilance in the future, threatening situation of the disciples. That is, they are to 'watch and pray' (again plural verbs) so that *they* might not enter into testing. The lesson of Jesus' experience is thus applied to the disciples."

[49] On "come into testing" (ἐισέλθητε εἰς πειρασμόν), DAVIES and ALLISON (*Matthew*, 3.499) state: "We give the phrase eschatological content: the disciples are to watch and pray so as not to be overcome by the last trial."

illustrate the tension between the willing spirit and the weak flesh. Jesus exemplifies how to overcome this tension in and through prayer. He voiced his own concerns of the "flesh" as he begged God to take away his cup of suffering and death. But in and through his prayer his "willing spirit" predominated over the "weak flesh" as he submitted his own will to that of God (26:39, 42).

When Jesus returned to the sleeping disciples after praying a third and final time (26:43-45), he exhorted them, "Get up, let us go!" (26:46). This indicates to the audience the powerful effect Jesus' prayer has on him and his disciples. Before he withdrew to pray, Jesus commanded his disciples to "sit here" (v. 36) and "remain here" (v. 38) while he prayed (v. 39). But after he has prayed, Jesus empowers his disciples to "get up" or "rise" (ἐγείρεσθε) from their inert, sleeping position and enables them to go with him – "let *us* go (ἄγωμεν)!" Now that Jesus has been strengthened through his prayer, he and his disciples can go together to play their respective roles in God's plan – the disciples to be scattered (26:31) and Jesus to be betrayed (26:45).[50]

The disciples and the audience must heed the transfiguration's mandate to listen (17:5) to Jesus' command for them to watch and pray (26:41; cf. 24:42-44). By praying the Gethsemane prayer of Jesus they can likewise submit their wills to God's will and follow Jesus' way of suffering and death, in order to share in the heavenly glory anticipated by his transfiguration. The Gethsemane prayer of Jesus empowers the audience to play their role in God's plan by watching and praying as they await Jesus' final coming in the glory prefigured by his transfiguration.

M. MATT 26:64: JESUS WILL BE SEEN SEATED AT GOD'S RIGHT AND COMING ON THE CLOUDS OF HEAVEN

When Jesus stands before the high priest and the assembly of Jewish leaders seeking false testimony in order to put him to death (26:3-4, 59), he further demonstrates the fortitude he gained through his Gethsemane prayer. To the high priest's command, "I charge you

---

[50] For a full discussion of Matt 26:36-46, see HEIL, *Death and Resurrection*, 42-49; see also J.D.M. DERRETT, "Sleeping at Gethsemane," *DRev* 114 (1996) 235-45.

under oath to the living God to tell us whether you are the Christ, the Son of God?" (26:63), Jesus replies with the indirect affirmation, "You have said it" (26:64), thus turning the oath back upon the high priest and indicating that his own words have condemned him of putting God's Messiah to death. Through his affirmation of his true messianic identity, however, Jesus courageously accepts the death to which it leads.[51]

Jesus goes on to valiantly proclaim his ultimate vindication and triumph over death to the assembly of Jewish leaders and to the audience by promising that "you will see the Son of Man seated at the right hand of the Power (Ps 110:1) and coming on the clouds of heaven (Dan 7:13; cf. Matt 24:30)!" (26:64). As the Son of Man, Jesus must suffer, die, and rise in accord with God's scriptural will (16:21; 17:9, 12, 22-23; 20:18-19, 28; 26:2, 24, 45). But as the Son of Man, Jesus, after the resurrection following his death, will be exalted by God ("the Power") and vindicated over his enemies (cf. Ps 110:1 in Matt 22:44) before his final coming in glory "on the clouds (νεφελῶν; cf. 24:30; 17:5) of heaven" (26:64).[52]

The transfiguration's mandate (17:5) bids the disciples (Peter is still present, 26:58) and the audience to listen to this courageous confession of Jesus. Just as Jesus gained courage by his prayer and by faith in his ultimate triumph over death, so the disciples and the audience can gain courage to endure possible suffering and death (10:17-21), in order to share in the heavenly glory presaged by the transfiguration of Jesus.

N. MATT 27:46-49: WILL ELIJAH COME TO SAVE JESUS FROM DEATH ON THE CROSS?

Some of the bystanders at Jesus' crucifixion attempt to prevent his death by twisting his prayer of lament from Ps 22:2, "My God (Ηλι), My God (Ηλι), why have you abandoned me?" (27:46), into a mocked

---

[51] HAGNER, *Matthew 14-28*, 799: "In Matthew's account of Jesus' response, given in the historical present tense for vividness, the words σὺ εἶπας, 'you have said,' rather than being strictly evasive (or negative), amount to an affirmative answer."

[52] On "the Power" as a "reverential substitute for God's name," see GUNDRY, *Matthew*, 545; HAGNER, *Matthew 14-28*, 801; DAVIES and ALLISON, *Matthew*, 3.529.

plea, "This one is calling Elijah!" (27:47).[53] After one of them offered Jesus vinegar to drink (27:48), the rest said, "Wait let us see if Elijah comes to save him!" (27:49).[54] In this further demonstration of blindness to the divine necessity of Jesus' death the audience experiences the irony that not even Elijah can rescue Jesus, because as Jesus himself stated, "But I say to you that Elijah has already come, yet they did not recognize him but did to him whatever they wished" (17:12). In the person of John the Baptist Elijah has already come and suffered the same fate Jesus is now suffering in accord with God's will (11:14; 14:1-12; 17:12-13). Furthermore, the transfiguration's mandate has urged the audience to listen (17:5) to Jesus' passion predictions, in order to understand that unlike the Elijah in the transfiguration epiphany, who attained heavenly glory without being put to death, Jesus must suffer a death perpetrated by the leaders of his people before attaining the heavenly glory foreshadowed by his transfiguration.

O. Matt 27:50-53: The death of Jesus initiates
the resurrection of the holy ones

As a direct result of the death of Jesus (27:50) the veil of the sanctuary in the temple was split in two from top to bottom; the earth was shaken, rocks were split, tombs were opened, and many bodies of the "holy ones" who "had fallen asleep" (died) were raised (27:51-52; see Ezek 37:1-14; Dan 12:2).[55] After the resurrection of Jesus these "holy ones" entered the "holy city" (Jerusalem, cf. 4:5) and appeared to many (27:53). That these "holy ones" were raised (ἠγέρθησαν, v. 52) and appeared to many after the resurrection (ἔγερσιν, v. 53) of Jesus confirms for the audience the predictions of Jesus that the transfiguration's pivotal mandate wants them to heed (17:5) – that not only would

---

[53] The vocative ἠλί meaning "my God" may also have been the shortened form of Elijah's name and therefore identical in sound to it, according to S.C. Layton, "Leaves from an Onomastician's Notebook," *ZAW* 108 (1996) 608-20.

[54] On Elijah as a helper of those in distress, see Öhler, *Elia*, 139-53.

[55] On "fallen asleep" (κεκοιμημένων) as a euphemistic metaphor for death, see M. Völkel, "κοιμάομαι," *EDNT* 2.302; BAGD, 437; Gundry, *Matthew*, 576; Davies and Allison, *Matthew*, 3.633.

he be raised (ἐγερθῆναι, 16:21; ἐγερθῇ, 17:9; ἐγερθήσεται, 17:23; 20:19) after being killed, but that those who lose their lives for his sake will find them and share in the vindication of his resurrection (10:38-39; 16:24-27).[56]

The "holy ones" include all of the innocent and righteous ones who have been unjustly put to death by the Jewish leadership (2:16; 14:1-12; 23:29-36).[57] The tombs (μνημεῖα) from which the holy ones are raised and come out (27:52-53) include the tombs (μνημεῖα) the Jewish leaders built and adorned for the righteous ones and prophets whom they murdered (23:29). The resurrection of the holy ones indicates to the audience God's vindication for the Jewish people's unjust killing not only of his righteous ones, prophets, wise men, and scribes (23:34; cf. 14:2) numbered among the holy ones but also of Jesus, his prophet (21:11, 46) and suffering innocent and righteous one (27:4, 19). In contrast to the prophets Moses and Elijah, who were not put to death by the people, but appeared (ὤφθη) in glory from heaven with the transfigured Jesus before the eyes of the disciples (17:3), the holy ones appeared (ἐνεφανίσθησαν) in glory to many only after having fallen asleep in death and coming out of their tombs (27:53).[58]

That the resurrected holy ones enter the holy city of Jerusalem and appear to many after Jesus' resurrection (27:53) continues the vindicating testimony against the Jewish people's acceptance of guilt for the unjust shedding of Jesus' blood (27:25), as indicated in Jesus' lament over this most holy of cities for rejecting him just as it killed the holy ones sent by God: "Jerusalem, Jerusalem, you who kill the prophets and stone those sent to you..." (23:37). The triumphant appearing of the holy ones to the many in the holy city of Jerusalem not only testifies against those who have killed Jesus and the other prophets and

---

[56] The resurrection of Jesus and the holy ones also confirms Jesus' teaching that there is a resurrection after death in 23:23-33.

[57] HAGNER, *Matthew 14-28*, 849: "The 'saints' or 'holy ones' here must be the righteous Jews (the δίκαιοι, 'righteous') of the time before Jesus, perhaps the patriarchs, prophets, or martyrs, although Matthew's readers will be thinking of the eventual resurrection of Christians." See also R.D. WITHERUP, "The Death of Jesus and the Raising of the Saints: Matthew 27:51-54 in Context," *SBLSP* 26 (1987) 581.

[58] On the glorified bodily resurrection from death of the holy ones, see S.P. BOTHA, "A Glorified Bodily Resurrection in Matthew 27:51b-53?: A Close Reading of the Text," *Hervormde Teologiese Studies* 52 (1996) 270-84.

holy ones God sent them, but also encourages the audience that they, like the holy ones, will share in the resurrection of Jesus prefigured in his transfiguration, if they are willing to take up the cross and lose their lives for the sake of Jesus (10:38-39; 16:24-27).[59]

P. MATT 27:54: THE CENTURION AND THOSE WITH HIM CONFESS THAT JESUS WAS THE SON OF GOD

When the three disciples heard the voice of God from the bright overshadowing cloud at the transfiguration, they fell upon their face and "were greatly frightened (ἐφοβήθησαν σφόδρα)" (17:6). After Jesus touched them and alleviated their fear (17:7), they still remained silent before the divine pronouncement, "This is my beloved Son, with whom I am well pleased" (17:5), even though Jesus was now the only one they saw (17:8). In contrast, when the centurion and those with him who were keeping watch over Jesus (cf. 27:36) saw the earthquake and the things that happened (cf. 27:50-53), they too "were greatly frightened (ἐφοβήθησαν σφόδρα)," but made the climactic confession of the entire narrative, "Truly this was the Son of God!" (27:54).

The soldiers' climactic confession indicates to the audience God's vindication of the trust Jesus has placed in God as his Son by remaining on the cross. By proclaiming that "this one" (οὗτος) was truly the Son of God (27:54), these gentile soldiers not only contradict the bystanders' misunderstanding that "this one" (οὗτος) is calling Elijah (27:47), but also transform their own mockery of the crucified Jesus – that "this one" (οὗτος) is Jesus, the King of the Jews (27:37) – into a profession of faith in the crucified Jesus' profound identity.[60] Their confession thus confirms not only that of Jesus himself before the high priest (26:63-64), that of Peter (16:16) and the disciples (14:33), but

---

[59] On 27:50-53, see HEIL, *Death and Resurrection*, 82-86.

[60] The gentile soldiers' statement in 27:54 is not a positive profession of faith and they remain wicked characters, merely expressing their sense of guilt and concession of defeat before God, according to D.C. SIM, "The 'Confession' of the Soldiers in Matthew 27:54," *HeyJ* 34 (1993) 401-24. For an OT parallel for how the soldiers have converted and come to faith, see B.T. VIVIANO, "A Psychology of Faith: Matt 27:54 in the Light of Exod 14:30-31," *RB* 104 (1997) 368-72.

also that of God himself at the baptism (3:17) and transfiguration of Jesus (17:5).

Once Jesus has died in faithful obedience to the divine will of his Father, then his true, profound identity as God's Son can be publicly proclaimed, even by Gentiles (27:54). The trustful submission to God's will (26:39, 42) that Jesus demonstrates in dying on the cross provides the audience with a model for their own obedient submission to God's will that they take up the cross and follow Jesus (10:38-39; 16:24-27). This is what the transfiguration's pivotal mandate has been urging them to hear (17:5) in order to understand that Jesus is truly God's beloved and favored Son by dying on the cross (unlike Moses and Elijah) with faith that God will vindicate him by raising him from death to the heavenly glory foreshadowed by his transfiguration.[61]

Q. MATT 28:1-10: AN ANGEL AND THE RISEN JESUS SEND THE WOMEN TO THE DISCIPLES

After Mary Magdalene and the other Mary came to see the tomb (28:1) where Jesus was buried (27:57-61), there was a great earthquake (cf. 27:51) as an angel of the Lord descended from heaven, approached, rolled back the stone sealing the tomb (27:60), and sat upon it in triumph (28:2). The angel's "appearance (εἰδέα) was like lightning and his clothing (ἔνδυμα) white (λευκὸν) as snow" (28:3).[62] This reminds the audience of the transfigured Jesus, whose "face (πρόσωπον) shone as the sun, while his clothes (ἱμάτια) became white (λευκὰ) as the light" (17:2). These similar but not identical descriptions of the face and clothing of Jesus and the angel confirm that

---

[61] On the significance of Jesus' death as the confirmation of his divine sonship and on Jesus' passion as a model for the disciples, see W. KRAUS, "Die Passion des Gottessohnes: Zur Bedeutung des Todes Jesu im Matthäusevangelium," *EvT* 57 (1997) 409-27.

[62] "Appearance" (εἰδέα) could also be translated as "face," according to BAGD, 220. The angel's "appearance" or "face" that was like lightening (ἀστραπὴ) resembles that of the heavenly man/angel in the Greek versions of Dan 10:6: "His face (πρόσωπον) was like the appearance of lightning (ἀστραπῆς)." And that "his clothing that was white as snow" (τὸ ἔνδυμα αὐτοῦ λευκὸν ὡς χιών) resembles that of the "Ancient One," God himself, in the Theodotion recension of Dan 7:9: "His clothing was like snow, white" (τὸ ἔνδυμα αὐτοῦ ὡσεὶ χιὼν λευκόν). See also DAVIES and ALLISON, *Matthew*, 3.666.

whereas the angel was permanently a heavenly figure, Jesus was only temporarily transfigured ("his clothes *became* white") into an angel-like, heavenly figure.[63]

After the guards, who had been posted at Jesus' tomb in an effort to further seal it (27:65-66), were shaken with fear and became as if dead (28:4) after the angel's epiphanic appearance (28:2-3), the angel told the women, "You need not be afraid (μὴ φοβεῖσθε)" (28:5). When the risen Jesus appeared to the women, he reinforced the angel's message as he also told them, "Do not be afraid (μὴ φοβεῖσθε)" (28:10). This reminds the audience that at the transfiguration when the disciples fell upon their face and were greatly frightened (17:6) upon hearing the epiphanic mandate of God from the overshadowing cloud (17:5), Jesus came forward, and touching them, said, "Arise and do not be afraid (μὴ φοβεῖσθε)" (17:7). Just as the elimination of the disciples' fear by the transfigured Jesus was meant to facilitate their obeying of the epiphanic mandate to listen to him (17:5), so the elimination of the women's fear by the angel and the risen Jesus is meant to facilitate their obeying of the epiphanic mandates to communicate to the disciples, who abandoned Jesus (26:56), the message of his resurrection and reunion with them in Galilee (28:7, 10).[64]

The angel's message that Jesus, the crucified one, has been raised (ἠγέρθη, 28:6, 7) from the dead "just as he said" (28:6) emphatically confirms the fulfillment of Jesus' predictions that he would indeed be raised (ἐγερθῆναι, 16:21; 26:32; ἐγερθῇ, 17:9; ἐγερθήσεται, 17:22; 20:19) from the dead, which the transfiguration's pivotal mandate has urged the disciples and audience to heed (17:5). Now that Jesus has been raised from the dead (ἠγέρθη ἀπὸ τῶν νεκρῶν, 28:7) the ban to silence that Jesus placed upon the disciples who witnessed his transfiguration – that they were to tell the vision to no one until the Son of Man has been raised from the dead (ἐκ νεκρῶν ἐγερθῇ, 17:9) – has been lifted.

---

[63] For a full discussion of the "transfiguration" of Jesus into an angel-like, heavenly figure, see chap. 4.

[64] On the allaying of fear with the μὴ φοβεῖσθε formula in the biblical tradition, see BALZ, "φοβέομαι," 430-31.

R. Matt 28:16-20: On a mountain in Galilee the risen Jesus promises his permanent presence

The final, climactic epiphany of the risen Jesus at the conclusion of Matthew's Gospel presents the audience with several narrative progressions relative to the epiphany of Jesus' transfiguration. The epiphanic appearance of the transfigured Jesus together with the heavenly Moses and Elijah to only three of the disciples on a mountain in Galilee (17:1-3) has now progressed to the epiphanic appearance of the risen Jesus to all eleven disciples on a mountain in Galilee (28:16-17).[65] After the three disciples witnessed the transfiguration epiphany, Peter wanted to build a tent to honor each epiphanic figure (17:4).[66] Now, after the eleven disciples see the risen Jesus, they worshipped him, although some doubted (28:17).[67]

That the eleven disciples saw (ἰδόντες) the risen Jesus in Galilee (28:17) fulfills his promise, which the transfiguration's mandate (17:5) urged the disciples and audience to heed, that after his resurrection he would go before them to Galilee (26:32). The angel reinforced this promise when he told the women the message they were to relay to the disciples – that in Galilee "you will see (ὄψεσθε) him" (28:7). Then the risen Jesus himself commissioned the women to tell the disciples that in Galilee "they will see (ὄψονται) me" (28:10).[68] Now that the eleven disciples have not only heard from the women, but seen for themselves that Jesus has been raised from the dead, the three disciples can tell of what they saw in the transfiguration epiphany (17:9). The disciples and audience can now tell of the transfiguration, because

---

[65] DONALDSON, *Jesus on the Mountain*, 175: "...the mountain of 28.16 functions as a literary symbol that binds each of the other mountain scenes, and themes developed in them, to the closing scene of the Gospel." KUPP, *Matthew's Emmanuel*, 204: "The final mountain has a coordinating and climactic role by which it summarizes and epitomizes the rhetorical and christological characteristics of Matthew's previous peak experiences."

[66] On the significance of the tents for the transfiguration epiphany, see chap. 6.

[67] On the interpretation of οἱ δὲ ἐδίστασαν as "but some doubted," see DAVIES and ALLISON, *Matthew*, 3.681-82. Note also the parallel grammatical construction in 26:67.

[68] On this emphatic reinforcement of the promise of the risen Jesus to appear to the disciples in Galilee, see ANDERSON, *Matthew's Narrative Web*, 169-72.

Jesus' resurrection from the dead makes clear that his transfiguration was a temporary anticipation of the heavenly glory he would attain only after suffering death at the hands of his people – unlike Moses and Elijah – and being raised by God.

After God's voice from the overshadowing cloud uttered the proclamation and mandate of the transfiguration epiphany (17:5), Jesus approached (προσῆλθεν) and touching the prostrate disciples, spoke to them (17:6-7). Now the risen Jesus approached (προσελθών) the prostrate disciples and himself uttered the proclamation and mandate of this resurrectional epiphany (28:18-20).[69] God's proclamation affirming his special favor upon the transfigured Jesus, "This is my beloved Son, with whom I am well pleased" (17:5), has now progressed to the risen Jesus' proclamation of that special favor, "All authority on heaven and earth has been given (ἐδόθη, divine passive) to me" (28:18; cf. 11:27).[70] God's mandate at the transfiguration for the disciples and audience to listen to Jesus (17:5) has now progressed to the risen Jesus' mandate for the disciples and audience to make disciples of all nations by baptizing them and teaching them to observe everything Jesus has commanded them (28:19-20). Whereas Jesus commanded (ἐνετείλατο) the disciples to tell no one of the transfiguration until he has been raised from the dead (17:9), now that he has been raised he empowers the disciples to teach everything I have commanded (ἐνετειλάμην) you" (28:20).[71]

---

[69] In Matthew only in 17:7 and 28:18 does Jesus "approach" someone. As MOSES (*Matthew's Transfiguration Story*, 149) notes, "in every other instance it is others who approach him. This usage is peculiar to Matthew, and on both occasions Jesus is portrayed in an extraordinary setting: in Matthew 17 it is the transfiguration, and in 28.18 it is the resurrected Jesus who comes."

[70] According to KUPP (*Matthew's Emmanuel*, 211), "we can assume that the divine passive of resurrection (ἠγέρθη in 28.6, 7) implies the same divine agent as ἐδόθη in 28.18b, i.e., resurrection in Matthew has meant both Jesus being raised from the dead and the bestowal of his unlimited authority."

[71] KUPP, *Matthew's Emmanuel*, 216: "The subjects of the four uses of ἐντέλλομαι in Matthew provide an illuminating pattern of the transition of the authority to give commands, from God in 4.6 (cf. 15.4), to Moses in 19.7, to Jesus in 17.9 and 28.20." DAVIES and ALLISON, *Matthew*, 3.686: "ἐνετειλάμην is a constative aorist and refers not to one command or to the Sermon on the Mount but to all of Jesus' teaching....But more than verbal revelation is involved, for such revelation cannot be separated from Jesus' life, which is itself a command. ἐνετειλάμην accordingly unifies word and deed and so recalls the entire book: everything is in view. The earthly ministry as a whole is an imperative."

To prolong the presence of Jesus, temporarily transfigured into a glorified, heavenly figure in conversation with Moses and Elijah, Peter offered to make a tent for each (17:4). But no tents are necessary to prolong the presence of the risen Jesus, who climaxes the mandate of this resurrectional epiphany with the promise, "And behold, I am with you all days until the end of the age" (28:20; cf. 1:23).[72] Now that Jesus has become the glorified, heavenly figure that was prefigured by his temporary transfiguration while on earth, he is able to remain permanently with his disciples and the audience.

S. CONCLUSION

The transfiguration's mandate in Matthew, "Listen to him!" (17:5), has pivoted the disciples and the audience back to Jesus' previous pronouncements for them to follow him on his way to suffering and death before being raised to heavenly glory (10:38-39; 16:21-27). It has also pivoted them forward to the subsequent predictions of the necessity for him (17:12, 22-23; 20:18-19; 21:33-46; 26:2, 12, 26-29, 31-35, 36-46) as well as them (20:20-28) to spend their lives in selfless, suffering service for others with the assurance of being raised from the dead (17:9; 22:23-33; 27:50-53) and seeing his final coming in the heavenly glory (24:30; 25:31; 26:64) prefigured by his transfiguration.

In the person of John the Baptist Elijah has already come (17:13), yet they put him to death (14:5; 17:12), as Jesus will be put to death. The audience realizes then that Elijah has not come first (17:10) as the heavenly figure the disciples witnessed in the transfiguration epiphany (17:3). Furthermore, Elijah will not come to save Jesus from death on the cross (27:46-49), because unlike the Elijah in the transfiguration epiphany, who attained heavenly glory without being put to death, Jesus must suffer death before attaining the heavenly glory foreshadowed by his transfiguration.

The disciples' great sadness at Jesus' prediction of his death and resurrection (17:23) further illustrates their "little faith" (17:20), their failure to share the firm faith of Jesus himself in God's power to heal

---

[72] For an analysis of Jesus' promise here, see KUPP, *Matthew's Emmanuel*, 216-19.

the possessed boy (17:14-20) and to raise Jesus from the dead to the heavenly glory indicated by his transfiguration.

The dramatic Gethsemane prayer of Jesus (26:36-46) empowers the audience to play their role in God's plan by watching and praying. By praying in imitation and on the strength of Jesus' prayer, they can submit their wills to God's will (26:39, 42) and follow Jesus' way of suffering and death, as they await Jesus' final coming in the glory prefigured by his transfiguration (16:27; 24:30; 25:31; 26:64).

The triumphant appearing of the "holy ones," who were raised from the dead when Jesus died (27:50-52), to the many in the holy city of Jerusalem after Jesus' resurrection (27:53) encourages the audience that they also will share in the resurrection of Jesus prefigured by his transfiguration, if they are willing to take up the cross and lose their lives for the sake of Jesus (10:38-39; 16:24-27).

The gentile soldiers' confession at the death of Jesus, "Truly this was the Son of God!" (27:54), confirms not only that of Jesus himself before the high priest (26:63-64), that of Peter (16:16) and the disciples (14:33), but also that of God himself at the baptism and transfiguration of Jesus – "This is my beloved Son, with whom I am well pleased!" (3:17; 17:5). The trustful submission to God's will (26:39, 42) that Jesus demonstrates in dying on the cross provides the audience with a model for their own obedient submission to God's will that they take up the cross and follow Jesus. The transfiguration's pivotal mandate has been urging the disciples and the audience to heed the challenge of Jesus' passion predictions in order to understand that Jesus is truly God's beloved and favored Son by dying on the cross (unlike Moses and Elijah) with faith that God will vindicate him by raising him from death to the heavenly glory foreshadowed by his transfiguration.

The angel's message that Jesus, the crucified one, has been raised from the dead "just as he said" (28:6) emphatically confirms the fulfillment of Jesus' predictions that he would indeed be raised from the dead (16:21; 17:9, 22; 20:19; 26:32), which the transfiguration's pivotal mandate has urged the disciples and audience to heed (17:5). The disciples and audience can now tell of the transfiguration (17:9), because Jesus' resurrection from the dead makes clear that his transfiguration was a temporary anticipation of the heavenly glory he would attain only after suffering death at the hands of his people – unlike Moses and Elijah – and being raised by God. Now

that Jesus has become the glorified, heavenly figure that was prefigured by his temporary transfiguration while on earth, he is able to
remain permanently with his disciples and the audience, so that they
can fulfill the risen Jesus' mandate that they make disciples of all
nations by baptizing them and teaching all that Jesus commanded
(28:19-20).

CHAPTER 12

LUKE 9:28-36 AND THE ANTECEDENT NARRATIVE

In this chapter we will demonstrate how the Lukan version of the transfiguration narrative functions as a "pivotal mandatory epiphany" in its narrative context. We will consider how the Lukan implied audience responds to the transfiguration narrative as a "mandatory e-piphany" based on its presupposed knowledge of biblical traditions and on what it has heard in the antecedent narrative. In the following chapter we will show how the Lukan transfiguration narrative as a "mandatory epiphany" prepares the implied audience for the subsequent Lukan narrative. These two chapters, then, will confirm the "pivotal" role of the transfiguration narrative in Luke.

A. LUKE 9:28

About eight days after these words, taking along Peter and John and James, he went up to the mountain to pray.

The temporal interval, "about eight days after these words" (9:28), leads the audience both to connect and to separate what is about to happen from what they have just heard in 9:18-27.[1] On the one hand, what is about to happen is closely connected to the preceding, occur-

---

[1] GREEN, *Luke*, 379: "The opening both separates temporally and associates thematically the transfiguration scene and the previous account of Peter's confession. Luke thus underscores the importance of Jesus' words and indicates that the scene now unfolding somehow builds on Jesus' teaching about his destiny and the shape of discipleship."

ring about a week after Peter's confession of Jesus as "the Christ of God" (9:20), of Jesus' first prediction of his suffering, death and resurrection (9:22), of his challenge for all to follow him in that suffering in order to share in the glory that follows it (9:23-26), and of his solemn promise that "there are some standing here who will not taste death until they see the kingdom of God" (9:27). Furthermore, there is a catch-word connection with the preceding. What is about to happen occurs about eight days after "these words" (τοὺς λόγους τούτους), that is, "my words" (τοὺς ἐμοὺς λόγους), the words of Jesus regarding his suffering, death and resurrection of which no one should be ashamed (9:26).[2]

On the other hand, what is about to happen occurs over a week later, indicating the initiation of a new and separate event. This means that what is about to happen is not limited to a relationship only with the immediately preceding words of Jesus, so that, for example, the transfiguration narrative would be simply the fulfillment of the promise given in 9:27.[3]

That Jesus took along "Peter and John and James" (9:28), three of the first four in the list of the specially chosen twelve apostles (6:14), begins to prepare the audience for a unique, private revelation of Jesus to these chosen three disciples, who were earlier associated as fishing partners (5:10). The audience remembers that Jesus allowed no one to enter with him into the house to witness the revelation of his power to raise the daughter of Jairus from death except "Peter and John and James" as well as the child's parents (8:51).[4] That these three were among "some of those standing here" (9:27) alerts the audience to the possibility that these three, as well as the audience, may experience something in the special, private event that is about to take place that will enable them to "see the kingdom of God" (9:27).

---

[2] Its catch-word connection with the expressions τοὺς ἐμοὺς λόγους in 9:26 and τοὺς λόγους τούτους in 9:44, both of which refer to Jesus' words, indicates that τοὺς λόγους τούτους in 9:28 likewise means "these words" rather than "these things." See REID, *Transfiguration*, 99.

[3] For past attempts at theological meanings for the temporal interval of "about eight days," see REID, *Transfiguration*, 100-102. She concludes: "These attempts at a theological explanation for ἡμέραι ὀκτώ are not persuasive" (p. 101).

[4] On the order Peter-John-James (cf. Mark 9:2; Matt 17:1) NOLLAND (*Luke 9:21-18:34*, 497) states: "Luke uses the names of his three companions in the order in which he has referred to the privileged inner group in 8:51."

While praying at his baptism (3:21), Jesus experienced the holy Spirit descending upon him while God's voice from heaven declared, "You are my beloved Son, with whom I am well pleased" (3:22). Jesus would regularly withdraw to deserted places and pray (5:16) in the context of his teaching and healing ministry (5:15, 17). Just as Jesus went out "to the mountain to pray" (εἰς τὸ ὄρος προσεύξασ-θαι), and spent the night in prayer to God (6:12), before calling his twelve apostles (6:13-16), so now he went up "to the mountain to pray (εἰς τὸ ὄρος προσεύξασθαι)" (9:28).[5] Jesus was praying in solitude with his disciples (9:18), before asking them the question that led to Peter's confession of him as "the Christ of God" (9:20). That Jesus "went up to the mountain to pray" (9:28), then, prepares the audience for yet another significant event to take place in the context of Jesus' praying.[6]

B. LUKE 9:29

And while he was praying the appearance of his face became different and his clothing dazzling white.

While Jesus was praying (προσευχομένου) at his baptism, he experienced the epiphany of heaven being opened and the holy Spirit descending in bodily form like a dove upon him (3:21-22).[7] Similarly, while Jesus is praying (προσεύχεσθαι) on the mountain where he went to pray (προσεύξασθαι), he and the three disciples he took along experience the epiphany of his transfiguration into a heavenly figure:

---

[5] On the relationship between the praying of Jesus in 3:21, 6:12, and 9:28, see FELDKÄM-PER, *Der betende Jesus*, 125-26. On Jesus' prayer and the transfiguration, see D. CRUMP, *Jesus the Intercessor: Prayer and Christology in Luke-Acts* (WUNT 49; Tübingen: Mohr, 1992) 42-48.

[6] H. BALZ, "προσευχή," *EDNT* 3.169: "Jesus prays at decisive junctures in the Gospel: after his baptism by John (Luke 3:21), before the calling of the Twelve (6:12), before Peter's confession (9:18), and before the Transfiguration (9:28f.). He demonstrates thereby in a special way his close relationship to the Father and thus becomes both a model and a teacher of prayer for the disciples, one who molds them into a praying community."

[7] Luke narrates the descent of the Spirit upon Jesus as an epiphany, whereas Mark (1:9-11) and Matthew (3:13-17) narrate it as a vision; see chap. 2.

"the appearance of his face became different and his clothing dazzling white" (9:29).[8]

Just as the descent of the holy Spirit "in bodily form" (σωματικῷ εἴδει) like a dove upon Jesus at his baptism (3:22), so now the dramatic difference in the "appearance" or "form" (εἶδος) of the face of Jesus indicates to the audience a physically visible and temporary epiphanic appearance. Jesus told the crowds that those "in glorious and luxurious clothing" (ἱματισμῷ ἐνδόξῳ καὶ τρυφῇ) dwell in royal palaces (7:25). That Jesus' "clothing" (ἱματισμὸς) became "dazzling white" (λευκὸς ἐξαστράπτων) indicates to the audience his momentary assimilation to those who dwell in the heavenly kingdom.[9] This dramatic change in the face and clothing of Jesus signals to the audience that he has been externally and temporarily transformed by God into a heavenly being while still on earth. It anticipates his future and permanent attainment of glory in heaven as promised to the righteous after their death.[10]

C. LUKE 9:30-31

Then behold two men were talking with him, who were Moses and Elijah, who, appearing in glory, were speaking about his exodus, which he was about to accomplish in Jerusalem.

The initial epiphanic transformation in the outward appearance and attire of Jesus (9:29) occurs implicitly for the three disciples, whom Jesus took along with him to the mountain (9:28), to see. It is immediately followed by an additional epiphanic appearance, introduced by "behold" or "look" (ἰδοὺ), which alerts the audience to share in what the disciples are privileged to view.[11]

---

[8] NOLLAND, *Luke 9:21-18:34*, 498: "The reference to prayer is repeated to make the link between transformation and prayer explicit." GREEN, *Luke*, 380: "Luke has it that *while Jesus was praying* he was transfigured (cf. 3:21-22)."

[9] REID, *Transfiguration*, 115: "The primary symbolism conveyed by Jesus' white clothing in 9:29 is that he is a heavenly being."

[10] On the significance and background of the change in the appearance of Jesus' face and of his dazzling white clothing, see chap. 4.

[11] GREEN, *Luke*, 381: "Luke has already employed words and phrases that privilege the sense of sight: 'appearance' and 'dazzling white'; to these he now adds 'Look!' and 'they

The word "behold" introduces the epiphanic appearance of "two men," identified as Moses and Elijah. The audience has heard Moses and Elijah mentioned individually in the previous narrative. Moses has been referred to as the giver of the Law (2:22; 5:14). Elijah has been mentioned in his role as a prophetic reformer (1:17) and wonder-working prophet (4:25-26), whom some think has reappeared in the person of Jesus (9:8, 19). But now Moses and Elijah appear together in glory and were speaking with the transfigured Jesus.

That Moses and Elijah "appeared" (ὀφθέντες) in glory from heaven in an epiphany (9:31) reminds the audience of the way that the angel of the Lord likewise "appeared" (ὤφθη) from heaven to Zechariah, the father of John the Baptist, in an epiphany (1:11). Their appearance "in glory" (ἐν δόξῃ) from heaven recalls the previous words of Jesus, in which he promised to come "in his glory" (ἐν τῇ δόξῃ αὐτοῦ), which is also the heavenly glory of the Father and the holy angels (9:26), after his death and resurrection (9:22). Their appearance in glory indicates that they are heavenly figures. That Jesus has been transformed into a heavenly figure enables the heavenly figures of Moses and Elijah to talk with him.[12]

Moses and Elijah were speaking with the transfigured Jesus about "his exodus" or "his departure" (ἔξοδον αὐτοῦ, 9:31), that is, the way that he will leave this earthly life by the death and resurrection he has just predicted (9:22).[13] His "exodus" or "departure" from earthly to

---

appeared,' and to these will be added the further affirmation, 'they saw' (v 32). This emphasis on seeing illuminates the transfiguration scene from the vantage point of the apostles, with Luke's focus set on the significance of this event for them. At the same time, Luke invites his audience to share their viewpoint through the use of 'Look!'"

[12] FITZMYER (*Luke I-IX*, 800) states that the appearance of Moses and Elijah in glory "clearly presents the two as heavenly figures." MARSHALL (*Luke*, 384) concurs: "Thereby they are shown to be visitors from heaven." NOLLAND, *Luke 9:21-18:34*, 499: "These figures appear in glory because they appear from heaven." GREEN, *Luke*, 381: "Luke tells concerning them what he has just shown concerning Jesus – namely, that they are present 'in glory,' sharing in the status of those who belong to the heavenly court."

[13] NOLLAND, *Luke 9:21-18:34*, 499-500: "ἔξοδος, 'exodus/departure,' is used in Jewish Greek of death ('departure [from life]'; see Wis 3:2; 7:6), but always with contextual clarification. V 22 is not close enough to allow a simple sense of death here, but that verse cannot be ignored in the search for the meaning of 'exodus' here....There must also be an allusion here to the exodus of the people of Israel from Egypt under Moses' leadership. It is surely, however, an excess to embrace in 'exodus' the whole Mosaic saga of deliverance from Egypt through to

heavenly life will be different from theirs.[14] Unlike Moses and Elijah, who have appeared "in glory" (9:31) – the heavenly glory they attained without being put to death by their people, Jesus will come "in his glory" (9:26), the glory prefigured by his temporary transformation into a heavenly figure (9:29), only after being rejected and killed by the Jewish leaders (9:22).[15] That Jesus "was about to accomplish" (ἤμελ-λεν πληροῦν) his exodus in Jerusalem expresses its divine inevitability, further linking it to the divine necessity (δεῖ) of his death and resurrection (9:22).[16] That Jesus will accomplish his exodus from the earthly to the heavenly realm "in Jerusalem" prepares the audience for his journey to the city where the elders, chief priests, and scribes will play their role in his exodus (9:22) that will lead to his coming in his glory (9:26).[17]

---

possession of the promised land...we need to recognize that our text is concerned with 'his exodus,' rather than an exodus of which he is moving force or leader." See also RINGE, "Luke 9:28-36," 92-93; S.R. GARRETT, "Exodus from Bondage: Luke 9:31 and Acts 12:1-24," *CBQ* 52 (1990) 656-80; M.L. STRAUSS, *The Davidic Messiah in Luke-Acts: The Promise and Its Fulfillment in Lukan Christology* (JSNTSup 110; Sheffield: Sheffield Academic Press, 1995) 271-72.

[14] Jesus' "exodus" is linked to the vindication of the righteous by P. DOBLE, *The Paradox of Salvation: Luke's Theology of the Cross* (SNTSMS 87; Cambridge: Cambridge University Press, 1996) 210-13. Doble states that "a reader recognises that the concept 'Exodus' is a whole package, comprising testing, humiliation, journeying, suffering at the hands of the 'ungodly' and ultimate vindication by God" (p. 213).

[15] For the significance of Moses and Elijah in the transfiguration narratives, see chap. 5. GREEN, *Luke*, 382: "Given the opening reference in this narrative unit to Jesus' words (v 28), which functions almost as a thematic heading, it is likewise difficult not to imagine that Jesus' own articulation of the divine purpose is related in a substantive way to this conversation about his 'exodus.' The point of their discussion, then, would be the nature of Jesus' journey through rejection and death to his exaltation."

[16] RADL, "μέλλω," 2.404: "μέλλω can express the necessity of an event that is based on the divine will and thus is certain to occur." RINGE, "Luke 9:28-36," 92: "...the verb πληρόω is most appropriate, in that it accentuates the notion that these events are part of God's foreordained salvific plan as Luke understood it." J.T. SQUIRES, *The Plan of God in Luke-Acts* (SNTSMS 76; Cambridge: Cambridge University Press, 1993) 113: "The epiphany of the transfigured Jesus signifies that his departure (ἔξοδον) to Jerusalem (9.31) will occur as part of God's plan for Jesus."

[17] GREEN, *Luke*, 382: "Because Jerusalem has already been established as the locus of the priesthood and the scribes (cf. 1:9-11; 2:46; 5:17) – who would be joined by the elders in rejecting Jesus (v 22) – this news also adds to the tension of the narrative as the Galilean section draws to a close....if Jerusalem is the place where Jesus' opposition will overtake him and bring him to his death, it is also the location where he will be vindicated through resurrection (v 22). The change of appearance he experiences on the mountain, after all, is an anticipatory vision of his coming in glory (cf. vv 26-27)."

D. LUKE 9:32

Now Peter and those with him had been overcome with sleep, but when they became wide awake, they saw his glory and the two men standing with him.

Peter and "those with him," that is, John and James (cf. 9:28), "had been overcome" or "had been weighed down" (ἦσαν βεβαρημένοι) with sleep (9:32).[18] Since the three disciples have been in a deep sleep, the audience realizes that they have not only been unaware of the epiphanic transfiguration of Jesus and the accompanying appearance of Moses and Elijah in glory, but, most significantly, have not heard the conversation about Jesus' approaching "exodus," which entails his death, in Jerusalem.[19]

Although they had been overcome with sleep at the outset, the disciples "became wide awake" (διαγρηγορήσαντες) in time to see the glory of the transfigured Jesus and "the two men standing with him" (9:32), that is, Moses and Elijah (9:30).[20] That upon awakening they only *saw* the two men "standing with him" (συνεστῶτας αὐτῷ) underlines for the audience that while the three disciples were asleep they failed to *hear* these same two men "talking with him" (συνελάλουν αὐτῷ, 9:30). That Moses and Elijah were "standing with" the transfigured Jesus associates his glory (δόξαν) with that of these "two men," who were likewise appearing in glory (δόξῃ, 9:31).

---

[18] BOCK, *Luke 1:1-9:50*, 870 n. 15: "It is clear that the disciples are in deep sleep, for the phrase βεβαρημένοι ὕπνῳ translates literally as 'weighed down with sleep.'" This same phrase is translated "heavy with sleep" by H. BALZ, "βαρέω," *EDNT* 1.198.

[19] REID, *Transfiguration*, 130: "...the disciples' sleep functions as a means to keep the disciples on the periphery during the event described in vv 29-31."

[20] Although διαγρηγορήσαντες could be translated "since they had kept awake" (see BAGD, 182; *EDNT* 1.298), doing so would seem to undermine if not defeat the point of the emphatic sleep motif. On this, see REID (*Transfiguration*, 130 n. 140), who states: "The phrase διαγρηγορήσαντες δὲ means 'becoming fully awake.' The prefix δια gives the intensive connotation 'fully' and the aorist is ingressive."

E. Luke 9:33

As they were separating from him, Peter spoke to Jesus, "Master, it is good that we are here, so let us make three tents, one for you and one for Moses and one for Elijah," not knowing what he was saying.

As "they," that is, Moses and Elijah, were separating from "him," that is, Jesus, indicating that their epiphanic appearance is coming to a close, Peter once again addresses Jesus as "master" (ἐπιστάτα) (9:33).[21] As the audience recalls, Peter, while accompanied by James and John (5:10), addressed Jesus as "master" (ἐπιστάτα, 5:5) when he obeyed Jesus' directive to lower the nets for a catch of fish (5:4). But the miraculously abundant catch of fish (5:6-7) at the word of Jesus indicated that he is much more than merely their "master." Indeed, Peter then addressed Jesus as "Lord" (κύριε, 5:8).

When the boat of disciples was in a sea storm, they cried out to Jesus, "Master, master (ἐπιστάτα ἐπιστάτα), we are perishing!" (8:24). But Jesus' epiphanic stilling of the sea storm revealed a dimension of his character much more profound than that of their "master." Indeed, it causes the disciples to query, "Who then is this that he commands even the winds and the water, and they obey him?" (8:25).

After a woman afflicted with hemorrhages was miraculously cured by merely touching the tassel of Jesus' cloak (8:43-44), Jesus asked, "Who touched me?" (8:45). While all were denying it, Peter in apparent exasperation replied, "Master (ἐπιστάτα), the crowds are pushing and shoving you around!" (8:45). But Jesus once again demonstrated to Peter, John and James (8:51) that he is much more than merely their

---

[21] In the NT the word ἐπιστάτης occurs only in Luke 5:5; 8:24, 45; 9:33, 49; 17:13. W. Grimm, "ἐπιστάτης," *EDNT* 2.37: "The etymology of the word (ἐπιστάτης = 'one who stands over another') and the contexts in which he uses it indicate a nuance in meaning. While Luke uses κύριε of messianic dignity (e.g., 2:11; 5:12; 7:6; 9:61) and διδάσκαλε of Jesus' teaching authority (e.g., 10:25; 18:18; 20:21, 28, 39), ἐπιστάτης is used of Jesus in his authoritative position within a definite group, his disciples...Ἐπιστάτης thus refers to Jesus' authority to instruct and to his special responsibility (cf. esp. Luke 8:24!) for the group of disciples that he has assembled." See also O. Glombitza, "Die Titel διδάσκαλος und ἐπιστάτης für Jesus bei Lukas," *ZNW* 49 (1958) 275-78.

"master," as he not only healed the hemorrhaging woman but raised Jairus's daughter from the dead (8:49-56).[22] Thus, when Peter, again accompanied by John and James, addresses the transfigured Jesus as "master" (ἐπιστάτα, 9:33), the audience is prepared for another revelation of how Jesus' more profound identity transcends that of "master" of his disciples.

After Peter addressed the transfigured Jesus as "master," he went on to say, "It is good that we are here, so let us make three tents, one for you and one for Moses and one for Elijah" (9:33). By suggesting that he make a tent each for Jesus, Moses, and Elijah, Peter would place each heavenly figure on the same level and in the same category. Peter apparently wants to prepare a dwelling place for each heavenly figure to prolong his glorious epiphanic appearance on earth, and thus to halt and render unnecessary the separation of Moses and Elijah from Jesus that has already begun (9:33). On analogy with the Tent of Meeting each tent would also provide a place for each heavenly figure possibly to offer divine communication.[23] But the audience experiences the irony that a heavenly communication, the conversation about Jesus' "exodus" in Jerusalem (9:31), has already taken place while the three disciples were asleep (9:32).

The narrator's aside, "not knowing what he was saying" (9:33), alerts the audience to the inappropriateness of Peter's offer.[24] Since Peter and his companions had been overcome with sleep (9:32), they did not hear the all-important conversation about Jesus' approaching "exodus" entailing his death in Jerusalem (9:31). Placing the transfigured Jesus, whose "glory" the awakened disciples saw (9:32), on the same level and in the same category as the heavenly figures of Moses and Elijah, who appeared in "glory" (9:31), implies that perhaps Jesus, despite his previous prediction about the necessity of his suffering and

---

[22] GREEN, *Luke*, 348: "In spite of what the disciples have seen, through Peter's response to Jesus we gather that they are not yet any closer to enlightenment. This is signaled by the nature of Peter's question, based on a lack of understanding. It is also indicated by the title with which he addresses Jesus, 'Master.' With this epithet Peter acknowledges Jesus' leadership, but little else regarding his identity or purpose."

[23] On the background and significance of the tents, see chap. 6.

[24] SHEELEY, *Narrative Asides*, 111: "The narrator breaks into the story at this point to inform the reader that Peter had no comprehension of the meaning of the occasion."

death before resurrection on the third day (9:22), has already or will attain heavenly glory like Moses and Elijah, that is, without being put to death by his people. Peter does not seem to realize that Jesus will attain the same heavenly glory he now momentarily shares with Moses and Elijah only after he has been put to death as a rejected prophet in Jerusalem.

F. LUKE 9:34

While he was saying these things, a cloud came and was overshadowing them. They were frightened as they entered into the cloud.

"While he was saying these things" (9:34) refers to the immediately preceding offer that Peter "spoke" to Jesus as Moses and Elijah were separating from him (9:33). This means that the further epiphanic appearance of the coming and overshadowing of the cloud, which occurs while Peter was speaking, also occurs simultaneous to the separation of Moses and Elijah from Jesus.[25] That a cloud, symbolic of God's presence, came and was overshadowing "them" (αὐτούς) refers to Moses and Elijah, the previous referent of "them" (αὐτοὺς) in the statement of their separation from Jesus. In accord with the vehicular function of clouds, with which the audience would be familiar from their knowledge of the biblical tradition, the cloud that overshadows Moses and Elijah facilitates and completes their separation from Jesus.[26]

With an alliterative Greek word play the epiphanic appearance of the cloud interrupts, ironically for the audience, Peter's inappropriate offer to make three "tents" (σκηνὰς, 9:33) for the three epiphanic figures. The cloud was "covering over" or "tenting over" (ἐπεσκίαζεν, 9:34) Moses and Elijah, thus completing their separation from the

---

[25] For the background and significance of the overshadowing cloud, see chap. 7.

[26] *Contra* REID (*Transfiguration*, 137) who states that "in 9:34 the cloud is not a vehicle of transport unless one interprets it as being the means by which Moses and Elijah depart from the scene. But this interpretation neglects the fact that at the beginning of v 33, Moses and Elijah are already said to be departing, before any mention of a cloud is made." Reid fails to realize here that in accord with Luke's grammatical constructions the coming and overshadowing of the cloud is simultaneous with the separation of Moses and Elijah from Jesus.

Jesus Peter wanted to make equal to them by making a tent or covering for each.

"They," that is, the three disciples, were frightened as "they," that is, Moses and Elijah, entered into the cloud (9:34). That "they" (αὐτούς) here refers to Moses and Elijah completes Luke's consistent use of this form of the Greek pronoun to refer exclusively to Moses and Elijah in the immediate context. In the statement that "they" were separating from him "they" (αὐτούς) obviously refers to Moses and Elijah as they are being separated "from him," Jesus (9:33). Consequently, in the statement that the cloud was overshadowing "them" the referent of "them" (αὐτούς) is again exclusively Moses and Elijah, the ones who are being separated from Jesus by the cloud (9:34). Finally, in the statement that "they" entered the cloud "they" (αὐτούς) once again refers exclusively to Moses and Elijah as they are departing from the scene via the cloud.[27]

As the audience recalls from their knowledge of the OT, only "Moses entered into the midst of the cloud" (εἰσῆλθεν Μωυσῆς εἰς τὸ μέσον τῆς νεφέλης, LXX Exod 24:18), when he along with Joshua and the children of Israel went up the mountain (Exod 24:13, 15), where the glory of the Lord in the cloud appeared as a flaming fire (Exod 24:17). Similarly now, only Moses and Elijah and not Jesus or the disciples "entered into the cloud" (εἰσελθεῖν αὐτοὺς εἰς τὴν νεφέλην, 9:34).[28]

A response of fear is common in witnesses of extraordinary, epiphanic, and miraculous phenomena. The audience has already heard how the shepherds at the birth of Jesus "were greatly frightened" or more literally, "were frightened with a great fear" (ἐφοβήθησαν φόβον μέγαν), at the magnificent epiphany of the angel of the Lord who

---

[27] With regard to the subject of the infinitive "entered" (εἰσελθεῖν) as referring here to Moses and Elijah and not including the disciples, LOHFINK (*Himmelfahrt Jesu*, 190) perceptively points out that "εἰσέρχομαι drückt eine aktive Bewegung aus. Davon kann bei den Aposteln keine Rede sein. Warum sollten sie in die Wolke *hineingehen*? Moses und Elias hingegen sind bereits in Bewegung – vergleiche das ἐν τῷ διαχωρίζεσθαι αὐτούς von Vers 33!" Wer εἰσελθεῖν αὐτούς auf die Apostel beziehen will, muß übersetzen: 'Sie fürchteten sich, als sie in die Wolke *hineingerieten*.' εἰσέρχομαι in der Bedeutung 'hineingeraten' is bei Lukas aber lediglich 22,40.46 belegt, und dort geht es um das 'Hineingeraten in die Versuchung.' Es handelt sich also nicht um eine reale Ortsbewegung wie in Lk 9,34."

[28] On Exod 24:15-18 as background here see chap. 7.   .

appeared to them and the glory of the Lord that shone around them (2:9).[29] After the disciples in the boat witnessed the epiphany of Jesus stilling the sea storm, they "were frightened and amazed" (φοβηθέντες δὲ ἐθαύμασαν, 8:25). Those who witnessed Jesus' miraculous exorcism of the Gerasene demoniac "were frightened" (ἐφοβήθησαν, 8:35). Similarly, the three disciples "were frightened" (ἐφοβήθησαν) as they witnessed the extraordinary epiphanic overshadowing of the cloud of God's presence into which Moses and Elijah entered (9:34) to complete their separation from the transfigured Jesus and thwart Peter's wish to build a tent for each epiphanic figure.

G. LUKE 9:35

Then a voice came from the cloud saying, "This is my chosen Son; to him listen!"

That "then a voice came *from* the cloud" (9:35) further indicates to the audience that the three disciples, whom the divine voice addresses, have remained outside of the cloud, representative of God's presence.[30] The voice comes "from" or "out of" (ἐκ) the cloud and speaks to the disciples.[31] Furthermore, that the voice emphatically directs the disciples to listen to Jesus (9:35) confirms for the audience that Jesus also is outside of the cloud. The cloud appropriately overshadows only the heavenly figures of Moses and Elijah, as it implicitly completes their separation from Jesus (9:33) and transports them back to heaven. This is ultimately confirmed at the end of the scene where it is stated that "when the voice came there was found Jesus alone" (9:36).

God's command to the disciples from the overshadowing cloud develops for the audience God's pronouncement to Jesus after his baptism:

---

[29] BALZ, "φοβέομαι," 430: "The revelation of God's power in extraordinary occurrences (Matt 27:54; Luke 2:9) and in Jesus' own deeds evokes astonishment, fear, and terror in witnesses."

[30] GREEN, *Luke*, 383: "God's presence is marked by the emphatic reference (three times!) to the cloud (a symbol for the divine presence), by its overshadowing presence, and by the voice from the cloud."

[31] See BAGD, 234, on ἐκ as denoting the direction from which something comes.

3:22: καὶ φωνὴν ἐξ οὐρανοῦ γενέσθαι, Σὺ εἶ ὁ υἱός μου ὁ ἀγαπητός ἐν σοὶ εὐδόκησα

9:35: καὶ φωνὴ ἐγένετο ἐκ τῆς νεφέλης λέγουσα, Οὗτός ἐστιν ὁ υἱός μου ὁ ἐκλελεγμένος, αὐτοῦ ἀκούετε

After Jesus' baptism the divine voice came "from heaven" (3:22), God's dwelling place. Now the divine voice comes "from the cloud" (9:35), symbolic of God's presence. After the baptism God told Jesus, "You are my beloved Son; with you I am well pleased!" (3:22). But now God tells the three disciples, "This is my chosen Son; to him listen!" (9:35).

Such characters as Mary, the mother of Jesus (1:32, 35), Jesus himself (3:22), the Devil (4:3, 9), the demons exorcized by Jesus (4:41; 8:28), and therefore the audience have already known the more profound identity of Jesus as God's unique Son. Herod has raised the question of who Jesus really is and expressed his desire to see him (9:9).[32] Now God's voice from the cloud reveals Jesus' profound identity directly to the three disciples: "This is my chosen Son" (9:35).[33] This divine proclamation from the overshadowing cloud corrects Peter's misunderstanding of the epiphanic appearance of Jesus. Peter would place the transfigured Jesus on the same level as the heavenly Moses and Elijah by making a tent for each (9:33). But with an emphatic "*this* one" (οὗτός), God points out that Jesus is not equal to Moses or Elijah, since he is "my chosen Son" (9:35). The disciples and the audience are to realize then that Jesus, as God's unique, "chosen Son," is much more than the mere "Master" (ἐπιστάτα) of Peter's address (9:33). He is not, as some in the narrative have thought, Elijah or one of the prophets of old (9:8, 19) such as Moses.[34] Indeed, there is even more to Jesus as God's own

---

[32] On Herod's question in 9:7-9, see J.A. DARR, *Herod the Fox: Audience Criticism and Lukan Characterization* (JSNTSup 163; Sheffield: Sheffield Academic Press, 1998) 163-72.

[33] GREEN, *Luke*, 384: "The importance of this divine intrusion into the narrative lies in the fact that Jesus' apostles have not heretofore been privy to information of this kind."

[34] DARR, *Herod the Fox*, 170: "That Jesus is not Elijah or 'a prophet of old' (Moses?) is further reinforced in the transfiguration scene (9.28-36), for there Jesus stands *alongside* these two figures as the voice from heaven designates him 'my son, my chosen one'" (Darr's emphasis). See also P. BÖHLEMANN, *Jesus und der Täufer: Schlüssel zur Theologie und Ethik des Lukas* (SNTSMS 99; Cambridge: Cambridge University Press, 1997) 255.

chosen Son than "the Christ of God" of Peter's previous confession (9:20).[35]

At Jesus' baptism God's declaration that "You are my beloved Son; with you I am well pleased!" (3:22) places God's seal of approval upon Jesus as the one equipped with the holy Spirit for his special God-given mission. For the audience one of the intertextual allusions here already hints that Jesus is to be linked to the Isaianic suffering servant of God. In Isa 42:1 God similarly gives his Spirit to the servant with whom he is pleased.[36]

At Jesus' transfiguration God's declaration to the disciples that "This is my chosen Son" (9:35) confirms for the audience that the Jesus to whom God gave the holy Spirit at his baptism will also play the role of the Isaianic suffering servant of God. The perfect passive participle ἐκλελεγμένος expresses that not only has Jesus already been "chosen" in the past – at his baptism, but that he is still "chosen" even now, especially now that he has predicted the necessity of his suffering and death before resurrection to glory (9:22-27).[37] God's declaration of Jesus as the Son God has "chosen" (ἐκλελεγμένος as divine passive) recalls for the audience God's similar declarations of Israel as his "chosen" servant in the LXX of Isa 42:1 (Ισραηλ ὁ ἐκλεκτός μου); 43:10 (ὁ παῖς, ὅν

---

[35] REID, *Transfiguration*, 139: "The message for the disciples is both a confirmation of Peter's declaration of Jesus' messiahship (9:20) and a corrective of his misunderstanding of what that entails (9:33)."

[36] FITZMYER, *Luke I-IX*, 486: "If the allusion is admitted, then the heavenly identification of Jesus would cast him in the role of the Servant of Yahweh. This would add a connotation to that of his sonship expressed in the first part of the declaration, a connotation of obedience and suffering, in that Jesus would be understood as the embodiment of the figure in Isaiah." GREEN, *Luke*, 187: "The second text [the first is Ps 2:7] foregrounded by the heavenly voice in 3:22 is Isa 42:1, a passage that also intimately links the object of divine pleasure with the anointing of the Spirit for divine mission. Our hearing an echo of Isa 42:1 also picks up on earlier intertextual connections with the Isaianic Servant in the Gospel – for example, Isa 42:6; 49:6 in 2:32." See also BOCK, *Luke 1:1-9:50*, 341-45; J. NOLLAND, *Luke 1-9:20* (WBC 35A; Dallas: Word Books, 1989) 163.

[37] J. ECKERT, "ἐκλέγομαι," *EDNT* 1.416: "In the Lukan literature fundamental theological statements are connected with ἐκλέγομαι....Jesus Christ is God's *chosen* Son, in whom the OT promises about the messianic Son of God (Ps 2:7), the elect suffering servant of God (Isa 42:1), and the prophet like Moses (Deut 18:15) are fulfilled (Luke 9:35)." BOCK, *Luke 1:1-9:50*, 874: "The use of the perfect participle shows that Jesus has already occupied the position of the 'elect one'."

ἐξελεξάμην; cf. MT); 44:2 (ὁ ἠγαπημένος Ισραηλ, ὅν ἐξελεξάμην; cf. Luke 3:22); and 49:7 (...Ισραηλ, καὶ ἐξελεξάμην σε).[38] That Jesus is God's "*chosen* Son" thus tells the disciples and the audience that although Jesus has been transfigured into a glorious figure like Moses and Elijah, he will attain that heavenly glory, unlike Moses and Elijah, only after undergoing the suffering and death for which God has chosen him as his beloved Son (3:22; 9:35).[39]

The urgent command of God from the cloud, "to him listen!," the mandate of this pivotal mandatory epiphany, "pivots" the audience back to and thus reinforces Jesus' own urgent appeals to "listen to" and understand his teaching:

8:8: "Whoever has ears to listen, let him listen (ἀκούειν ἀκουέτω)!"
8:18: "Watch, then, how you listen (ἀκούετε)!"[40]
9:35: "To him listen (ἀκούετε)!"

God's mandate for the disciples, "to him listen" (αὐτοῦ ἀκούετε, 9:35) reminds the audience of Moses's promise that God would raise up from and for the people of Israel a prophet like Moses, so that "to him shall you listen" (αὐτοῦ ἀκούσεσθε, LXX Deut 18:15).[41] God

---

[38] DOBLE (*Paradox of Salvation*, 213-14) links Jesus as God's "chosen one" to the vindicated righteous who are also God's elect in Wis 3:9; 4:14-15: "Luke's version of the transfiguration, anticipating the complex events of Jesus' final days during *Pesah* in Jerusalem, not only named that complex ἔξοδος but further echoed Wisdom in speaking of this δίκαιος as God's chosen one." That the "chosen one" involves royal-messianic as well as Isaianic servant imagery is maintained by STRAUSS, *Davidic Messiah in Luke-Acts*, 264-67.

[39] REID, *Transfiguration*, 141: "The further designation of Jesus as ὁ ἐκλελεμένος brings into greater relief the direct relationship between Jesus' special status as God's Son and his election by God to follow the path of suffering to glory....In Luke 9:35 the voice is directed to the disciples and Luke advances the previous understanding of Jesus as ὁ ἀγαπητός to that of Jesus as suffering servant conveyed by ὁ ἐκλελεμένος. Ironically, it is precisely because Jesus is God's unique Son that he is chosen to undergo the passion." See also G. SCHRENK, "ἐκλέγομαι," *TDNT* 4.189; MARSHALL, *Luke*, 388.

[40] J.A. DARR, "'Watch How You Listen' (Lk. 8.18): Jesus and the Rhetoric of Perception in Luke-Acts," *The New Literary Criticism and the New Testament* (JSNTSup 109; eds. E.S. Malbon and E.V. McKnight; Sheffield: Sheffield Academic Press, 1994) 104: "At the level of discourse, Jesus' words about perception serve to *program* the authorial audience's hearing/reading of Luke's story" (Darr's emphasis).

[41] FITZMYER, *Luke I-IX*, 803: "The Lucan order is closer to the LXX of Deut 18:15...Heaven's word thus substitutes Jesus, its chosen messenger and Son, for the withdrawing heavenly figures of old." NOLLAND, *Luke 9:21-18:34*, 502: "In that the words 'hear him'

himself reinforced the promise of a prophet like Moses, and added: "I will place my word in his mouth, and he will speak to them as I command him" (LXX Deut 18:18). But now the disciples and the audience are to listen to Jesus not just as a prophet like Moses (or Elijah) but as God's own chosen Son, who speaks as God, his Father, commands him. Although Peter and his fellow disciples have not heard the conversation between Jesus and Moses and Elijah (9:31), since they were asleep (9:32), Peter's offer to make three tents would provide a place – on analogy with the Tent of Meeting – for possible divine communication from each of the three epiphanic heavenly figures. But God's mandate indicates that they should not be so much concerned with what the heavenly Moses and Elijah might have to say as with what Jesus, as God's chosen Son, has had and will have to say to them. The audience's recall of Deut 18:15-18, then, reinforces for them that what they have already heard and what they will hear from Jesus is the very word of God himself.[42]

The divine mandate to listen to Jesus as God's chosen Son especially refers the disciples and the audience back to what Jesus has just spoken in the scene (9:21-27) preceding the transfiguration.[43] Attentively listening to what Jesus has just said would enable the disciples and the audience to grasp the more profound identity of the transfigured Jesus as God's chosen Son in contrast to the heavenly figures of Moses and Elijah. After Peter as spokesman for the disciples confessed Jesus to be "the Christ of God" (9:20), Jesus, in rebuking them, ordered them not to tell this to anyone (9:21), saying, "It is necessary for the Son of Man to suffer many things and to be rejected by the

---

echo Deut 18:15 (cf. Acts 3:22; 7:37) a further Mosaic link is here established, but should not be pressed in terms of a Moses typology." See also STRAUSS, *Davidic Messiah in Luke-Acts*, 270-71.

[42] REID, *Transfiguration*, 139: "A new note is struck by emphasizing that Jesus is the one to whom disciples must listen and whom disciples must heed. He is the word of God for them. This emphasis on the person of Jesus is evident in v 35...with the placement of αὐτοῦ, the personal pronoun referring to Jesus, before the imperative ἀκούετε."

[43] R.C. TANNEHILL, *The Narrative Unity of Luke-Acts: Volume 1: The Gospel According to Luke* (FFNT; Philadelphia: Fortress, 1986) 223: "A connection is apparent in the reference to Jesus' 'departure' in 9:31, which is related to the announcement of Jesus' coming death in 9:22, and in the command to 'hear him' in 9:35, which is divine confirmation of the authority of Jesus' words in 9:22-27 and later."

elders and the chief priests and the scribes, and to be killed, but to be raised on the third day" (9:22). Therefore, although Jesus' temporary transfiguration into a heavenly figure indicates that he will ultimately attain heavenly glory like Moses and Elijah, unlike them he will do so only as he is raised by God after being rejected and put to death by the leaders of his own people. This is why the disciples and audience must heed the epiphanic mandate to "listen to him!" (9:35).[44]

There has been no indication that Peter or the disciples have really heard and understood what Jesus has said with regard to his death and resurrection. Attentively listening to what Jesus told "all" (πάντας) of the disciples would enable Peter, James, and John, as well as the audience, to realize that they must all follow Jesus on his way of suffering and death, by denying themselves and taking up their cross daily (9:23), if they are to join him in the ultimate and permanent heavenly glory that his transfiguration prefigures. They must lose their lives for the sake of Jesus in order to save them (9:24). They must not be ashamed of Jesus and "my words" (9:26), especially his words about the necessity for his suffering and death before resurrection (9:22) and his word about the necessity to follow him in that suffering and death (9:23-25), in order to join him in heavenly glory. That Jesus, as the Son of Man, is still to come "in his glory" (ἐν τῇ δόξῃ αὐτοῦ) and that of the Father and the holy angels (9:26) confirms that "his glory" (τὴν δόξαν αὐτοῦ) that the disciples witnessed during his transfiguration (9:32) is but a temporary anticipation of his final glory yet to come as God's chosen Son (9:35).[45]

---

[44] NOLLAND, *Luke 9:21-18:34*, 501-2: "The point is to hear what Jesus has been seeking to teach them. This is the response to Peter's desire to preserve inviolate the scene of glory that the three have witnessed. The glory they have seen is the glory to which Jesus is destined as chosen Son, but what they have glimpsed in this anticipatory scene comes to its fulfillment only by way of the cross. God here throws his weight behind Jesus' words in vv 22-27." R.C. TANNEHILL, *Luke* (ANTC; Nashville: Abingdon, 1996) 162: "The principal application in context is to Jesus' teaching about suffering and death in 9:22-26, but this command is also a preface to all Jesus' teaching of disciples on his journey to Jerusalem, teaching designed to prepare them for their tasks when he is no longer with them."

[45] REID, *Transfiguration*, 131-32: "An important step is taken in the NT when δόξα, which had been used in relation to God (e.g., Luke 2:9; 7:55) is now used of Jesus. The phrase εἶδον τὴν δόξαν αὐτοῦ has echoes of Num 12:8, where it is said that Moses saw the glory of God, τὴν δόξαν κυρίου εἶδεν. The expression also calls to mind OT eschatological promises of seeing God's glory...Against this background, εἶδον τὴν δόξαν αὐτοῦ in 9:32 can also be

Attentively listening to Jesus' words about the necessity to follow him on his way to suffering and death would enable the three disciples and the audience to realize how the transfiguration epiphany prepares them to fulfill Jesus' promise that "there are some standing here who will not taste death until they see the kingdom of God" (9:27). The temporary transfiguration of Jesus into a heavenly figure assures the three disciples and the audience that he will ultimately and permanently achieve the heavenly glory of God's kingdom after his necessary suffering, rejection, and death. The transfiguration epiphany will thus enable them to see the kingdom of God already in some sense in Jesus' death and resurrection which some of them will witness before they "taste"[46] the bitterness of their own death as followers of Jesus.[47]

H. Luke 9:36

When the voice came there was found Jesus alone. And they kept silent and reported to no one in those days any of the things they had seen.

Simultaneous with or immediately after the sounding of God's voice from the overshadowing cloud, *"This* is my chosen Son; *to him* listen!"* (9:35), Jesus was found alone.[48] This emphatically underlines for the disciples and the audience that the divine voice refers to Jesus in contrast to Moses and Elijah, who have disappeared in the cloud, so

---

understood as a proleptic vision of Jesus' eschatological glory. This interpretation agrees with Luke's use elsewhere of δόξα in reference to Jesus, where it is a future glory into which he will enter: 9:26; 21:27; 24:26."

[46] "Taste" in the frequently occurring phrase, "taste death," implies the moment of suffering according to VAN DER MINDE, "γεύομαι," 1.246.

[47] On Luke's concept and use of "the kingdom of God" U. LUZ ("βασιλεία," *EDNT* 1.204) states: "He thus rejects a temporally determined imminent expectation considered in temporal terms...Alongside sayings about the future βασιλεία there are isolated sayings which assume its presence already in heaven (Luke 23:42f.; cf. 16:19-31). The concepts are not harmonized in Luke."

[48] FITZMYER (*Luke I-IX*, 803) translates, "once that voice had spoken," or literally, "in the happening of the voice" (ἐν τῷ γενέσθαι τὴν φωνὴν).

that Jesus now stands there alone.[49] That Jesus is now found by the disciples to be alone indicates that his temporary transfiguration into a heavenly figure for the purpose of conversing with the heavenly figures of Moses and Elijah has concluded. That Jesus is the only one left there before the disciples places them in a position to obey the epiphanic mandate to listen to him. They have apparently not really listened in the past, especially to what Jesus said in predicting his death and resurrection and their role in it as his disciples (9:21-27). Will they listen in the future?

That the three disciples "kept silent" (9:36) stands in contrast to Peter's previous impromptu outburst suggesting the making of a tent for each epiphanic heavenly figure. The narrator told the audience at that time that Peter did not know what he was saying (9:33). Are Peter and his companions now so non-understanding of what has happened in the transfiguration epiphany that they have been reduced to complete silence?

That the silenced disciples "reported" (ἀπήγγειλαν) to no one in those days any of the things they had seen (9:36) in the miraculous transfiguration epiphany stands in contrast to previous reportings of Jesus' miracles. The disciples of John the Baptist reported (ἀπήγγειλαν) to him "concerning all these things" (7:18), which includes the miracles Jesus had just performed (7:1-17). When Jesus sent John's disciples back to him, he told them to report (ἀπαγγείλατε) what they had seen and heard, namely, his healing miracles and his preaching of the good news to the poor (7:22). After the swineherds witnessed Jesus' miraculous exorcism of the Gerasene demoniacs, they reported (ἀπήγγειλαν) it publicly "in the city and in the fields" (8:34). Those who witnessed this miracle reported (ἀπήγγειλαν) to those who came to see what happened how the possessed man was saved (8:36). And the hemorrhaging woman publicly reported (ἀπήγγειλαν) before "all the people" how she had been miraculously cured by Jesus (8:47). But now the miraculous transfiguration

---

[49] MARSHALL, *Luke*, 389: "Luke's briefer phrasing, culminating in μόνος, brings out more forcefully the fact that Jesus alone remained with them." NOLLAND, *Luke 9:21-18:34*, 502: "Luke tightens the link between the voice and the new scene in which Jesus is quite alone: the aloneness of Jesus is an aloneness that is divinely orchestrated and used to underline the thrust of the words spoken to the disciples."

remains a silently private matter of the disciples. They curiously and mysteriously do not "report" it publicly, adding to the suspense for the audience.[50]

After Peter as spokesman of the disciples confessed Jesus to be "the Christ of God" (9:20), Jesus, in rebuking them, commanded them to tell "no one" (μηδενὶ) this (9:21). They are to tell no one that Jesus is the Christ until they understand what kind of Christ he is, namely, one that must suffer, die, and rise, as well as what being a disciple of this Christ entails, namely, denying oneself, taking up the cross daily, and losing one's life to save it (9:22-27). But now the transfiguration's epiphanic mandate, which urges the disciples to listen to these words of Jesus to understand not only how he is "the Christ of God" but how he is "the chosen Son" of God (9:35) has rendered the disciples so silent that they reported to "no one" (οὐδενὶ) in those days any of the things they had seen (9:36). This further adds to the suspense for the audience as to whether the disciples have understood the significance of the transfiguration epiphany.

That the disciples kept silent and reported to no one "in those days" any of the things they had seen (9:36) implies that they did report what they had experienced at a later time, after they understood the significance of the transfiguration epiphany by heeding the epiphanic mandate to listen to what Jesus has already said and what he still may say about the divine necessity for his suffering and death before entering into the heavenly glory prefigured in his transfiguration. The use of the perfect tense in referring to the things "they had seen" (ἑώρακαν) expresses the enduring effect upon them of what they had experienced in this miraculous but mysterious epiphanic event. It further hints to the audience that what the disciples have seen cannot remain silent and will eventually be reported.[51]

---

[50] On Luke's use of ἀπαγγέλλω in the reporting of Jesus' miracles, see I. BROER, "ἀγγέλλω," *EDNT* 1.13.

[51] With regard to Luke's use of the perfect tense here MARSHALL (*Luke*, 389) states that "it brings out the continued importance of an event which for the time being had to remain silent. Only later was its signficance to become fully apparent."

I. Conclusion

Since Jesus has prayed before very significant events in his ministry (3:21; 5:16; 6:12; 9:18), that he took along Peter and John and James when he went up to the mountain to pray (9:28) prepares the audience for yet another very significant event. While Jesus was praying on the mountain, there suddenly occurs a spectacular epiphany of his transfiguration into a heavenly figure, as "the appearance of his face became different and his clothing dazzling white" (9:29). This dramatic change in the face and clothing of Jesus signals to the audience that he has been externally and temporarily transformed by God into a heavenly being while still on earth. It anticipates his future and permanent attainment of glory in heaven as promised to the righteous after their death.

The initial epiphanic transfiguration of Jesus in the presence of the three disciples is immediately followed by an additional epiphanic appearance of two men, Moses and Elijah, who appear in glory and talk with Jesus about his "exodus," which he was about to accomplish in Jerusalem (9:30-31). Jesus' "exodus" or "departure" refers to the way that he will leave this earthly life by the death and resurrection he has just predicted (9:22). Unlike Moses and Elijah, who have attained heavenly glory without being put to death by their people, Jesus will attain the glory prefigured by his temporary transformation into a heavenly figure only after being rejected and killed by the Jewish leaders (9:22). That Jesus "was about to accomplish" his exodus in Jerusalem expresses its divine inevitability, further linking it to the divine necessity of his death and resurrection. That Jesus will accomplish his exodus from the earthly to the heavenly realm "in Jerusalem" prepares the audience for his journey to the city where the elders, chief priests, and scribes will play their role in his exodus that will lead to his ultimate coming in glory (9:26).

Although the three disciples had been overcome with sleep so that they did not hear the conversation about Jesus' approaching "exodus," they became wide awake in time to see the glory of the transfigured Jesus and that of Moses and Elijah standing with him (9:32). That upon awakening they only *saw* the two men standing with him underlines for the audience that while the three disciples were asleep they failed to *hear* these same two men talking with him. That Moses and Elijah were standing with the transfigured Jesus associates his glory with that of these two men, who were likewise appearing in glory (9:31).

The narrator tells the audience that Peter did not know what he was saying when he offered that they make a tent for each epiphanic figure. Peter wants to prepare a dwelling place for each heavenly figure to prolong his epiphanic appearance on earth, and thus to halt and render unnecessary the separation of Moses and Elijah from Jesus that has already begun (9:33). On analogy with the Tent of Meeting each tent would also provide a place for each heavenly figure to offer divine communication. But the audience experiences the irony that a heavenly communication, the conversation about Jesus' "exodus" in Jerusalem (9:31), has already taken place while the three disciples were asleep (9:32).

Placing the transfigured Jesus on the same level and in the same category as the heavenly figures of Moses and Elijah implies that perhaps Jesus, despite his previous prediction about the necessity of his suffering and death before resurrection on the third day (9:22), has already or will attain heavenly glory like Moses and Elijah, that is, without being put to death by his people. Peter does not seem to realize that Jesus will attain the same heavenly glory he now momentarily shares with Moses and Elijah only after he has been put to death as a rejected prophet in Jerusalem.

But Peter is interrupted by yet another sudden and unexpected epiphanic appearance as a cloud overshadowed Moses and Elijah, implicitly transporting them back to heaven. The disciples responded with fear as Moses and Elijah entered into the cloud (9:34). After Jesus' baptism God's voice from heaven told Jesus, "You are my beloved Son; with you I am well pleased!" (3:22). But now God tells the three disciples, "This is my chosen Son; to him listen!" (9:35). This confirms for the audience that the Jesus to whom God gave the holy Spirit at his baptism will also play the role of the Isaianic suffering servant of God.

God's voice from the cloud (9:35) serves as the pivotal mandate that distinguishes Jesus from Moses and Elijah as God's chosen Son and commands the disciples and the audience to listen to Jesus. The mandate thus "pivots" them back to the previous teaching of Jesus (8:8, 18), especially his teaching about the necessity for him and his followers to suffer and be put to death (9:21-27) before entering into

the heavenly glory of God's kingdom anticipated by Jesus' transfiguration.   The pivotal mandatory epiphany concludes with Jesus again
alone with the disciples, who kept silent and reported to no one in
those days any of the things they had seen (9:36). Will the disciples and
the audience heed the pivotal epiphanic mandate and listen to Jesus in
order to understand the way that he and they will attain the heavenly
glory anticipated by his transfiguration?   Only by truly listening to
Jesus will they be able to break their silence and report in the days to
come what they have experienced in the transfiguration epiphany.

CHAPTER 13

LUKE 9:28-36 AND THE SUBSEQUENT NARRATIVE

In the preceding chapter we considered how the Lukan transfiguration narrative functions as a pivotal mandatory epiphany in relation to the antecedent Lukan narrative. More specifically, we saw how the mandate, "To him listen!" (9:35), pivoted the audience back especially to Jesus' pronouncement of the necessity for his disciples to follow him on his way to suffering and death before being raised to heavenly glory (9:21-27) as a key to understanding the significance of the transfiguration epiphany. In this chapter we will consider how the Lukan transfiguration epiphany, especially its pivotal mandate, relates to and prepares the audience for the rest of Luke's Gospel.

A. LUKE 9:41: JESUS WILL NOT BE WITH THEM MUCH LONGER

Jesus' lamentful question to the "faithless and perverse generation" (9:41; cf. Deut 32:5, 20) represented by the crowd (9:37), the father who brought his son to Jesus (9:38-39), and the disciples who failed to heal him (9:40) – "How long am I to be with you and bear with you?" (9:41; cf. Num 14:27) – expresses an ironic double meaning. On the one hand, it expresses the extreme length of time Jesus has had to endure their lack of faith. On the other hand, it warns of the short period Jesus will still be with them before his approaching death, as anticipated by his absence from them during his transfiguration. The audience realizes that in the future the disciples must have the faith to heal such cases on their own, since Jesus will not always be there to do it for them.[1]

---

[1] NOLLAND, *Luke 9:21-18:34*, 510: "Clearly in mind is the exodus to come in Jerusalem (v 31), which will put an end to the present situation." GREEN, *Luke*, 389: "Jesus is already anticipating his execution (9:22, 44), after which his followers will share responsibility in the divine mission, and they are in a deplorable state of readiness."

B. Luke 9:44-45: The disciples still do not understand Jesus' prediction of his passion

While all the people were amazed at all the things Jesus was doing, especially his miraculous deeds such as the remarkable exorcism, which his disciples were unable to perform (9:37-42), but that amazed everyone (9:43), Jesus told his disciples: "As for you, place into your ears these words – the Son of Man is about to be delivered into the hands of men" (9:44).[2] While everyone else is overwhelmed by the miracles, the disciples, "you" (ὑμεῖς), to whom it has been given to know the mysteries of the kingdom of God (8:10), are to focus on the divine necessity of Jesus' passion.[3]

Jesus' appeal for the disciples to "place into your ears (ὦτα) these words" (9:44) not only recalls his earlier appeal after the parable of the sower, "Whoever has ears (ὦτα) to listen, let him listen!" (8:8; cf. 1:44; 4:21; 8:18), but especially reinforces the epiphanic pivotal mandate of God's voice from the overshadowing cloud at the transfiguration, "To him listen!" (9:35).[4] That mandate "pivoted" the disciples and the audience back especially to "these words" (τοὺς λόγους τούτους) after which the transfiguration epiphany took place (9:28), that is, "these words of mine" (τοὺς ἐμοὺς λόγους, 9:26), which refers to Jesus' pronouncement of the necessity not only for his own death and resurrection but for the disciples to follow him by denying themselves, taking up their cross daily, and losing their lives for his sake (9:21-25). That mandate also "pivoted" the disciples and the audience ahead to the future words of Jesus, "these words" (τοὺς λόγους τούτους) predicting his passion, which Jesus now urges the disciples

---

[2] This translation attempts to bring out the force of the emphatic ὑμεῖς ("as for you") and the epexegetic sense of γάρ. MARSHALL, *Luke*, 393: "...most scholars take 'these words' to be the immediately following prediction of the passion, with γάρ epexegetic."

[3] This puts "the impending passion of the Son of Man in the starkest contrast to the *wonder of the miracles* (vv. 43-44)," according to R.J. DILLON, *From Eye-Witnesses to Ministers of the Word* (AnBib 82; Rome: Biblical Institute, 1978) 35 (Dillon's emphasis).

[4] TANNEHILL, *Narrative Unity*, 1.226: "Three leading apostles were told by a heavenly voice to 'hear him,' and Jesus introduces his statement in v. 44 with a similar command to hear."

to place in their ears in order to really listen to and understand them (9:44).[5]

"These words" of Jesus, namely, his words that as the Son of Man he "is about to" (μέλλει) be delivered into the hands of men (9:44) remind the audience of the conversation between the transfigured Jesus and Moses and Elijah about his "exodus," which he "was about to" (ἤμελλεν) accomplish in Jerusalem (9:31). That Jesus will be delivered into the hands of men is part of his "exodus" from death to resurrection and heavenly exaltation that "is about to" take place in Jerusalem in accord with the necessity of God's plan of salvation.[6]

That Jesus "is about to be delivered into the hands of men" (9:44) abbreviates the fuller prediction that the disciples and audience have already heard of his rejection by the Jewish leaders, death, and resurrection on the third day (9:22).[7] That Jesus as the Son of "Man" is about to be delivered (by God, divine passive) into the hands of "men" forms a word-play expressing the irony that rather than being welcomed by men, Jesus, as God's messianic agent, "the Son of Man," will be delivered into their destructive power.[8] Before Jesus as the Son of Man comes in his final glory (9:26), a glory prefigured by his transfiguration (9:32), he must as the Son of Man be delivered into the hands of men (9:44) to be put to death (9:22).[9]

---

[5] M. VÖLKEL, "οὖς," *EDNT* 2.547: "Οὖς always means the natural ear in the NT, esp. insofar as it entails the capacity of hearing. It is rarely described with the term for the process of hearing (Luke 1:44; 4:21; Acts 11:22). In Luke 9:44 the phrase θέσθε εἰς τὰ ὦτα simply refers to the understanding of the one who hears."

[6] The verb μέλλω, "is about to," expresses here the necessity of an event that is certain to occur in accord with the divine will; see RADL, "μέλλω" 2.404.

[7] TANNEHILL, *Narrative Unity*, 1.226: "The passion announcement is shortened to the single sentence...The disciples (and the readers) should be able to recall the rest from the previous announcement."

[8] FITZMYER, *Luke I-IX*, 814; NOLLAND, *Luke 9:21-18:34*, 514: "If it is right to find a deliberative word-play with serious purpose in the juxtaposition of 'Son of Man' and 'men,' then the handing over will need to be, after all, by God: he who should be welcomed by men is instead handed over (by God) to their destructive will."

[9] The LXX of Dan 7:25 offers a close parallel to the Son of Man being delivered (παραδίδοσθαι) into the hands of men, according to C.C. CARAGOUNIS, *The Son of Man: Vision and Interpretation* (WUNT 38; Tübingen: Mohr-Siebeck, 1986) 199. In reference to Dan 7:25 NOLLAND (*Luke 9:21-18:34*, 513) states: "There, the saints of the Most High (the equivalent to the 'one like a son of man' of the vision of v 13) shall be delivered up (LXX uses

Despite God's epiphanic mandate to listen to Jesus (9:35), reinforced by Jesus' urgent command for the disciples to place the words of his passion prediction into their ears (9:44), they fail to listen with understanding. Their failure is expressed most emphatically: "But they did not understand this saying and it was hidden from them so that they did not comprehend it, and they were afraid to ask him about this saying" (9:45).[10] There seems to be both a divine and human reason for this failure. That "it was hidden" (παρακεκαλυμμένον) from them suggests a divine passive, that it was purposefully hidden from them and continued to be hidden (perfect tense) at this time as part of God's plan.[11] On the other hand, God gave the disciples the knowledge of the mysteries of the kingdom of God (8:10, 18) and they have already heard the first passion prediction (9:22), so that they should be capable of listening with understanding.[12] That they are able to obey neither the transfiguration's pivotal mandate nor the command of Jesus creates a major suspense for the audience.[13]

---

the same verb, παραδιδόναι) into the hands of the final king of the kingdom represented by the fourth beast of Daniel's vision of 7:1-14. If this is the correct background for our text, then Son of Man here is already Danielic, and it is so precisely in its reference to suffering, rather than (as with other texts) in connection with vindication and glory." On the various nuances of παραδίδοσθαι in Luke 9:44 – "delivered," "handed over," "betrayed," etc., see IBID., 514; W. POPKES, "παραδίδωμι," *EDNT* 3.20.

[10] GREEN, *Luke*, 390: "The disciples' lack of perception is emphatic. It is accentuated, first, by Jesus' apparent need to urge the disciples to internalize his words, to hear and to perceive (cf. 8:10). Following this, Luke outlines their failure to hear in four phrases: they lacked understanding, its meaning was concealed, they lacked perception, and they declined to discuss this subject further on account of their fear (cf. 8:25)."

[11] MARSHALL, *Luke*, 394: "The saying was hidden from them; the use of παρακαλύπτω with ἀπό is a Hebraism, and the passive again indicates divine action; this is confirmed by the ἵνα clause which should be understood as expressive of purpose..." See also FITZMYER, *Luke I-IX*, 814.

[12] TANNEHILL, *Narrative Unity*, 1.227: "If we assume that 9:45 does not tarnish the image of the disciples, since God did not intend them to understand at this point, we depart from the viewpoint of Jesus, for he clearly wants and expects the disciples to understand now ('Put into your ears these words'). The tension between Jesus and the disciples at this point highlights the reality and seriousness of the disciples' blindness, which dominate the scene even if there is a hint that God can use human blindness for a divine purpose."

[13] With regard to the narrative aside in 9:45, SHEELEY (*Narrative Asides*, 109) states: "This aside begins the process of putting distance between the narrator and the reader on the one hand and the disciples on the other."

C. Luke 9:51-56: Jesus sets his face to go to Jerusalem

Jesus begins his final journey to Jerusalem with the notice that "when the days were completed for his being taken up, he set his face to go to Jerusalem" (9:51). This reminds the audience of the conversation the glorified Moses and Elijah had with the transfigured Jesus "about his exodus, which he was about to accomplish in Jerusalem" (9:31). Both Jesus' "exodus" and his being "taken up" refer to his suffering, death, and resurrection that must occur in Jerusalem before he attains the heavenly glory of Moses and Elijah prefigured by his temporary transfiguration. But the connotation of his being "taken up" develops that of his "exodus." Whereas the "exodus" (ἔξοδον) of Jesus focuses upon his "departure" or "going *out* (ἔξ)" of this earthly life by way of his death and resurrection, his being "taken up" (ἀναλήμψεως) focuses upon his "ascension" or "going *up* (ἀνα)" to heavenly glory by way of his death and resurrection (cf. Acts 1:2, 11, 22).[14]

Jesus' being "taken up" (ἀναλήμψεως) recalls Elijah's being "taken up" (ἀνελήμφθη in 4 Kgdms 2:9, 11; 1 Macc 2:58; ἀναλημφθεὶς in Sir 48:9) into heaven without dying.[15] But the audience knows that Jesus, unlike the prophet Elijah, will be "taken up" into heaven only after being put to death by his own people and raised from the dead by God (9:22).[16]

---

[14] On the meaning of Jesus' being "taken up" in Luke 9:51 and in Acts 1:2, 11, 22, see P.A. van Stempvoort, "The Interpretation of the Ascension in Luke and Acts," *NTS* 5 (1958-59) 30-42; J.B. Tyson, *The Death of Jesus in Luke-Acts* (Columbia: University of South Carolina Press, 1986) 98-99; M.C. Parsons, *The Departure of Jesus in Luke-Acts: The Ascension Narratives in Context* (JSNTSup 21; Sheffield: JSOT, 1987) 130-32; R.C. Tannehill, *The Narrative Unity of Luke-Acts: Volume 2: The Acts of the Apostles* (FFNT; Minneapolis: Fortress, 1990) 11; Zwiep, *Ascension*, 80-86. According to Zwiep, "the possibility must be emphasised that we have here a progressive parallelism, the statement in v. 51 (ascension) expanding the imagery of v. 31 (departure from life)" (p. 86).

[15] See chap. 5.

[16] According to Zwiep (*Ascension*, 86), "ἀνάλημψις recalls the biblical Elijah tradition, ἔξοδος is derived from the biblical Moses tradition, perfectly fitting in the context of the Transfiguration scene." But it should be noted that ἀναλαμβάνω (*Mos.* 2.291) and ἀνάλημψις (A.-M. Denis, ed., *Fragmenta pseudepigraphorum quae supersunt graeca una cum historicorum et auctorum Judaeorum hellenistarum fragmentis* [PVTG 3; Leiden: Brill, 1970] 63-64) are used also to refer to the heavenly "ascension" of Moses. And Jesus' "exo-

That Jesus now set his face (πρόσωπον, 9:51), the same face (προσώπου, 9:29) the audience knows was temporarily transformed into a face of heavenly glory, to go to Jerusalem expresses his determined resolve to undergo his "exodus" (9:31) and submit himself to the divine necessity that he be put to death by the Jewish leaders in Jerusalem before being raised by God (9:22).[17] The focused play on the *face* of Jesus continues as "he sent messengers before his face (προσώπου)," who went into a village of the Samaritans to prepare for him (9:52).[18] But the Samaritans did not receive him, because "his face (πρόσωπον) was going to Jerusalem" (9:53).[19] Thus, Jesus sent messengers before his *face*, the *face* resolutely going to Jerusalem, and persevered despite rejection of that *face* set for suffering and death, so that the *face* of Jesus can be permanently transformed into heavenly glory by way of his resurrection.

---

dus" in 9:31 alludes primarily to the exodus of the people of Israel rather than to the exodus of Moses (Josephus in *A.J.* 4.8.2 §189 refers to the death of Moses as his "exodus from life [ἐπ' ἐξόδῳ τοῦ ζῆν]").

[17] According to G. SCHNEIDER ("στηρίζω," *EDNT* 3.276), that Jesus set his face (πρόσωπον ἐστήρισεν) "evokes the language of similar OT formulations (Jer 3:12; 21:10; Ezek 6:2, and elsewhere)" and expreses how Jesus "submits resolutely to the realization of the divine plan (cf. Luke 9:22)." NOLLAND, *Luke 9:21-18:34*, 535: "Jesus sets out resolutely to make the trip to Jerusalem for which 9:21-50 have been a focused preparation. The specific mention of Jerusalem as the place of destiny has thus far been restricted to 9:31, but reference to the leadership group in v 22 has already implied a Jerusalem setting clearly enough." See also SQUIRES, *Plan of God*, 168; C.A. EVANS, "'He Set His Face': On the Meaning of Luke 9:51," *Luke and Scripture: The Function of Sacred Tradition in Luke-Acts* (C.A. Evans and J.A. Sanders; Minneapolis: Fortress, 1993) 93-105.

[18] That Jesus "sent messengers before his face (ἀπέστειλεν ἀγγελους πρὸ προσώπον αὐτοῦ)," who "entered" (εἰσῆλθον) into a Samaritan village "to prepare" (ἐτοιμάσαι) for him (9:52) exhibits a remarkable linguistic similarity to the LXX of Exod 23:20: "And behold I am sending my messenger before your face (ἀποστέλλω τὸν ἀγγελον μου πρὸ προσώπου σου), to guard you on the way, so that he might lead you into (εἰσαγάγη) the land, which I have prepared (ἡτοίμασά) for you" (cf. LXX Mal 3:1). Thus the exodus of the Israelites from Egypt to the promised land continues to be played upon as background for the "exodus" of Jesus from death on earth to life in heaven, which is to take place at Jerusalem (9:31).

[19] On the traditional animosity between Jews and Samaritans, see GREEN (*Luke*, 404-5), who states: "That Jesus is rejected precisely on the terms in which his prophetic resolution had first been expressed is reminiscent of Jesus' rejection by the people of Nazareth (4:16-30). Like them, these Samaritan villagers rebuff Jesus because they cannot accept his understanding and embodiment of the divine purpose."

The audience heard how Peter, in suggesting the building of a tent for each of the three heavenly figures in the transfiguration scene (9:33), failed to understand how Jesus differs from Moses and Elijah, because he and his companions were asleep (9:32) during the conversation about Jesus' "exodus" to be accomplished in Jerusalem (9:31). Now Peter's companions at the transfiguration, James and John (9:28), similarly misunderstand how Jesus differs from the prophet Elijah as he begins his fateful journey to Jerusalem. Just as Elijah called down fire from heaven to destroy representatives of Ahaziah, king of Samaria, who did not recognize the God of Israel (2 Kgs 1:10, 12), so James and John suggest that they call down fire from heaven to destroy the Samaritans who will not welcome Jesus (9:54).[20] Whereas at the transfiguration God's voice from the overshadowing cloud in effect rebuked Peter's incongruous suggestion (9:35), now Jesus turns and rebukes James and John, before they go on to another village (9:55-56).[21]

As Jesus begins his fateful journey to Jerusalem (9:51-56), then, the suspense continues for the audience regarding the disciples' failure to heed the transfiguration's pivotal mandate to listen (9:35) with understanding to Jesus' predictions of the divine necessity for him to go to Jerusalem to suffer much, be rejected by the leaders, and put to death before rising (9:22, 44) to the glory foreshadowed by his transfiguration (9:32).

D. LUKE 10:39: MARY WAS LISTENING TO THE WORD OF JESUS

While Jesus continues on his final and fateful journey to Jerusalem, a woman named Martha welcomes him to share the hospitality of a

---

[20] GREEN, LUKE, 406: "The inadequacy of the disciples at this juncture is underscored by their explicit identification as James and John. These two were among the trio who accompanied Jesus in the scene of transfiguration, and who thus heard Jesus and his message legitimated in the most profound way possible, by God himself (9:28-36). Had they in fact 'listened to him,' would they not have remembered his words regarding the divine necessity of his rejection?"

[21] On the Elijah background in 9:51-56, see T.L. BRODIE, "The Departure for Jerusalem (Luke 9,51-56) as a Rhetorical Imitation of Elijah's Departure for the Jordan (2 Kgs 1,1-2,6)," *Bib* 70 (1989) 96-109. For a recent argument for the longer Byzantine reading in 9:54-56, see L. RAMAROSON, "Mise en oeuvre de l'"ecclectisme intégral' à propos de Jn 8,57 et de Lc 9,54-56," *ScEs* 49 (1997) 181-85.

meal in her home (10:38).[22]　That Martha's sister Mary was listening (ἤκουεν) to the word of Jesus in the position of a disciple, "sitting alongside at the feet of the Lord" (10:39),[23] alerts the audience to her obedience of God's pivotal mandate to the disciples at the transfiguration of Jesus, "This is my chosen Son; to him listen (ἀκούετε)!" (9:35). By attentively listening to the word of Jesus, Mary, a female disciple, is in a position to understand the necessity of Jesus' journey to suffer and die in Jerusalem, which the male disciples are unable to understand at this point (9:45). Through this meal scene the audience realizes that before a disciple can appropriately "serve" Jesus, as Martha wants to do (10:40-42), he or she must first listen to the word of Jesus like Mary, the word that calls disciples to a selfless service that follows Jesus on the divinely necessary way of his suffering and death, in order to share in the resurrection to glory (9:22-26) anticipated by his transfiguration.

E. LUKE 13:33-35: JESUS WILL TRIUMPH OVER HIS DEATH AS A PROPHET IN JERUSALEM

After some Pharisees warn Jesus to flee because Herod wants to kill him (13:31), Jesus asserts that it is divinely necessary (δεῖ; cf. 9:22) to continue his journey, and thus accomplish his "exodus" at Jerusalem (9:31), "for it is not possible that a prophet die outside of Jerusalem" (13:33).[24] In Jesus' following lament over Jerusalem it becomes clear to the audience that the prophet Jesus (cf. 7:16, 39; 9:8, 19) will not just perish or die (ἀπολέσθαι) a natural death in Jerusalem, but that he will be *killed* by the people, especially by the Jewish leaders (9:22; 11:49-

---

[22] On 10:38-42 as a meal scene, see J.P. HEIL, *The Meal Scenes in Luke-Acts: An Audience-Oriented Approach* (SBLMS 52; Atlanta: Society of Biblical Literature, 1999) 67-79.

[23] J.A. FITZMYER, *The Gospel According to Luke X-XXIV* (AB 28A; Garden City: Doubleday, 1985) 893: "Her position is that of a listening disciple."

[24] SQUIRES (*Plan of God*, 169) points out how in 13:33 "Luke emphasizes the essentially inevitable nature of God's plan." Both of the impersonal constructions in 13:33, "it is necessary" (δεῖ) and "it is not possible" (οὐκ ἐνδέχεται), place the activity of Jesus within God's will, according to L.T. JOHNSON, *The Gospel of Luke* (SacPag 3; Collegeville: Liturgical Press, 1991) 218. TANNEHILL (*Luke*, 224) points out that 13:33 "is an exaggeration, making the point that Jerusalem especially, as symbolic center and seat of authority, is responsible for the deaths of the prophets. Thus it is the appropriate site of Jesus' death."

51), since Jerusalem "kills (ἀποκτείνουσα; cf. ἀποκτανθῆναι in 9:22; ἀποκτενοῦσιν in 11:49) the prophets and stones those sent to her" (13:34).[25] To be killed by Jerusalem, the central and representative city of the Jewish people, is the usual fate of prophets like Jesus.[26]

This explicitly confirms for the audience what was implied in the transfiguration, namely, that unlike the prophets Moses and Elijah, who avoided the destiny of rejected prophets and achieved their heavenly glory without being put to death by their people, the prophet Jesus will undergo the usual destiny of a rejected prophet and be killed by the people of Jerusalem.[27]   But, as prefigured by his transfiguration into heavenly glory (9:29-32), Jesus' death as a rejected prophet will be vindicated by God raising him (9:22). Then the people of Jerusalem, after they have rejected and killed Jesus, will ultimately see him coming in glorious triumph over death, when the time comes for them to exclaim the words of Ps 118:26: "Blessed is the one who comes in the name of the Lord" (13:35; cf. 9:26).[28]

F. LUKE 18:31-34: THE TWELVE DO NOT UNDERSTAND JESUS' PREDICTION OF HIS DEATH AND RESURRECTION

As Jesus takes along (παραλαβὼν) the Twelve, reminding the audience how he earlier took along (παραλαβὼν) three of the Twelve

---

[25] In 13:33 ἀπολέσθαι has the sense of die or perish; see A. KRETZER, "ἀπόλλυμι," *EDNT* 1.136. S. CUNNINGHAM, *'Through Many Tribulations': The Theology of Persecution in Luke-Acts* (JSNTSup 142; Sheffield: Sheffield Academic Press, 1997) 113: "Jerusalem is the city of Jesus' death, and he must not only die in, but at the hand of, Jerusalem."

[26] For scriptural background to Luke's theme of the destiny of prophets, see DOBLE, *Paradox of Salvation*, 134; FITZMYER, *Luke X-XXIV*, 1032; D.L. TIEDE, *Prophecy and History in Luke-Acts* (Philadelphia: Fortress, 1980); D.P. MOESSNER, *Lord of the Banquet: The Literary and Theological Significance of the Lukan Travel Narrative* (Harrisburg: Trinity, 1989).

[27] R.I. DENOVA, *The Things Accomplished Among Us: Prophetic Tradition in the Structural Pattern of Luke-Acts* (JSNTSup 141; Sheffield: Sheffield Academic Press, 1997) 157: "Luke presents Jesus of Nazareth as a prophet...And, as a prophet, Jesus conforms to the biblical tradition of the 'rejected prophet', with his ultimate rejection resulting in death." See also CUNNINGHAM, *'Through Many Tribulations'*, 112-15.

[28] On 13:35 as a reference to the eschatological coming of Jesus at his parousia after his resurrection from death as a rejected prophet, see NOLLAND, *Luke 9:21-18:34*, 742; C.A. EVANS, "Prophecy and Polemic: Jews in Luke's Scriptural Apologetic," *Luke and Scripture:*

– Peter, James, and John – to witness his transfiguration and hear the pivotal mandate to listen to him (9:28; cf. 6:14), he solemnly announces to them, "Behold we are going up to Jerusalem" (18:31). Jesus had resolutely set his face for Jerusalem (9:51, 53), in order to accomplish his "exodus" there, the topic of his conversation with the heavenly Moses and Elijah at his transfiguration (9:31). Thus Jesus' "exodus" from earthly life to the heavenly glory anticipated by his transfiguration is imminent.

At this point Jesus pronounces the most elaborate prediction yet of his resurrection after a humiliating suffering and death: "All the things written by the prophets will be fulfilled for the Son of Man.[29] For he will be delivered to the Gentiles and he will be ridiculed and insulted and spat upon; and after scourging him they will kill him, but on the third day he will rise" (18:31-33; cf. 9:22, 44; 12:50; 17:25).[30] Even now, after the Twelve have accompanied Jesus on his purposeful journey to Jerusalem, they emphatically fail to listen with understanding to the words of Jesus: "And they understood nothing of these things, and this saying was hidden from them, and they did not know what was being said" (18:34).

The response of the Twelve resembles that of the whole group of disciples to Jesus' urgent plea to really hear his passion prediction shortly after the transfiguration (9:45). If anything the failure of the Twelve is even more emphatic: "They understood *nothing* (οὐδὲν) of these things!" (18:34). Just as the saying was hidden (παρακεκαλυμμένον) from the disciples (9:45), so now it is hidden (κεκρυμμένον) from the Twelve (18:34), again indicating that it was purposefully hidden from them and continued to be hidden (perfect tense) by God (divine passive). Although their non-understanding is ultimately part of God's plan, nevertheless the disciples have once again failed to listen with understanding to the words of Jesus.[31] They

---

The Function of Sacred Tradition in Luke-Acts (C.A. Evans and J.A. Sanders; Minneapolis: Fortress, 1993) 178-79.

[29] NOLLAND, Luke 9:21-18:34, 895: "'All things' points to the way in which Luke thinks not just of the passion but of a program of events leading on to the glorification of Jesus beyond resurrection (cf. 24:26; 9:31, 51)."

[30] For a comparison of the passion prediction in 18:31-34 with those in 9:22 and 9:43-45, see CUNNINGHAM, "Through Many Tribulations", 116-19.

[31] TANNEHILL, Luke, 273: "In 18:34 the sentence 'What he said was hidden from them' is sometimes understood to say that God was hiding it from the disciples. This may be so, but

have obviously heard the words of Jesus, but they have simply understood nothing of their significance, they have not listened with understanding.[32] Nevertheless it is urgently important for the disciples and
the audience to heed God's pivotal mandate and continue to listen to
Jesus (9:35), in order eventually to be given by God to understand the
necessity for Jesus to be killed before being raised to the heavenly
glory prefigured by his transfiguration.[33]

G. LUKE 20:9-19: AS GOD'S BELOVED SON JESUS WILL BE KILLED BUT VINDICATED

After Jesus has entered the temple, he addresses a parable (20:9-19)
to the people in which he tells how the owner (God) of the vineyard
finally sends to the tenants (Jewish leadership), who have already beat-
en and insulted three of his servants (prophets) (20:9-12), "my beloved
son" (τὸν υἱόν μου τὸν ἀγαπητόν), thinking that they will respect him
(20:13). This reminds the audience of the transfiguration's pivotal mandate uttered by God's voice from the cloud: "This is my chosen Son (ὁ
υἱός μου ὁ ἐκλελεγμένος); to him listen!" (9:35; cf. 3:22). That the
tenants killed (ἀπέκτειναν, 20:15) the beloved son, after saying to one
another, "Let us kill (ἀποκτείνωμεν) him, so that the inheritance will
be ours" (20:14), recalls Jesus' predictions that he will be killed (ἀποκτανθῆναι, 9:22; ἀποκτενοῦσιν, 18:32) by both the Jewish leaders and
the Gentiles. The prophecy that Jesus, the beloved Son, represents "the
stone which the builders rejected (ἀπεδοκίμασαν)" (20:17) in his quotation of Ps 117:22 (LXX) echoes his predictions that it is divinely

---

the disciples are not thereby relieved of responsibility...Jesus clearly regards it important for
the disciples to understand his passion announcements (cf. 9:44: 'Let these words sink into
your ears')."

[32] D.L. BOCK, *Luke 9:51-24:53* (BECNT 3B; Grand Rapids: Baker, 1996) 1499: "In all
probability Luke does not mean that Jesus' message was unintelligible, but that the disciples
could not understand how his death could fit into the divine plan for Jesus...The focus is on
comprehending how God's plan works, not on understanding the words themselves."

[33] D.L. TIEDE, *Luke* (Minneapolis: Augsburg, 1988) 316: "The passive voice, 'it was
hid,' is again the most telling, for this is a 'theological passive.' Jesus is telling them what God
has not yet revealed to them. These are the 'secret matters' which will yet be made known,
and they must be 'heard' with care so that they may later be explicated (8:17-18)."

necessary that he be rejected (ἀποδοκιμασθῆναι) by the elders, the chief priests, and the scribes (9:22) as well as by "this generation" (17:25).[34] The transfiguration's mandate invites the disciples and the audience to listen to this parable in order to understand that Jesus, as God's chosen Son, will be killed by the leaders of his own people.

Realizing that the parable was directed against them, the scribes and the chief priests were seeking to lay hands on Jesus that very hour, but they feared the people (20:19; cf. 19:47-48). But the audience knows that this will not prevent the Jewish leaders from eventually putting Jesus to death. That the tenants of the parable killed the beloved son after beating and insulting and wounding the servants, who represent the prophets (20:10-12), further confirms for the audience how Jesus will suffer the fate of a rejected prophet. After the tenants wounded the third servant, they threw him out (ἐξέβαλον, 20:12), just as the people of Nazareth threw out (ἐξέβαλον) Jesus (4:29), after he stated that no prophet is accepted in his native place (4:24). Furthermore, the audience has already heard Jesus state that some of the prophets and apostles sent by God will be persecuted and killed (11:49), and that Jerusalem kills the prophets and stones those sent to her (13:34).[35] Unlike the prophets Moses and Elijah, who attained heavenly glory (9:30-31) without being killed by their people, Jesus will attain the heavenly glory prefigured by his transfiguration only after being killed by his own people as a rejected prophet.

Although Jesus, "the stone," will be rejected and killed, God will marvelously vindicate him by transforming him into the "cornerstone" or "head of the corner" (20:17), which implies his resurrection from the dead.[36] The transfiguration's pivotal mandate (9:35) bids the disci-

---

[34] CUNNINGHAM, *"Through Many Tribulations"*, 124: "This prophecy particularly stands in line with two previous formal passion predictions, each containing ἀποδοκιμάζω as a linking word (9.22; 17.25; cf. 20.17). These three verses, in fact, contain the only uses of ἀποδοκιμάζω in Luke-Acts. The prediction takes on additional significance, for the narrator has just heightened the intensity in the level of opposition on the part of the religious leaders who are now attempting to destroy Jesus (19.47)."

[35] IBID.

[36] GREEN, *Luke*, 709: "Jesus is pointing first to scriptural warrant for (and thus to the divine necessity of) the sequence of events outlined in the parable, including the demise of the son; and second to the certainty that the death of the son would not be the last word, but a prelude to exaltation...This interpretive move yields a stone that is rejected but vindicated..."

ples and audience to listen with the understanding that although Jesus will be rejected and killed like a prophet, as God's beloved and chosen Son, he will be vindicated and ultimately attain the heavenly glory anticipated by his transfiguration.

H. LUKE 20:27-39: JESUS TEACHES THAT GOD WILL RAISE THE DEAD TO LIFE

In refuting the attempt of some Sadducees to debunk the concept of resurrection from the dead as contradicting the direct teaching of the Torah (20:27-39), Jesus points out that those deemed worthy to attain the resurrection of the dead are "angel-like" (20:35-36).[37] When Jesus was transfigured, his "face became different and his clothing dazzling white" (9:29), indicating that he has temporarily become like an angel.[38] Jesus' transfiguration into an angel-like heavenly figure, which foreshadows his future resurrection from the dead, reinforces for the audience his assertion that those who attain the resurrection of the dead enter into a heavenly existence that transcends earthly categories – they neither marry nor die again, but become children of God (20:34-36).

Jesus demonstrates that the dead are raised by pointing to Moses, who called the Lord "the God of Abraham, the God of Isaac, and the God of Jacob" (Exod 3:6), thus indicating that "he is not the God of the dead but of the living, for to him all are alive" (20:37-38).[39] Since the three patriarchs were already long dead when God pronounced this to Moses, the implication is that God has raised them from the dead. In other words, since God in his covenantal fidelity to the people of Israel promises to be the saving God not of those who are "dead" but of those

---

[37] The Sadducees' teaching is even more evident in Luke's version, according to E. MAIN, "Les Sadducéens et la résurrection des morts: Comparison entre Mc 12,18-27 et Lc 20,27-38," *RB* 103 (1996) 411-32.

[38] On the transfigured Jesus as an angel-like heavenly figure, see chap. 4.

[39] GREEN, *Luke*, 722: "Drawing on Exod 3:6, 15, he (1) notes that when God was speaking to Moses he was still the God of the long-dead patriarchs Abraham, Isaac, and Jacob; (2) infers the absurdity that God would broadcast a covenant relationship with persons whose existence had expired; (3) concludes that Abraham, Isaac, and Jacob must therefore still be alive; and (4) deduces that, in relating the story about the bush, Moses himself attested resurrection-belief."

who are "living," the patriarchs of Israel – Abraham, Isaac, and Jacob – cannot remain dead but are still living, "for to him all are alive" (20:38; cf. 4 Macc 7:19; 16:25), so that there is a resurrection of the dead.[40] If the disciples and the audience heed the transfiguration's pivotal mandate to listen to Jesus (9:35), they will hear in this pronouncement that although Jesus, unlike Moses and Elijah, will be put to death, he will surely be raised from the dead like the patriarchs, since God is "not the God of the dead but of the living" (20:38). That all are alive for God gives them hope that God will raise them to a new and different heavenly life after they have given their lives to God for the sake of Jesus (9:24; 17:33).

I. Luke 21:27: Jesus is still to come on a cloud with much power and glory

During his teaching of the people in the temple Jesus discloses that at the end of the world (21:25-26) people will see him as "the Son of Man coming on a cloud with much power and glory" (21:27; cf. Dan 7:13-14). Whereas Moses and Elijah were transported by the divine overshadowing cloud (νεφέλη) back to heaven after their appearance in glory with the transfigured Jesus on earth (9:34), Jesus, after his death and resurrection to heavenly glory, will be transported on a cloud (ἐν νεφέλῃ) from heaven to earth, as a sign that redemption is near (21:28).

That Jesus as the Son of Man is still to come "on a cloud with much power and glory (δόξης)" (21:27) reminds the audience of Jesus' previous prediction that as the Son of Man he is still to come "in his glory (δόξῃ) and that of the Father and of the holy angels" (9:26; cf. 11:30; 12:8, 40; 17:22, 24, 26, 30; 18:8).[41] Between these two predictions the three disciples saw the glory (δόξαν, 9:32) of the transfigured

---

[40] TANNEHILL, *Luke*, 296: "By New Testament times, when a belief in resurrection was shared by many Jews, the understanding of God's faithful protection for Abraham, Isaac, and Jacob could be extended to include life after death (something assumed for the patriarchs in 13:28; 16:22-31)."

[41] GREEN, *Luke*, 740: "Throughout his Gospel, Luke repeatedly identifies Jesus as the Son of Man and, more recently, has laid the groundwork for his readers to anticipate the coming of Jesus as Son of Man. Luke 21:27 portrays the most exalted picture yet, however."

Jesus, together with that of Moses and Elijah, who appeared with him in glory (δόξῃ, 9:31). The transfiguration's pivotal mandate to listen to Jesus (9:35) thus directs the disciples and the audience backward (9:26) and forward (21:27) to these two pronouncements about Jesus' future coming in glory, so that they will realize that the transfigured glory of Jesus before his suffering and death is only a preliminary glimpse of his final coming in glory after his suffering, death and resurrection (9:22, 44; 17:24-25; 18:31-33).

J. Luke 22:14-27: The disciples do not understand the significance of Jesus' sacrificial death

After another reference to the fact that he must "suffer" (παθεῖν, 22:15), reminding the audience of his pronouncements of the divine necessity that he "suffer much" (πολλὰ παθεῖν, 9:22; 17:25), Jesus interprets the eating of the bread and drinking of the cup of wine after his final Passover meal with his disciples as a symbolic anticipation of the sacrificial death (22:19-20) he must undergo before he partakes of the eschatological banquet in the kingdom of God (22:16-18, 30).[42] The cup of wine that is the new covenant in Jesus' blood "which is being poured out for you" (22:20) parallels and complements the bread that is his body "which is being given for you" (22:19). By eating the bread that unites them to the sacrificial body of Jesus and drinking the wine that unites them to the sacrificial blood of Jesus, the disciples already begin to receive the salvific benefits of the death of Jesus in their sharing with him of the close fellowship of the sacrificial and covenantal meal he has provided for them before his death.

This new and unique addition to the Passover meal, which they are to "keep doing in remembrance" of him (22:19), will not only keep them and future disciples (the audience) always in union with his salvific, sacrificial, and covenantal death, but also anticipates their reunion

---

[42] On Jesus' interpretation of the bread and cup of wine as symbolic of his sacrificial body and blood – his sacrificial death – that effects atonement, see HEIL, *Meal Scenes in Luke-Acts*, 173-80; F.G. CARPINELLI, "'Do This as *My* Memorial' (Luke 22:19): Lucan Soteriology of Atonement," *CBQ* 61 (1999) 74-91.

with him at the final banquet in God's kingdom (22:16-18).[43] The transfiguration's pivotal mandate (9:35) thus enjoins the disciples and the audience to listen to these words of Jesus in order to understand that his transfiguration into a heavenly figure portends his future partaking of the heavenly banquet in the kingdom of God that will occur only after his sacrificial death.

Jesus' shocking pronouncement that "the hand of the one delivering/betraying (παραδιδόντος) me is with me at the table" (22:21), but woe to that man by whom the Son of Man is delivered/betrayed (παραδίδοται, 22:22), reminds the audience of his previous predictions that as the Son of Man (18:31) he will be delivered/betrayed (παραδοθήσεται) to the Gentiles (18:32) and that as the Son of Man he is going to be delivered/betrayed (παραδίδοσθαι) into the hands of men (9:44).[44] The questioning that ensues among the disciples as to which of them it could be who was going to betray Jesus (22:23) develops into a quarrel as to which of them seemed to be greatest (22:24).

This quarrel reminds the audience of the previous argument that arose within the disciples as to which of them might be greatest (9:46). Occurring immediately after Jesus' prediction that he was going to be betrayed into the hands of men (9:44), an argument about their individual greatness appeared rather incongruous to the audience. It demonstrated the disciples' emphatic, fearful lack of understanding regarding Jesus' prediction (9:45). Now a quarrel about their greatness similarly appears rather incongruous after Jesus' pronouncement that he is being betrayed by one of them (22:21-23).[45] It continues to demonstrate the disciples' total non-understanding of Jesus' prediction of his passion, death, and resurrection (18:34), which they have just ritually anticipat-

---

[43] On the salvific significance of Jesus' death in 22:19-20, see A. BÜCHELE, *Der Tod Jesu im Lukasevangelium: Eine redaktionsgeschichtliche Untersuchung zu Lk 23* (FTS 26; Frankfurt: Knecht, 1978) 167-69; B.D. EHRMAN, "The Cup, The Bread, and the Salvific Effect of Jesus' Death in Luke-Acts," *SBLSP* 30 (1991) 576-91; I.J. DU PLESSIS, "The Saving Significance of Jesus and His Death on the Cross in Luke's Gospel – Focusing on Luke 22:19b-20," *Neot* 28 (1994) 523-40.

[44] POPKES, "παραδίδωμι," 3.18; BAGD, 614-15.

[45] The various connections between the dispute about betrayal in 22:23 and the quarrel about greatness in 22:24 are pointed out by P.K. NELSON, *Leadership and Discipleship: A Study of Luke 22:24-30* (SBLDS 138; Atlanta: Scholars Press, 1994) 141. Nelson adds: "These connections imply that for the apostles to prize greatness is not unlike betrayal."

ed in Jesus' last supper (22:19-20). They have failed to understand that Jesus is in their midst "as the one who serves" (22:27) and that the new Passover meal he has given them should issue in a leadership that imitates his humble life and sacrificial death, a leadership concerned not with the greatness of public acclaim but with the paradoxical greatness of lowly, selfless service of others (22:24-27). Thus, the disciples are still unable to heed the transfiguration's pivotal mandate to listen to Jesus with understanding (9:35), so that the tension continues to mount for the audience.

K. LUKE 22:39-46: JESUS ACCEPTS DEATH THROUGH PRAYER WHILE HIS DISCIPLES SLEEP

When Jesus went out to the Mount (Ὄρος) of Olives, followed by the disciples (22:39), he himself prayed (προσηύχετο, 22:41) after he urged the disciples, "Pray (Προσεύχεσθε) lest you enter into temptation" (22:40). This reminds the audience of how Jesus earlier took along three of the disciples to the mountain (ὄρος) to pray (προσεύξασθαι, 9:28), before being transfigured into a heavenly figure while praying (ἐν τῷ προσεύχεσθαι, 9:29). But there are noteworthy developments. The anonymous mountain of the transfiguration in Galilee has become the specific Mount of Olives in Jerusalem, the place for the accomplishment of Jesus' "exodus" (9:31). Now all the disciples, not just three of them, are with Jesus. And whereas Jesus alone prayed during his transfiguration, he now exhorts the disciples to pray and thus to join him in praying.[46]

Jesus' praying on the Mount of Olives both exemplifies and empowers the disciples (and the audience) how to pray not to enter into temptation (22:40, 46; cf. 21:36; 11:4), that is the Satan-inspired

---

[46] FELDKÄMPER (*Der betende Jesus*, 235) notes the development that has occurred regarding the disciples' participation in the praying of Jesus. After spending the night in prayer on the mountain (6:12), Jesus called to himself the twelve disciples whom he named apostles (6:13-16). In 9:18 the disciples (and in 9:28-29 a chosen three of the disciples) were with Jesus as he prayed alone. In 11:1 the disciples were so impressed with the praying of Jesus that they asked him to teach them to pray like him. And now after commanding the disciples to pray (22:40), Jesus exemplifies how they should pray in imitation of him (22:41-42).

"temptation" or "testing" (πειρασμόν, cf. 4:1-13; 8:13; 22:3, 28, 31), which includes avoiding the divine necessity of suffering and death before heavenly glorification.[47]   In and through his praying Jesus is enabled to overcome the temptation not to submit to God's will that he suffer and die, as he prays, "Father, if you are willing, take this cup away from me; yet not my will but yours be done" (22:42). The image of drinking the "cup" expresses the God-willed destiny of suffering and death which is part of his "exodus" that he was about to accomplish in Jerusalem (9:31).[48]

The praying of Jesus that resulted in his temporary transfiguration into the glory of a heavenly figure (9:29, 32) included the epiphanic appearing in glory of the heavenly figures of Moses and Elijah, who spoke about his "exodus" in Jerusalem (9:31). It provided a proleptic experience of the ultimate heavenly glory that will follow the "exodus," the divinely necessary "going out" of the earthly realm by way of suffering and death before entering the heavenly realm of glory by way of resurrection. This praying of Jesus thus offered heavenly encouragement to him as well as to the disciples and the audience, whom Jesus has called to participate in his "exodus," his necessary suffering and death (9:23-27).[49]

But now the heavenly encouragement that comes from the praying of Jesus is even more dramatically and explicitly pronounced, as "there appeared to him an angel from heaven strengthening him" (22:43). Similar to the epiphanic appearing (ὀφθέντες) of Moses and Elijah in glory to the transfigured Jesus (9:31), the epiphanic appearance (ὤφθη) of the angel provides Jesus the heavenly encouragement to pray more earnestly in his agony.[50]   That "his sweat became like drops of blood

---

[47] W. POPKES, "πειράζω," EDNT 3.66: "It remains correct that the Passion is the time determined by God when Satan again vehemently attacks Jesus."

[48] PATSCH, "ποτήριον," 142: "The image of the cup has the same meaning 'fate of death' in Jesus' prayer in Gethsemane (Mark 14:36 par. Matt 26:39/Luke 22:42) and when Jesus restrains Peter at his arrest (John 18:11)."

[49] On the encouragement from the glorification that occurred while Jesus was praying during his transfiguration, CRUMP (Jesus the Intercessor, 42) remarks: "The proleptic experience of glorification must, at least partially, by interpreted as heavenly encouragement for Jesus as he begins his journey to the God-ordained city of eventual death and resurrection."

[50] We are accepting as authentic the textually uncertain reading in Luke 22:43-44. For arguments against its authenticity, see FITZMYER, Luke X-XXIV, 1443-44; B.D. EHRMAN and

falling to the ground" (22:44) expresses the external, physical manifestation of his intense inner, spiritual struggle (sweat) to accept the necessary death (blood; cf. 22:20) God wills for him.[51]

In the scene of the transfiguration the three disciples "had been overcome with sleep" (9:32), so that they did not hear the conversation about Jesus' "exodus" of suffering and death to be accomplished in Jerusalem (9:31). Because he was asleep and did not hear the conversation, Peter did not know what he was saying when he suggested the making of a tent for each epiphanic figure (9:33). Now, after Jesus has been strengthened in and through his prayer, he finds the whole group of disciples "sleeping because of grief" (22:45). Evidently they have been so overwhelmed by grief in light of Jesus' warnings about Satanic testings and temptations (22:31, 40) that they have fallen asleep, thus lacking the strength to fulfill Jesus' command for them to "pray lest you enter into temptation" (22:40).[52] The divine voice of the transfiguration's mandate urged the disciples, who had fallen asleep so that they were unable to hear about Jesus' "exodus," to listen to Jesus (9:35). Now, similarly, Jesus commands the disciples, who had fallen asleep from grief so

---

M.A. PLUNKETT, "The Angel and the Agony: The Textual Problem of Luke 24:43-44," *CBQ* 45 (1983) 401-16. For arguments in favor of its authenticity, see G. SCHNEIDER, "Engel und Blutschweiss (Lk 22,43-44): 'Redaktionsgeschichte' im Dienste der Textkritik," *BZ* 20 (1976) 112-16; J.H. NEYREY, "The Absence of Jesus' Emotions – the Lucan Redaction of Lk 22,39-46," *Bib* 61 (1980) 153-71; J.B. GREEN, "Jesus on the Mount of Olives (Luke 22.39-46): Tradition and Theology," *JSNT* 26 (1986) 35-36; T. BAARDA, "Luke 22:42-47a: The Emperor Julian as a Witness to the Text of Luke," *NovT* 30 (1988) 289-96; BROWN, *Death of the Messiah*, 180-86; CRUMP, *Jesus the Intercessor*, 117-21. After presenting the evidence for and against authenticity, Crump concludes that "it is possible to be fairly confident in asserting that the weight of the internal evidence more than answers the objections made against these verses, and tips the scales very strongly in favour of the authenticity of Lk. 22:43-44" (p. 121).

[51] For the significance of Jesus' sweat, see FELDKÄMPER, *Der betende Jesus*, 247.

[52] With regard to the "grief" (λύπη) of the disciples here, NEYREY ("Absence of Jesus' Emotions," 169) states: "Λύπη, then, is Luke's term for summarizing the disciples' lack of strength...This weakness, moreover, contrasts them with Jesus, who is not subject to λύπη but is strong (ἐνισχύων) and struggles against λύπη...We noted earlier how λύπη is defined as fear of imminent conflict – either pain or death; it causes loss of strength and paralysis...Now in Luke the disciples were warned of impending conflicts (notably 22,40, but see also 22,22.28.31); and the text suggests that in the face of their impending conflict, they were, in fact, overcome by grief and fear, became weak, and shrank to the ground, and contracted themselves in sleep."

that they were unable to pray with Jesus, to "pray, so that you do not enter into temptation" (22:46).[53]

In and through his praying Jesus was strengthened with heavenly encouragement to overcome the temptation not to submit his will to God's will that he suffer and die before being raised to the heavenly glory prefigured by his transfiguration. By following his example of prayer the disciples and the audience can likewise overcome the temptation not to submit their wills to God's will that they participate in Jesus' way of suffering and death before sharing in the heavenly glory prefigured by his transfiguration.[54] Since Jesus was able to pray when the disciples were not able because they were asleep, Jesus' prayer is not only an example but the empowerment of the prayer of the disciples and the audience. Whereas they could not obey Jesus' initial command to pray lest they enter into temptation (22:40), now that Jesus has prayed when they could not, they have been empowered to obey his renewed command that they pray so that they do not enter into temptation (22:46).[55] The disciples and the audience can now pray not only in imitation of but on the strength of Jesus' prayer.[56]

L. LUKE 22:69-70: AS GOD'S SON JESUS WILL BE SEATED AT THE RIGHT HAND OF THE POWER OF GOD

Jesus further demonstrates the strength and encouragement he gained through his prayer on the Mount of Olives, when he stands on

---

[53] The structural parallels between the scenes of the transfiguration (9:28-36) and of the prayer on the Mount of Olives (22:39-46) are noted by SCHNEIDER, "Engel und Blutschweiss," 116.

[54] FELDKÄMPER, *Der betende Jesus*, 249: "Wenn Jesus nun sie, die Traurig-Schlafenden und Unverständigen zum Gebet auffordert, wie er soeben gebetet hat, dann ist damit gemeint: Sie sollen sich wie er im Gebet um Erkenntnis des Willens des Vaters bemühen und sich zu einem 'Ja' zu diesem Willen durchringen, d.h. zu einer Annahme des Leidenwegs, damit sie so in der Versuchung nicht zu Fall, d.h. Abfall (vgl. 8,13) kommen."

[55] Although only a minor difference in grammatical style, the difference in wording between the initial command of Jesus, "Pray lest you enter (μὴ εἰσελθεῖν) into temptation" (22:40), and the renewed, concluding command, "Pray, so that you do not enter (ἵνα μὴ εἰσέλθητε) into temptation" (22:46), indicates the changed situation. Now that Jesus has prayed when the disciples could not, they can fulfill the command to pray not to enter into temptation.

[56] On the prayer of Jesus on the Mount of Olives as both example and empowerment, see FELDKÄMPER, *Der betende Jesus*, 249-50.

trial before the Sanhedrin (22:66). After they ask him whether he is the Christ (22:67), Jesus courageously proclaims: "But from now on the Son of Man will be seated at the right hand of the power of God!" (22:69; cf. Ps 110:1). As heard on the level of the Sanhedrin seeking evidence to destroy Jesus, this powerful, prophetic pronouncement of Jesus assures the audience that "from now on" (ἀπὸ τοῦ νῦν),[57] that is, now that the time of "your hour and the power of darkness" (22:53) has begun, now that the Sanhedrin are beginning to fulfill the passion predictions, and now that they definitely "will not believe" (22:67), Jesus, as the heavenly, transcendent and exalted "Son of Man," will ultimately triumph over them. The audience thus experiences the surprising irony that the Sanhedrin, in attempting to triumph over Jesus through their Satanic "power of darkness," are, as the unwitting victims of the irony, actually bringing about the triumph of Jesus over them through the "power of God." Through this irony the audience experiences the mysterious paradox of Jesus' becoming the exalted and triumphant Son of Man not only despite but in and through the attempt of the Jewish leaders to condemn him to death.

Based upon reminiscence of the passion predictions, the audience hears this prophetic pronouncement as a climactic development of Jesus' revelation of himself as the messianic "Son of Man." The audience is now called to believe not only that Jesus as the messianic "Son of Man" must suffer, die and rise again (9:22, 44; 17:24-25; 18:31-33), but also that he will be exalted as the heavenly, transcendent "Son of Man" endowed with the "power of God" (22:69; cf. 21:27). The Sanhedrin then correctly infer from Jesus' proclamation his more profound identity – that he is indeed not only the Christ and the Son of Man but the very "Son of God" (22:70).[58]

---

[57] For similar uses of this phrase as expressions of climactic turning points in the narrative of Luke-Acts, see Luke 1:48; 5:10; 12:52; 22:18; Acts 18:6. See also M.L. SOARDS, *The Passion According to Luke: The Special Material of Luke 22* (JSNTSup 14; Sheffield: JSOT, 1987) 95.

[58] J.P. HEIL, "Reader-Response and the Irony of Jesus Before the Sanhedrin in Luke 22:66-71," *CBQ* 51 (1989) 271-84; J. PLEVNIK, "Son of Man Seated at the Right Hand of God: Luke 22,69 in Lucan Christology," *Bib* 72 (1991) 331-47; P. TREMOLADA, *"E fu annoverato fra iniqui": Prospettive di lettura della Passione secondo Luca alla luce di Lc 22,37 (Is 53,12d)* (AnBib 137; Rome: Biblical Institute, 1997) 184-93.

This further confirms the message of the transfiguration. As the chosen Son of God (9:35) Jesus will ultimately triumph over the suffering and death of his "exodus" in Jerusalem (9:31) and attain the exaltation of the Son of Man (22:69; 9:26) prefigured by his temporary transfiguration into heavenly glory (9:29, 32). The transfiguration's mandate thus urges the disciples and the audience to listen (9:35) to this courageous confession of Jesus. Just as Jesus gained courage by his prayer and by faith in his ultimate triumph over death, so the disciples and the audience can gain courage to endure possible suffering and death (21:12-19), in order to share in the heavenly glory presaged by the transfiguration of Jesus.

M. LUKE 23:11: HEROD CLOTHES JESUS IN A BRIGHT SHINING GARMENT

Herod's contempt and ridicule of Jesus (23:11) falls short of the death sentence the Jewish leaders seek. Their insidious attempt suffers further frustration as Herod sends Jesus back to Pilate, who earlier refused to comply with their charges against Jesus (23:1-5). But at the same time that Herod is thwarting the designs of the Jewish authorities, the audience perceives the irony that, by "ridiculing" Jesus and "treating him with contempt," Herod is actually carrying forward God's hidden salvific design, as previously predicted by Jesus in his passion prophecies (9:22, 44; 17:25; 18:31-33).

The intriguing motif of Herod clothing Jesus with a "bright shining garment" contributes to the irony. On the surface level of the narrative it continues to express the ridicule and mockery of Jesus.[59] But on the deeper level, that of Herod unconsciously furthering God's hidden plan, the audience realizes that Herod is dressing Jesus in the clothing of heavenly beings, appropriate to his future exaltation and glory as the Son of Man (22:69). In the scene of Jesus' transfiguration the disciples saw "his glory" (9:32) after his clothing (ἱματισμὸς) became "dazzling white" (λευκὸς ἐξαστράπτων, 9:29), indicating his temporary trans-

---

[59] On the significance of the garment DARR (*Herod the Fox*, 201) states that "it was a dramatic and sardonic way of indicating to Pilate that Herod had found nothing worthy of death in Jesus."

formation into a heavenly being. That Herod clothes Jesus in a "bright shining garment" (ἐσθῆτα λαμπρὰν) fit for a heavenly being, then, further assures the audience that Jesus will attain the heavenly glory signaled by the dazzling white clothing of his transfiguration after he has accomplished his "exodus" of suffering, death and resurrection in Jerusalem (9:31).[60]

N. LUKE 23:35: THE CRUCIFIED JESUS IS MOCKED AS GOD'S CHOSEN ONE

While the people stood watching the crucified Jesus, the leaders were sneering, "He saved others, let him save himself, if he is the Christ of God, the chosen one!" (23:35). Their ridicule of the dying Jesus as "the chosen one" (ὁ ἐκλεκτός) ironically confirms God's voice at the transfiguration, "This is my chosen (ὁ ἐκλελεγμένος) Son; to him listen!" (9:35). The audience experiences the irony that it is by dying on the cross as "the Christ of God" (cf. 9:20) and God's "chosen one" that Jesus is saving not only himself but others in a more profound way. He is undergoing his "exodus" of suffering and death that he must accomplish in Jerusalem (9:31) in accord with God's will before being raised to the ultimate salvation of heavenly glory (9:32) prefigured by his transfiguration and promised to others (9:26).[61] By dying on the cross Jesus models for the disciples and the audience his provocative challenge, which the transfiguration's mandate urged them to hear – "whoever wants to save his life will lose it, but whoever loses his life for my sake will save it" (9:24).

---

[60] That the "bright shining garment" placed on Jesus is the kind of clothing worn by heavenly beings is confirmed by the exact verbal parallel in Acts 10:30, where the "man" who appears to Cornelius from heaven is dressed in a "bright shining garment" (ἐσθῆτι λαμπρᾷ). See also J.P. HEIL, "Reader-Response and the Irony of the Trial of Jesus in Luke 23:1-25," *ScEs* 43 (1991) 182.

[61] STRAUSS, *Davidic Messiah*, 267: "The Jewish leaders cry out that if Jesus is God's chosen Christ (i.e. the royal messiah), he should save himself from death. Luke knows, however, that God's choice and anointing is for this very purpose: the messiah must first suffer and die (as servant) before entering his glory (Lk. 9.31-32; 24.26)." See also GREEN, *Luke*, 281; BÜCHELE, *Tod Jesu*, 48.

O. LUKE 24:4-11: TWO MEN IN DAZZLING GARMENTS REVEAL JESUS' RESURRECTION

While the women are puzzled at not finding the body of Jesus in his tomb (24:3), they become the recipients of a dramatic epiphany as "two men" suddenly came upon them in "dazzling garments" (24:4). This reminds the audience of the transfiguration epiphany. The epiphanic introduction of these two angelic "men" is identical to that of the heavenly figures of Moses and Elijah at the transfiguration: "and behold two men" (καὶ ἰδοὺ ἄνδρες δύο; 24:4; 9:30; see also 9:32).[62] That these two angelic men appear in "dazzling garments" (ἐσθῆτι ἀστραπτούσῃ) indicative of their heavenly status recalls not only Herod's clothing of Jesus in a "bright shining garment" (ἐσθῆτα λαμπρὰν) fit for a heavenly being (23:11), but also Jesus' transfiguration into a heavenly being when his clothing becoming "dazzling" (ἐξαστράπτων) white (9:29).[63]

In the transfiguration epiphany the temporary transformation of Jesus into the glory (9:32) of a heavenly figure, as well as his conversation with the two men appearing in heavenly glory (9:31), indicated to the disciples and the audience the ultimate heavenly glory Jesus would attain after his divinely necessary "exodus" – his suffering, death, and resurrection – in Jerusalem (9:31). Unlike these two heavenly men – Moses and Elijah, Jesus will attain ultimate heavenly glory only after being raised by God after suffering the destiny of a prophet – death at the hands of his own people. Now that Jesus has been put to death by his people, the two angelic men at the empty tomb reveal his resurrection to the women: "Why do you seek the living one among the dead? He is not here, but has been raised!" (24:5-6).

---

[62] DILLON, *From Eye-Witnesses*, 22: "The visitation of heavenly figures, cryptically designated as ἄνδρες δύο, occurs on three occasions in Lk-Acts, and the three may intentionally echo one another: the transfiguration scene (Lk 9,30), the empty tomb (Lk 24,4), and the ascension (Acts 1,10)."

[63] M.L. RIGATO, "'"Remember"...Then They Remembered': Luke 24:6-8," *Luke and Acts* (eds. G. O'Collins and G. Marconi; New York: Paulist, 1993) 101: "We may regard the two men-angels in dazzling clothes (24:4) as two messengers of the risen Jesus who possess, as it were, his characteristics."

In urging the women to remember what Jesus spoke to them while still in Galilee (24:6), namely, his prophecy of the divine necessity that he be crucified but raised on the third day (24:7), the two angelic men are complementing for the audience God's pivotal mandate at the transfiguration, which urged the disciples to listen (9:35) especially to Jesus' passion predictions. That the women remembered his words (24:8; cf. 22:61) confirms the fulfillment of all of Jesus' passion prophecies, now that he has been raised from the dead (24:6). Nevertheless, when the women reported "all these things to the eleven and to all the rest" (24:9), the apostles did not believe them (24:10-11). Hence the dramatic tension for the audience regarding the disciples' total non-understanding (9:45; 18:34) of the divine necessity for Jesus to suffer and be put to death before being raised to the heavenly glory foreshadowed by his transfiguration poignantly persists.[64]

P. LUKE 24:25-46: THE RISEN JESUS EXPLAINS HIS NECESSARY DEATH TO THE DISCIPLES

The risen Jesus chastises the two Emmaus disciples: "Oh, how foolish you are and how slow of heart to believe in all that the prophets have spoken!" (24:25). Their foolishness and slowness of heart further explains for the audience the disciples' incapacity to understand and believe (9:45; 18:34) not only what Jesus, "a prophet powerful in deed and word" (24:19), spoke in his passion and resurrection predictions (9:22, 44; 17:25; 18:31-33; 24:6-7), which the transfiguration's pivotal mandate urged them to heed (9:35), but also *all* that the prophets have spoken" (cf. 18:31).

With a persuasive question introduced by οὐχί, demanding an affirmative answer, the risen Jesus himself begins to convince his non-understanding, unbelieving disciples: "Was it not necessary that the Christ should suffer these things and enter into his glory?" (24:26). As the audience recalls, as soon as Peter finally identified Jesus as the

---

[64] J. PLEVNIK, "The Eyewitnesses of the Risen Jesus in Luke 24," *CBQ* (1987) 94: "There exists, however, a tension between all the facts surrounding the empty tomb, including the apparent readiness of the women to believe, and the belief of the disciples. In fact, the 'eleven' and 'all the rest' remain incredulous. This tension alone must still be resolved."

"Christ of God" (9:20), Jesus rebuked the disciples and instructed them not to tell this to anyone (9:21). After Jesus then predicted the divine necessity of his suffering, death, and resurrection (9:22), he invited all his followers to appropriate his suffering and death into their own lives (9:23-25), in order ultimately to share in his glory (ἐν τῇ δόξῃ αὐτοῦ, 9:26), when he comes as the exalted Son of Man with much power and glory (δόξης, 21:27).

Eight days later three of the disciples experienced the transfiguration of Jesus, in which they saw his glory (τὴν δόξαν αὐτοῦ, 9:32) and that of the "two men" with him – Moses and Elijah, who likewise appeared in glory (ἐν δόξῃ, 9:31), after they awakened from sleep (9:32). But their sleep prevented them from hearing about "his exodus" in Jerusalem (9:31). The risen Jesus now begins to rectify this as he explains to two of his disciples the necessity for him as the Christ to suffer the death of a prophet, which Moses and Elijah, though rejected as prophets, did not suffer, before "entering into his glory (εἰς τὴν δόξαν αὐτοῦ)" (24:26). For the audience his entrance (εἰσελθεῖν) into heavenly glory (24:26) thus complements his exodus (ἔξοδον) of suffering, death, and resurrection (9:31).[65]

The risen Jesus goes on to interpret for the Emmaus disciples "the things concerning himself" in fulfillment of what was prophesied "in *all* the scriptures" (24:27). The audience is overwhelmed by the totality of the prophetic scriptural witness that predicted the prophetic fate of Jesus – "all" (24:25) that "all" the prophets have spoken in "all" the scriptures (24:27). This underlines for the audience how the suffering, death, resurrection, and exaltation into glory of Jesus as the messianic, rejected prophet (24:19-21, 26) fulfills all that was predicted by both the prophetic scriptural words and lives of all the prophets who prece-

---

[65] DILLON, *From Eye-Witnesses*, 143: "Not only does εἰσελθεῖν respond to the dominical ἔξοδος discussed by the heavenly figures (Lk 9,31), but the vision on the mount was declared by Lk (9,32) to be a vision of *his glory*." On the close connection between the vision of Jesus' glory and the appearance of Moses and Elijah, Dillon further elaborates: "The connection is that the figures already belong to the realm of δόξα, as v. 31 says of them: οἳ ὀφθέντες ἐν δόξῃ. Moses and Elia already resided in the realm which Jesus *entered* after his death. They too, in their time and fashion, had experienced the divine vindication of which the persecuted prophet can be certain" (Dillon's emphasis). Although persecuted as prophets, neither Moses nor Elijah was put to death by their own people. That is the crucial difference between how they achieved heavenly glory and how Jesus "entered into his glory" (24:26).

ded him in all the scriptures.[66] By entering into his glory after suffering death (24:26), Jesus even achieved the heavenly vindication that the two rejected prophets, Moses and Elijah, achieved without being put to death as prophets.

The dramatic tension of the disciples' failure to understand begins to be resolved for the audience, as the two Emmaus disciples voiced to one another their exuberant, exclamatory question: "Were not our hearts burning within us while he was speaking to us on the way, while he was opening to us the scriptures?" (24:32). Their coming to understand and believe while he was speaking to them on the way to Emmaus finally shatters for the audience the suspense of the disciples' total non-understanding (9:45; 18:34) of Jesus' prophetic predictions of the divine necessity of his suffering, death, and resurrection. The audience realizes that before the Emmaus disciples' eyes could be opened to recognize the risen Jesus, he had to open for them the scriptures, which contain all the prophecies that confirm his predictions that it was divinely necessary for him as the Christ to suffer death before entering into the glory (24:26) anticipated by his transfiguration (9:32).

The risen Jesus' statement to the whole group of disciples gathered in Jerusalem, "These are my words which I spoke to you while I was still with you" (24:44), recalls and reinforces for the audience the transfiguration's pivotal mandate to listen to the words of Jesus (9:35), especially the words of his passion predictions. The risen Jesus explained the meaning of his previously non-understood passion predictions to the Emmaus disciples (24:25-27) by opening the scriptures for them (24:32). So now to the Jerusalem assembly of disciples he explains the divine necessity of his death and resurrection as the Christ in prophetic fulfillment of all that was written about him in the Law of Moses, in the Prophets, and in the Psalms (24:44-46) by opening their mind to understand the scriptures (24:45).[67] This finally and climactically resolves for the audience the suspense of the disciples' total non-

---

[66] TANNEHILL, *Luke*, 356: "The Messiah in his earthly ministry lived the life of a prophet, and prophets are regularly rejected, persecuted, and even killed (cf. 4:24; 6:22-23; 11:47-51; 13:33-34; Acts 7:52). Scripture and the story of Jesus are being read in light of a presumed pattern of prophetic destiny that includes suffering."

[67] FITZMYER, *Luke X-XXIV*, 1582: "It is not so much the words themselves that Christ recalls for them as their meaning, which the following statements (vv. 44b,45,46) make clear."

understanding (9:45; 18:34) of Jesus' prophetic predictions of the divine necessity of his suffering, death, and resurrection (9:22, 44; 17:25; 18:31-33), which God's voice in the transfiguration's pivotal mandate urged them to heed (9:35).

Thus, the risen Jesus himself has enabled the disciples and the audience to understand that, now that he has been put to death and accomplished "his exodus" in Jerusalem (9:31), he has entered into the glory (24:26) anticipated by his transfiguration (9:32). By continuing to heed the transfiguration's pivotal mandate (9:35) to listen to Jesus' exhortation to appropriate his suffering and death into their lives (9:22-25), the disciples and the audience can look forward to sharing in the heavenly glory (24:26) of the risen Jesus when he comes again as the exalted Son of Man (9:26; 21:27).

Q. Luke 24:51: The risen Jesus is taken up to heaven

After the risen Jesus led the disciples as far as Bethany (24:50), and while he was blessing them, "he departed from them and was taken up to heaven" (24:51).[68] The risen Jesus who stood (ἔστη) in the midst of the group of disciples in Jerusalem (24:36) has now departed (διέστη) from them. That Jesus departed and was taken up (ἀνεφέρετο) by God (divine passive) to heaven completes his "departure" or "exodus" (ἔξοδον, 9:31) discussed at his transfiguration and his "taking up" (ἀναλήμψεως, 9:51) to be accomplished in Jerusalem.[69] That Jesus "departed" and was taken up "to heaven" by God means that he has now gone where the overshadowing divine cloud of the transfiguration epiphany took the "separating" (διαχωρίζεσθαι) Moses and Elijah (9:33-34). By suffering the death of a rejected prophet, Jesus has now attained the heavenly

---

[68] For a text-critical argument in favor of the short reading of 24:51, which omits the words "was taken up to heaven," see PARSONS, *Departure of Jesus*, 29-52. But for the more convincing and more widely accepted argument in favor of the longer reading, see A.W. ZWIEP, "The Text of the Ascension Narratives (Luke 24.50-3; Acts 1.1-2, 9-11)," *NTS* (1996) 219-44.

[69] J. KREMER, "ἀναφέρω," *EDNT* 1.94: "A more precise definition of διέστη is achieved by describing the process (impf.) of the ascension as Jesus' experience of being carried away."

glory the rejected prophets Moses and Elijah attained without being put to death.[70]

Now that the disciples and the audience have experienced the ascension to heavenly glory of Jesus after his suffering and death, which was prefigured by his temporary transfiguration into a heavenly being (9:29, 32), they no longer need keep silent about the things they saw in the transfiguration epiphany (9:36). By continuing to heed the transfiguration's pivotal mandate to listen to Jesus (9:35), the disciples and the audience will witness to the necessity for Jesus to suffer and be put to death (24:44-49), and for his followers to appropriate that suffering and death in their own lives (9:22-26). They may then look forward to participating in the celestial exaltation of Jesus, when he comes again from heaven in his glory (9:26; 21:27; Acts 1:9-11).

R. Conclusion

The transfiguration's mandate in Luke, "To him listen!" (9:35), has pivoted the disciples and the audience back to Jesus' previous pronouncement for them to appropriate into their lives the suffering and death he will undergo before being raised to heavenly glory (9:22-26). It has also pivoted them forward to the subsequent predictions of the necessity for him to suffer and be put to death as a rejected prophet in Jerusalem (9:44, 51-56; 13:33-35; 18:31-33; 20:9-19; 22:14-23, 39-46; 24:4-7, 25-27, 44-46) as well as for them to spend their lives in selfless, suffering service for others (9:41; 10:39; 22:24-27; 23:35) with the assurance of being raised from the dead (20:27-39) and sharing in the heavenly glory (21:27; 22:69-70; 23:11; 24:26, 51) prefigured by his transfiguration. Obeying the transfiguration's mandate to listen especially to Jesus' passion predictions was necessary so that the risen Jesus could explain to the non-understanding disciples (9:45, 54-55;

---

[70] GREEN, *Luke*, 861-62: "'Into heaven' signifies both the finality of Jesus' departure (until the parousia) and Jesus' glorified status...The glory and regal power anticipated of Jesus (9:26, 32, 51; 19:12) is now made visible to his followers; they are thus provided with incontrovertible evidence that Jesus' humility and humiliation on the cross, far from disqualifying divine sanction of his mission, are actually embraced by God. God's verdict reverses and supersedes the verdict of those who rejected, condemned, and executed Jesus."

18:34; 22:24-27; 24:8-11) the necessity for his suffering and death before entering into the glory (24:25-27, 44-46) anticipated by his transfiguration.

The eventual absence of Jesus with his extraordinary healing power, anticipated at his transfiguration, challenges the audience to have the faith to continue the healing mission of Jesus (9:41; cf. 9:1-6; 10:1-9). That Jesus resolutely set his "face" for the accomplishment of his "exodus" (9:31) in Jerusalem (9:51-53), the same "face" that was temporarily transfigured into glory (9:29), models for the audience the determination they need to undergo suffering and death before attaining heavenly glory (9:22-26). By attentively listening to the word of Jesus (10:39), Mary is a model of obedience to the transfiguration's mandate to listen to Jesus (9:35). By following her example the audience will realize that the words of Jesus call disciples to a selfless service that follows Jesus on the divinely necessary way of his suffering and death (9:21), in order to share in the resurrection to glory (9:22-26) anticipated by his transfiguration.

Unlike the rejected prophets Moses and Elijah, the prophet Jesus will not only be rejected but killed by the people of Jerusalem (13:33-34), although he is God's beloved and chosen Son (20:13; 9:35). But his transfiguration into heavenly glory (9:29-32) assures the audience that Jesus' death as a rejected prophet will be vindicated by God raising him (9:22; 20:17), so that he will come again in glory (9:26; 13:35).

Jesus' transfiguration into an angel-like heavenly figure (9:29), which foreshadows his future resurrection from the dead, reinforces for the audience his assertion that those who attain the resurrection of the dead enter into a heavenly existence that transcends earthly categories (20:34-36). If the audience heeds the transfiguration's mandate to listen to Jesus (9:35), they will hear that although Jesus, unlike Moses and Elijah, will be put to death, he will surely be raised from the dead like the patriarchs, since God is "not the God of the dead but of the living" (20:38).

The transfiguration's pivotal mandate to listen to Jesus (9:35) directs the audience backward (9:26) and forward (21:27) to pronouncements about Jesus' future coming in glory, so that they will realize that the transfigured glory of Jesus before his suffering and death is only a preliminary glimpse of his final coming in glory after his suffering, death and resurrection. It enjoins the audience to listen to the words of Jesus at his last supper in order to understand that his transfiguration into a heavenly figure portends his future partaking of the heavenly banquet in the kingdom of God that will occur only after his sacrificial death (22:14-20).

By following Jesus' example of prayer (22:39-46) the audience can overcome the temptation not to submit their wills to God's will that they participate in Jesus' way of suffering and death before sharing in heavenly glory. The audience can now pray not only in imitation of but on the strength of Jesus' prayer. Just as Jesus gained courage by his prayer and by faith in his ultimate triumph over death (22:69), so the disciples and the audience can gain courage to endure possible suffering and death (21:12-19), in order to share in the heavenly glory presaged by the transfiguration of Jesus.

That Herod clothes Jesus in a bright shining garment (23:11) fit for a heavenly being further assures the audience that Jesus will attain the heavenly glory signaled by the dazzling white clothing of his transfiguration (9:29). By dying on the cross as God's "chosen one" (23:35; cf. 9:35), Jesus models for the audience his provocative challenge, which the transfiguration's mandate urged them to heed – "whoever wants to save his life will lose it, but whoever loses his life for my sake will save it" (9:24; cf. 23:35).

Even after two angelic men revealed Jesus' resurrection to the women at the tomb, the disciples did not believe the women (24:4-11). But the risen Jesus himself enabled first the Emmaus disciples (24:25-27, 32) and then the whole group of disciples in Jerusalem (24:44-46) and thus the audience to understand that, now that he has been put to death and accomplished "his exodus" in Jerusalem (9:31), he has entered into the glory (24:26) anticipated by his transfiguration (9:32). By continuing to heed the transfiguration's pivotal mandate (9:35) to listen to Jesus' exhortation to appropriate his suffering and death into their lives (9:22-25), the audience can look forward to sharing in the heavenly glory (24:26) of the risen Jesus when he comes again as the exalted Son of Man (9:26; 21:27). Indeed, now that Jesus has ascended to heaven (24:51) and rejoined the heavenly Moses and Elijah, the audience no longer needs to keep silent about the things the disciples saw in the transfiguration epiphany (9:36).

CHAPTER 14

CONCLUSION

After a brief indication of past research and of our new methodological approach, we illustrated how all three versions of the transfiguration narrative exhibit their own unique characteristics. Nevertheless, each narrates essentially the same sequence of literary motifs. We concluded that each version presents a unified, consistent narrative that is of the same basic literary genre, evoking in general the same basic responses from their respective implied Gospel audiences familiar with the genre (chap. 1).

Having demonstrated the difference between the literary genres of "theophany," "vision," and "epiphany," we illustrated how the transfiguration story exhibits the literary characteristics of a rather complex epiphany, with some very rough precedents in the angelophanies to Gideon (Judg 6:11-24) and to Manoah and his wife (Judg 13:2-24). Since the entire transfiguration epiphany is oriented to and issues in the climactic, authoritative *mandate* from the divine voice out of the overshadowing cloud, "Listen to him!" (Mark 9:7; Matt 17:5; Luke 9:35), we concluded that it can be more specifically designated as a "mandatory epiphany" (chap. 2).

The mandatory epiphanies to Balaam (Num 22:31-35), to Joshua (Josh 5:13-15), and to Heliodorus (2 Macc 3:22-34) provide literary precedents for the Gospel audiences to recognize and understand the literary genre of the transfiguration narrative as that of a similar "pivotal mandatory epiphany," in which the climactic mandate serves as a pivotal focus. In the transfiguration mandatory epiphany the pivotal mandate not only points out that Jesus, rather than Moses or Elijah, is God's beloved/chosen Son, but also directs the disciples and the audience to listen to Jesus in order to understand the significance of the epiphanic appearance of the transfigured Jesus in conversation with Moses and Elijah. The words of Jesus that the disciples and the audience are to heed are the words predicting his passion, death and resurrection, a recurring theme of pivotal significance in each of the Gospel narratives in which the transfiguration occurs (chap. 3).

The "transfiguration" of Jesus, that is, the extraordinary change in the appearance of his face and clothing so that they became extremely white and radiant, is an epiphanic motif describing his external, proleptic, and temporary transformation by God into a heavenly being while still on earth. This epiphanic "transfiguration" of Jesus performs a twofold narrative function: It enables Jesus, while still on earth, to appear and speak with the heavenly figures of Moses and Elijah before the eyes of the disciples; and it points to Jesus' future and permanent attainment of glory in heaven as promised to the righteous after their death (chap. 4).

The prophets Moses and Elijah appear from heaven in conversation with the transfigured Jesus to contrast the way that he will ultimately attain the same heavenly glory they enjoy. Elijah, although he suffered persecution as a prophet, attained heavenly glory by ascending directly into heaven without dying the death of a rejected prophet. Moses, although he suffered rebellion and opposition from his people, was never put to death as a rejected prophet. He died and was buried in a very extraordinary way, honored and revered by his people. Later Jewish traditions indicate that the great prophet Moses attained heavenly glory either at the time of his mysterious death and burial or, like the prophet Elijah, without dying at all. The Gospel audiences know that Jesus, unlike Moses and Elijah, will attain heavenly glory only after being unjustly put to death as a prophet rejected by his people and raised from the dead by God (chap. 5).

From their knowledge and familiarity with the various "tent" traditions the Gospel audiences may think that Peter wants to make three tents as temporary dwelling places (1) to honor each individual heavenly figure and commemorate what God has done in bringing about this marvelous manifestation of each of the three heavenly figures, analogous to the commemorative role of the tents at the Feast of Tabernacles; (2) to provide fitting locations for each of the heavenly, prophetic figures to continue his glorious appearance and communicate divine instructions to the disciples on earth, analogous to the role of the tent as a place for divine communication in the Tent of Meeting; (3) to furnish on earth appropriate hospitable habitations for their sojourn similar to the habitations that Abraham, the patriarchs, and all the righteous enjoy in heaven. Since the audience realizes that Peter's offer to make three tents was inappropriate, only the remainder of the transfiguration epiphany will reveal which, if any, of these traditions are relevant (chap. 6).

By the end of each transfiguration narrative the audience realizes that the epiphanic cloud has overshadowed *only Moses and Elijah*. The cloud of God's presence has not only concealed Moses and Elijah from the eyes of the disciples but has also separated them from Jesus, so that the disciples no longer see Moses and Elijah, but only Jesus. This is confirmed by the *oracular* function of the cloud, in which the voice of God speaks "from the cloud" to the disciples outside the cloud and directs them to listen to Jesus also outside of the cloud. By making a tent – analogous to the Tent of Meeting – for each of the epiphanic figures, Peter would place each on the same level, honoring each with an equal opportunity to speak and thus prolong the epiphanic event. But the overshadowing cloud ironically interrupts Peter's offer to make a "tent" or "covering" for each as it "covers over" or "tents over" Moses and Elijah. Adding to the irony, the voice of God himself utters the mandate of this pivotal mandatory epiphany, directing the disciples and the audience to listen not to Moses and Elijah at tents but to Jesus as God's Son. In accord with its *vehicular* function the overshadowing cloud implicitly transports Moses and Elijah back to heaven, bringing the entire transfiguration event to an abrupt conclusion, as the disciples see Jesus left there alone, restored to his pre-transfigured, earthly state (chap. 7).

That no bleacher *on the earth* could thus whiten his clothes that became very radiantly white in Mark's account (9:3) confirms for the audience the heavenly nature of Jesus' transformed clothing. That the three disciples became terrified at the epiphany of the transfigured Jesus in conversation with Moses and Elijah was the reason Peter did not know what to reply (9:6), when he responded to the revelation of the more profound identity of Jesus in relation to Moses and Elijah by suggesting the making of a tent for each (9:5). After Jesus' baptism God's voice from the heavens told Jesus, "You are my beloved Son; with you I am well pleased!" (1:11). But now God's voice from the cloud tells the three disciples, "This is my beloved Son; listen to him!" (9:7). What the audience (1:1, 11) and the demonic world have already known (3:11; 5:7), namely that Jesus is the Son of God, God now reveals directly to the three disciples (9:7). God's voice from the cloud serves as the pivotal mandate that distinguishes Jesus from Moses and Elijah as God's beloved Son and commands the disciples and the audience to listen to Jesus. The mandate thus "pivots" them back to the previous teaching of Jesus (4:2-3, 9, 23-24; 7:14; 8:18), especially his teaching about the necessity for him and his followers to suffer and to lose their lives (8:31-38) before entering into the heavenly glory of God's kingdom anticipated by Jesus' transfiguration (chap. 8).

The mandate of the Markan transfiguration epiphany (9:7) also pivoted the disciples and the audience forward to the subsequent predictions of the necessity for Jesus (9:12, 31-32; 10:32-34; 12:1-12; 14:8, 22-25, 27-31, 32-42) as well as them (10:35-45) to give their lives in humble, suffering service for others with the assurance of being raised from the dead (9:9; 12:18-27; 16:5-8) and seeing his final coming in the heavenly glory (13:26; 14:62) prefigured by his transfiguration. The audience is to realize that Elijah has not come (9:11) as the heavenly figure the disciples witnessed in the transfiguration epiphany (9:4). And Elijah will not come to take Jesus down from the cross (15:35-36), because unlike the Elijah in the transfiguration epiphany, Jesus must suffer death before attaining heavenly glory. Because he listened to how Jesus revealed himself to be Son of God by dying on the cross, the centurion confirmed for the audience God's own voice at the transfiguration (9:7; cf. 1:11). By praying in imitation and on the strength of Jesus' prayer, the audience can submit their wills to God's will and follow Jesus' way of suffering and death (14:32-42). The Markan narrative challenges the audience to tell others of the significance of Jesus' transfiguration (9:9) as the assurance that resurrection to heavenly glory follows suffering and death for the gospel of Jesus (16:5-8) (chap. 9).

That "his face shone as the sun, while his clothes became white as the light" in Matthew's version (17:2) confirms for the audience the heavenly nature of Jesus' transformed face and clothing. God's voice from the cloud confirms the disciples' (14:33) and Peter's (16:16) previous confessions of Jesus' divine sonship. It also reinforces God's declaration from the heavens at Jesus' baptism (3:17) and God's voice from a fulfillment quote (12:17-18) that Jesus, now on his way to suffering and death (16:21), is still "my beloved Son, with whom I am well pleased" (17:5). God's mandate to listen to Jesus (17:5) "pivots" the disciples and the audience back to Jesus' previous teaching about the kingdom of heaven, especially his teaching about the necessity for him and his followers to suffer and be put to death (16:21-27) before entering into the glory of the kingdom of heaven anticipated by Jesus' transfiguration. Only in Matthew does Jesus utter words that complement the voice of God from the cloud by encouraging the fearful disciples and the audience to heed the divine mandate (chap. 10).

The transfiguration's mandate in Matthew (17:5) also pivoted the disciples and the audience forward to the subsequent predictions of the necessity for him (17:12, 22-23; 20:18-19; 21:33-46; 26:2, 12, 26-29, 31-35, 36-46) as well as them (20:20-28) to spend their lives in selfless, suffering service for others with the assurance of being raised from the dead (17:9; 22:23-33; 27:50-53) and seeing his final coming in the heavenly glory (24:30; 25:31; 26:64) prefigured by his transfiguration. By praying in imitation and on the strength of Jesus' prayer, the audience can submit their wills to God's will (26:39, 42) that they take up the cross and lose their lives for the sake of Jesus (10:38-39; 16:24-27). The appearing of the "holy ones," who were raised from the dead when Jesus died (27:50-52), encourages the audience that they also will share in the resurrection of Jesus. The audience can now tell of the transfiguration (17:9), because Jesus' resurrection makes clear that his transfiguration was a temporary anticipation of the heavenly glory he would attain only after suffering death at the hands of his people – unlike Moses and Elijah – and being raised by God. Now that Jesus has become the glorified, heavenly figure that was prefigured by his temporary transfiguration, he is able to remain permanently with the audience, so that they can fulfill the risen Jesus' mandate to make disciples of all nations by baptizing them and teaching all that Jesus commanded (28:19-20) (chap. 11).

In Luke, while Jesus was praying, "the appearance of his face became different and his clothing dazzling white" (9:29), indicating that he has been externally and temporarily transformed by God into a heavenly being while still on earth. Moses and Elijah appear in glory and talk with Jesus about his "exodus," which he was about to accomplish in Jerusalem (9:30-31), referring to the way that he will leave this earthly life by the death and resurrection he has just predicted (9:22). Although the three disciples had been overcome with sleep so that they did not hear the conversation about Jesus' approaching "exodus," they became wide awake in time to see the glory of the transfigured Jesus and that of Moses and Elijah standing with him (9:32). When Peter offered to make a tent for each epiphanic figure to halt and render unnecessary the separation of Moses and Elijah from Jesus that has already begun (9:33), he does not realize that Jesus will attain the same heavenly glory he now momentarily shares with Moses and Elijah only after he has been put to death as a rejected prophet in Jerusalem. God's voice from the cloud (9:35) serves as the pivotal mandate that distinguishes Jesus from Moses and Elijah as God's chosen Son and commands the disciples and the audience to listen to Jesus. The mandate thus "pivots" them back to his teaching about the necessity for him and his followers to suffer and be put to death (9:21-27) before entering into the heavenly glory of God's kingdom anticipated by Jesus' transfiguration (chap. 12).

The transfiguration's mandate in Luke (9:35) also pivoted the disciples and the audience forward to the subsequent predictions of the necessity for Jesus to suffer and be put to death as a rejected prophet in Jerusalem (9:44, 51-56; 13:33-35; 18:31-33; 20:9-19; 22:14-23, 39-46; 24:4-7, 25-27, 44-46) as well as for them to spend their lives in selfless, suffering service for others (9:41; 10:39; 22:24-27; 23:35) with the assurance of being raised from the dead (20:27-39) and sharing in the heavenly glory (21:27; 22:69-70; 23:11; 24:26, 51) prefigured by his transfiguration. That Jesus resolutely set his "face" for the accomplishment of his "exodus" (9:31) in Jerusalem (9:51-53), the same "face" that was transfigured into glory (9:29), models for the audience the determination they need to undergo suffering and death before attaining heavenly glory (9:22-26). By following the example of Mary, who listened to Jesus (10:39), the audience will realize that the words of Jesus call disciples to a selfless service that follows Jesus on the divinely necessary way of his suffering and death (9:21).

The words of the Lukan Jesus at his last supper enable the audience to understand that his transfiguration into a heavenly figure portends his future partaking of the banquet in the kingdom of God that will occur only after his sacrificial death (22:14-20). By following Jesus' example of prayer (22:39-46) the audience can overcome the temptation not to submit their wills to God's will that they participate in Jesus' way of suffering and death. That Herod clothes Jesus in a bright shining garment (23:11) fit for a heavenly being further assures the audience that Jesus will attain the heavenly glory signaled by the dazzling white clothing of his transfiguration (9:29). By dying on the cross as God's "chosen one" (23:35; cf. 9:35), Jesus models for the audience his provocative challenge, which the transfiguration's mandate urged them to heed – "whoever wants to save his life will lose it, but whoever loses his life for my sake will save it" (9:24; cf. 23:35). Now that Jesus has ascended to heaven (24:51) and rejoined the heavenly Moses and Elijah, the audience can report the things the disciples saw in the transfiguration epiphany (9:36) (chap. 13).

The above interpretation of Jesus' transfiguration has significant theological ramifications. That Jesus attained the heavenly glory anticipated at his transfiguration by suffering the humiliating death of a rejected prophet, which Moses and Elijah avoided, signifies a profound affirmation of the totality of our human condition. It gives new meaning to suffering and death for all Christians. Heavenly glory lies not in the wish to escape but in the courage to embrace rejection, suffering, and death.

BIBLIOGRAPHY

ABEL, F.-M. "L'apparition du chef de l'armée de Yahveh à Josué (Jos. V,13-15)." *Miscellanea Biblica et Orientalia: Athanasio Miller Oblata.* Studia Anselmiana 27. Rome: Herder, 1951. 109-13.

– *Les Livres des Maccabées.* Ebib. Paris: Gabalda, 1949.

ALLISON, D.C. "Elijah Must Come First." *JBL* 103 (1984): 256-58.

ALSUP, J. E. "Theophany in the NT." *IDBSup*, 898-900.

AMIT, Y. *The Book of Judges: The Art of Editing.* BIS 38. Leiden: Brill, 1999.

ANBAR, M. "La 'reprise'." *VT* 38 (1988): 385-98.

ANDERSEN, F.I. "2 (Slavonic Apocalypse of) Enoch." *OTP* 1.91-213.

ANDERSON, J.S. *Matthew's Narrative Web: Over, and Over, and Over Again.* JSNTSup 91. Sheffield: JSOT, 1994.

ANDERSON, J.C. "The Social Function of Curses in the Hebrew Bible." *ZAW* 110 (1998): 223-37.

ASHLEY, T.R. *The Book of Numbers.* NICOT. Grand Rapids: Eerdmans, 1993.

AUNE, D.E. *Revelation 1-5.* WBC 52A. Dallas: Word Books, 1997.

– *Revelation 6-16.* WBC 52B. Nashville: Nelson, 1998.

– *Revelation 17-22.* WBC 52C. Nashville: Nelson, 1998.

BAARDA, T. "Luke 22:42-47a: The Emperor Julian as a Witness to the Text of Luke." *NovT* 30 (1988): 289-96.

BALTENSWEILER, H. *Die Verklärung Jesu: Historisches Ereignis und synoptische Berichte.* ATANT 33. Zürich: Zwingli, 1959.

BALZ, H. "βαρέω." *EDNT* 1.198.

– "μαστιγόω." *EDNT* 2.395-96.

– "προσευχή." *EDNT* 3.164-69.

– "φοβέομαι." *EDNT* 3.429-32.

BARRÉ, M. "The Portrait of Balaam in Numbers 22-24." *Int* 51 (1997): 254-66.

BARRETT, C.K. *The Acts of the Apostles: Volume I: Preliminary Introduction and Commentary on Acts I-XIV*. ICC. Edinburgh: Clark, 1994.

BARTH, G. "ὀλιγοπιστία." *EDNT* 2.506.

BASSER, H.W. "The Jewish Roots of the Transfiguration." *Bible Review* 14 (1998) 30-35.

BAUCKHAM, R. *Jude and the Relatives of Jesus in the Early Church*. Edinburgh: Clark, 1990.

– ed. *The Gospels for All Christians: Rethinking the Gospel Audiences*. Grand Rapids: Eerdmans, 1998.

BEALE, G.K. *The Book of Revelation*. NIGTC. Grand Rapids: Eerdmans, 1999.

BEGG, C. "'Josephus's Portrayal of the Disappearances of Enoch, Elijah, and Moses': Some Observations." *JBL* 109 (1990): 691-93.

BERGER, K. "πρόσωπον," *EDNT* 3.180-81.

BEYERLE, S. *Der Mosesegen im Deuteronomium: Eine text-, kompositions- und form-kritische Studie zu Deuteronomium 33*. BZAW 250. New York: De Gruyter, 1997.

BIEBERSTEIN, K. *Josua-Jordan-Jericho: Archäologie, Geschichte und Theologie der Landnahmeerzählungen Josua 1-6*. OBO 143. Göttingen: Vandenhoeck & Ruprecht, 1995.

BINDER, D.D. *Into the Temple Courts: The Place of the Synagogues in the Second Temple Period*. SBLDS 169. Atlanta: Society of Biblical Literature, 1999.

BIRNBAUM, E. *The Place of Judaism in Philo's Thought: Israel, Jews, and Proselytes*. BJS 290. Atlanta: Scholars Press, 1996.

BLACKBURN, B. *Theios Aner and the Markan Miracle Traditions: A Critique of the Theios Aner Concept as an Interpretative Background of the Miracle Traditions Used by Mark*. WUNT 40. Tübingen: Mohr Siebeck, 1991.

BLOCK, D.I. "Will the Real Gideon Please Stand Up?: Narrative Style and Intention in Judges 6-9." *JETS* 40 (1997): 353-66.

Bock, D.L. *Luke 1:1-9:50*. BECNT 3A. Grand Rapids: Baker, 1994.

– *Luke 9:51-24:53*. BECNT 3B. Grand Rapids: Baker, 1996.

BÖHLEMANN, P. *Jesus und der Täufer: Schlüssel zur Theologie und Ethik des Lukas*. SNTSMS 99. Cambridge: Cambridge University Press, 1997.

BOLING, R.G. and G.E. WRIGHT. *Joshua: A New Translation with Notes and Commentary*. AB 6. New York: Doubleday, 1982.

BOOBYER, G.H. *St. Mark and the Transfiguration Story*. Edinburgh: Clark, 1942.

BORGEN, P. "Heavenly Ascent in Philo: An Examination of Selected Passages." *The Pseudepigrapha and Early Biblical Interpretation*. Eds. J.H. Charlesworth and C.A. Evans. JSPSup 14. Sheffield: JSOT, 1993. 246-68.

– *Philo of Alexandria: An Exegete for His Time*. NovTSup 86. Leiden: Brill, 1997.

BOTHA, S.P. "A Glorified Bodily Resurrection in Matthew 27:51b-53?: A Close Reading of the Text." *Hervormde Teologiese Studies* 52 (1996): 270-84.

BOUGHTON, L.C. "'Being Shed for You/Many': Time-Sense and Consequences in the Synoptic Cup Citations." *TynBul* 48 (1997): 249-70.

BRAY, G. "La transfiguration." *Revue Réformée* 50 (1999): 85-91.

BRODIE, T.L. "The Departure for Jerusalem (Luke 9,51-56) as a Rhetorical Imitation of Elijah's Departure for the Jordan (2 Kgs 1,1-2,6)." *Bib* 70 (1989): 96-109.

BROER, I. "ἀγγέλλω." *EDNT* 1.12-13.

BROWER, K. "Mark 9:1: Seeing the Kingdom in Power." *JSNT* 6 (1980): 17-41.

BROWN, R.E. *The Death of the Messiah: From Gethsemane to the Grave: A Commentary on the Passion Narratives in the Four Gospels*. ABRL. New York: Doubleday, 1994.

BRUCE, F.F. *1 & 2 Thessalonians*. WBC 45. Waco: Word Books, 1982.

BÜCHELE, A. *Der Tod Jesu im Lukasevangelium: Eine redaktionsgeschichtliche Untersuchung zu Lk 23*. FTS 26. Frankfurt: Knecht, 1978.

BUDD, P.J. *Numbers*. WBC 5. Waco: Word Books, 1984.

BÜHNER, J.-A. "λευκός." *EDNT* 2.350-51.

– "σκηνή." *EDNT* 3.251-52.

BURCHARD, C. "Markus 15:34." *ZNW* 74 (1983): 1-11.

BURRIDGE, R.A. "About People, by People, for People: Gospel Genre and Audiences." *The Gospels for All Christians: Rethinking the Gospel Audiences*. Ed. R. Bauckham. Grand Rapids: Eerdmans, 1998. 113-45.

CARAGOUNIS, C.C. *The Son of Man: Vision and Interpretation*. WUNT 38. Tübingen: Mohr-Siebeck, 1986.

CARPINELLI, F.G. "'Do This as *My* Memorial' (Luke 22:19): Lucan Soteriology of Atonement." *CBQ* 61 (1999): 74-91.

CARRELL, P.R. *Jesus and the Angels: Angelology and the Christology of the Apocalypse of John*. SNTSMS 95. Cambridge: Cambridge University Press, 1997.

CARTER, W. *Households and Discipleship: A Study of Matthew 19-20*. JSNTSup 103. Sheffield: JSOT, 1994.

CARTER, W. and J.P. HEIL. *Matthew's Parables: Audience-Oriented Perspectives*. CBQMS 30. Washington: Catholic Biblical Association, 1998.

CASEY, M. *Aramaic Sources of Mark's Gospel*. SNTSMS 102. Cambridge: Cambridge University Press, 1998.

CASTELLO, G. "Balaam e Balak: Approccio narrativo a Nm 22-24." *Oltre il Racconto: Esegesi ed ermeneutica: alla ricerca del senso*. BTN. Naples: M. D'Auria Editore, 1994. 29-48.

CASTELOT, J.J. and A. CODY, "Religious Institutions of Israel." *NJBC*. 1253-83.

CHILDS, B.S. *The Book of Exodus: A Critical, Theological Commentary*. OTL. Philadelphia: Westminster, 1974.

CHILTON, B.D. "The Transfiguration: Dominical Assurance and Apostolic Vision." *NTS* 27 (1981) 115-24.

CLARKE, E.G. *Targum Pseudo-Jonathan: Deuteronomy: Translated, with Notes*. Aramaic Bible 5B. Collegeville: Liturgical Press, 1998.

CLIVAZ, C. "La Transfiguration au risque de la compréhension du disciple: Mc 9/2-10." *ETR* 70 (1995): 493-508.

COATS, G.W. "Legendary Motifs in the Moses Death Report." *CBQ* 39 (1977): 34-44.

COGAN, M. and H. TADMOR. *II Kings: A New Translation with Introduction and Commentary*. AB 11. New York: Doubleday, 1988.

COLLINS, J.J. *Daniel: A Commentary on the Book of Daniel*. Hermeneia. Minneapolis: Fortress, 1993.

COOK, S.L. "The Metamorphosis of a Shepherd: The Tradition History of Zechariah 11:17 + 13:7-9." *CBQ* 55 (1993): 453-66.

CRUMP, D. *Jesus the Intercessor: Prayer and Christology in Luke-Acts*. WUNT 49. Tübingen: Mohr, 1992.

CUNNINGHAM, S. *'Through Many Tribulations': The Theology of Persecution in Luke-Acts*. JSNTSup 142. Sheffield: Sheffield Academic Press, 1997.

DANOVE, P. *The End of Mark's Story: A Methodological Study*. BIS 3. Leiden: Brill, 1993.

– "The Characterization and Narrative Function of the Women at the Tomb (Mark 15,40-41.47; 16,1-8)." *Bib* 77 (1996): 375-97.

DARR, J.A. "'Watch How You Listen' (Lk. 8.18): Jesus and the Rhetoric of Perception in Luke-Acts." *The New Literary Criticism and the New Testament*. Eds. E.S. Malbon and E.V. McKnight. JSNTSup 109. Sheffield: Sheffield Academic Press, 1994. 87-107.

– *Herod the Fox: Audience Criticism and Lukan Characterization*. JSNTSup 163. Sheffield: Sheffield Academic Press, 1998.

DAUBE, D. *The New Testament and Rabbinic Judaism*. New York: Arno, 1973.

DAVIES, W.D. and D.C. ALLISON. *The Gospel According to Saint Matthew: Volume I: Introduction and Commentary on Matthew I-VII*. ICC. Edinburgh: Clark, 1988.

– *The Gospel According to Saint Matthew: Volume II: Commentary on Matthew VIII-XVIII*. ICC. Edinburgh: Clark, 1991.

– *The Gospel According to Saint Matthew: Volume III: Commentary on Matthew XIX-XXVIII*. ICC. Edinburgh: Clark, 1997.

DEL AGUA, A. "The Narrative of the Transfiguration as a Derashic Scenification of a Faith Confession (Mark 9.2-8 Par.)." *NTS* 39 (1993) 340-54.

DENIS, A.-M., ed. *Fragmenta pseudepigraphorum quae supersunt graeca una cum historicorum et auctorum Judaeorum hellenistarum fragmentis*. PVTG 3. Leiden: Brill, 1970.

DENOVA, R.I. *The Things Accomplished Among Us: Prophetic Tradition in the Structural Pattern of Luke-Acts*. JSNTSup 141. Sheffield: Sheffield Academic Press, 1997.

DERRETT, J.D.M. "Peter and the Tabernacles (Mark 9,5-7)." *DRev* 108 (1990): 37-48.

– "Sleeping at Gethsemane." *DRev* 114 (1996): 235-45.

DESPLANQUE, C. "Mystère divin et ambiguïté humaine dans l'historie de Balaam." *Hokhma* 64 (1997): 1-16.

DE VAULX, J. *Les Nombres*. SB. Paris: Gabalda, 1972.

DILLON, R.J. *From Eye-Witnesses to Ministers of the Word*. AnBib 82. Rome: Biblical Institute, 1978.

DOBLE, P. *The Paradox of Salvation: Luke's Theology of the Cross*. SNTSMS 87. Cambridge: Cambridge University Press, 1996.

DONALDSON, T.L. *Jesus on the Mountain: A Study in Matthean Theology*. JSNTSup 8. Sheffield: JSOT, 1985.

DORAN, R. *Temple Propaganda: The Purpose and Character of 2 Maccabees*. CBQMS 12. Washington: Catholic Biblical Association of America, 1981.

DOWD, S.E. *Prayer, Power, and the Problem of Suffering: Mark 11:22-25 in the Context of Markan Theology*. SBLDS 105. Atlanta: Scholars Press, 1988.

DU PLESSIS, I.J. "The Saving Significance of Jesus and His Death on the Cross in Luke's Gospel—Focusing on Luke 22:19b-20." *Neot* 28 (1994): 523-40.

DURHAM, J.I. *Exodus*. WBC 3. Waco: Word Books, 1987.

ECKERT, J. "ἐκλέγομαι." *EDNT* 1.416-17.

EHRMAN, B.D. "The Cup, The Bread, and the Salvific Effect of Jesus' Death in Luke-Acts." *SBLASP* 30 (1991): 576-91.

EHRMAN, B.D. and M.A. PLUNKETT. "The Angel and the Agony: The Textual Problem of Luke 24:43-44." *CBQ* 45 (1983): 401-16.

ELLIOTT, J.K. *The Language and Style of the Gospel of Mark*. NovTSup 71. Leiden: Brill, 1993.

ERNST, J. *Das Evangelium nach Markus*. RNT. Regensburg: Pustet, 1981.

EVANS, C.A. "'He Set His Face': On the Meaning of Luke 9:51." *Luke and Scripture: The Function of Sacred Tradition in Luke-Acts*. C.A. Evans and J.A. Sanders. Minneapolis: Fortress, 1993. 93-105.

– "Prophecy and Polemic: Jews in Luke's Scriptural Apologetic." *Luke and Scripture: The Function of Sacred Tradition in Luke-Acts*. C.A. Evans and J.A. Sanders. Minneapolis: Fortress, 1993. 171-211.

FAIERSTEIN, M.M. "Why Do the Scribes Say That Elijah Must Come First?" *JBL* 100 (1981): 75-86.

FELDKÄMPER, L. *Der betende Jesus als Heilsmittler nach Lukas*. VMSAB 29. St. Augustin, West Germany: Steyler, 1978.

FELDMAN, L.H. "Prolegomenon." *The Biblical Antiquities of Philo*. M.R. James. New York: KTAV, 1971. ix-clxix.

– "Prophets and Prophecy in Josephus." *JTS* 41 (1990): 386-422.

– "Josephus' Portrait of Moses." *JQR* 82 (1992): 285-328.

– "Josephus' Portrait of Moses: Part Two." *JQR* 83 (1993): 7-50.

– "Josephus' Portrait of Moses: Part Three." *JQR* 83 (1993): 301-30.

– *Josephus's Interpretation of the Bible*. Berkeley: University of California Press, 1998.

– *Studies in Josephus' Rewritten Bible*. JSJSup 58. Leiden: Brill, 1998.

FISCHER, T. "Heliodor im Tempel zu Jerusalem: Ein `hellenistischer' Aspekt der 'frommen Legende'." *Prophetie und geschichtliche Wirklichkeit im alten Israel: Festschrift für Siegfried Herrmann zum 65. Geburtstag*. Eds. R. Liwak and S. Wagner. Stuttgart: Kohlhammer, 1991. 122-33.

FITZER, G. "στίλβω." *TDNT* 7.665-66.

FITZMYER, J.A. *The Gospel According to Luke I-IX*. AB 28. Garden City: Doubleday, 1981.

– *The Gospel According to Luke X-XXIV*. AB 28A. Garden City: Doubleday, 1985.
– "More About Elijah Coming First." *JBL* 104 (1985): 295-96.

– *The Acts of the Apostles: A New Translation with Introduction and Commentary*. AB 31. New York: Doubleday, 1998.

FLETCHER-LOUIS, C.H.T. *Luke-Acts: Angels, Christology and Soteriology*. WUNT 94. Tübingen: Mohr Siebeck, 1997.

FOSSUM, J.E. *The Name of God and the Angel of the Lord: Samaritan and Jewish Concepts of Intermediation and the Origin of Gnosticism.* WUNT 36. Tübingen: Mohr Siebeck, 1985.

– "Ascensio, Metamorphosis: The 'Transfiguration' of Jesus in the Synoptic Gospels." *The Image of the Invisible God: Essays on the Influence of Jewish Mysticism on Early Christology.* NTOA 30. Göttingen: Vandenhoeck & Ruprecht, 1995. 71-94.

FRENSCHKOWSKI, M. *Offenbarung und Epiphanie: Band 2: Die verborgene Epiphanie in Spätantike und frühen Christentum.* WUNT 80. Tübingen: Mohr Siebeck, 1997.

FRITZ, V. *Das Buch Josua*, HAT 7. Tübingen: Mohr Siebeck, 1994.

GARRETT, S.R. "Exodus from Bondage: Luke 9:31 and Acts 12:1-24." *CBQ* 52 (1990): 656-80.

– *The Temptations of Jesus in Mark's Gospel.* Grand Rapids: Eerdmans, 1998.

GIBLIN, C.H. "The Beginning of the Ongoing Gospel (Mk 1,2-16,8)." *The Four Gospels 1992: Festschrift Frans Neirynck.* Ed. F. Van Segbroeck, et al. BETL 100. Leuven: Leuven University, 1992. 975-85.

GINZBERG, L. *The Legends of the Jews.* 7 vols. Philadelphia: Jewish Publication Society, 1909-38.

GLOBE, A. "The Text and Literary Structure of Judges 5,4-5." *Bib* 55 (1974): 168-78.

GLOMBITZA, O. "Die Titel διδάσκαλος und ἐπιστάτης für Jesus bei Lukas." *ZNW* 49 (1958): 275-78.

GNILKA, J. *Das Evangelium nach Markus: (Mk 1,1-8,26).* EKKNT 2/1. Zürich: Benziger, 1978.

– *Das Evangelium nach Markus: (Mk 8,27-16,20).* EKKNT 2/2. Zürich: Benziger, 1979.

– *Das Matthäusevangelium: Kommentar zu Kap. 14,1 - 28,20 und Einleitungsfragen.* HTKNT 1. Freiburg: Herder, 1988.

GNUSE, R. "Dream Genre in the Matthean Infancy Narratives." *NovT* 32 (1990): 97-120.

GOLDINGAY, J.E. *Daniel.* WBC 30. Dallas: Word Books, 1989.

GOLDSTEIN, J.A. *II Maccabees: A New Translation with Introduction and Commentary.* AB 41A. New York: Doubleday, 1983.

GOODENOUGH, E.R. *By Light, Light: The Mystic Gospel of Hellenistic Judaism.* Amsterdam: Philo, 1969.

GÖRG, M. *Das Zelt der Begegnung: Untersuchung zur Gestalt der sakralen Zelttraditionen Altisraels.* BBB 27. Bonn: Hanstein, 1967.

– "שכב." TWAT 7.1137-47.

GREEN, J.B. "Jesus on the Mount of Olives (Luke 22.39-46): Tradition and Theology." *JSNT* 26 (1986): 29-48.

– *The Gospel of Luke*. NICNT. Grand Rapids: Eerdmans, 1997.

GRIMM, W. "ἐπιστάτης." *EDNT* 2.37.

GROSSFELD, B. *The Targum Onqelos to Exodus: Translated, with Apparatus and Notes*. Aramaic Bible 7. Wilmington: Glazier, 1988.

– *The Targum Onqelos to Deuteronomy: Translated, with Apparatus, and Notes*. Aramaic Bible 9. Wilmington: Glazier, 1988.

GROSS, W. *Bileam: Literar- und formkritische Untersuchung der Prosa in Num 22-24*. SANT 38. Munich: Kösel, 1974.

GUNDRY, R.H. *The Use of the Old Testament in St. Matthew's Gospel*. NovTSup 18. Leiden: Brill, 1967.

– *Matthew: A Commentary on His Literary and Theological Art*. Grand Rapids: Eerdmans, 1982.

– *Mark: A Commentary on His Apology for the Cross*. Grand Rapids: Eerdmans, 1993.

– Review of Moses, *Matthew's Transfiguration Story*. *JBL* 116 (1997): 560-62.

GUNNEWEG, A.H.J. "Das Gesetz und die Propheten: Eine Auslegung von Ex 33,7-11; Num 11,4-12,8; Dtn 31,14f.; 34,10." *ZAW* 102 (1990): 169-80.

HAACKER, K. and P. SCHÄFER. "Nachbiblische Traditionen vom Tod des Mose." *Josephus-Studien: Untersuchungen zu Josephus, dem antiken Judentum und dem Neuen Testament: Festschrift O. Michel*. Ed. O. Betz, et al. Göttingen: Vandenhoeck & Ruprecht, 1974. 147-74.

HAGNER, D.A. *Matthew 14-28*. WBC 33B. Dallas: Word Books, 1995.

HARRINGTON, D.J. "Pseudo-Philo." *OTP* 2.297-377.

HARTLEY, J.E. *Leviticus*. WBC 4. Dallas: Word Books, 1992.

HARTMAN, L.F. and A.A. DI LELLA. *The Book of Daniel*. AB 23. New York: Doubleday, 1978.

HAWK, L.D. *Every Promise Fulfilled: Contesting Plots in Joshua*. Louisville: Westminster John Knox, 1991.

HEGERMANN, H. "δόξα." *EDNT* 1.344-48.

HEIL, J.P. *Jesus Walking on the Sea: Meaning and Gospel Functions of Matt 14:22-33, Mark 6:45-52 and John 6:15b-21*. AnBib 87. Rome: Biblical Institute, 1981.

– "Reader-Response and the Irony of Jesus Before the Sanhedrin in Luke 22:66-71." *CBQ* 51 (1989): 271-84.

– "Mark 14,1-52: Narrative Structure and Reader-Response." *Bib* 71 (1990): 305-32.

– "Reader-Response and the Irony of the Trial of Jesus in Luke 23:1-25." *ScEs* 43 (1991): 175-86.

– *The Death and Resurrection of Jesus: A Narrative-Critical Reading of Matthew 26-28*. Minneapolis: Fortress, 1991.

– "The Narrative Structure of Matthew 27:55-28:20." *JBL* 110 (1991): 419-38.

– "Reader-Response and the Narrative Context of the Parables About Growing Seed in Mark 4:1-34." *CBQ* 54 (1992): 271-86.

– *The Gospel of Mark as a Model for Action: A Reader-Response Commentary*. New York: Paulist, 1992.

– "The Progressive Narrative Pattern of Mark 14,53-16,8." *Bib* 73 (1992): 331-58.

– "Ezekiel 34 and the Narrative Strategy of the Shepherd and Sheep Metaphor in Matthew." *CBQ* 55 (1993): 698-708.

– "The Fifth Seal (Rev 6,9-11) as a Key to the Book of Revelation." *Bib* 74 (1993): 220-43.

– *Blood and Water: The Death and Resurrection of Jesus in John 18-21*. CBQMS 27. Washington: Catholic Biblical Association, 1995.

– "The Narrative Strategy and Pragmatics of the Temple Theme in Mark." *CBQ* 59 (1997): 76-100.

– "The Double Meaning of the Narrative of Universal Judgment in Matthew 25.31-46." *JSNT* 69 (1998): 3-14.

– "A Note on 'Elijah with Moses' in Mark 9,4." *Bib* 80 (1999): 115.

– *The Meal Scenes in Luke-Acts: An Audience-Oriented Approach*. SBLMS 52. Atlanta: Society of Biblical Literature, 1999.

HESTER, J.D. "Dramatic Inconclusion: Irony and the Narrative Rhetoric of the Ending of Mark." *JSNT* 57 (1995): 61-86.

HIEBERT, T. "Theophany in the OT." *ABD* 6.505-11.

HILL, A.E. *Malachi: A New Translation with Introduction and Commentary*. AB 25D. New York: Doubleday, 1998.

HOFIUS, O. "'Für euch gegeben zur Vergebung der Sünden': Vom Sinn des Heiligen Abendmahls." ZTK 95 (1998): 313-37.

HOLTZ, T. "ἥλιος." *EDNT* 2.117-18.

HOOKER, M.D. "'What Doest Thou Here, Elijah?': A Look at St Mark's Account of the Transfiguration." *The Glory of Christ in the New Testament*. Eds. L.D. Hurst and N.T. Wright. Oxford: Clarendon, 1987.

– *The Gospel According to Saint Mark*. Peabody, MA: Hendrickson, 1991.

HOUTMAN, C. *Der Himmel im Alten Testament: Israels Weltbild und Weltanschauung*. OTS 30. Leiden: Brill, 1993.

HUMPHREY, E.M. "Collision of Modes?—Vision and Determining Argument in Acts 10:1-11:18." *Textual Determinacy Volume II*. Eds. R.B. Robinson and R.C. Culley. *Semeia* 71. Atlanta: Scholars Press, 1995. 65-84.

HUSSER, J.-M. *Le songe et la parole: Etude sur le rêve et sa fonction dans l'ancien Israël*. BZAW 210. Berlin: De Gruyter, 1994.

ISAAC, E. "1 (Ethiopic Apocalypse of) Enoch." *OTP* 1.5-89.

JACKSON, H.M. "The Death of Jesus in Mark and the Miracle from the Cross." *NTS* 33 (1987): 16-37.

JACOB, E. "Une théopanie mysterieuse: Josué 5,13-15." *Ce Dieu Qui vient: Mélanges offerts à Bernard Renaud*. LD 159. Paris: Cerf, 1995. 130-35.

JACOBSON, H. *A Commentary on Pseudo-Philo's Liber Antiquitatum Biblicarum: With Latin Text and English Translation*. AGJU 31. Leiden: Brill, 1996.

JAGERSMA, H. "Doe je schoen van je voet: Een onderzoek naar de achtergrond en betekenis van Jozua 5:13-15." *Tekst & Interpretatie: Studies over getallen, teksten, verhalen en geschiednis in het Oude Testament*. Nijkerk: Callenbach, 1990. 108-18.

JEREMIAS, J. *Theophanie: Die Geschichte einer alttestamentlichen Gattung*. WMANT 10. Neukirchen: Neukirchener Verlag, 1977.

– "Theophany in the OT." *IDBSup*, 896-98.

JOHNSON, L.T. *The Gospel of Luke*. SacPag 3. Collegeville: Liturgical Press, 1991.

JOOSTEN, J. *People and Land in the Holiness Code: An Exegetical Study of the Ideational Framework of the Law in Leviticus 17-26*. VTSup 67. Leiden: Brill, 1996.

JOUBERT, S.J. "Facing the Past: Transtextual Relationships and Historical Understanding in the Letter of Jude." *BZ* 42 (1998): 56-70.

KEE, H.C. "The Transfiguration in Mark: Epiphany or Apocalyptic Vision?" *Understanding the Sacred Text: Essays in Honor of Morton S. Enslin on the Hebrew Bible and Christian Beginnings*. Ed. J. Reumann. Valley Forge: Judson, 1972. 135-52.

KELLERMANN, D. "מִשְׁכָּן." *TWAT* 5.62-69.

KLEINE, H. "ὄρος." *EDNT* 2.533-34.

KLIJN, A.F.J. "2 (Syriac Apocalypse of) Baruch." *OTP* 1.615-52.

KNOWLES, M. *Jeremiah in Matthew's Gospel: The Rejected-Prophet Motif in Matthaean Redaction*. JSNTSup 68. Sheffield: JSOT, 1993.

KOCH, K. "אהל," *TDOT* 1.118-30.

KRAFT, R.A., ed. *The Testament of Job According to the SV Text: Greek Text and English Translation*. SBLTT 5. Missoula: Scholars Press, 1974.

KRAUS, W. "Die Passion des Gottessohnes: Zur Bedeutung des Todes Jesu im Matthäusevangelium." *EvT* 57 (1997): 409-27.

KREMER, J. "ἀναλαμβάνω." *EDNT* 1.83-84.

– "ἀναφέρω." *EDNT* 1.94.

– "ὁράω." *EDNT* 2.526-29.

KRETZER, A. "ἀπόλλυμι." *EDNT* 1.135-36.

– "παραλαμβάνω." *EDNT* 3.29-30.

KÜBEL, P. "Epiphanie und Altarbau." *ZAW* 83 (1971): 225-31.

KUHN, P. *Offenbarungsstimmen im Antiken Judentum: Untersuchungen zur Bat Qol und verwandten Phänomenen*. TSAJ 20. Tübingen: Mohr Siebeck, 1989.

KUPP, D.D. *Matthew's Emmanuel: Divine Presence and God's People in the First Gospel*. SNTSMS 90. Cambridge: Cambridge University Press, 1996.

LANE, W.L. *The Gospel According to Mark: The English Text with Introduction, Exposition and Notes*. NICNT. Grand Rapids: Eerdmans, 1974.

LAUTERBACH, J.Z. *Mekilta de-Rabbi Ishmael*. Philadelphia: Jewish Publication Society, 1961.

LAYTON, S.C. "Leaves from an Onomastician's Notebook." *ZAW* 108 (1996): 608-20.

LÉGASSE, S. "εὐδοκέω." *EDNT* 2.75.

LENTZEN-DEIS, F. *Die Taufe Jesu nach den Synoptikern: Literarkritische und gattungsgeschichtliche Untersuchungen*. FTS 4. Frankfurt: Knecht, 1970.

LEVINE, B.A. *Numbers 1-20: A New Translation with Introduction and Commentary*. AB 4A. New York: Doubleday, 1993.

LEVINE, E. *The Aramaic Version of the Bible: Contents and Context*. BZAW 174. Berlin: De Gruyter, 1988.

LIEFELD, W.L. "Theological Motifs in the Transfiguration Narrative." *New Dimensions in New Testament Study*. Eds. R.N. Longenecker and M.C. Tenney. Grand Rapids: Zondervan, 1974. 162-79.

LOEWENSTAMM, S.E. "The Death of Moses." *Studies on the Testament of Abraham*. Ed. G.W.E. Nickelsburg. SBLSCS 6. Missoula: Scholars Press, 1972. 185-217.

LOHFINK, G. *Die Himmelfahrt Jesu: Untersuchungen zu den Himmelfahrts- und Erhöhungstexten bei Lukas*. SANT 26. Munich: Kösel, 1971.

Lührmann, D. "Epiphaneia: Zur Bedeutungsgeschichte eines griechischen Wortes." *Tradition und Glaube: Das frühe Christentum in seiner Umwelt: Festgabe für Karl Georg Kuhn zum 65. Geburtstag.* G. Jeremias, et al. Göttingen: Vandenhoeck & Ruprecht, 1971. 185-99.

Luomanen, P. *Entering the Kingdom of Heaven: A Study on the Structure of Matthew's View of Salvation.* WUNT 101. Tübingen: Mohr Siebeck, 1998.

Lust, J., E. Eynikel, and K. Hauspie. *A Greek-English Lexicon of the Septuagint.* 2 Parts. Stuttgart: Deutsche Bibelgesellschaft, 1992, 1996.

Luzarraga, J. *Las tradiciones de la nube en la Biblia y en el Judaismo primitivo.* AnBib 54. Rome: Biblical Institute, 1973.

Luz, U. *Das Evangelium nach Matthäus.* EKKNT 1/2. Zürich: Benziger, 1990.

– "βασιλεία." *EDNT* 1.201-5.

MacDonald, J. "The Samaritan Doctrine of Moses." *SJT* 3 (1960): 149-62.

– *The Theology of the Samaritans.* NTL. London: SCM, 1964.

Mach, M. "Christus Mutans: Zur Bedeutung der 'Verklärung Jesu' im Wechsel von jüdischer Messianität zur neutestamentlichen Christologie." *Messiah and Christos: Studies in the Jewish Origins of Christianity: Festschrift D. Flusser.* Ed. I. Gruenwald, et al. TSAJ 32. Tübingen: Mohr Siebeck, 1992. 177-98.

Magness, J.L. *Sense and Absence: Structure and Suspension in the Ending of Mark's Gospel.* Atlanta: Scholars Press, 1986.

Maher, M. *Targum Pseudo-Jonathan: Exodus: Translated, with Notes.* Aramaic Bible 2. Collegeville: Liturgical Press, 1994.

Main, E. "Les Sadducéens et la résurrection des morts: Comparison entre Mc 12,18-27 et Lc 20,27-38." *RB* 103 (1996): 411-32.

Malbon, E.S. "Fallible Followers: Women and Men in the Gospel of Mark." *The Bible and Feminist Hermeneutics.* Ed. M.A. Tolbert. *Semeia* 28. Chico: Scholars Press, 1983. 29-48.

– *Narrative Space and Mythic Meaning in Mark.* San Francisco: Harper & Row, 1986.

Manicardi, E. *Il cammino di Gesù nel Vangelo di Marco: Schema narrativo e tema cristologico.* AnBib 96. Rome: Biblical Institute, 1981.

Marais, J. *Representation in Old Testament Narrative Texts.* BIS 36. Leiden: Brill, 1998.

Marcus, J. The *Way of the Lord: Christological Exegesis of the Old Testament in the Gospel of Mark.* Louisville: Westminster/Knox, 1992.

Marshall, C.D. *Faith as a Theme in Mark's Narrative.* SNTSMS 64. Cambridge: Cambridge University Press, 1989.

MARSHALL, I.H. *The Gospel of Luke*. Grand Rapids: Eerdmans, 1978.

McCURLEY, F.R. "'And After Six Days' (Mark 9:2): A Semitic Literary Device." *JBL* 93 (1974) 67-81.

McGUCKIN, J.A. *The Transfiguration of Christ in Scripture and Tradition*. Studies in the Bible and Early Christianity 9. Lewiston: Mellen, 1986.

McNAMARA, M. *Targum Neofiti I: Deuteronomy: Translated, with Apparatus and Notes*. Aramaic Bible 5A. Collegeville: Liturgical Press, 1997.

McNAMARA, M. and R. HAYWORD. *Targum Neofiti I: Exodus: Translated, with Introduction and Apparatus and Notes*. Aramaic Bible 2. Collegeville: Liturgical Press, 1994.

MENKEN, M.J.J. "The Quotation from Isaiah 42,1-4 in Matthew 12,18-21: Its Textual Form." *ETL* 75 (1999): 32-52.

METZGER, B.M. *A Textual Commentary on the Greek New Testament*. New York: United Bible Societies, 1971.

— "The Fourth Book of Ezra." *OTP* 1.517-59.

MICHAELIS, W. "λευκός" *TDNT* 4.241-50.

— "ὁράω." *TDNT* 5.315-82.

— "σκηνή." *TDNT* 7.368-94.

MILGROM, J. *Leviticus 1-16: A New Translation with Introduction and Commentary*. AB 3. New York: Doubleday, 1991.

MILLER, K.E. "The Nuptial Eschatology of Revelation 19-22." *CBQ* 60 (1998): 301-18.

MILLER, R.J. "Historicizing the Trans-Historical: The Transfiguration Narrative (Mark 9:2-8, Matt 17:1-8, Luke 9:28-36)." *Forum* 10 (1994): 219-48.

— "Is There Independent Attestation for the Transfiguration in 2 Peter?" *NTS* 42 (1996): 620-25.

— "Source Criticism and the Limits of Certainty: The Lukan Transfiguration Story as a Test Case." *ETL* 74 (1998): 127-44.

MOBERLY, R.W.L. *At the Mountain of God: Story and Theology in Exodus 32-34*. JSOTSup 22. Sheffield: JSOT, 1983.

MOESSNER, D.P. *Lord of the Banquet: The Literary and Theological Significance of the Lukan Travel Narrative*. Harrisburg: Trinity, 1989.

MORRIS, L. *The Gospel According to Matthew*. Grand Rapids: Eerdmans, 1992.

MOSES, A.D.A. *Matthew's Transfiguration Story and Jewish-Christian Controversy*. JSNTSup 122. Sheffield: Sheffield Academic Press, 1996.

MÜLLER, P.-G. "ἐπιφάνεια." *EDNT* 2.44-45.

MURPHY, F.J. *The Structure and Meaning of Second Baruch.* SBLDS 78. Atlanta: Scholars Press, 1985.

– *Pseudo-Philo: Rewriting the Bible.* New York: Oxford University Press, 1993.

MYERS, C. *Binding the Strong Man: A Political Reading of Mark's Story of Jesus.* Maryknoll, NY: Orbis, 1988.

MYERS, J.M. *I and II Esdras: Introduction, Translation and Commentary.* AB 42. New York: Doubleday, 1974.

NARDONI, E. "A Redactional Interpretation of Mark 9:1." *CBQ* 43 (1981): 365-84.

NELSON, P.K. *Leadership and Discipleship: A Study of Luke 22:24-30.* SBLDS 138. Atlanta: Scholars Press, 1994.

NELSON, R.D. *Joshua: A Commentary.* OTL. Louisville: Westminster John Knox, 1997.

NEYREY, J.H. "The Absence of Jesus' Emotions—the Lucan Redaction of Lk 22,39-46." *Bib* 61 (1980): 153-71.

– "The Apologetic Use of the Transfiguration in 2 Peter 1:16-21." *CBQ* 42 (1980): 504-19.

NIEMAND, C. *Studien zu den Minor Agreements der synoptischen Verklärungsperiko-pen: Eine Untersuchung der literarkritischen Relevanz der gemeinsamen Abwei-chungen des Matthäus und Lukas von Markus 9,2-10 für die synoptische Frage.* Frankfurt: Lang, 1989.

NOLLAND, J. *Luke 1-9:20.* WBC 35A. Dallas: Word Books, 1989.

– *Luke 9:21-18:34.* WBC 35B. Dallas: Word Books, 1993.

NOTH, M. *Das Buch Josua.* HAT 7. Tübingen: Mohr Siebeck, 1953.

– *Numbers: A Commentary.* OTL. Philadelphia: Westminster, 1968.

NÜTZEL, J.M. *Die Verklärungserzählung im Markusevangelium: Eine redaktionsge-schichtliche Untersuchung.* FB 6. Bamberg: Echter, 1973.

– "μεταμορφόω." *EDNT* 2.415.

O'CONNELL, R.H. *The Rhetoric of the Book of Judges.* VTSup 63. Leiden: Brill, 1996.

OEPKE, A. "νεφέλη." *TDNT* 4.902-10.

ÖHLER, M. "Die Verklärung (Mk 9:1-8): Die Ankunft der Herrschaft Gottes auf der Erde." *NovT* 38 (1996): 197-217.

– *Elia im Neuen Testament: Untersuchungen zur Bedeutung des alttestamentlichen Propheten im frühen Christentum.* BZNW 88. Berlin: De Gruyter, 1997.

– "The Expectation of Elijah and the Presence of the Kingdom of God." *JBL* 118 (1999): 461-76.

OHMANN, H.M. "Some Remarks on the Use of the Term 'Theophany' in the Study of the Old Testament." *Unity in Diversity: Studies Presented to Dr. Jelle Faber on the Occasion of His Retirement.* Ed. R. Faber. Hamilton, Ont.: Senate of the Theological College of the Canadian Reformed Churches, 1989. 2-12.

OLLEY, J.W. "YHWH and His Zealous Prophet: The Presentation of Elijah in 1 and 2 Kings." *JSOT* 80 (1998) 25-51.

OLSON, D.T. *Deuteronomy and the Death of Moses: A Theological Reading.* OBT. Minneapolis: Fortress, 1994.

OTTO, R.E. "The Fear Motivation in Peter's Offer to Build Τρεῖς Σκηνάς." *WTJ* 59 (1997): 101-12.

PAMMENT, M. "Moses and Elijah in the Story of the Transfiguration." *ExpTim* 92 (1981): 338-39.

PARSONS, M.C. *The Departure of Jesus in Luke-Acts: The Ascension Narratives in Context.* JSNTSup 21. Sheffield: JSOT, 1987.

PATSCH, H. "ποτήριον." *EDNT* 3.141-42.

PAX, E. *Epiphaneia: Ein religionsgeschichtlicher Beitrag zur Biblischen Theologie.* Munich: Zink, 1955.

– "Epiphanie." *RAC* 5 (1962): 832-909.

PENNER, J.A., "Revelation and Discipleship in Matthew's Transfiguration Account," *BSac* 152 (1995): 201-10.

PEPPERMÜLLER, R. "ἔξοδος." *EDNT* 2.8.

PLEVNIK, J. "The Eyewitnesses of the Risen Jesus in Luke 24." *CBQ* (1987): 90-103.

– "Son of Man Seated at the Right Hand of God: Luke 22,69 in Lucan Christology." *Bib* 72 (1991): 331-47.

POPKES, W. "δεῖ." *EDNT* 1.279-80.

– "παραδίδωμι." *EDNT* 3.18-20.

– "πειράζω." *EDNT* 3.64-67.

POWELL, M.A. "A Typology of Worship in the Gospel of Matthew." *JSNT* 57 (1995): 3-17.

– Review of Moses, *Matthew's Transfiguration Story. CBQ* 59 (1997): 585-87.

PROPP, W.H. "The Skin of Moses' Face — Transfigured or Disfigured?" *CBQ* 49 (1987): 375-86.

RADL, W. "μέλλω." *EDNT* 2.403-4.

– "φωνή." *EDNT* 3.446-47.

RAMAROSON, L. "Mise en oeuvre de l''eclectisme intégral' à propos de Jn 8,57 et de Lc 9,54-56." *ScEs* 49 (1997): 181-85.

REFOULÉ, F. "Jésus, nouveau Moïse, ou Pierre, nouveau Grand Prêtre? (Mt 17,1-9; Mc 9,2-10)." *RTL* 24 (1993): 145-62.

REID, B.E. "Voices and Angels: What Were They Talking About at the Transfiguration?: A Redaction-Critical Study of Luke 9:28-36." *BR* 34 (1989): 19-31.

– *The Transfiguration: A Source- and Redaction-Critical Study of Luke 9:28-36.* CahRB 32. Paris: Gabalda, 1993.

REINMUTH, E. *Pseudo-Philo und Lukas: Studien zum Liber Antiquitatum Biblicarum und seiner Bedeutung für die Interpretation des lukanischen Doppelwerks.* WUNT 74. Tübingen: Mohr Siebeck, 1994.

RICHARD, E.J. *First and Second Thessalonians.* SacPag 11. Collegeville: Liturgical Press, 1995.

RIESENFELD, H. *Jésus transfiguré: L'arrière-plan du récit évangélique de la transfiguration de Notre-Seigneur.* ASNU 16. Copenhagen: Munksgaard, 1947.

RIGATO, M.L. ""Remember"...Then They Remembered': Luke 24:6-8." *Luke and Acts.* Eds. G. O'Collins and G. Marconi. New York: Paulist, 1993. 93-102.

RINGE, S.H. "Luke 9:28-36: The Beginning of an Exodus." *The Bible and Feminist Hermeneutics. Semeia* 28. Ed. M. A. Tolbert. Chico: Scholars Press, 1983. 83-99.

RITT, H. "φῶς." *EDNT* 3.447-48.

ROBBINS, V.K. "Pronouncement Stories from a Rhetorical Perspective." *Forum* 4,2 (1988) 3-32.

RÖSEL, M. "Wie einer vom Propheten zum Verführer wurde: Tradition und Rezeption der Bileamgestalt," *Bib* 80 (1999): 506-24.

RÖMHELD, K.F.D. "Von den Quellen der Kraft (Jdc 13)." *ZAW* 104 (1992): 28-52.

ROUILLARD, H. "L'ânesse de Balaam: Analyse littéraire de Nomb., XXII, 21-35." *RB* 87 (1980): 5-37, 211-41.

– *La péricope de Balaam (Nombres 22-24): La prose et les "oracles."* Ebib 4. Paris: Gabalda, 1985.

ROWLAND, C. *The Open Heaven: A Study of Apocalyptic in Judaism and Early Christianity.* New York: Crossroad, 1982.

SABOURIN, L. "The Biblical Cloud: Terminology and Traditions." *BTB* 4 (1974): 290-311.

SALDARINI, A.J. *The Fathers According to Rabbi Nathan: A Translation and Commentary.* SJLA 11. Leiden: Brill, 1975.

SANDERS, E. P. "Testament of Abraham." *OTP* 1.871-902.

SCHÄFER-LICHTENBERGER, C. *Josua und Salomo: Eine Studie zu Autorität und Legitimität des Nachfolgers im Alten Testament.* VTSup 58. Leiden: Brill, 1995.

SCHILDGEN, B.D. *Crisis and Continuity: Time in the Gospel of Mark.* JSNTSup 159. Sheffield: Sheffield Academic Press, 1998.

SCHMITT, H.-C. "Der heidnische Mantiker als eschatologischer Jahweprophet: Zum Verständnis Bileams in der Endgestalt von Num 22-24." *"Wer ist wie du, HERR, unter den Göttern?": Studien zur Theologie und Religionsgeschichte Israels für Otto Kaiser zum 70. Geburtstag.* Ed. I. Kottsieper, et al. Göttingen: Vandenhoeck & Ruprecht, 1994. 180-98.

SCHNEIDER, G. "Engel und Blutschweiss (Lk 22,43-44): 'Redaktionsgeschichte' im Dienste der Textkritik." *BZ* 20 (1976): 112-16.

– "ἀγάπη." *EDNT* 1.8-12.

– "εἶδος." *EDNT* 1.385-86.

– "ἐπισκιάζω." *EDNT* 2.34-35.

– "ῥαββί." *EDNT* 3.205-6.

– "στηρίζω." *EDNT* 3.276.

SCHRENK, G. "ἐκλέγομαι." *TDNT* 4.168-192.

SCHULZ, S. "σκιά." *TDNT* 7.394-400.

SEEBASS, H. "Zur literarischen Gestalt der Bileam-Perikope." *ZAW* 107 (1995): 409-19.

SHEELEY, S.M. *Narrative Asides in Luke-Acts.* JSNTSup 72. Sheffield: JSOT, 1992.

SIEVERS, J. "Josephus and the Afterlife," *Understanding Josephus: Seven Perspectives.* JSPSup 32. Ed. S. Mason. Sheffield: Sheffield Academic Press, 1998. 20-34.

SIM, D.C. "The 'Confession' of the Soldiers in Matthew 27:54." *HeyJ* 34 (1993): 401-24.

– *The Gospel of Matthew and Christian Judaism: The History and Social Setting of the Matthean Community.* Edinburgh: Clark, 1998.

SMELIK, K.A.D. "Een ezel stoot zich in't gemeen..Een verkenning van Numeri 22-24." *Amsterdamse Cahiers Voor Exegese en Bijbelse Theologie* 13 (1994): 14-30.

SMITH, M. "The Origin and History of the Transfiguration Story." *USQR* 36 (1980) 39-44.

SOARDS, M.L. *The Passion According to Luke: The Special Material of Luke 22.* JSNTSup 14. Sheffield: JSOT, 1987.

SOGGIN, J.A. *Joshua.* OTL. Philadelphia: Westminster, 1972.

– *Judges: A Commentary.* OTL. Philadelphia: Westminster, 1981.

SONNET, J.-P. *The Book Within the Book: Writing in Deuteronomy.* BIS 14. Leiden: Brill, 1997.

SPICQ, C. *Theological Lexicon of the New Testament*. 3 vols. Peabody: Hendrickson, 1994.

SPILSBURY, P. *The Image of the Jew in Flavius Josephus' Paraphrase of the Bible*. TSAJ 69. Tübingen: Mohr Siebeck, 1998.

SPITTLER, R.P. "Testament of Job." *OTP* 1.829-68.

SQUIRES, J.T. *The Plan of God in Luke-Acts*. SNTSMS 76. Cambridge: Cambridge University Press, 1993.

STANDAERT, B. "Adonai Shalom (Judges 6-9): The Persuasive Means of a Narrative and the Strategies of Inculturation of Yahwism in a New Context." *Rhetoric, Scripture, & Theology: Essays from the 1994 Pretoria Conference*. Eds. S.E. Porter and T.H. Olbricht. JSNTSup 133. Sheffield: Sheffield Academic Press, 1996. 195-202.

STEGNER, W.R. "The Use of Scripture in Two Narratives of Early Jewish Christianity (Matthew 4.1-11; Mark 9.2-8)." *Early Christian Interpretation of the Scriptures of Israel: Investigations and Proposals*. JSNTSup 148. Eds. C.A. Evans and J. A. Sanders. Sheffield: Sheffield Academic Press, 1997. 98-120.

STEIN, R.H. "Is the Transfiguration (Mark 9:2-8) a Misplaced Resurrection Account?" *JBL* 95 (1976) 79-96.

STIPP, H.-J. "Samson, der Nasiräer." *VT* 45 (1995): 337-69.

STOCK, K. *Boten aus dem Mit-Ihm-Sein: Das Verhältnis zwischen Jesus und den Zwölf nach Markus*. AnBib 70. Rome: Biblical Institute, 1975.

– "Das Bekenntnis des Centurio: Mk 15,39 im Rahmen des Markusevangeliums." *ZKT* 100 (1978): 289-301.

STONE, M.E., trans. *The Testament of Abraham: The Greek Recensions*. SBLTT 2. Missoula: Society of Biblical Literature, 1972.

– "Greek Apocalypse of Ezra." *OTP* 1.561-79.

– *Fourth Ezra: A Commentary on the Book of Fourth Ezra*. Hermeneia. Minneapolis: Fortress, 1990.

STRAUSS, M.L. *The Davidic Messiah in Luke-Acts: The Promise and Its Fulfillment in Lukan Christology*. JSNTSup 110. Sheffield: Sheffield Academic Press, 1995.

TABOR, J.D. "'Returning to the Divinity': Josephus's Portrayal of the Disappearance of Enoch, Elijah, and Moses." *JBL* 108 (1989): 225-38.

TANNEHILL, R.C. *The Sword of His Mouth*. Philadelphia: Fortress, 1975.

– "Attitudinal Shift in Synoptic Pronouncement Stories." *Orientation by Disorientation: Studies in Literary Criticism and Biblical Literary Criticism*. Ed. R.A. Spencer; Pittsburgh: Pickwick, 1980, 183-97.

– "Introduction: The Pronouncement Story and Its Types." *Pronouncement Stories. Semeia* 20. Ed. R.C. Tannehill. Chico: Scholars Press, 1981, 1-13.

– "Varieties of Synoptic Pronouncement Stories." *Pronouncement Stories. Semeia* 20. Ed. R.C. Tannehill. Chico: Scholars Press, 1981, 101-19

– *The Narrative Unity of Luke-Acts: Volume 1: The Gospel According to Luke.* FFNT. Philadelphia: Fortress, 1986.

– *The Narrative Unity of Luke-Acts: Volume 2: The Acts of the Apostles.* FFNT. Minneapolis: Fortress, 1990.

– LUKE. ANTC. Nashville: Abingdon, 1996.

TANNER, J.P. "The Gideon Narrative as the Focal Point of Judges." *BSac* 149 (1992): 146-61.

TAYLOR, J. "The Coming of Elijah, Mt 17,10-13 and Mk 9,11-13: The Development of the Texts." *RB* 98 (1991): 107-19.

THEISSEN, G. *Urchristliche Wundergeschichten: Ein Beitrag zur formgeschichtlichen Erforschung der synoptischen Evangelien.* SNT 8. Gütersloh: Mohn, 1974.

THRALL, M.E. "Elijah and Moses in Mark's Account of the Transfiguration." *NTS* 16 (1969-70): 305-17.

TIEDE, D.L. *Prophecy and History in Luke-Acts.* Philadelphia: Fortress, 1980.

– *Luke.* Minneapolis: Augsburg, 1988.

TOLBERT, M.A. *Sowing the Gospel: Mark's World in Literary-Rhetorical Perspective.* Minneapolis: Fortress, 1989.

TREMOLADA, P. *"E fu annoverato fra iniqui": Prospettive di lettura della Passione secondo Luca alla luce di Lc 22,37 (Is 53,12d).* AnBib 137. Rome: Biblical Institute, 1997.

TRITES, A.A. "The Transfiguration in the Theology of Luke: Some Redactional Links." *The Glory of Christ in the New Testament.* Eds. L.D. Hurst and N.T. Wright. Oxford: Claredon, 1987. 71-81.

TROMP, J. *The Assumption of Moses: A Critical Edition with Commentary.* SVTP 10. Leiden: Brill, 1993.

TYSON, J.B. *The Death of Jesus in Luke-Acts.* Columbia: University of South Carolina Press, 1986.

ULFGARD, H. *Feast and Future: Revelation 7:9-17 and the Feast of Tabernacles.* ConBNT 22. Stockholm: Almqvist & Wiksell International, 1989.

– *The Story of Sukkot: The Setting, Shaping, and Sequel of the Biblical Feast of Tabernacles.* BGBE 34. Tübingen: Mohr Siebeck, 1998.

VAN DER MINDE, H.-J. "γεύομαι." EDNT 1.245-46.

VAN HENTEN, J.W. *The Maccabean Martyrs as Saviours of the Jewish People: A Study of 2 and 4 Maccabees.* JSJSup 57. Leiden: Brill, 1997.

VAN IERSEL, B.M.F. *Mark: A Reader-Response Commentary.* JSNTSup 164. Sheffield: Sheffield Academic Press, 1998.

VAN SETERS, J. "Joshua's Campaign of Canaan and Near Eastern Historiography." *SJOT* 4 (1990): 1-12.

– "From Faithful Prophet to Villain: Observations on the Tradition History of the Balaam Story." *A Biblical Intinerary: In Search of Method, Form and Content: Essays in Honor of George W. Coats.* Ed. E.E. Carpenter. JSOTSup 240. Sheffield: Sheffield Academic Press, 1997. 126-32.

VAN STEMPVOORT, P.A. "The Interpretation of the Ascension in Luke and Acts." *NTS* 5 (1958-59): 30-42.

VIGNOLO, R. "Una finale reticente: interpretazione narrativa di Mc 16,8." *RivB* 38 (1990): 129-89.

VIVIANO, B.T. "Rabbouni and Mark 9:5." *RB* 97 (1990): 207-18.

– "A Psychology of Faith: Matt 27:54 in the Light of Exod 14:30-31." *RB* 104 (1997): 368-72.

– Review of Moses, *Matthew's Transfiguration Story. RB* 105 (1998): 618-20.

Völkel, M. "κοιμάομαι." *EDNT* 2.301-2.

– "οὖς." *EDNT* 2.547-48.

WADSWORTH, M. "The Death of Moses and the Riddle of the End of Time in Pseudo-Philo." *JJS* 28 (1977): 12-19.

WAHL, O. *Apocalypsis Esdrae, Apocalypsis Sedrach, Visio Beati Esdrae.* PVTG 4. Leiden: Brill, 1977.

WALSH, J.T. "Elijah," *ABD* 2.463-66.

WANAMAKER, C.A. *The Epistles to the Thessalonians.* NIGTC. Grand Rapids: Eerdmans, 1990.

WANKE, J. "καλός." *EDNT* 2.244-45.

WATTS, J.W. "The Legal Characterization of Moses in the Rhetoric of the Pentateuch." *JBL* 117 (1998): 415-26.

WATTS, R.E. *Isaiah's New Exodus and Mark.* WUNT 88. Tübingen: Mohr Siebeck, 1997.

WEAVER, D.J. *Matthew's Missionary Discourse: A Literary Critical Analysis.* JSNTSup 38. Sheffield: JSOT, 1990.

WENHAM, D. and A.D.A. MOSES. "'There Are Some Standing Here..': Did They Become the 'Reputed Pillars' of the Jerusalem Church? Some Reflections on Mark 9:1, Galatians 2:9 and the Transfiguration." *NovT* 36 (1994): 146-63.

WEVERS, J.W. *Notes on the Greek Text of Exodus.* SBLSCS 30. Atlanta: Scholars Press, 1990.

– *Notes on the Greek Text of Genesis.* SBLSCS 35. Atlanta: Scholars Press, 1993.

– *Notes on the Greek Text of Deuteronomy.* SBLSCS 39. Atlanta: Scholars Press, 1995.

– *Notes on the Greek Text of Leviticus.* SBLSCS 44. Atlanta: Scholars Press, 1997.

– *Notes on the Greek Text of Numbers.* SBLSCS 46. Atlanta: Scholars Press, 1998.

WIARDA, T. "Peter as Peter in the Gospel of Mark." *NTS* 45 (1999): 19-37.

WIEFEL, W. *Das Evangelium nach Matthäus.* THKNT 1. Leipzig: Evangelische Verlagsanstalt, 1998.

WILKINS, M.J. *The Concept of Disciple in Matthew's Gospel.* NovTSup 59. Leiden: Brill, 1988.

WINTERMUTE, O.S. "Apocalypse of Zephaniah." *OTP* 1.497-515.

WINTHER-NIELSEN, N. *A Functional Discourse Grammar of Joshua: A Computer-Assisted Rhetorical Structure Analysis.* ConBOT 40. Stockholm: Almqvist & Wiksell, 1995.

WISCHMEYER, O. "Herrschen als Dienen—Mk 10,41-45." *ZNW* 90 (1999): 28-44.

WITHERUP, R.D. "The Death of Jesus and the Raising of the Saints: Matthew 27:51-54 in Context." *SBLASP* 26 (1987): 574-85.

YAMASAKI, G. *John the Baptist in Life and Death: Audience-Oriented Criticism of Matthew's Narrative.* JSNTSup 167. Sheffield: Sheffield Academic Press, 1998.

YARBRO COLLINS, A. "The Signification of Mark 10:45 Among Gentile Christians." *HTR* 90 (1997): 371-82.

ZEITLIN, S. *The Second Book of Maccabees.* New York: Harper & Brothers, 1954.

ZELLER, D. "Elija und Elischa im Frühjudentum." *BK* 41 (1986): 154-60.

– "La métamorphose de Jésus comme épiphanie (Mc 9,2-8)." *L'Évangile exploré: Mélanges offerts à Simon Légasse à l'occasion de ses soixante-dix ans.* LD 166. Ed. A. Marchadour. Paris: Cerf, 1996. 167-86.

– "Bedeutung und religionsgeschichtlicher Hintergrund der Verwandlung Jesu (Markus 9:2-8)." *Authenticating the Activities of Jesus.* NTTS 28. Eds. B. Chilton and C. A. Evans. Leiden: Brill, 1999. 303-21.

ZERWICK, M. *Biblical Greek.* Rome: Biblical Institute, 1963.

ZERWICK, M. and M. GROSVENOR. *A Grammatical Analysis of the Greek New Testament.* Rome: Biblical Institute, 1974.

ZIESLER, J.A. "The Transfiguration Story and the Markan Soteriology." *ExpTim* 81 (1970): 263-68.

ZMIJEWSKI, J. "ἀστραπή." *EDNT* 1.174-75.

ZWIEP, A.W. "The Text of the Ascension Narratives (Luke 24.50-3; Acts 1.1-2, 9-11)." *NTS* (1996): 219-44.

– *The Ascension of the Messiah in Lukan Christology.* NovTSup 87. Leiden: Brill, 1997.

SCRIPTURAL INDEX

Genesis
5:24...98, 112
12:7...156 n. 16, 205
16:1-16...72 n. 37
17:1...156 n. 16, 205
18:1-16...72 n. 37
18:1-15...49
19:1-22...52 n. 1
22:12...154
22:14...154, 154 n. 11

Exodus
2:11-15...101
3:2-5...60 n. 17
3:2...156 n. 16, 205
3:5...62, 63 n. 22, 65
3:6...186, 238, 293
3:8...63 n. 22
15-16...101
16:9...132
16:10-11...132-33, 133 n. 11
16:10...132, 132 n. 9, 133 n. 10
16:12...132
19:3...155
19:9...133-34
19:11...155
19:16-20...155
19:16-19...37 n. 5, 133
19:20...135
23:20...286 n. 18
24:9-10...155
24:13...136, 155, 267

24:15-18...134-36, 267 n. 28
24:15...134, 135, 136, 267
24:16...134, 135, 138 n. 24, 152 n. 2, 201 n. 1, 210
24:17...134, 135, 136, 155, 210, 267
24:18...135, 136, 267
29:42-43...124
32...101
32:1...104
33:7-11...117
33:7...117, 123, 125
33:8...124
33:9...124, 136
33:10...125
33:11...124, 136
34:29...78-79
34:35...157, 157 n. 20, 206
40:35...136, 137, 138, 139

Leviticus
23:40...121
23:42-43...116, 122

Numbers
7:89...140 n. 31
9:15-23...141 n. 32
9:18-23...139-40, 139 n. 26
9:18...139, 140
9:20...140
9:22...139
9:23...140, 140 n. 30

AUTHOR INDEX

Burchard, C., 196 n. 54
Burridge, R.A., 35 n. 1

Caragounis, C.C., 283 n., 9
Carpinelli, F.G., 295 n. 42
Carrell, P.R., 82 nn. 18-19, 89 n. 43
Carter, W., 22 n. 5, 233 n. 26, 235 n. 30, 236 nn. 33-34, 237 n. 35, 238 n. 37
Casey, M., 176 n. 7
Castello, G., 52 n. 2
Castelot, J.J., 117 n. 3
Childs, B.S., 122 n. 19, 132 n. 8, 133 nn. 10-11
Chilton, B.D., 161 n. 29
Clarke, E.G. 102 n. 21
Clivaz, C., 21 n. 1
Coats, G.W., 103 n. 24
Cody, A., 117 n. 3
Cogan, M., 101 n. 17
Collins, J.J., 81 n. 16, 86 n. 32, 91 n. 49, 217 nn. 41-43
Cook, S.L., 190 n. 42
Crump, D., 259 n. 5, 298 n. 49, 299 n. 50
Cunningham, S., 289 nn. 25, 27, 290 n. 30, 292 n. 34

Danove, P., 197 n. 57, 198 n. 60
Darr, J.A., 269 nn. 32, 34, 271 n. 40, 302 n. 59
Daube, D., 138 n. 24
Davies, W.D., 38 n. 8, 78 n. 10, 118 nn. 6-7, 130 n. 2, 135 n. 15, 203 n. 4, 205 n. 11, 206 n. 14, 207 n. 17, 209 n. 20, 214 n. 34, 217 n. 43, 219 n. 47, 227 nn. 9-10, 228 n. 11, 242 n. 46, 243 n. 49, 245 n. 52, 246 n. 55, 249 n. 62, 251 n. 67, 252 n. 71
Del Agua, A., 23 n. 10
Denis, A.-M., 285 n. 16

Denova, R.I., 289 n. 27
Derrett, J.D.M., 118 n. 11, 244 n. 50
Desplanque, C., 52 n. 2
de Vaulx, J., 139 n. 26, 140 n. 29
Di Lella, A.A., 81 n. 16
Dillon, R.J., 282 n. 3, 304 n. 62, 306 n. 65
Doble, P., 262 n. 14, 271 n. 38, 289 n. 26
Donaldson, T.L., 201 n. 1, 204 n. 5, 251 n. 65
Doran, R., 66 n. 26, 67 n. 27, 68 n. 30
Dowd, S.E., 181 n. 21
du Plessis, I.J., 296 n. 43
Durham, J.I., 122 n. 19, 124 n. 25

Eckert, J., 270 n. 37
Ehrman, B.D., 296 n. 43, 298 n. 50
Elliott, J.K., 152 n. 3
Ernst, J., 151 n. 2
Evans, C.A., 286 n. 17, 289 n. 28
Eynikel, E., 135 n. 16, 139 n. 28
Faierstein, M.M., 177 n. 9
Feldkämper, L., 77 n. 5, 259 n. 5, 297 n. 46, 299 n. 51, 300 nn. 54, 56
Feldman, L.H., 88 n. 38, 101 n. 17, 103 nn. 25-26, 104 n. 27, 105 nn. 31-32
Fischer, T., 66 n. 26, 67 n. 27, 68 n. 29, 69 n. 33, 70 n. 34
Fitzer, G., 91 n. 48
Fitzmyer, J.A., 29 n. 19, 77 n. 5, 79 n. 10, 116 n. 2, 120 n. 16, 130 n. 3, 147 n. 42, 177 n. 9, 261 n. 12, 270 n. 36, 271 n. 41, 274 n. 48, 283 n. 8, 284 n. 11, 288 n. 23, 289 n. 26, 298 n. 50, 307 n. 67
Fletcher-Louis, C.H.T., 78 n. 8
Fossum, J.E., 78 n. 9, 113 n. 56
Frenschkowski, M., 39 n. 9
Fritz, V., 59 n. 14

Garrett, S.R., 159 n. 23, 192 n. 46, 262 n. 13

Schildgen. B.D., 153 n. 4
Schmitt, H.-C., 52 n. 2
Schneider, G., 77 n. 6, 138 n. 22, 159 n. 24, 212 n. 30, 286 n. 17, 299 n. 50, 300 n. 53
Schrenk, G., 271 n. 39
Schulz, S., 139 n. 28
Seebass, H., 52 n. 2
Sheeley, S.M., 162 n. 31, 265 n. 24, 284 n. 13
Sievers, J., 106 n. 34
Sim, D.C., 202 n. 3, 248 n. 60
Smelik, K.A.D., 52 n. 2
Smith, M., 22 n. 9
Soards, M.L., 301 n. 57
Soggin, J.A., 45 nn. 21-22, 46 nn. 24, 26, 60 n. 18
Sonnet, J.-P., 102 n. 19, 103 n. 22
Spicq, C., 78 n. 7, 191 n. 45
Spilsbury, P., 103 n. 25, 106 n. 33
Spittler, R.P., 142 n. 34
Squires, J.T., 262 n. 16, 286 n. 17, 288 n. 24
Standaert, B., 45 n. 20
Stegner, W.R., 23 n. 11
Stein, R.H., 22 n. 6
Stipp, H.-J., 47 n. 27
Stock, K., 96 n. 4, 153 nn. 6-7, 183 n. 23, 195 n. 52
Stone, M.E., 82 n. 20, 83 nn. 24-25, 84 n. 26, 126 n. 28, 145 n. 38, 148 n. 45
Strauss, M.L., 262 n. 13, 271 n. 38, 272 n. 41, 303 n. 61

Tabor, J.D., 105 n. 31
Tadmor, H., 101 n. 17
Tannehill, R.C., 72 n. 37, 167 n. 45, 272 n. 43, 273 n. 44, 282 n. 4, 283 n. 7, 284 n. 12, 285 n. 14, 288 n. 24, 290 n. 31, 294 n. 40, 307 n. 66
Tanner, J.P., 45 n. 20

Taylor, J., 24 n. 13
Theissen, G., 39 n. 9
Thrall, M.E., 99 n. 15
Tiede, D.L., 289 n. 26, 291 n. 33
Tolbert, M.A., 151 n. 1, 175 n. 4, 190 n. 43
Tremolada, P., 301 n. 58
Trites, A.A., 21 n. 3
Tromp, J., 109 nn. 43-44, 46, 110 nn. 47-49, 111 n. 50
Tyson, J.B., 285 n. 14

Ulfgard, H., 89 n. 40, 117 n. 3, 120 n. 15

van der Minde, H.-J., 168 n. 47, 215 n. 35, 274 n. 46
van Henten, J.W., 68 n. 30, 71 n. 36
van Iersel, B.M.F., 152 n. 2, 155 n. 13, 169 n. 49, 176 n. 5, 178 n. 14, 180 n. 18, 184 nn. 27-28, 186 n. 30, 190 n. 42
Van Seters, J., 52 n. 2, 61 n. 19
van Stempvoort, P.A., 285 n. 14
Vignolo, R., 198 n. 60
Viviano, B.T., 78 n. 10, 159 n. 24, 248 n. 60
Völkel, M., 246 n. 55, 283 n. 5

Wadsworth, M., 108 n. 38
Wahl, O., 148 n. 45
Walsh, J.T., 101 n. 18
Wanamaker, C.A., 146 n. 40
Wanke, J., 160 n. 28, 208 n. 19
Watts, J.W., 102 n. 19
Watts, R.E., 155 n. 12
Weaver, D.J., 234 nn. 27-28
Wenham, D., 24 n. 12
Wevers, J.W., 102 n. 21, 103 n. 23, 122 n. 18, 123 n. 21, 132 n. 9, 133 n. 10, 134 nn. 13-14, 136 n. 18, 137 n. 20, 138 n. 24, 139 n. 27, 140 n. 30, 154 n. 11, 157 n. 20, 166 n. 42

Finito di stampare
nel mese di novembre 2000

presso la tipografia
"Giovanni Olivieri" di E. Montefoschi
00187 Roma - Via dell'Archetto, 10,11,12